LIVING LANGUAGE

Living Language
Reading, Thinking, and Writing

Alleen Pace Nilsen

Arizona State University

Allyn and Bacon

Boston London Toronto Sydney Tokyo Singapore

Vice President: Eben W. Ludlow
Editorial Assistant: Tania Sanchez
Executive Marketing Manager: Lisa Kimball
Cover Administrator: Linda Knowles
Composition Buyer: Linda Cox
Manufacturing Buyer: Meghan Cochran
Production Coordinator: Deborah Brown
Editorial-Production Service: Anne Rebecca Starr
Text Designer: Melinda Grosser, *silk*

Copyright © 1999 by Allyn and Bacon
A Viacom Company
160 Gould Street
Needham Heights, Massachusetts 02494

Internet: www.abacon.com

Many of the designations used by manufacturers and sellers to distinguish their products are claimed as trademarks. Where those designations appear in this book, and Allyn and Bacon was aware of a trademark claim, the designations have been printed in caps or initial caps.

Library of Congress Cataloging-in-Publication Data
Nilsen, Alleen Pace.
   Living language : reading, thinking, and writing / Alleen Pace
Nilsen.
      p.   cm.
   Includes index.
   ISBN 0-205-27091-3
   1. Readers—Language and languages.   2. Language and languages—
Problems, exercises, etc.   3. Critical thinking—Problems,
exercises, etc.   4. Report writing—Problems, exercises, etc.
5. English language—Rhetoric.   6. College readers.   I. Title.
PE1127.L47N55   1998
808'.0427—dc21   98-30375
                                                                      CIP

Text credits appear on pages 477–479 and are considered an extension of the copyright page.

Printed in the United States of America
10   9   8   7   6   5   4   3   2   1   03   02   01   00   99   98

CONTENTS

③ COMMUNICATION CHALLENGES   89

6 LANGUAGE TO PERSUADE   255

7 THE MASS MEDIA 313

8 TECHNOLOGY AND LANGUAGE CHANGE 379

9 CHANGING WORDS IN A CHANGING WORLD   427

INDEX   481

Rhetorical Contents

Comparison/Contrast

Definition/Illustration

Deduction/Illustration

Description

Induction

NARRATION

 # PREFACE

Living Language: Reading, Thinking, and Writing examines many topics that today's bright young people like to think and write about. And in keeping with the philosophy that English classes are an appropriate place for students to learn about language processes, I have selected contributors who look at today's important issues through the perspective of communication practices.

In addition to essays written by such talented and well-known commentators as Maya Angelou, James Baldwin, Rita Braver, Sandra Cisneros, Peter Farb, J. N. Hook, Garrison Keillor, Anna Quindlen, Amy Tan, Deborah Tannen, and Malcolm X and Alex Haley, *Living Language* contains essays by new writers on such current topics as e-mail privacy, celebrity authors, group names, the proliferation of rumors on the Internet, road rage, talk radio, free speech, humor in politics, holiday greetings, shaming penalties, sports mascots, and graffiti and tagging.

I have included models for writing that range from traditional essays to newspaper columns and from letters to the editor to a television documentary. Headlines, soundbites, advertisements, a sweepstakes offer, bumper stickers, and roadside signs also illustrate the variety of formats for written communication. And for today's visually oriented students, photos, cartoons, charts, and collages of newspaper headlines have been included to enhance understanding and provide stimuli for class discussion.

Eleven workshops scattered throughout the book supply raw material for analyzing the processes through which language changes. The workshops include Brain Teasers, questions that require students to search their memories as well as to make original observations and engage in critical thinking. Because not all students will be able to figure out the answers to all questions—in fact, some of the questions do not have clear-cut answers—these activities are good for cooperative learning either in small or class-size groups. Each chapter also includes Living Language boxes made up of short news summaries, word etymologies, linguistic anecdotes, and interesting language facts. These boxes are designed to help students make connections between what they study in class and what they see in their daily lives.

Living Language is organized in concentric circles moving out from the reader. It begins with a chapter on personal names—that bit of language that is closest to each of us—and ends with a chapter on worldwide communication (Chapter 9). The chapters in between tell about the miracle of language and how all cultures and all human beings develop systems of communication. Chapter 2 moves away from the personal names in Chapter 1 to how people learn language and how the world developed language. Chapters 3 and 4 look at social and political complications inherent in today's society. Chapter 5 illustrates some of the ways in which humor works both as a social lubricant and a cohesive bond. Chapter 6 looks at specific techniques used for persuasion, while Chapter 7 shows how our lives are influenced by the mass media. Chapter 8 illustrates how advances in knowledge and technology require new vocabulary to describe discoveries, procedures, inventions, customs, concepts, and changing social conditions and values. Because of these advances and mass media's power to introduce new words and new meanings, the English language changes on a daily basis.

Understanding and appreciating processes of language change has both practical and pleasurable rewards. When people see the double meaning in a sign, smile at the pun in a newspaper headline, understand the second level of a name, and catch on to clever allusions, they live fuller and more creative lives. And from a practical standpoint, individuals need to understand the tools of persuasion and principles of linguistic inbonding that people use with members of their own group as they outbond or exclude others. Communities, both local and national, need people who are literate in many different senses. For example, in Chapter 8, Judith Stone observes that even though we can't all be Einsteins, we are nevertheless *de facto* scientific advisors when we cast votes on issues relating to pesticides, acid rain, and protecting the ozone layer. In a similar way, ordinary citizens make decisions on language-related issues including what to do about graffiti and how to protect children from obscenity while also protecting free speech. The spreading of rumors and false information through new kinds of media means that discerning readers must be brave enough to ask the right questions. Society also needs informed citizens to participate in the organizations that draw up selection guidelines for school and public libraries, decide the hours of family viewing of television, and make decisions about what words will get a student expelled or a teacher fired. And without some background knowledge, we can't discuss—much less give helpful advice on—the complicated issues surrounding "Official Language" and "English Only" laws, nor can we ask intelligent questions about Ebonics or the relative benefits of extended versus early-exit bilingual programs.

Suggested Topics for Writing and Information Sources for Writing appear at the end of each chapter to encourage students to think and write. An Instructor's Manual for *Living Language: Reading, Thinking, and Writing* that provides answers to the questions along with supplemental discussion material is available from the publisher. Also, I will be happy to hear comments and to answer questions from students or teachers, either through regular mail

(Arizona State University English Department, Tempe, AZ 85287-0302) or through e-mail <Alleen.Nilsen@ASU.EDU>.

ACKNOWLEDGMENTS

Practically everyone I know needs to be acknowledged for contributing either tidbits or large chunks to this book. First, it was a family affair. My husband and colleague, Don L. F. Nilsen, professor of English linguistics here at Arizona State University, answered questions on a daily basis. It was also wonderful to have three grown children to call on. One of my sons, Kelvin, provided computer science information, and the other, D. Sean, answered legal questions about shaming penalties and laws on married women's surnames. My daughter, Nicolette, helped me understand differences between English and Japanese. She also proofread and edited out many of the mistakes that would have appalled composition teachers. I humbly apologize for those that remain.

Colleagues and friends at ASU were wonderfully helpful. They include Karen Adams, Carina Andreade, Charles Conley, Lucy Cruz, Ken Donelson, Greg Glau, Nancy Gutierrez, Kate Harts, Mary Jones, Julie Knapp, Jim Konz, Myrna Morgan, John Ramage, Thelma Richard, Duane Roen, Kristin and Gene Valentine, and Teresa Wells. From outside ASU, I am indebted to names expert Ed Callary, composition teacher David Carroll, advertising specialist Don Hauptman, and linguist Jerrie Cobb Scott. Also, thanks to the Changing Hands Bookstore in Tempe for letting me take pictures of their books, and thanks to my niece, Gina Harrop, for taking the pictures of her husband, Lance, that appear on pp. 49 and 104–105.

Thanks also to the following reviewers for their helpful comments: Cynthia A. Bily, Adrian College; Boyd Davis, University of North Carolina at Charlotte; Robert Funk, Eastern Illinois University; R. Gerald Nelms, Southern Illinois University at Carbondale; Carol A. Roper, Dutchess Community College; Sally K. Slocum, the University of Akron; and John Webster, University of Washington.

A. P. N.

LIVING LANGUAGE

MS. or MRS.?

Elvis' name regi

names for new babies

Don't first-name me!
Call me 'Mister'

Baelyn

Waylan

Kyoung-Ho

Jermar

LaJanae

Cruz

Seiichi

Keanu

Barte

As

LA Police overuse of guns calle
'John Wayne' syndrome

Bad boys, bad boys...

Yogi and Barnacle Bill—
rock stars on Mars

Roseanne dropping Arnold from her name –
joining Cher, Madonna, Ann-Margret

In a state   issued by the Associated Press, Rosanne Arnold's agent

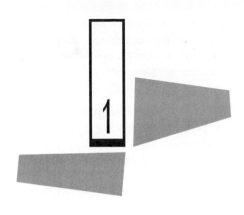

You and Your Names

With rare exceptions, every human community has developed some kind of systematic naming practice to distinguish individual group members. In the first few months of their lives, people learn to recognize the sound patterns of their own names and forever after relate to these particular sounds on a deep psychological level. Parents report that their infants get a happy smile on their faces and listen transfixed as grandparents lovingly repeat their names in long distance phone calls. Researchers find that when people are connected to earphones with a different message coming to each ear, they will choose one of the messages to listen to and ignore the other. However, if their name is spoken in the nondominant message, their focus quickly changes.

The line from the familiar theme song of television's *Cheers*, "You want to go where everybody knows your name," touches a sympathetic chord because most people spend so much time among strangers that they are nostalgic about having a home away from home. People are fascinated not only with the sounds of their own names, but also with the written forms. News magazines surprise their subscribers with personally identified inserts, while advertisers shock the receivers of mass mailings into paying attention by boldly printing individual's names in such blanks as "_____ is a winner" and "_____ has been approved for. . . ." Other marketers tempt customers with monogrammed shirts, towels, and briefcases; engraved pens and pencils; personalized luggage and name plates; and individualized greeting cards. Grandparents are an easy mark for companies selling books and audiotapes featuring characters named after a designated child. And perhaps the pleasure that gang members get from seeing their names painted on highway overpasses is similar to that which authors get from seeing their names on book covers, actors from seeing their names on movie posters or theater marquees, and business people and politicians from seeing their names on office doors. In this chapter you will read articles and work with concepts exploring these ideas and illustrating the many ways that:

- names are an important part of language systems.
- personal names, both literally and at a deep psychological level, help define people's identities.
- naming patterns differ from culture to culture and change as the cultures change.
- language communities use names for many purposes beyond identification.

TWO NEWSPAPER ARTICLES

Because there's always a new generation coming along, the naming of babies is a popular subject for newspaper feature stories. The first article reprinted here was published in an Arizona newspaper and appropriately reflects the demographics of a state with a higher than average number of Hispanic and Native American citizens. The second one, published in the *New York Times,* pays more attention to African-American naming practices. But notice how both authors say that the trend of giving unusual names to children is not limited to minority groups.

DENNY? VITO? RITCHIE? OLD MONIKERS CONQUERED BY CREATIVE COININGS IN BABY-NAME GAME

Deborah Ross

1   New parents wield extraordinary power when they choose a baby name. They can go the traditional route and give more Johns and Marys to the world. They can pay tribute to their favorite movie stars with such names as Keanu and Demi. Or they can get totally creative and follow the suit of comedian Damon Wayans, who chose the name Fuddy for his child.

2   But there's another trend in modern American baby-naming: letting the name reflect the child's ethnic, religious or cultural heritage.

3   Current baby-name guides promise 10,000, 20,000, even 30,000 names for expectant couples to pore over. With titles like *The Melting Pot Book of Baby Names* and *Bebes Preciosos: 5001 Hispanic Baby Names,* they also promise a multicultural perspective.

4   "People are more interested in the style of names these days . . . in finding names that really have some meaning for them," said Pamela Redmond Satran, co-author of the popular name guide *Beyond Jennifer & Jason.* Often,

parents choose baby names that honor living or deceased relatives. A name might also pay homage by reflecting the family's heritage, Satran noted.

5   "The whole world of ethnic names is a way for people to find names that have solid tradition behind them, but are different," she said.

6   Gherarda Castillo of Phoenix loves her Hispanic-flavored first name. Now 27, she said that as a child she didn't appreciate its uniqueness.

7   "My parents badly wanted a child, and they promised their first child would be named after St. Gerard, the patron saint of motherhood," Castillo said, adding that the name was feminized and the "h" was added for an Italian spelling to reflect her mother's background.

8   Choosing the name of a saint or biblical figure, in many cases one who shares their child's birthday, is a common practice among Catholic Latino parents, according to Rose Mare Arce and Maité Junco, authors of *Bebes Preciosos*. Their book includes a list of significant saints' birth dates or dates on which they are remembered.

9   Also listed are names from literature and popular culture and Hispanic variations on given names from other languages, such as Daví or Davito for David.

A glance at the shelves of most bookstores will show a surprising variety of books designed to help new parents choose a name for their baby.

10   Native Americans have many interesting traditions behind baby-naming.

11   Melody Whiteshield of Phoenix, as an elder in her Hopi family, has had the responsibility of naming two babies, a grandson and a goddaughter. In both cases, she's drawn inspiration from her clan name, Coyote.

12   Her grandson is named Cruz Wyiacha Kennedy-Silas, the first name being a translation of "little coyote pup who plays" and the second name meaning "lightning bug" or "one who blinks" in Sioux, Whiteshield said, adding that the 9-month-old is already living up to his playful name.

13   Her goddaughter, a grand-niece, is named Mariahs Skye, the first name translating to "foxy little coyote girl" from Hopi. The 2½-year-old has both Hopi and Sioux heritage.

14   Whiteshield conducted baby-naming ceremonies in the traditional manner by washing the babies' hair at sunrise, declaring the names, then taking the babies out to greet the sun and say morning prayers. Their families carried corn, representing the mother who stays with them through life and follows them into the spirit world.

15   Many of the colorful names in Native American families come from observance of nature, such as Wenutu for "sky clearing after being cloudy" and Nikiti for "round and smooth like an abalone shell," according to *The New Age Baby Name Book* by Sue Browder. It provides 10,000 entries from cultures around the world.

16   Kim Ayiyi of Phoenix drew from her African-American family heritage as well as her husband's Nigerian roots to name her two young sons.

17   Hope Kirby Osaze Ayiyi, almost 5, is named after, respectively, his father, his mother's stepfather and a Nigerian word for "gift from God." Chrisdeón (pronounced Christain) Efosa Ayiyi, 3, has Nigerian names, the middle name also meaning "gift from God," their mother said.

18   "The idea was to incorporate it (the children's African heritage) in American life as much as possible, which is something that at my age I'm just learning about myself," said Kim Ayiyi, noting the ordinariness of her given name.

19   When the boys were babies, she said, she would make up ditties using their full names and sing them often so that they got to know their names.

20   Shelby Livingston, formerly of Phoenix and author of the 1,000-name *African-American Baby Name Workbook,* said she sees a trend of naming babies after African warriors. Also, many couples like to combine their given names to create a new name, such as *Jermar* for a combination of Jerry and Mary, Livingston said.

21   She compiled the book in an unusual way: by simply stopping African-Americans wherever she could to ask them their first names. The result is a list with such lyrical monikers as LaJanae, Amisstika, Jaymez and Vercius.

22   "Twenty years ago, everybody wanted to be *Patty* and *Susie* and fit in" with mainstream American culture, Satran said. Now ethnic pride is reasserting itself, not just in African-Americans and Arab-Americans, but also

in Jews, those of Irish descent, Asian-Americans and people of various European heritages.

23   Couples of mixed racial or ethnic backgrounds are making interesting compromises in baby-naming when they want their children to carry on names that reflect both sides of the family, Satran said.

24   Her children, for instance, are named Rory and Owen to carry on their mother's Irish heritage.

25   With her co-author on *Beyond Jennifer & Jason*, Linda Rosenkrantz, Satran has written *Beyond Shannon and Sean: An Enlightened Guide to Irish Baby Naming*, as well as *Beyond Sarah and Sam: An Enlightened Guide to Jewish Baby Naming* and *Beyond Charles and Diana: An Anglophiles' Guide to Baby Naming*, all published in 1992.

From DeVon to LaDon, Invented Names Proclaim "I Am"

Karen De Witt

I have fallen in love with American names,
The sharp gaunt names that never get fat,
The snakeskin titles of mining-claims,
The plumed war-bonnet of Medicine Hat,
Tucson and Deadwood and Lost Mule Flat.

1   In "American Names," the poet Stephen Vincent Benet celebrated the rich lyrical creativity of Americans when it comes to naming things, whether places or themselves. Mr. Benet harked back to an earlier era when regional distinctions marked a man named Beauregard as Southern gentry, just as one named Quincy Lowell could only be a Bostonian toff.

2   Over the years, immigrants added names ending in vowels and others made mostly of consonants. Hollywood renamed with a vengeance, turning Marion Morrison into macho John Wayne and Archibald Leach into suave Cary Grant. But for sheer inventive verve, nothing beats black Americans for naming themselves.

3   Shaniqua, Laquanda, Starletta, DeVon. Kadesha, Kanisha, LaToya, LaDon.

4   Rhythmic and melodious, idiosyncratically spelled, these names are uniquely black. These names are not the African or Islamic names like Kwame or Hakim that found favor in a wave of black pride that re-emerged in the 1960's and that continue to be chosen today. And some blacks object to the trend, seeing the names as racial markers that stigmatize a child in school or later in the job market. Most etymologists, however, say that while blacks may be more inclined toward such invention, the phenomenon is growing throughout the English-speaking world. It is, they say, human creativity, individualism, a way of forging a new identity.

5   E. Ethelbert Miller, director of the African-American Resource Center at Howard University, said he sees the newly invented names as "a form of black style."

6   "It's like not tucking in a shirt or wearing a hat backwards," Mr. Miller said. "It makes your child appear unique by giving it a name that stands out."

7   Leonard Ashley, professor of English at Brooklyn College, who is past president of the American Name Society, said he sees the names as part of a "sad psychology" of "trying to be somebody" in a society that continues to exclude blacks.

8   "From everything we know," Mr. Ashley said, "a unique name is counter-indicated. Studies show you do better in society if your name is not unusual."

9   But Sonia Sanchez, a poet, professor of English at Temple University and author of the forthcoming collection *Wounded in the House of a Friend* (Africa World Press), said the creation of such names is positive energy in situations where little may be positive.

10   "These names may not be truly African, but they have the same polysyllabic flavor," said Ms. Sanchez, who was born Wilsonia Benetta. "LaTanya— You know that is an African-American name right away. Listen to it. It tells you—I am."

11   Name experts say such creativity reflects the rise of a global culture, and is not limited to blacks.

12   "People are exposed to more names from other countries," said Cleveland Kent Evans, a psychologist at Bellevue College in Nebraska, who wrote *Unusual and Most Popular Baby Names* (Signet, 1992). "Then the culture of celebrity . . . is worldwide and an obvious place for finding unusual names." He recalls a flood of Ariels after Disney's *Little Mermaid* and Jasmines after Jasmine Guy of *A Different World.*

13   At times, entertainers' names sound made-up: Take Arsenio Hall or Winona Ryder or Wynonna Judd. Arsenio is from the Greek "arsenikos" meaning "manly" or "virile." Winona, in all its variant spellings, is an American Indian name that is also a re-occurring place name. Whoopi Goldberg, though, is neither.

14   Such artful names challenge assumptions. "There is nothing weirder about Shaniqua or LaKisha than Vanessa, which Jonathan Swift invented for his poem 'Cadenus and Vanessa,' " said Mr. Evans. Esther Van Homerigh, a

friend of Swift, was the inspiration for a name that combined her first and last names.

15   The power of names and naming has occasionally been co-opted by the state to stigmatize or maintain a cultural heritage. During the Middle Ages, Poland and Russia made Jewish citizens take German-sounding names to set them apart. And living in overcrowded ghettos, many adopted names that alluded to the countryside like Rosenblum (rose bloom) or Lilienthal (lily valley), according to Charles Panati's *Browser's Book of Beginnings* (Houghton-Mifflin, 1984).

16   In Germany, local rulers enriched their treasuries by requiring that Jews pay to adopt Germanic names. The mellifluous sounding Morgenstern (morning star) and Silverberg (silver mountain) were among the most expensive. Trade names like Kaufman (merchant) or Schneider (tailor) were moderately priced.

17   In the Soviet Union during the 1930s and after World War II, the Soviet Government often encouraged parents to show their commitment to Communism and state programs by naming their children Marlen, a combination of Marx and Lenin, or Elem, for the first letters of their names.

18   And sometimes people change their names so they won't stand out.

19   "My name is made up," said Dr. Amitai Etzioni, a professor of sociology at George Washington University. "I was born Werner Falk, but when my family immigrated to Israel when I was a first grader, my parents were told that the kids would tease me because of the name. Half of Israel seems to have new names. My first name means truth in Hebrew, and Etzioni is a region in Israel."

20   But Mr. Ashley pointed out that what is unique today may not be tomorrow. "What is an unusual name?" he said. "Because of Shaquille O'Neal, the name Shaquille doesn't raise an eyebrow."

COMPREHENSION

1. Words to talk about:

   - *Bebes Preciosos* [from the book title]
   - But for sheer *inventive verve*
   - *idiosyncratically* spelled
   - Most *etymologists*
   - the *mellifluous sounding*

2. De Witt says that someone "named Quincy Lowell could only be a Bostonian toff." From the context, can you guess what *toff* means? What clues help?

3. Each of these authors begins with something different, a lead, designed to hook readers. Describe the power of those beginnings. Which was the most interesting to you?
4. Find the paragraph in each article where the lead ended and the author stated her thesis; that is, established the point to be developed in the rest of the article.
5. De Witt says that Jonathan Swift invented the name Vanessa to honor his friend Esther Van Homerigh. Trace the connection.

Discussion

1. What is the main trend that Ross and De Witt focus on?
2. Both authors offer explanations for the trend they are discussing. Cite three of the reasons they give and talk a little about your own observations in relation to their hypotheses.
3. Find the paragraph in De Witt's piece that is actually a poem, even though it is not divided into stanzas. Read it aloud. How does it illustrate the point made in the paragraph that follows?
4. Ross says that people are looking for names that "have solid tradition behind them, but are different." What example does she use to illustrate her point? Explain how it is both solidly traditional and different.
5. When Ross cites the Native-American boy named Cruz Wyiacha Kennedy-Silas, she misses an opportunity to point out that his hyphenated last name is evidence of another trend that is taking place. Why do you think she didn't mention the hyphenated last name?
6. When newspaper-feature writers want to give a new slant to an old story, they often come up with an idea and then go looking for two or three people whose stories exemplify the point they want to make. Since everybody in the world has a name and a story that goes with it, reporters could easily find examples of practically any kind of naming pattern. What evidence besides individual examples and anecdotes do the writers give to lend support to their thesis that today's parents are looking for baby names that reflect family heritage?
7. One way of checking out the accuracy of these commentaries is to gather data from your classmates. In groups of four, take four sheets of paper divided into male and female columns. Identify one sheet of paper as your grandparents' generation (over 60); another as your parents' generation (between 40 and 60); another as young adults (between 20 and 40); and the last one as children. Pass the sheets so that each person in your group can list the given names of extended family members in the appropriate columns. When all four of you have contributed

to each sheet, ponder the lists to see what you can observe about changes over time or about changes related to the ethnicity of group members.

- Are there more female than male names?
- Do the female names tend to be more creative than the male names?
- Have the names changed over the generations? If so, how?
- Do you see any reasons for the popularity of particular names?

LIVING LANGUAGE 1.1

Names in the News

These news stories exemplify various ways that names go beyond the simple matter of identification.

- A Jordanian couple decided to honor the peace efforts of the slain Israeli prime minister by naming their first-born son Yitzhak Rabin. Angry neighbors forced them to move four different times. When the baby was five months old, a sympathetic factory owner in Tel Aviv provided the parents with jobs and a place to live while explaining, "I hope an Israeli couple will soon name their child after King Hussein, our partner in peace." (*Sydney* [Australia] *Morning Herald,* July 12, 1996)
- As a mark of affection, Chinese parents and other relatives refer to young children by a double version of their given names. A similar feeling of affection and protectiveness may be the reason for giving giant pandas, an animal native only to China, such double names as Ling-Ling and Hsing-Hsing at the Washington National Zoo, Chia-Chia at the London Zoo, Shao-Shao at the Madrid Zoo, and Ying-Ying at the Chapultepec Zoo in Mexico City. (*Names,* Dec. 1985)
- As a high school writer in 1916–17, Ernest Hemingway was so fascinated with his own name that he used all of these bylines: Ernest Hemingway, Ernest Miller Hemingway, Ernest MacNamara Hemingway, Ernest Monahan Hemingway, Ernest Hemingway. (with a period), Ernest Michealowitch Hemingway, B. S., and just E. H. (Associated Press, May 6, 1994)
- In 1992, the French Parliament suspended an 1803 law severely limiting naming practices. The new freedoms were soon tested when the parents of a girl in La Rochelle named her Marie Marie Marie. A lower court disallowed the name,

- Are names repeated from one generation to another? If so, why? Are repeated names more likely to be male than female?
- Can you find evidence supporting the contentions of the two authors that people today are looking more to their ethnic heritages and are also feeling more free to create names or to choose names from foreign countries?

As a group, discuss your results and present your conclusions, illustrated by specific examples, to the class.

---

which was approved after an appeal. The parents chose the triple name because at birth the girl weighed 3.33 kilos, her head and chest measured 33 centimeters, and her mother was 33 years old. (*New York Post,* Jan. 22, 1993)

- While some people glory in having unusual names, others take pride in sharing their names and belonging to groups of like-named people. In 1992, the Mikes of America elected Michael Jordan as their "Mike of the Year," while country music singer George Strait was named "George of the Year" by fellow Georges. The Jim Smith society has over 1,500 members, and as the wife of one of them wrote to "Dear Abby" (Dec. 16, 1993) the hardest part of the annual conventions is keeping their hotel bills from being confused.
- Lance Morrow in a *Time* magazine essay used the name George Herbert Walker Bush to illustrate the point that names possess a "peculiar indelible power." He said that to Democrats "the full inventory of the pedigree, formally decanted, produced a piled-on, Connecticut preppie Little Lord Fauntleroy effect that went nicely with the populist crack that Bush 'was born on third base and thought he had hit a triple.' " (March 8, 1993)
- When comedian Roseanne Barr married actor Tom Arnold, she was surprisingly successful in changing her name to Roseanne Arnold, but when the couple divorced she sent a letter to the Academy of Television Arts & Sciences asking that any mention she might receive in relation to the Emmy awards should refer to her as "Roseanne. Period." She signed the letter "Roseanne Arnold" with a slash through Arnold. (*Arizona Republic,* July 8, 1994)

My Name

Sandra Cisneros

No matter how hard parents try to choose an appropriate name for a new baby, many babies grow into children who wish they were named something else. While most people have strong feelings about their names, they aren't as articulate as Sandra Cisneros is in this chapter from her book *The House on Mango Street.*

1   In English my name means hope. In Spanish it means too many letters. It means sadness, it means waiting. It is like the number nine. A muddy color. It is the Mexican records my father plays on Sunday mornings when he is shaving, songs like sobbing.

2   It was my great-grandmother's name and now it is mine. She was a horse woman too, born like me in the Chinese year of the horse—which is supposed to be bad luck if you're born female—but I think this is a Chinese lie because the Chinese, like the Mexicans, don't like their women strong.

3   My great-grandmother. I would've liked to have known her, a wild horse of a woman, so wild she wouldn't marry. Until my great-grandfather threw a sack over her head and carried her off. Just like that, as if she were a fancy chandelier. That's the way he did it.

4   And the story goes she never forgave him. She looked out the window her whole life, the way so many women sit their sadness on an elbow. I wonder if she made the best with what she got or was she sorry because she couldn't be all the things she wanted to be. Esperanza. I have inherited her name, but I don't want to inherit her place by the window.

5   At school they say my name funny as if the syllables were made out of tin and hurt the roof of your mouth. But in Spanish my name is made out of a softer something, like silver, not quite as thick as sister's name—Magdalena—which is uglier than mine. Magdalena who at least can come home and become Nenny. But I am always Esperanza.

6   I would like to baptize myself under a new name, a name more like the real me, the one nobody sees. Esperanza as Lisandra or Maritza or Zeze the X. Yes. Something like Zeze the X will do.

COMPREHENSION

1. What is it about her name that Esperanza does not like?
2. Why is Esperanza so interested in her own name? Which reasons are stated specifically, and which ones are implied?
3. Find two or three metaphors or similes (figurative comparisons) in this chapter, and explain how they are both efficient and effective in communicating Esperanza's feelings.

DISCUSSION

1. Cisneros often uses short, choppy statements, including what some critics call "minor" or "incomplete" sentences. Find several of these short and/or minor sentences and explain their effects on you as a reader.
2. The narrator is more than half-way into her story before she says that her name is Esperanza. Why does she wait?
3. What does Esperanza hope to gain with a new name? Why does the author make her sound so tentative as she works her way toward Zeze the X?
4. In *The Great Gatsby*, F. Scott Fitzgerald introduces his title character with:

   James Gatz—that was really, or at least legally, his name. He had changed it at the age of seventeen and at the specific moment that witnessed the beginning of his career—when he saw Dan Cody's yacht drop anchor over the most insidious flat on Lake Superior. It was James Gatz who had been loafing along the beach that afternoon in a torn green jersey and a pair of canvas pants, but it was already Jay Gatsby who borrowed a rowboat, pulled out to the *Tuolumne* and informed Cody that a wind might catch him and break him up in half an hour.
   I suppose he'd had the name ready for a long time, even then.

   How does Fitzgerald's James Gatz compare with Cisneros's Esperanza? What motivates them to want new names? Do we view the two characters differently because Cisneros's Esperanza is just daydreaming, while Fitzgerald's character actually changes his name?
5. Have you ever wanted to change your name? If so, why? If you've changed your name, how did it affect you? Your friends and family?
6. Even if you haven't changed your name, do you go by different names in different situations? For example, are you called something different in a foreign language class or in a religious setting? Do people you are close to have a pet name for you? If so, do you feel different because of the different name?

FROM I KNOW WHY THE CAGED BIRD SINGS

Maya Angelou

In this part of Angelou's best-selling autobiography, she tells about being sent to work with a friend of the family, Miss Glory, who had worked for twenty years as Mrs. Cullinan's maid. At the time of the story, Maya (Margaret) is ten and is still traumatized by having been raped. She hardly speaks and is probably sent off with Miss Glory in hopes the experience will be therapeutic. Also, she will be learning the intricacies of a white woman's kitchen in preparation for her own career as a maid.

1   On our way home one evening, Miss Glory told me that Mrs. Cullinan couldn't have children. She said that she was too delicate-boned. It was hard to imagine bones at all under those layers of fat. Miss Glory went on to say that the doctor had taken out all her lady organs. I reasoned that a pig's organs included the lungs, heart and liver, so if Mrs. Cullinan was walking around without those essentials, it explained why she drank alcohol out of unmarked bottles. She was keeping herself embalmed.

2   When I spoke to Bailey [Maya's older brother] about it, he agreed that I was right, but he also informed me that Mr. Cullinan had two daughters by a colored lady and that I knew them very well. He added that the girls were the spitting image of their father. I was unable to remember what he looked like, although I had just left him a few hours before, but I thought of the Coleman girls. They were very light-skinned and certainly didn't look very much like their mother (no one ever mentioned Mr. Coleman).

3   My pity for Mrs. Cullinan preceded me the next morning like the Cheshire cat's smile. Those girls, who could have been her daughters, were beautiful. They didn't have to straighten their hair. Even when they were caught in the rain, their braids still hung down straight like tamed snakes. Their mouths were pouty little cupid's bows. Mrs. Cullinan didn't know what she missed. Or maybe she did. Poor Mrs. Cullinan.

4   For weeks after, I arrived early, left late and tried very hard to make up for her barrenness. If she had had her own children, she wouldn't have had to ask me to run a thousand errands from her back door to the back door of her friends. Poor old Mrs. Cullinan.

5   Then one evening Miss Glory told me to serve the ladies on the porch. After I set the tray down and turned toward the kitchen, one of the women

asked, "What's your name, girl?" It was the speckled-faced one. Mrs. Cullinan said, "She doesn't talk much. Her name's Margaret."

6   "Is she dumb?"

7   "No. As I understand it, she can talk when she wants to but she's usually quiet as a little mouse. Aren't you, Margaret?"

8   I smiled at her. Poor thing. No organs and couldn't even pronounce my name correctly.

9   "She's a sweet little thing, though."

10   "Well, that may be, but the name's too long. I'd never bother myself. I'd call her Mary if I was you."

11   I fumed into the kitchen. That horrible woman would never have the chance to call me Mary because if I was starving I'd never work for her. I decided I wouldn't pee on her if her heart was on fire. Giggles drifted in off the porch and into Miss Glory's pots. I wondered what they could be laughing about.

12   Whitefolks were so strange. Could they be talking about me? Everybody knew that they stuck together better than the Negroes did. It was possible that Mrs. Cullinan had friends in St. Louis who heard about a girl from Stamps being in court and wrote to tell her. Maybe she knew about Mr. Freeman.

13   My lunch was in my mouth a second time and I went outside and relieved myself on the bed of four-o'clocks. Miss Glory thought I might be coming down with something and told me to go on home, that Momma would give me some herb tea, and she'd explain to her mistress.

14   I realized how foolish I was being before I reached the pond. Of course Mrs. Cullinan didn't know. Otherwise she wouldn't have given me the two nice dresses that Momma cut down, and she certainly wouldn't have called me a "sweet little thing." My stomach felt fine, and I didn't mention anything to Momma.

15   That evening I decided to write a poem on being white, fat, old and without children. It was going to be a tragic ballad. I would have to watch her carefully to capture the essence of her loneliness and pain.

16   The very next day, she called me by the wrong name. Miss Glory and I were washing up the lunch dishes when Mrs. Cullinan came to the doorway. "Mary?"

17   Miss Glory asked, "Who?"

18   Mrs. Cullinan, sagging a little, knew and I knew. "I want Mary to go down to Mrs. Randall's and take her some soup. She's not been feeling well for a few days."

19   Miss Glory's face was a wonder to see. "You mean Margaret, ma'am. Her name's Margaret."

20   "That's too long. She's Mary from now on. Heat that soup from last night and put it in the china tureen and, Mary, I want you to carry it carefully."

21   Every person I knew had a hellish horror of being "called out of his name." It was a dangerous practice to call a Negro anything that could be

loosely construed as insulting because of the centuries of their having been called niggers, jigs, dinges, blackbirds, crows, boots and spooks.

22   Miss Glory had a fleeting second of feeling sorry for me. Then as she handed me the hot tureen she said, "Don't mind, don't pay that no mind. Sticks and stones may break your bones, but words . . . You know, I been working for her for twenty years."

23   She held the back door open for me. "Twenty years. I wasn't much older than you. My name used to be Hallelujah. That's what Ma named me, but my mistress give me 'Glory,' and it stuck. I likes it better too."

24   For a few seconds it was a tossup over whether I would laugh (imagine being named Hallelujah) or cry (imagine letting some white woman rename you for her convenience). My anger saved me from either outburst. I had to quit the job, but the problem was going to be how to do it. Momma wouldn't allow me to quit for just any reason.

25   "She's a peach. That woman is a real peach." Mrs. Randall's maid was talking as she took the soup from me, and I wondered what her name used to be and what she answered to now.

26   For a week I looked into Mrs. Cullinan's face as she called me Mary. She ignored my coming late and leaving early. Miss Glory was a little annoyed because I had begun to leave egg yolk on the dishes and wasn't putting much heart in polishing the silver. I hoped that she would complain to our boss, but she didn't.

27   Then Bailey solved my dilemma. He had me describe the contents of the cupboard and the particular plates she liked best. Her favorite piece was a casserole shaped like a fish and green glass coffee cups. I kept his instructions in mind, so on the next day when Miss Glory was hanging out clothes and I had again been told to serve the old biddies on the porch, I dropped the empty serving tray. When I heard Mrs. Cullinan scream, "Mary!" I picked up the casserole and two of the green glass cups in readiness. As she rounded the kitchen door I let them fall on the tiled floor.

28   I could never absolutely describe to Bailey what happened next, because each time I got to the part where she fell on the floor and screwed up her ugly face to cry, we burst out laughing. She actually wobbled around on the floor and picked up shards of the cups and cried, "Oh, Momma. Oh, dear Gawd. It's Momma's china from Virginia. Oh, Momma, I sorry."

29   Miss Glory came running in from the yard and the women from the porch crowded around. Miss Glory was almost as broken up as her mistress. "You mean to say she broke our Virginia dishes? What we gone do?"

30   Mrs. Cullinan cried louder, "That clumsy nigger. Clumsy little black nigger."

31   Old speckled-face leaned down and asked, "Who did it, Viola? Was it Mary? Who did it?"

32   Everything was happening so fast I can't remember whether her action preceded her words, but I know that Mrs. Cullinan said, "Her name's

Margaret, goddam it, her name's Margaret!" And she threw a wedge of the broken plate at me. It could have been the hysteria which put her arm off, but the flying crockery caught Miss Glory right over her ear and she started screaming.

33   I left the front door wide open so all the neighbors could hear.

34   Mrs. Cullinan was right about one thing. My name wasn't Mary.

COMPREHENSION

1. Words to talk about:

   - make up for her *barrenness*
   - in the china *tureen*
   - picked up *shards*

2. Why is it dangerous to call a Negro "out of his name"?

DISCUSSION

1. Give a couple of examples of Margaret's statements that let readers know how young and naive she is.
2. Even though Angelou writes this story through the voice of a twelve-year-old, she includes some poetic descriptions that are simple enough for readers to feel they are coming from a child. Give an example.
3. What increasingly serious steps does Margaret take to express her unhappiness about being called Mary?
4. Why does Angelou leave it up to readers to decide whether or not Mrs. Cullinan throws the plate at Miss Glory? If it is on purpose, why does she do it?

FROM A WORLD WITHOUT SURNAMES

J. N. Hook

If you want to learn more about your surname and how you came to have the particular name that you have, a good place to look would be in J. N. Hook's book, *Family Names* (Macmillan, 1982), from which this piece is reprinted. He began this particular chapter by writing, "When the world's population was small and even a city might hold only a few thousand people, and when most folks never got more than ten or fifteen miles from their birthplace (usually walking), and when messages were sent by personal messenger rather than by impersonal post, there was hardly a necessity for more than one name." But, as he goes on to show, the world became more complicated, and because of that, people needed more complete ways of keeping track of each other; hence, the development of surnames.

1   Suppose that you were living in England in the Middle Ages. Suppose further that your name was John. Not John Something—just John. The Somethings did not yet exist in England. King or commoner, you were just John.

2   Your male ancestors had also been John, or Thomas, Robert, Harold, Richard, William, or more anciently Eadgar or Eadwine or Aelfred, and their wives may have been Alice, Joan, Berthe, Blanche, Beatrice, Margaret, Marie, Inga, or Grette. Most names of your day were Norman French, since the descendants of William the Conqueror and his followers ruled the land. . . .

3   In Yorkshire in the fourteenth century, in a list of 19,600 mixed male and female names, C. L. Ewen found that John accounted for 17 percent of the total, followed by William, Thomas, and Robert, with Alice (5 percent) and Joan (4 percent in various spellings) the most popular names for women. There were some biblical names other than John—almost 2 percent Adam, for example—but the popularity of Peter, Paul, Abraham, David, and others was still in the future.

4   England, like other countries in the Middle Ages, was mainly a rural and male-dominated society. There were no large cities. Some groups of people lived within the walls of a castle or nearby; still others clustered in villages from which workers trudged short distances each day to tend the crops or the livestock, or where they remained to do their smithing, wagon making, tailoring, or other tasks. Women often worked beside the men in the fields, and in a family wealthy enough to have its own cow or a few pigs or sheep, the women were likely to be responsible for the animals' care. Women's libera-

tion was centuries away and largely undreamed of—although older England had had some strong queens, and Shakespeare's plays would later reflect some influence of women on medieval national affairs. In general, women were subservient, and their subservience was to be shown in the naming processes getting under way.

5   Almost all the occupational names, for example, refer to work done mainly or entirely by men in the Middle Ages, and countless fathers but few mothers were memorialized in names that would become family names. Had women's prestige been higher we would today have many persons with names like Milkmaid, Buxom, and Margaretson.

6   If the Middle Ages had been urbanized, no doubt the use of second names would have accelerated. If a city has three thousand Williams, ways must be found to indicate which William one talks about. A typical medieval village, though, might have had only five or ten Williams, a similar number of Johns, and maybe two or three Roberts or Thomases.

7   Even so, distinctions often needed to be made. If two villagers were talking about you (John, you remember, is who you are), misunderstandings would arise if each had a different John in mind. So qualifications were added, as in imaginary bits of conversation like these:

"A horse stepped on John's foot."
"John from the hill?"
"No. John of the dale."

"John the son of William?"
"No. John the son of Robert."

"John the smith?
"No. John the tailor."

"John the long?"
"No. John the bald."

8   In the rush of conversation the little, unimportant words could drop out or be slurred over so that John from the hill became John hill, and the other persons could be John dale, John William's son, John Robert's son, John smith, John tailor, John long, and John bald (or ballard, which means "the bald one"). The capital letters that we now associate with surnames are only scribal conventions introduced later on.

9   Distinctions like those illustrated in the conversations were a step toward surnames. But the son of John the smith might be Robert the wainwright (wagon maker). That is, he did not inherit the designation smith from his father. There were no true English surnames—family names—until Robert the son of John smith became known as Robert smith (or Smith) even though his occupation was a wainwright, a fletcher (arrow maker), a tanner or barker (leather worker), or anything else. Only when the second name was passed down from one generation to the next did it become a surname.

10   That step did not occur suddenly or uniformly, although throughout most of Europe it was a medieval development. Ewen has described the details of the development in England, basing his scholarly analysis on thousands of entries in tax rolls, court records, and other surviving documents. He has pointed out that before the fourteenth century most of the differentiating adjuncts were prefaced by *filius* (son of), as in Adam fil' Gilberti (Adam, son of Gilbert), by *le* (the), as in Beaudrey le Teuton, by *de* (of, from), as in Rogerius de Molis (Roger from the mills), or by *atta* (at the), as in John atte Water (John at the water), which later might be John Atwater. These particles often dropped out. Thus a fourteenth-century scribe began writing his name as David Tresruf, but other evidence shows that Tresruf was simply a place name and that David de Tresruf was the way the scribe earlier wrote his name.

11   Almost all English and Continental surnames fall into the four categories I have illustrated:

Place Names	John Hill, John Atwater
Patronyms (or others based on personal names)	John Robertson, John Williams, John Alexander
Occupational Names	John Smith, John Fletcher
Descriptive Names	John Long, John Armstrong

12   With a few exceptions the million-plus surnames that Americans bear are of these four sorts. If we were mainly an Oriental or an African nation, the patterns would be different. But we are primarily European in our origins, and in Europe it seemed natural to identify each person during the surname-giving period according to location, parentage, occupation, appearance or other characteristics.

13   It never used to occur to me that my name and almost everyone else's name has a meaning, now often unknown even to its possessors. My own name, I found, is a place name. A *hook* is a sharp bend in a stream or a peninsula or some odd little corner of land. My paternal ancestors, who came from Somerset in southern England, lived on such a hook, probably one of the many irregularly shaped bits of land in Somerset. The numerous Hookers, like General Joseph Hooker in the Civil War, lived in similar places in the name-giving period. Hocking(s), Hoke(r), Horn(e), and Horman(n) are other English or German names that share the meaning of Hook, so they are my cousins, by semantics though not by blood. So are the Dutch Hoekstra, van Hoek, and Haack, who lived in their own odd little corners in the Netherlands. . . .

14   The fourfold identification of people by place, ancestry, occupation, or description has worked well, and only science fiction writers today ever suggest that our names may or should be replaced by numbers or number-letter combinations. Even an ordinary name like William Miller, George Rivers, or Anne Armstrong can acquire an individuality and a rememberable quality hard to imagine for 27–496–3821 or Li94T8633. I'd probably not enjoy a love affair with American names that looked like mere license plate identifications. . . .

15   Often, superficially different American surnames turn out to be essentially the same name in meaning when translated from the foreign language into English. I've already mentioned some of the foreign equivalents of the occupational name Smith and the patronym Johnson.

16   Place names, often unique or nearly so, are not likely to be internationally duplicated except when they refer to geographically common features like bodies of water or land masses. We may illustrate the possibilities with the English surname Hill, whose German equivalent may be Buhl, Buehler, Knor(r), or Piehl, paralleled by Dutch Hoger and Hoogland (literally "high land"), French Depew and Demont, Italian Costa and Colleti, Finnish Maki (one of Finland's most common names), Hungarian Hegi, Scandinavian Berg, Bergen, Bagge, and Haugen, and Slavic Kopec, Kopecky, and Pagorak, all of which mean "hill" or "small mountain."

17   Differences in size or in skin or hair coloration are international, as many of our personal descriptive surnames confirm. English Brown and Black, for instance, may refer to either dark skin or brown or black hair. (*Black,* however sometimes comes from Old English *blac,* related to our *bleach* and meaning "white" or "light," so Mr. Black's ancestors may have been either fair or dark.) Blake is a variant of Black. The French know the dark person as Le Brun or Moreau, the Germans as Braun, Brun, Mohr, or Schwartz, the Italians as Bruno, the Russians as Chernoff. Pincus refers to a dark-skinned Jew, Mavros to a dark Greek. Dark Irishmen may be named, among other possibilities, Carey, Duff, Dunn(e), Dolan, Dow, or Kearns. Hungarian Fekete has a dark skin. Czechoslovakian Cerny or Czerny (black) reveals linguistic similarity to Polish Czarnik, Czarniak, or Czarnecki and Ukrainian Corney. Spanish Negron is a very dark person.

18   Many names spelled identically are common to two or more languages, and a considerable number of such names have more than a single meaning. So Gray, although usually an English name meaning "gray haired," in a few instances is French for a person from Gray (the estate of Gradus) in France. Gray must therefore be classified both as a personal descriptor and a place name. Hoff is usually German for a farm or an enclosed place, but less often is English for Hoff (pagan temple), a place in Westmoreland. Many Scandinavian names are identical in Denmark, Norway, and Sweden, although spelling variants such as *-sen* and *-son* suggest the likelihood of one country rather than another. In general a person must know at least a little about his or her ancestry before determining with assurance the nationality and most likely meaning of his or her name.

19   A small percentage of names, few of them common in the United States, is derived from sources other than the basic four. For example, a few Jewish names are based on acronyms or initials. Thus Baran or Baron sometimes refers to *Ben Rabbi Nachman,* and *Brock* to *Ben Rabbi Kalman.* Zak, abbreviating *zera kedoshim* (the seed of martyrs) is often respelled Sack, Sacks, or Sachs, although these may also be place names for people from Saxony. Katz is sometimes based on *kohen tzedek* (priest of righteousness), and Segal (in several spellings) can be from *segan leviyyah,* (member of the tribe of Levi).

20   Other Jewish names are somewhat arbitrary German or Yiddish pairings, usually with pleasant connotations, like Lowenthal (lion's valley), Gottlieb (God's love), or Finkelstein (little finch stone). Some modern Swedes have replaced their conventional patronyms (Hanson, Jorgenson, etc.) with nature words or pairings of nature words like Lind (linden), Lindstrom (linden stream), Asplund (aspen grove), and Ekberg (oak mountain).

21   Numerous Norwegian surnames are a special variety of place names called farm names. Many Norwegian farms have held the same name for hundreds of years, and people from a given farm have come to be known by its name. So Bjornstad, for instance, means "Bjorn's farm," and Odega(a)rd means "dweller on uncultivated land."

22   Japanese names are comparable to some of the Jewish and Swedish names mentioned a moment ago, in that they frequently combine two words, one or both of which may refer to nature. So Fujikawa combines two elements meaning "wisteria" and "river," Hayakawa is "early river," Tanaka is "ricefield, middle," Inoue is "well (noun), upper," and Kawasaki is "river, headland."

23   Chinese surnames are very few—perhaps nine or ten hundred in all—and endlessly repeated. A few dozen of them are especially widely used, like the familiar Wong, which may mean either "field" or "large body of water," Chin (the name of the first great dynasty, of more than two thousand years ago), Wang "yellow" or "prince," Le "pear tree," and Yee "I." . . .

24   Not more than one American surname in twenty, however, can be classified with assurance in any category other than the big four: places, patronyms, occupations, and descriptors.

Comprehension

1. Words to talk about:

   - Most names of your day were *Norman French*
   - people from *Saxony*
   - influence of women on *medieval* national affairs
   - the *name-giving* period
   - cousins, *by semantics though not by blood*

2. Hook writes directly to his reader beginning with "Suppose that you. . . ." What is the effect of addressing *you* directly?

Discussion

1. For the Middle Ages, he lists many fewer women's than men's names. There were probably just as many women as men and they must have

had names. Can you figure out why he doesn't list equivalent numbers?

2. Hook explained how his own surname was a "semantic cousin" to such names as Hocking, Hoke(r), van Hoek, and Horn. By using your knowledge of word meanings, plus Hook's information, look at the surnames in the left column and try to find one or more "semantic cousins" in the right column.

LeGrande	Knorr/Piehl
Fletcher	Waggoner
Atwater	Ekberg
Linden	Wickman
Tanner	Gross/Gordo/Nagy
Chandler	Lindstrom
Redman	Miller
Wainwright	Barker
Mueller	Parker
Hill	Rivers
Forrester	Rousse
Oakland	Arrowsmith

3. How is it that someone with the surname of Black might have ancestors whose coloring was either unusually dark or unusually light?
4. What do some Jewish, Swedish, and Japanese names have in common?
5. Explain the reasoning behind Hook's statement that "If the Middle Ages had been urbanized, no doubt the use of second names would have accelerated."
6. Why were so many names of the Middle Ages French? For example, why in old records do we find names preceded by *filius* to mean "son of," by *le* to mean "the," or by *de* to mean "of" or "from"?
7. What does it mean that the same scribe sometimes wrote his name David de Tresruf and sometimes David Tresruf?
8. In a December 13, 1993, story about Prince Charles and Princess Diana of Wales, *Time* magazine wrote "This Thursday marks the first anniversary of the Waleses' official separation. . . ." How does referring to Charles and Diana as "the Waleses," relate to the naming customs that Hook described?
9. Records from Chaucer's time have found listings for such names as Fleming, French, and Holland, apparently given to travelers from those regions. Look through a local telephone directory and see if you can find modern equivalents. What are they?
10. Hook described the practice of putting capitals at the beginning of names as a "scribal convention." What are some other writing customs that English speakers have agreed to follow?

Workshop 1.1

Names: Common and Uncommon

Hook refers to his "love affair" with names as something he wouldn't have if all of us were identified by numbers or codes. Names and naming appeal to the intellectually curious partly because there are so many quirks in the system.

PART I: NAMES WITH A SMILE

BRAIN TEASERS

1. Tom Swifties are puns that get their name from the *Tom Swift* books popular with kids in the 1940s. The jokes are as old as " 'Let's Run,' Tom said swiftly," and as new as " 'We're leaving Bosnia,' Tom said acerbicly." Other examples include " 'Can I get you a martini?' Tom asked drily," " 'I'll make the coffee,' she said perkily," and " 'Get to the back of the boat,' Tom said sternly." Create two or three Tom Swifties of your own. Once you think of some adverbs (those adjectives changed into adverbs by an *-ly* ending), then it's fairly easy to think of a beginning that will relate in different ways to your adverb. The funniest ones will have a surprise pun hidden under the obvious appropriateness.

2. A similar, but more literary, wordplay game that is making the rounds on e-mail is for the listener to guess the title of a book being referred to as in, " 'I don't care how earnest you are,' he said wildly." The answer is Oscar Wilde's *The Importance of Being Earnest*. Figure out the answers to these others:
   ■ "But Rochester, you already have a wife!" she said airily.
   ■ "Where's my wife?" Gatsby asked lackadaisically.
   ■ "God bless us everyone," he said timidly.
   Try your hand at making up a new example.

3. Puns that rely on the double meanings of people's names include, "Is Helen Reddy?" "Will Buckley Gore Vidal?" "Take the Monet and run," "Hello, Dali," and "Cezanne's Greetings." When Donald Trump failed to make a $30 million loan payment, the *Miami Herald* headlined its story with "Donald Ducks!" Working in small groups, make a list of twenty or thirty names that would be recognized by your classmates; for example, local politicians, performers, or other celebrities. Examine the names for possible double meanings and see if you can create one or two funny statements modeled on the pattern shown here.

4. When baseball writer Peter Schmuck moved to the *Baltimore Sun* from California he wrote an introductory column about himself explaining that Schmuck "is my real name," and that "I never considered changing it." He gave his reason for leaving California: "I could no longer tolerate a state that once turned down my request for a personalized license plate on the grounds that my surname is 'obscene and offensive to public decency' " (*Miami Herald*, Feb. 4, 1990). Schmuck had learned to make fun of his name, perhaps inspired by the slogan of the people who make

"What he thinks of the book hardly matters. He won't be able to resist dropping a name like T. Coraghessan Boyle."

Source: Cartoon by Ed Fisher © 1993 The Chronicle of Higher Education/ Reprinted by permission of Ed Fisher.

jam: "With a name like Smuckers, you have to be good." Have you known anyone whose name has unpleasant connotations? If so, how did they handle the situation? Were they able to joke about it? Give an example of their patter.

5. Celebrity parents who appear in the news for having given their children unusual names include country singer Billy Ray Cyrus and his wife Leticia, who named

continued

WORKSHOP 1.1

Names: Common and Uncommon   continued

their son Braison Chance, and actor Woody Harrelson and wife Laura, who named their daughter Denni Montana. Ron Howard has said that he names his children after the places of their conception. Before they separated, Bruce Willis said he was still hoping for a son because he and Demi Moore agreed that he would name the boys and she would name the girls. He prefers plain names while Demi likes exotic ones. So far, they have three daughters: Rumer Glenn, Scout (after the girl in the well-known novel *To Kill a Mockingbird*), and Tallulah Belle. Do you know of other interesting names that celebrities have chosen for their children? Why do we know so much about their names?

PART II: GENERIC EPONYMS: THE MOST COMMON OF PROPER NAMES

In the early 1990s, Michalene Busico wrote an article entitled "Hi, I'm Bob" for the *San Jose Mercury News*. She wrote that "somewhere along the line, Bob stopped being just a name and became a three-letter (OK. two-letter) shorthand for an uncomplicated way of life, an unassuming attitude, and unsophisticated look. Which means, although you may not be named Bob, you can be a Bob."

The article commemorated the movie *What About Bob?* that was premiering in San Jose. Busico's article illustrated the playful way in which people are attracted to some particular common names. Besides the film, Busico cited *The Bob Book;* a Nissan commercial featuring signs for "Bob's Road," "Bob's Expressway," and "Yield to Bob"; Twin Peaks' evil BOB; the singing group called the Bobs; and Bob's Big Boy restaurants. A couple of years later, she could have also cited a major promotional campaign for an easy-to-use software program named Bob; presidential candidate Bob Dole, who painted the name BOB on his airplane; and the BOB (Bank One Ballpark), home of the Arizona Diamondbacks baseball team.

BRAIN TEASERS

1. What literary purpose do you think is filled by finding a name such as Bob to stand for the ordinary guy?
2. Like Bob, several other common names have found their way into English where they are used almost like "anonymous" or "generic" eponyms in that they cannot be traced to a particular individual. The most anonymous of the generic eponyms are legal terms for people who cannot or do not want to be identified: John Doe, Richard Roe, Mary Moe, and Jane Doe or Jane Roe. One of the most controversial legal cases of our time was filed under one of these anonymous eponyms. What was it? How does that kind of anonymity differ from the kind implied in this

line from Max Shulman's novel *Barefoot Boy with Cheek*, "It's getting hard enough to handle the votes without letting every Tom, Dick, and Harry in on the election"?

3. How is "a good ol' Joe," different from "a Bob"? Here are several uses of Joe as a generic eponym listed in alphabetical order. Rearrange them so that they are roughly in chronological order based on when they came into popular use.

   ■ GI (from "General Issue") Joe = a soldier
   ■ Holy Joe = a chaplain
   ■ J. Random Hacker = a computer Joe
   ■ Joe Blow = a blowhard
   ■ Joe Camel = the controversial cartoon character who in 1997 lost his job of advertising Camel cigarettes
   ■ Joe College or Joe Prep = a college student
   ■ Joe Cool = a cool dude
   ■ Joe Schmo = a fool
   ■ Joe Six-Pack = a beer drinker
   ■ Joe Water = trademark name for caffeine enhanced bottled water

4. Jack is associated with the common worker as seen in the phrase, "Jack of all trades; master of none." In fourteenth-century France, aristocrats referred to peasants as Jacque and to the 1358 peasant revolt as "the Jacquerie." In *A Tale of Two Cities*, Charles Dickens amuses readers by showing a Monsieur and Madame Defarge in conversation with a group of men identified as "Jacques One, Jacques Two, Jacques Three, Jacques Four, and Jacques Five"—quite literally "every man Jack." Try to think of a half-dozen work-related terms in common use that include the name *jack*. It has been used in this sense for so long that often the name is not capitalized.

5. John is an alternate form of Jack and is used almost as often. John Bull personifies Great Britain, Johnny Reb is a Confederate soldier, and John Barleycorn is an alcoholic drink. A Johnny-come-lately jumps on the bandwagon after everyone else is aboard. Poor John and Cheap John have negative connotations as do "john" for a prostitute's customer, a Dear John letter for a brush-off, johnny for a hospital gown, long johns for winter underwear, and john for toilet, which in 1994 inspired the creation of a "Justice for John Committee." Why, if it has so many negative connotations, do parents keep giving the name to their sons?

6. Far fewer work terms are based on women's names, but the religious and charitable organization of the Salvation Army is sometimes referred to as Sal, Sally Ann, and Sally. Can you figure out why? Also, what contributed to the Bell Telephone Company being personified as Ma Bell? And what does it say about the

continued

WORKSHOP 1.1

Names: Common and Uncommon   continued

female presence of women in banking when lenders give a human touch to big bureaucracy by talking about "getting *Fannie Mae's* approval" rather than "the approval of the *Federal National Mortgage Association*"?

7. Nancy is a diminutive of the name Ann derived from a Hebrew word meaning "grace." From this noble beginning, the name has been adapted to some less-than-positive uses. Can you think of any?

8. Jenny is a nickname for Jane and Janet. A "spinning jenny" got its name from the fact that women most often did the spinning. How has the name been adopted into the animal kingdom?

9. Jill used to be such a common name that it stood for any girl as in the nursery rhyme, "Jack and Jill went up the hill. . . ." Jills probably didn't spurn their lovers anymore than Suzies or Janes did, but their name nevertheless became a verb meaning "to drop one's lover in an insensitive fashion." What's the word?

10. A different kind of anonymous eponym relies for its effect on a descriptive word being put with a name, as when speakers use rhyme such as Starvin' Marvin, alliteration as in Gloomy Gus, and assonance as in Alibi Ike or Screaming Meemie. Try to think of a couple of other such names based on (1) rhyming, (2) assonance (the vowels are the same), and (3) alliteration (they start with the same consonants).

PART III: SOURCES OF SURNAMES

Go through this list of well-known individuals and divide their surnames into the four basic categories that Hook identified: place names, patronyms, occupational names, personal descriptions. If you don't know the meaning of some of the names, see if you can get a clue from looking in a dictionary for such words as *bank, cart, ford,* and *warren.*

Terry Anderson	Paul Newman
Russell Baker	Oliver North
Tallulah Bankhead	Tyrone Power
James Brown	Pat Robertson
Eddie Cantor	Diane Sawyer
Jimmy Carter	Peter Sellers
Winston Churchill	Oliver Stone
Clint Eastwood	Donald Sutherland
Gerald Ford	Margaret Thatcher
Alan Greenspan	Harry Truman
Jesse Jackson	Earl Warren
Steven King	H. G. Wells
David Lean	Vanna White
Walter Mondale	Woodrow Wilson

Now examine the surnames of your classmates and see how many names you can trace back to one of those categories of creation.

MAKING A NAME FOR YOURSELF

Leslie Dunkling

In news stories about celebrities, it's almost a cliché to have lines such as this one about Toni Morrison when she won the Nobel Prize in literature: "Morrison was born Chloe Anthony Wofford in the steel-mill city of Lorain, Ohio." When Tiny Tim suffered a heart attack, one reporter wrote, "Tim, whose given name is Herbert Khaury, is best known for his 1968 hit, 'Tiptoe Through the Tulips,' " and in a story about country singer Boxcar Willie doing CPR on a fan who suffered a heart attack, the reporter wrote, "Boxcar Willie, whose real name is Cecil Martin, learned CPR in the air force." In this excerpt from the sixth edition of the 1993 *Guinness Book of Names,* Leslie Dunkling writes about some of the reasons that people change their names.

1   A great many people have a burning ambition to make a name for themselves. Although "name" here is used for "reputation," the name itself remains of great importance. If it is to be widely used and remembered, other people must be able to say it and spell it easily, and it must not suggest anything undesirable or silly. At the same time, a slight dash of the unusual is welcome to provide the necessary individuality. Many of our surnames, casually bestowed centuries ago and badly treated since, do not fulfill these criteria. Bearers of such names are left with little alternative but to change them if they really are set on a public life. They must begin quite literally by making a name for themselves.

STAGE NAMES

2   The world of entertainment naturally comes immediately to mind. Stage names are an accepted part of the profession. Among those who have adapted their real surnames to some purpose are Dirk Bogarde, originally named Derek Gentron Gaspart Ulric van den Bogaerde; Fred Astaire—Frederick Austerlitz; Danny Kaye—David Daniel Kaminsky; Jerry Lewis—Joseph Levitch; Greta Garbo—Greta Gustafsson. The smallest possible change was made by Warren Beatty, formerly Beaty. His sister, Shirley Maclean Beaty, emerged as Shirley MacLaine. Liberace is one who retained his real surname but dropped the Wladziu Valentino that preceded it. Others have preferred to take more

drastic action and forget the old surname completely. Well-known examples include Diana Dors, formerly Diana Fluck; Judy Garland—Frances Gumm; Kirk Douglas—Issur Danielovitch Demsky; Engelbert Humperdinck—Arnold Dorsey.

3   Politicians can hardly be described as entertainers, but they also need names that the public can cope with. Spiro Agnew understandably adapted his Greek family name, Anagnostopoulos, for this reason. Such changes differ from the adoption of political pseudonyms, which have been used in countries such as Russia. Stalin "steel," was chosen by I. V. Dzhugashvili, whose real name derived from a word meaning "dross." Lenin's name was meant to be a reminder of political disturbances on the River Lena in Siberia, though it exists as a real name, derived from Alexander. Lenin's real name was Ulyanov.

4   Mention of Russian names brings us back to stage names, for in certain circles, such as the ballet, they have great prestige. Those not as fortunate as Rudolf Nureyev, who was able to use his real name, have sometimes adopted one that has a suitably Russian-sounding flavor. Alice Marks became Alicia Markova, while Patrick Healey-Kay changed to Anton Dolin. The dignity and romanticism of such names contrasts interestingly with the names of some other dancers, who appear in the Parisian Crazy Horse Cabaret. The latter appear under such evocative names (and little else) as Pamela Boum-Boum, Polly Underground, and Rita Cadillac.

PEN NAMES

5   Writers' pseudonyms have been used far longer than stage names and often for different reasons. The desire is not necessarily to escape from an unfortunate name, but genuinely to conceal the writer's true identity. In the past it was sometimes thought that readers would be prejudiced against women writers, so many of them wrote as men or tried to conceal their sex in noncommittal names, such as those used by the Brontë sisters, Currier, Ellis, and Acton Bell. Other authors have been ashamed of their works for one reason or another and have not wished anyone to know their true identities. In modern times there are authors who would flood the market if they used their own name all the time, and a string of pseudonyms becomes necessary. A single pen name can, on the other hand, conceal the fact that several different authors are writing the stories concerned. Finally, if an author has made himself something of an authority in one area, he may feel that another name is required when he turns to pastures new.

6   One would expect authors to choose pen names that have linguistic point to them. Lewis Carroll has a suitably etymological connection with Charles Lutwidge Dodgson, its inventor. Lutwidge is a form of Ludwig, which can be directly translated as Lewis. Charles is Carolus in Latin, and Carroll simply

adapts it slightly. The 19th-century writer Ouida looks as if she transferred her name from the city of that name in Morocco, but she herself explained it as a natural linguistic development. It represented her own attempt as a child to pronounce her middle name, Louise.

ALIASES

7   These last examples once again retain a definite link with the real name, which many people who adopt a new name consider to be necessary. Traces of name magic are revealed here, for this hints at a deep-rooted belief that one's real name is somehow part of one's real self, and that complete abandonment of it will have evil consequences. Criminal records support this contention strongly, for an analysis of aliases that have been used shows that the adopted surnames normally have the same initial, number of syllables and basic sound as the originals. What appears to be a totally new name is more often drawn from the namer's immediate onomastic environment. It will be the mother's maiden name or the surname of a close friend, or a name transferred from a street or place that has strong personal associations. The link with the real past is maintained.

8   As we have seen, immigration into an English-speaking country can be another reason for name change and here again an attempt is often made to link with the original name. The Ukrainian Vasyl Mykula who became William McCulla showed one way of doing it. Other Russian-English pairs are Prishchipenko—Price, Chernyshev—Chester, Grushko—Grey. Direct translation, e.g. of German Muller, French Meunier, Hungarian Molnar, Dutch Mulder, into English Miller achieves a similar result. But by far the commonest reason for a surname change is marriage. . . .

OTHER SURNAME CHANGES

9   Meanwhile, however, a large number of ordinary people who are not seeking public fame or trying to conceal their identities, change their surnames every year. They make use of a very simple legal process to rid themselves of a name which for one reason or another is an embarrassment to them. Who can possibly blame the Mr. Bugg who became a Howard, or the gentlemen called Bub, Holdwater, Poopy, Piddle, Honeybum, Leakey, Rumpe, and Teate who quietly dropped these surnames a century ago? Curiously enough, they were criticized at the time, though the criticisms were directed at the names they adopted, thought to be too high and mighty for ordinary citizens.

10   Personally, I can only wonder why more people do not follow the sensible example set by these name-changes. Why on earth do I, for example, put up with Dunkling, which is frequently converted into Dumpling by the

hard-of-hearing or malicious? I have had its replacement standing by for years, an easy-to-spell, easy-to-say, pleasant-sounding name with the most respectable literary and other associations, and not, to my knowledge, at present attached to any other family. If I do not adopt it, is it because—not being an actor by nature—I would not be able to live out my life behind an onomastic disguise? Or am I conceited enough to think that I can overcome the natural disadvantages of my name and win through anyway?

11   Ideas about what is unusual also change with the passing of time. At one time somebody named Petard, which derives from a word meaning "to break wind," would presumably have wanted to change it: today his friends might simply associate him vaguely with a passage in *Hamlet* and he would not feel under attack. A Belcher, on the other hand, was quite happy when others interpreted his name as bel chiere, "pretty face." The forgetting of this early meaning has left him sadly exposed.

12   Other men are quite happy with their names until they reach adulthood and take up a profession. They then fall victim to the inevitable comments about their being Berriman, the undertaker, or D. Kaye, the dentist. Partnership names such as Reid and Wright for Belfast printers, and Doolittle and Dally for estate agents are also much commented on, although they do have the advantage of attracting publicity.

13   If you are seriously thinking of changing your surname you would do well for your descendants' sake to begin it with a letter near the front of the alphabet. The custom when groups of people are gathered together for any purpose of working through them in alphabetical order has had a serious effect on people named Young and the like, psychologists tell us. They are constantly made to feel insignificant because they are dealt with last.

COMPREHENSION

1. Words to talk about:

   - the adoption of *political pseudonyms*
   - appear under such *evocative* names
   - has a suitably *etymological* connection
   - from the namer's immediate *onomastic environment*
   - by the hard-of-hearing or *malicious*

2. What criteria does Dunkling give for a name that is to be widely used and remembered?
3. How do reasons for pennames differ from reasons for stage names?
4. What other reasons did Dunkling give for people changing their names?

Discussion

1. Go through the name changes that Dunkling writes about in the first paragraph under "Stage Names" and see if you can figure out why the changes were made. How did the new names affect the performer's status?

2. What is high status for one field may not be high status for another. As you look at the following name changes, all of which were devised to mark new and more prestigious roles in life, decide which of these other reasons contributed to the desire for a change.
   (a) To increase individuality and memorability
   (b) To connect the person to his or her career goals
   (c) To get rid of an unpleasant connotation
   (d) To show (or hide) a religious or ethnic identification
   Also, look for relationships between the old and the new names and see if you can make observations about the onomastic (study of proper names) environments of some of the names.

   - When Margaret Mitchell turned in her manuscript of *Gone with the Wind,* her Irish heroine was named Pansy. An editor sent Mitchell back to try again, and she returned with Scarlett O'Hara.
   - Akebono, the first American to win the Japanese sumo wrestling championship, was born Chad Rowan in Oahu, Hawaii.
   - When Geraldo Rivera practiced law in New York City he did so under the name of Jerry Rivers.
   - A couple of generations ago, Irish writers John Cassidy and John Phelan changed their names to Sean O'Casey and Sean O'Faiolain, respectively.
   - An aspiring New York comedian changed her name from Caryn Johnson to Whoopi Goldberg.
   - Boxer Cassius Clay changed his name to Mohammad Ali.
   - In the early 1800s, Louisa May Alcott's father, Bronson, changed their family name from Allcox to Alcott.
   - In his first movie, Arnold Schwarzenegger appeared under the name of Arnold Strong, but then decided to go back to his German name.
   - The first sexy movie star of the 1920s was Alan Bolt, better known as Rudolph Valentino.
   - The uniquely named singers Simon and Garfunkel started their career as Tom and Jerry, appearing as such on Dick Clark's *American Bandstand.*

TWO ARTICLES ABOUT WOMEN AND SURNAMES

The discussions currently taking place in relation to women adopting (or not adopting) their husbands' surnames when they marry is a clear illustration of the principle that as a culture changes so, too, will its language. Until the last few decades, most people assumed that women were legally required to take their husbands' surnames, but during the late 1970s and 1980s, a variety of court decisions and scholarly as well as popular articles upheld and publicized the fact that people have the right to take whatever surname they desire as long as it is not for fraudulent purposes. Following are two articles presenting some of the different viewpoints on the issue. The first is written by Anna Quindlen, a novelist and columnist for the *New York Times;* the second is a news story by Karen De Witt, which also appeared in the *New York Times,* eight years later.

THE NAME IS MINE

Anna Quindlen

1 I am on the telephone to the emergency room of the local hospital. My elder son is getting stitches in his palm, and I have called to make myself feel better, because I am at home, waiting, and my husband is there, holding him. I am 34 years old, and I am crying like a child, making a slippery mess of my face. "Mrs. Krovatin?" says the nurse, and for the first time in my life I answer "Yes."

2 This is a story about a name. The name is mine. I was given it at birth, and I have never changed it, although I married. I could come up with lots of reasons why. It was a political decision, a simple statement that I was somebody and not an adjunct of anybody, especially a husband. As a friend of mine told her horrified mother, "He didn't adopt me, he married me."

3 It was a professional and a personal decision, too. I grew up with an ugly dog of a name, one I came to love because I thought it was weird and unlovable. Amid the Debbies and Kathys of my childhood, I had a first name only my grandmothers had and a last name that began with a strange letter. "Sorry,

the letters I, O, Q, U, V, X, Y and Z are not available," the catalogues said about monogrammed key rings and cocktail napkins. Seeing my name in black on white at the top of a good story, suddenly it wasn't an ugly dog anymore.

4   But neither of these are honest reasons, because they assume rational consideration, and it so happens that when it came to changing my name, there was no consideration, rational or otherwise. It was mine. It belonged to me. I don't even share a checking account with my husband. Damned if I was going to be hidden beneath the umbrella of his identity.

5   It seemed like a simple decision. But nowadays I think the only simple decisions are whether to have grilled cheese or tuna fish for lunch. Last week, my older child wanted an explanation of why he, his dad and his brother have one name, and I have another.

6   My answer was long, philosophical and rambling—that is to say, unsatisfactory. What's in a name? I could have said disingenuously. But I was talking to a person who had just spent three torturous, exhilarating years learning names for things, and wanted to communicate to him that mine meant something quite special to me, had seemed as form-fitting as my skin, and as painful to remove. Personal identity and independence, however, were not what he was looking for; he just wanted to make sure I was one of them. And I am—and then again, I am not. When I made this decision, I was part of a couple. Now, there are two me's, the me who is the individual and the me who is part of a family of four, a family of four in which, in a small way, I am left out.

7   A wise friend who finds herself in the same fix says she never wants to change her name, only to have a slightly different identity as a family member, an identity for pediatricians' offices and parent-teacher conferences. She also says that the entire situation reminds her of the women's movement as a whole. We did these things as individuals, made these decisions about ourselves and what we wanted to be and do. And they were good decisions, the right decisions. But we based them on individual choice, not on group dynamics. We thought in terms of our sense of ourselves, not our relationships with others.

8   Some people found alternative solutions: hyphenated names, merged names, matriarchal names for the girls and patriarchal ones for the boys, one name at work and another at home. I did not like those choices; I thought they were middle grounds, and I didn't live much in the middle ground at the time. I was once slighlty disdainful of women who went all the way and changed their names. But I now know too many smart, independent, terrific women who have the same last names as their husbands to be disdainful anymore. (Besides, if I made this decision as part of a feminist world view, it seems dishonest to turn around and trash other women for deciding as they did.)

9   I made the choice. I haven't changed my mind. I've just changed my life. Sometimes I feel like one of those worms I used to hear about in biology, the

ones that, chopped in half, walked off in different directions. My name works fine for one half, not quite as well for the other. I would never give it up. Except for that one morning when I talked to the nurse at the hospital, I always answer the question, "Mrs. Krovatin?" with "No, this is Mr. Krovatin's wife." It's just that I understand the down side now.

10   When I decided not to disappear beneath my husband's umbrella, it did not occur to me that I would be the only one left outside. It did not occur to me that I would ever care—not enough to change, just enough to think about the things we do on our own own and what they mean when we aren't on our own anymore.

STAND-BY-YOUR-MAN "MRS." MAKES A COMEBACK

Karen De Witt

1   Women who threw away their bras, went off to work and took husbands without taking husband's names are in for a surprise.

2   Mrs. is back.

3   Even if they have established professional identities, women who march down the aisle are apparently becoming more willing to exchange their surnames for their husbands' along with the wedding vows.

4   The shift is a gentle one, and not one that many people are counting. But a personal declaration of independence—my name!—that had become orthodoxy in certain circles is taking some flak from a new generation.

5   Here, for example, is Crystal Dozier, a 29-year-old product-research manager for the McGraw-Hill Continuing Education Center in Washington, who took her husband's name when she got married two years ago.

6   "I wanted to buck that feminist viewpoint that in order to be a real woman you have to have your identity and it's defined by what you're called. I know who I am, and I'm going to follow the tradition that I chose."

7   James Madden, associate publisher at *American Demographics* magazine, said he isn't surprised.

8   "The 'baby bust' generation," he said, "tends to be a little more traditional, waiting longer to get married, and when they do, looking for more-traditional marriages."

9   Chalk it up to nostalgia from a generation whose mothers shucked tradition for careers and the work force. Maybe those who grew up admiring *The Brady Bunch* couldn't imagine Carol Brady having any name other than "Mrs. Brady," and decided that they would like to be called Mrs., too.

10   Some speculate about a reaction to the more strident feminists, who saw in the matronly honorific a symbol of male oppression.

11   Others, like William Dunn, author of *The Baby Bust: A Generation Comes of Age* (American Demographics, 1993), argue that those born after the 1960s are more frequently the children of divorce or single-parent households and are more conservative in general than their parents' generation.

12   It's not that the old tradition ever came undone, really, except among well-educated professional women who established careers and professional identities before marriage.

13   A survey last year in *American Demographics* showed that 14 percent of women under age 40 had kept their maiden names, as against 10 percent of women in their 40s and 5 percent of women 50 or older.

14   The gap was consistent with educational differences between the age groups. Fewer than 5 percent of wives who had only a high-school education used something other than their husband's names, compared with 15 percent of those with bachelor's degrees and more than 20 percent of those with post-graduate degrees.

15   But the daughters and younger sisters of that last group seem to be losing interest in the cause.

16   No less a source than *Bride's* magazine has acknowledged, in its December-January issue, that something is afoot, noting that keeping a maiden name is "a thorny issue."

17   "It's a highly personal decision," said Millie Martini Bratten, editor in chief of the magazine. "But many younger women are taking their husbands' names. Even some older women said they were having difficulty making the decision, particularly if they knew they were going to have children."

18   The decision entails all kinds of complications.

19   "I always assumed that I would take my husband's name when I got married, but it did seem odd at the beginning," said Lori Boswell, born Lori Perry, who is a 25-year-old administrative assistant at a biotechnology company in Boston. "My first inclination was to use 'Perry Boswell,' but that was a mouthful, so I went ahead and had everything changed. It made life easier having the same name as your husband: You can say you're the Boswells."

20   Crystal Dozier had another concern.

21   "You have to look at it from the man's point of view," she said. "I think it's an ego booster for a man to have his wife take her husband's name, especially for a professional black woman. It makes a statement to the world that 'Even though I'm professional, I still stand by my man.' "

COMPREHENSION

1. Words to talk about:
   - an *adjunct* of anybody
   - I could have said *disingenuously*
   - had become *orthodoxy* in certain circles
2. How does Quindlen draw readers into the problem she's discussing?
3. Besides the dramatic effect of Quindlen's introduction, what information does her lead impart?
4. Compare Quindlen's lead to De Witt's. How did De Witt draw readers into her article?

DISCUSSION

1. Compare the data presented by the two writers. Why didn't Quindlen get some statistics for her piece?
2. What do De Witt's statistics show? Do they fit with your experience?
3. One of Quindlen's techniques for being efficient in communicating complicated thoughts is to use original metaphors. Find and explain three or four such metaphors.
4. What did Quindlen mean when she said, "If I made this decision [to keep Quindlen as her name] as part of a feminist world view, it seems dishonest to turn around and trash other women for deciding as they did"?
5. One of the women that De Witt quoted identified herself as a "professional black woman." Is ethnicity a factor in such a decision as this one? What other factors will influence a couple as they decide how to "make two into one"?
6. Quindlen mentioned people finding alternative solutions to the naming problem. In a minifeature about Washington power couples, those "whose careers are brilliantly synergistic," *Time* magazine (Aug. 23, 1993) listed several Washington, D.C., couples under the heading, "Honey, I've Asked the Macbeths in for Drinks." The best known of the couples are listed below. (At the time the article was published, some were engaged but are now married.) Identify the naming pattern the woman goes by. If you know anything about the couple, perhaps you can conjecture on why a particular pattern was chosen. Keep in mind that before the 1970s, it was almost unheard of for a woman to keep her family name.

(a) The woman kept only her given name and adopted her husband's surname.
(b) The woman kept her family surname as a middle name and adopted her husband's surname.
(c) The woman kept her family surname without adopting her husband's surname.

Bob and Elizabeth Dole

Ruth Bader Ginsburg and Martin Ginsburg

Marian Wright Edelman and Peter Edelman

Alan Greenspan and Andrea Mitchell

Bruce and Hattie Babbitt

James Carville and Mary Matalin

Al Hunt and Judy Woodruff

Kerry Kennedy Cuomo and Andrew Cuomo

Bob Barnett and Rita Braver

Susan Molinari and Bill Paxon

7. Thirty years ago a listing such as the one above would never have been published; first, because such dual career couples were rare, and second, because magazines and newspapers had style sheets that carefully prescribed how the names of married women should be written. The list would probably have started off with "Mr. and Mrs. Bob Dole." Under what circumstances do you think that form is appropriate?

■
Suggested Topics for Writing

CLASS PROJECTS

1. Prepare an annotated bibliography of information on choosing baby names. If each person in the class finds one good source on the Internet or finds and skims a book designed to help parents choose a name for a new baby, the class could put together a useful bibliography that could help parents decide which information source would best fit their needs. Each student could write a brief (about 200 words) description.

For a book, include the title, author, length, and cost; a description of its contents (does it just list names and their meanings or does it include discussions, and, if so, on what?); the philosophy from which it is written; how convenient it is to use and find (is it available at local libraries or bookstores?); the qualifications of the author; and any other characteristics that are unique. For an Internet source, include how to find the listing; whether it's a chat-room with different people offering their opinions or whether it provides some documented information; and whatever other information you think would be helpful to someone wanting to browse efficiently.

2. Draw up a Living Language box on aptronyms. In 1678, John Bunyan started the custom of giving aptronymic names to characters when he published his allegorical *Pilgrim's Progress*. Among his characters were Christian, Giant Despair, Giant Grim, Faithful, Mr. Moneylove, Mr. Pickthank, Everyman, Mr. Great-Heart, Mr. Honest, Standfast, Mr. Valiant-for-Truth, Mr. Despondency's daughter, Mr. Fearing, Mr. Feeble-Mind, Mr. Brisk, Mrs. Bats-Eyes, and Madam Bubble. Two centuries later, Charles Dickens was equally creative in devising appropriate names for his characters. Today, Ursula LeGuin in her four fantasies about Earthsea gives her characters three different names: a birth name, a use name, and a sacred name. In a much lighter tone, Toni Cade Bambara also gave multiple names to the characters in her humorous short story "Gorilla, My Love." To make a Living Language box on the subject, each class member could contribute a brief paragraph about an especially memorable name or set of names. Besides literature for a general adult audience, you could look at cartoon characters, children's literature and folk tales, and characters on television.

INDIVIDUAL PROJECTS

1. Write the story of your given name. You can look at it from a private and/or a public stance. The private part would be your own story, while in the public part you could write about such things as the meaning and the connotations of your name and what famous or infamous people share it.
2. Do some research and write a history of your family name. Think of the audience for your paper as members of your extended family. Maybe you can distribute it as a family newsletter or send it out as a more-interesting-than-usual holiday greeting.
3. Write a report on the given names chosen by your extended family over the last three or four generations. How have they changed? Can you make any generalizations from them? Has your family grown closer to or further from its ethnic heritage?

4. If you have friends or relatives with a new baby, interview them and write a report that they can save for the baby. Find out the meaning of the name, who else has had the name, how its spelling was chosen, and what hopes the parents have for the name.

5. Write an essay on some aspect of the changes taking place in patterns of married women's surnames. Until early in the 1800s, most married women in the United States were addressed as "Mrs.," followed by their given names and their husband's surnames; for example, Mrs. Martha Washington and Mrs. Dolley Madison. But then it became fashionable, although first viewed as affected or snobbish, for women to share in their husband's accomplishments by using for example, the form Mrs. George Bush. Some women even took their husband's honorary titles as in Mrs. Judge Simmons or Mrs. Doc Heywood.

INFORMATION SOURCES FOR WRITING

Most libraries and bookstores will have recently written books, and perhaps even one or two computer programs, designed to help parents choose names for their babies. Interest groups can be found on the Internet, and a computer assisted search under "Names" will provide titles of news stories and magazine feature articles in which names play a part. Some university libraries subscribe to *Names: A Journal of Onomastics,* which has been published since 1951 by The American Name Society. The titles of some useful books are listed below.

All Those Wonderful Names: A Potpourri of People, Places and Things, by J. N. Hook. New York: Wiley, 1991.

Beyond Jennifer & Jason: An Englightened Guide to Naming Your Baby, by Linda Rosenkrantz and Pamela R. Satran. New York: St. Martin, 1988. In keeping up with the current trend toward Americans naming their children to celebrate their ethnic heritages, the same authors have also written *Beyond Shannon and Sean: An Englightened Guide to Irish Baby Naming; Beyond Sarah and Sam: An Enlightened Guide to Jewish Baby Naming;* and *Beyond Charles and Diana: An Anglophiles' Guide to Baby Naming.*

Cassell Dictionary of Proper Names, by Adrian Room. Florida: Cassell, 1994.

A Collector's Compendium of Rare and Unusual, Bold and Beautiful, Odd and Whimsical Names, by Paul Dickson. New York: Delacorte, 1986.

Everyday Words from Names of People & Places, by Allan Wolk. New York: Elsevier/Nelson, 1980.

Family Names: How Our Surnames Came to America, by J. N. Hook. New York: Macmillan, 1982.

Family Names: The Origins, Meanings, Mutations, and History of More than 2,800 American Names, by J. N. Hook. New York: Collier, 1983.

First Names First, by Leslie Dunkling. New York: Universe, 1977.

The Guinness Book of Names, 6th edition, by Leslie Dunkling. London: Guinness, 1993.

The Language of Names, by Justin Kaplan and Anne Bernays. New York: Simon & Schuster, 1997.

Our Names, Our Selves: The Meaning of Names in Everyday Life, by Mary Lassiter. London: Heinemann, 1983.

Parents Book of Baby Names, by Martin Kelly. New York: Ballantine, 1985.

Surnames for Women: A Decision-Making Guide, by Susan J. Kupper. Jefferson, North Carolina: McFarland, 1990.

New Words Enter Dictionarie

Summer enrollment doubles for sign language classes

By Luke P. Wroblewski
ASSOCIATED PRESS
CHICAGO-

ore: Plain English

Pediatricians prescribing reading to

Proposed phoni ontroversial fo ucation comn

Hersheler
TED PRESS
are rethinking their hopes for a unified

Linguist tries to save endangered languages

By RON J. I
ASSOCIAT
PHILAD
Dr. Lesl
turn to a
from of
commun
it is now
inside of
believes
that it can

Research Sugges
bulary in fir

THE WONDER OF WORDS

This chapter explores the miracle of language both from very personal viewpoints and from the collective learning of linguists. It begins with the personal reminiscences of Chris Arthur, a lecturer at the University of Wales, and goes on to well-known stories told by Helen Keller, Frederick Douglass, and Malcolm X. From there, linguist David Crystal, writes about language acquisition viewed from the outside rather than the inside. He tells what observers and linguists know, and what they are still hoping to learn, about the amazing intellectual accomplishment that virtually all children achieve in mastering the art of speech during their first three or four years of life.

The chapter then moves to the broader picture of the history of languages and to the surprising new theory that someday we may be able to trace all languages back to a "mother tongue." Jack Rosenthal's "On Language Fossilizing" is a light-hearted look at how words move into a language and stay there even if speakers lack the experience to understand their origins. The chapter ends with a workshop on appropriation, which illustrates connections between language change and the way the human mind works. It hints at how many symbols are floating in the collective unconscious of a group of speakers. When speakers want to communicate a new thought or create a memorable name, their chances of success are increased if they pick something already in the pool of community symbols and then figure out a way to claim ownership of the symbol by adapting it to their specific purposes.

FOUR STORIES ABOUT ACQUIRING LANGUAGE AND LITERACY

The four excerpts printed here each tell a story about how the author acquired a particular level of skill with language. In the first one, Chris Arthur tries to go back to "that strange dead ground which occupies so much of everyone's biography—time we have inhabited but have no memory of passing through." He is musing on, and wondering about, the miracle of language acquisition. Although the next three essays do not answer the questions that Arthur poses, they offer interesting insights. Each writer developed a particular stage of language later in life than do most people, which means that they were old enough to have memories of doing so. And because they were unusually intelligent and motivated, they became masterful communicators, as shown by their individual stories.

FROM "FERRULE"

Chris Arthur

1 Like almost everyone, I picked up language like a dog running through a field of burrs. Suddenly, without any effort or deliberation, you find yourself peppered with words. The first one or two will be noticed by those around you. After all, they spend a lot of time throwing them, hoping they will stick. But soon they cover you so completely that their continuing accretion goes unnoticed. Grammar, pronunciation, vocabulary stealthily sink their hooks into the deepest furrows of the mind and take root there.

2   A burr-covered dog will roll and groom until his coat is clear. Language clings to us unshakably, sending its tendrils to creep through us like ivy, finding some purchase even in the most intimate interstices of silence. So thorough is this subtle penetration, at once empowering and imprisoning, that it becomes hard to imagine what life without language would be like.

3   No exertion of memory can retrieve, intact and intelligible, the way in which we acquired this second skin of words. The genesis even of the most vital parts of our vocabulary is lost, hidden in that strange dead ground which occupies so much of everyone's biography—time we have inhabited but have no memory of passing through, our presence here, articulate and grown, the only evidence of ever having been there.

4   Can anyone bring to mind that moment of epiphany when they realized they had a name, or when mute shapes on paper—mother, tree, dog, grass— first spoke the burden of their meaning to us? Who can remember when they first heard the sound of *genocide* and took into mind all the terrible dimensions of its menacing enormity? Or when the eye first met *redolent* on the page and translated its net of sound and sense into another gentle weapon in meaning's potent armory? . . . Such moments, however epochal, are lost as surely within our individual horizons as the first words spoken by Homo sapiens are lost in the dwarfing silence of prehistory.

THE LIVING WORD

Helen Keller

Helen Keller was born in 1880. Although she was both deaf and blind, she perhaps had an advantage over similarly afflicted children in that her condition was brought on by an illness after the first year and a half of her life, so she had been exposed to sounds and speech. Laura Bridgman, the woman she mentions as having dressed the doll that Annie Sullivan brought her from the Perkins Institute in Baltimore, was the first deaf and blind person taught to communicate in sign language. She too had heard speech as an infant. "The Living Word" is an excerpt from Keller's book, *The Story of My Life*.

1 The most important day I remember in all my life is the one on which my teacher, Anne Mansfield Sullivan, came to me. I am filled with wonder when I consider the immeasurable contrast between the two lives which it connects. It was the third of March, 1887, three months before I was seven years old.

2   On the afternoon of that eventful day, I stood on the porch, dumb, expectant. I guessed vaguely from my mother's signs and from the hurrying to and fro in the house that something unusual was about to happen, so I went to the door and waited on the steps. The afternoon sun penetrated the mass of honeysuckle that covered the porch and fell on my upturned face. My fingers lingered almost unconsciously on the familiar leaves and blossoms

which had just come forth to greet the sweet southern spring. I did not know what the future held of marvel or surprise for me. Anger and bitterness had preyed upon me continually for weeks and a deep languor had succeeded this passionate struggle.

3   Have you ever been at sea in a dense fog, when it seemed as if a tangible white darkness shut you in, and the great ship, tense and anxious, groped her way toward the shore with plummet and sounding-line, and you waited with beating heart for something to happen? I was like that ship before my education began, only I was without compass or sounding-line, and had no way of knowing how near the harbor was. "Light! give me light!" was the wordless cry of my soul, and the light of love shone on me in that very hour.

4   I felt approaching footsteps. I stretched out my hand as I supposed to my mother. Someone took it, and I was caught up and held close in the arms of her who had come to reveal all things to me, and, more than all things else, to love me.

5   The morning after my teacher came she led me into her room and gave me a doll. The little blind children at the Perkins Institution had sent it and Laura Bridgman had dressed it; but I did not know this until afterward. When I had played with it a little while, Miss Sullivan slowly spelled into my hand the word "d-o-l-l." I was at once interested in this finger play and tried to imitate it. When I finally succeeded in making the letters correctly I was flushed with childish pleasure and pride. Running downstairs to my mother I held up my hand and made the letters for doll. I did not know that I was spelling a word or even that words existed; I was simply making my fingers go in monkey-like imitation. In the days that followed I learned to spell in this uncomprehending way a great many words, among them *pin, hat, cup* and a few verbs like *sit, stand* and *walk.* But my teacher had been with me several weeks before I understood that everything has a name.

6   One day, while I was playing with my new doll, Miss Sullivan put my big rag doll into my lap also, spelled "d-o-l-l" and tried to make me understand that "d-o-l-l" applied to both. Earlier in the day we had had a tussle over the words "m-u-g" and "w-a-t-e-r." Miss Sullivan had tried to impress it upon me that "m-u-g" is *mug* and that "w-a-t-e-r" is *water,* but I persisted in confounding the two. In despair she had dropped the subject for the time, only to renew it at the first opportunity. I became impatient at her repeated attempts and, seizing the new doll, I dashed it upon the floor. I was keenly delighted when I felt the fragments of the broken doll at my feet. Neither sorrow nor regret followed my passionate outburst. I had not loved the doll. In the still, dark world in which I lived there was no strong sentiment or tenderness. I felt my teacher sweep the fragments to one side of the hearth, and I had a sense of satisfaction that the cause of my discomfort was removed. She brought me my hat, and I knew I was going out into the warm sunshine. This thought, if a wordless sensation may be called a thought, made me hop and skip with pleasure.

Today educators of the hearing impaired have three different philosophies about learning to communicate. One group advocates that deaf children learn lip reading and be taught to speak, even if they will never sound "normal." Another group advocates the kind of finger spelling that Anne Sullivan taught to Helen Keller, while still a third group advocates a system of signing that works much like pictographs. Look at these photos of Lance Harrop, a signer at Arizona State University, and see if you can match the pictures to these meanings: *daughter, telephone, tree,* and *surprise.* Which system is he using? Why wouldn't this system work for Helen Keller? What advantages does it have? What disadvantages? Could all three systems be used by the same person? Under what circumstances? Nine out of ten deaf children are born into hearing families. What are some of the ramifications of this for education and communication?

7   We walked down the path to the well-house, attracted by the fragrance of the honeysuckle with which it was covered. Some one was drawing water and my teacher placed my hand under the spout. As the cool stream gushed over one hand she spelled into the other the word *water*, first slowly, then rapidly. I stood still, my whole attention fixed upon the motions of her fingers. Suddenly I felt a misty consciousness as of something forgotten—a thrill of returning thought; and somehow the mystery of language was revealed to me. I knew then that "w-a-t-e-r" meant the wonderful cool something that was flowing over my hand. That living word awakened my soul, gave it light, hope, joy, set it free! There were barriers still, it is true, but barriers that could in time be swept away.

8   I left the well-house eager to learn. Everything had a name, and each name gave birth to a new thought. As we returned to the house every object which I touched seemed to quiver with life. That was because I saw everything with the strange, new sight that had come to me. On entering the door I remembered the doll I had broken. I felt my way to the hearth and picked up the pieces. I tried vainly to put them together. Then my eyes filled with tears; for I realized what I had done, and for the first time I felt repentance and sorrow.

9   I learned a great many new words that day. I do not remember what they all were; but I do know that *mother, father, sister, teacher* were among them— words that were to make the world blossom for me, "like Aaron's rod, with flowers." It would have been difficult to find a happier child than I was as I lay in my crib at the close of that eventful day and lived over the joys it had brought me, and for the first time longed for a new day to come.

LEARNING TO READ AND WRITE

Frederick Douglass

Frederick Douglass was born into slavery in Maryland in 1817. His mother was African American, while his father was white. He escaped from the South in 1838 when he was twenty-one years old. He became a leading abolitionist, a writer, newspaper editor, and lecturer, and eventually the U.S. minister to Haiti. This excerpt is taken from his 1841 autobiography, *The Narrative of the Life of Frederick Douglass: An American Slave.*

1   I lived in Master Hugh's family about seven years. During this time, I succeeded in learning to read and write. In accomplishing this, I was compelled

to resort to various stratagems. I had no regular teacher. My mistress, who had kindly commenced to instruct me, had, in compliance with the advice and direction of her husband, not only ceased to instruct, but had set her face against my being instructed by any one else. It is due, however, to my mistress to say of her, that she did not adopt this course of treatment immediately. She at first lacked the depravity indispensable to shutting me up in mental darkness. It was at least necessary for her to have some training in the exercise of irresponsible power, to make her equal to the task of treating me as though I were a brute.

2   My mistress was, as I have said, a kind and tender-hearted woman; and in the simplicity of her soul she commenced, when I first went to live with her, to treat me as she supposed one human being ought to treat another. In entering upon the duties of a slaveholder, she did not seem to perceive that I sustained to her the relation of a mere chattel, and that for her to treat me as a human being was not only wrong, but dangerously so. Slavery proved as injurious to her as it did to me. When I went there, she was a pious, warm, and tender-hearted woman. There was no sorrow or suffering for which she had not a tear. She had bread for the hungry, clothes for the naked, and comfort for every mourner that came within her reach. Slavery soon proved its ability to divest her of these heavenly qualities. Under its influence, the tender heart became stone, and the lamblike disposition gave way to one of tiger-like fierceness. The first step in her downward course was in her ceasing to instruct me. She now commenced to practice her husband's precepts. She finally became even more violent in her opposition than her husband himself. She was not satisfied with simply doing as well as he had commanded; she seemed anxious to do better. Nothing seemed to make her more angry than to see me with a newspaper. She seemed to think that here lay the danger. I have had her rush at me with a face made all up of fury, and snatch from me a newspaper, in a manner that fully revealed her apprehension. She was an apt woman; and a little experience soon demonstrated, to her satisfaction, that education and slavery were incompatible with each other.

3   From this time I was most narrowly watched. If I was in a separate room any considerable length of time, I was sure to be suspected of having a book and was at once called to give an account of myself. All this, however, was too late. The first step had been taken. Mistress, in teaching me the alphabet, had given me the *inch*, and no precaution could prevent me from taking the *ell*.

4   The plan which I adopted, and the one by which I was most successful, was that of making friends of all the little white boys whom I met in the street. As many of these as I could, I converted into teachers. With their kindly aid, obtained at different times and in different places, I finally succeeded in learning to read. When I was sent on errands, I always took my book with me, and by going one part of my errand quickly, I found time to get a lesson before my return. I used also to carry bread with me, enough of which was always in the house, and to which I was always welcome; for I was much better off in this

regard than many of the poor white children in our neighborhood. This bread I used to bestow upon the hungry little urchins, who, in return, would give me that more valuable bread of knowledge. I am strongly tempted to give the names of two or three of those little boys, as a testimonial of the gratitude and affection I bear them; but prudence forbids;—not that it would injure me, but it might embarrass them; for it is almost an unpardonable offence to teach slaves to read in this Christian country. It is enough to say of the dear little fellows, that they lived on Philpot Street, very near Durgin and Bailey's shipyard. I used to talk this matter of slavery over with them. I would sometimes say to them, I wished I could be as free as they would be when they got to be men. "You will be free as soon as you are twenty-one, *but I am a slave for life!* Have not I as good a right to be free as you have?" These words used to trouble them; they would express for me the liveliest sympathy, and console me with the hope that something would occur by which I might be free.

5   I was now about twelve years old, and the thoughts of being *a slave for life* began to beat heavily upon my heart. Just about this time, I got hold of a book entitled "The Columbian Orator" [a textbook teaching argument and rhetoric]. Every opportunity I got, I used to read this book. Among much of other interesting matter, I found in it a dialogue between a master and his slave. The slave was represented as having run away from his master three times. The dialogue represented the conversation which took place between them, when the slave was retaken the third time. In this dialogue, the whole argument in behalf of slavery was brought forward by the master, all of which was disposed of by the slave. The slave was made to say some very smart as well as impressive things in reply to his master—things which had the desired though unexpected effect; for the conversation resulted in the voluntary emancipation of the slave on the part of the master.

6   In the same book, I met with one of Sheridan's mighty speeches on and in behalf of Catholic emancipation [in England, where Catholics were not allowed to vote until 1829]. These were choice documents to me. I read them over and over again with unabated interest. They gave tongue to interesting thoughts of my own soul, which had frequently flashed through my mind, and died away for want of utterance. The moral which I gained from the dialogue was the power of truth over the conscience of even a slaveholder. What I got from Sheridan was a bold denunciation of slavery, and a powerful vindication of human rights. The reading of these documents enabled me to utter my thoughts, and to meet the arguments brought forward to sustain slavery; but while they relieved me of one difficulty, they brought on another even more painful than the one of which I was relieved. The more I read, the more I was led to abhor and detest my enslavers. I could regard them in no other light than a band of successful robbers, who had left their homes, and gone to Africa and stolen us from our homes, and in a strange land reduced us to slavery. I loathed them as being the meanest as well as the most wicked

of men. As I read and contemplated the subject, behold! that very discontentment which Master Hugh had predicted would follow my learning to read had already come, to torment and sting my soul to unutterable anguish. As I writhed under it, I would at times feel that learning to read had been a curse rather than a blessing. It had given me a view of my wretched condition, without the remedy. It opened my eyes to the horrible pit, but to no ladder upon which to get out. In moments of agony, I envied my fellow-slaves for their stupidity. I have often wished myself a beast. I preferred the condition of the meanest reptile to my own. Any thing, no matter what, to get rid of thinking! It was this everlasting thinking of my condition that tormented me. There was no getting rid of it. It was pressed upon me by every object within sight or hearing, animate or inanimate. The silver trump of freedom had roused my soul to eternal wakefulness. Freedom now appeared, to disappear no more forever. It was heard in every sound, and seen in every thing. It was ever present to torment me with a sense of my wretched condition. I saw nothing without seeing it, I heard nothing without hearing it, and felt nothing without feeling it. It looked from every star, it smiled in every calm, breathed in every wind, and moved in every storm.

7   I often found myself regretting my own existence, and wishing myself dead; and but for the hope of being free, I have no doubt but that I should have killed myself, or done something for which I should have been killed. While in this state of mind, I was eager to hear any one speak of slavery. I was a ready listener. Every little while, I could hear something about the abolitionists. It was some time before I found what the word meant. It was always used in such connections as to make it an interesting word to me. If a slave ran away and succeeded in getting clear, or if a slave killed his master, set fire to a barn, or did any thing very wrong in the mind of a slaveholder, it was spoken of as the fruit of *abolition*. Hearing the word in this connection very often, I set about learning what it meant. The dictionary afforded me little or no help. I found it was "the act of abolishing"; but then I did not know what was to be abolished. Here I was perplexed. I did not dare to ask any one about its meaning, for I was satisfied that it was something they wanted me to know very little about. After a patient waiting, I got one of our city papers, containing an account of the number of petitions from the north, praying for the abolition of slavery in the District of Columbia, and of the slave trade between the States. From this time I understood the words *abolition* and *abolitionist,* and always drew near when that word was spoken, expecting to hear something of importance to myself and fellow-slaves. The light broke in upon me by degrees. I went one day down on the wharf of Mr. Waters; and seeing two Irishmen unloading a scow of stone, I went, unasked, and helped them. When we had finished, one of them came to me and asked me if I were a slave. I told him I was. He asked, "Are ye a slave for life?" I told him that I was. The good Irishman seemed to be deeply affected by the statement. He said to the other that

it was a pity so fine a little fellow as myself should be a slave for life. He said it was a shame to hold me. They both advised me to run away to the north; that I should find friends there, and that I should be free. I pretended not to be interested in what they said, and treated them as if I did not understand them; for I feared they might be treacherous. White men have been known to encourage slaves to escape, and then, to get the reward, catch them and return them to their masters. I was afraid that these seemingly good men might use me so; but I nevertheless remembered their advice, and from that time I resolved to run away. I looked forward to a time at which it would be safe for me to escape. I was too young to think of doing so immediately; besides, I wished to learn how to write, as I might have occasion to write my own pass. I consoled myself with the hope that I should one day find a good chance. Meanwhile, I would learn to write.

8   The idea as to how I might learn to write was suggested to me by being in Durgin and Bailey's ship-yard, and frequently seeing the ship carpenters, after hewing, and getting a piece of timber ready for use, write on the timber the name of that part of the ship for which it was intended. When a piece of timber was intended for the larboard side, it would be marked thus—"L." When a piece was for the starboard side, it would be marked thus—"S." A piece for the larboard side forward, would be marked thus—"L.F." When a piece was for starboard side forward, it would be marked thus—"S.F." For larboard aft, it would be marked thus—"L.A." For starboard aft, it would be marked thus—"S.A." I soon learned the names of these letters, and for what they were intended when placed upon a piece of timber in the ship-yard. I immediately commenced copying them, and in a short time was able to make the four letters named. After that, when I met with any boy who I knew could write, I would tell him I could write as well as he. The next word would be, "I don't believe you. Let me see you try it." I would then make the letters which I had been so fortunate as to learn, and ask him to beat that. In this way I got a good many lessons in writing, which it is quite possible I should never have gotten in any other way. During this time, my copy-book was the board fence, brick wall, and pavement; my pen and ink was a lump of chalk. With these, I learned mainly how to write. I then commenced and continued copying the Italics in Webster's Spelling Book, until I could make them all without looking on the book. By this time, my little Master Thomas had gone to school, and learned how to write, and had written over a number of copybooks. These had been brought home, and shown to some of our near neighbors, and then laid aside. My mistress used to go to class meeting at the Wilk Street meetinghouse every Monday afternoon, and leave me to take care of the house. When left thus, I used to spend the time in writing in the spaces left in Master Thomas's copybook, copying what he had written. I continued to do this until I could write a hand very similar to that of Master Thomas. Thus after a long, tedious effort for years, I finally succeeded in learning how to write.

FROM THE AUTOBIOGRAPHY OF MALCOLM X

Malcolm X and Alex Haley

Malcolm Little took the surname of "X" when he converted to Islam while serving a prison term for armed robbery. He was released from prison in 1952 and by 1959 was the chief spokesperson for the Nation of Islam. While in the southern states Martin Luther King Jr. was advocating passive resistance, in the northern states Malcolm X was talking about "The Hate that Hate Produced" and declaring that justice would be achieved "by whatever means necessary." When he met with Fidel Castro in 1960, the FBI became even more interested in his activities. In 1964, Malcolm X formally split with the Nation of Islam and formed a new group, Muslim Mosque, Inc. The next year, he was assassinated while giving a speech in New York City. Three Black Muslims were convicted of the murder, but even today some people wonder if Malcolm's death was arranged by federal agents. His autobiography, which he narrated to Alex Haley, was published shortly after his death. He was fortunate in getting the then-unknown Haley as a co-author. Ten year later, Haley would become almost as famous as Malcolm X for his best-selling *Roots*, which told the story of Haley's ancestors and was made into a successful television miniseries.

1   I've never been one for inaction. Everything I've ever felt strongly about, I've done something about. I guess that's why, unable to do anything else, I soon began writing to people I had known in the hustling world, such as Sammy the Pimp, John Hughes, the gambling house owner, the thief Jumpsteady, and several dope peddlers. I wrote them all about Allah and Islam and Mr. Elijah Muhammad. I had no idea where most of them lived. I addressed their letters in care of the Harlem or Roxbury bars and clubs where I'd known them.

2   I never got a single reply. The average hustler and criminal was too uneducated to write a letter. I have known many slick sharp-looking hustlers, who would have you think they had an interest in Wall Street; privately, they would get someone else to read a letter if they received one. Besides, neither would I have replied to anyone writing me something as wild as "the white man is the devil."

3   What certainly went on the Harlem and Roxbury wires was that Detroit Red was going crazy in stir, or else he was trying some hype to shake up the warden's office.

4   During the years that I stayed in the Norfolk Prison Colony, never did any official directly say anything to me about those letters, although, of course, they all passed through the prison censorship. I'm sure, however, they monitored what I wrote to add to the files which every state and federal prison keeps on the conversion of Negro inmates by the teachings of Mr. Elijah Muhammad.

5   But at that time, I felt that the real reason was that the white man knew that he was the devil.

6   Later on, I even wrote to the Mayor of Boston, to the Governor of Massachusetts, and to Harry S. Truman. They never answered; they probably never even saw my letters. I handscratched to them how the white man's society was responsible for the black man's condition in this wilderness of North America.

7   It was because of my letters that I happened to stumble upon starting to acquire some kind of a homemade education.

8   I became increasingly frustrated at not being able to express what I wanted to convey in letters that I wrote, especially those to Mr. Elijah Muhammad. In the street, I had been the most articulate hustler out there—I had commanded attention when I said something. But now, trying to write simple English, I not only wasn't articulate, I wasn't even functional. How would I sound writing in slang, the way I would *say* it, something such as, "Look, daddy, let me pull your coat about a cat, Elijah Muhammad—"

9   Many who today hear me somewhere in person, or on television, or those who read something I've said, will think I went to school far beyond the eighth grade. This impression is due entirely to my prison studies.

10   It had really begun back in the Charlestown Prison, when Bimbi first made me feel envy of his stock of knowledge. Bimbi had always taken charge of any conversation he was in, and I had tried to emulate him. But every book I picked up had few sentences which didn't contain anywhere from one to nearly all of the words that might as well have been in Chinese. When I just skipped those words, of course, I really ended up with little idea of what the book said. So I had come to the Norfolk Prison Colony still going through only book-reading motions. Pretty soon, I would have quit even these motions, unless I had received the motivation that I did.

11   I saw that the best thing I could do was get hold of a dictionary—to study, to learn some words. I was lucky enough to reason also that I should try to improve my penmanship. It was sad. I couldn't even write in a straight line. It was both ideas together that moved me to request a dictionary along with some tablets and pencils from the Norfolk Prison Colony school.

12   I spent two days just riffling uncertainly through the dictionary's pages. I'd never realized so many words existed! I didn't know *which* words I needed to learn. Finally, just to start some kind of action, I began copying.

13   In my slow, painstaking, ragged handwriting, I copied into my tablet everything printed on that first page, down to the punctuation marks.

14   I believe it took me a day. Then, aloud, I read back, to myself, everything I'd written on the tablet. Over and over, aloud, to myself, I read my own handwriting.

15   I woke up the next morning, thinking about those words—immensely proud to realize that not only had I written so much at one time, but I'd written words that I never knew were in the world. Moreover, with a little effort,

I also could remember what many of these words meant. I reviewed the words whose meanings I didn't remember. Funny thing, from the dictionary first page right now, that "aardvark" springs to my mind. The dictionary had a picture of it, a long-tailed, long-eared, burrowing African mammal, which lives off termites caught by sticking out its tongue as an anteater does for ants.

16   I was so fascinated that I went on—I copied the dictionary's next page. And the same experience came when I studied that. With every succeeding page, I also learned of people and places and events from history. Actually the dictionary is like a miniature encyclopedia. Finally the dictionary's *A* section had filled a whole tablet—and I went on into the *B*'s. That was the way I started copying what eventually became the entire dictionary. It went a lot faster after so much practice helped me to pick up handwriting speed. Between what I wrote in my tablet, and writing letters, during the rest of my time in prison I would guess I wrote a million words.

17   I suppose it was inevitable that as my word-base broadened, I could for the first time pick up a book and read and now begin to understand what the book was saying. Anyone who has read a great deal can imagine the new world that opened. Let me tell you something: From then until I left that prison, in every free moment I had, if I was not reading in the library, I was reading on my bunk. You couldn't have gotten me out of books with a wedge. Between Mr. Muhammad's teachings, my correspondence, my visitors . . . and my reading of books, months passed without my even thinking about being imprisoned. In fact, up to then, I never had been so truly free in my life.

COMPREHENSION

1. Words and phrases to talk about:
   - their continuing *accretion*
   - finding some *purchase*
   - the most intimate *interstices* of silence
   - sound of *genocide*
   - first met *redolent*
   - meaning's potent *armory*
   - first words spoken by *Homo sapiens*
   - make the world bloom for me like *"Aaron's rod with flowers."*
   - Mistress . . . had given me the *inch*, and no precaution could prevent me from taking the *ell*
   - in behalf of Catholic *emancipation*
   - a piece of timber was intended for the *larboard* side
   - for *larboard aft*, it would be marked
   - continued copying the *Italics* in Webster's Spelling Book
   - Detroit Red was going crazy in *stir*

2. Why didn't the dictionary help Frederick Douglass learn the meaning of *abolitionist*?
3. How did Frederick Douglass use his oral skills to learn to write?

Discussion

1. Why does Chris Arthur tell his story mostly through similes and metaphors?
2. What words does Chris Arthur mention that bring a change in tone to the cheerful homage he was paying to the miracle of language?
3. Even though each of these pieces is about learning a different aspect of language, the writers went through some of the same experiences. What were they?
4. When Helen Keller first learned finger spelling, she said she was just making her fingers go in "monkey-like imitation." She could "spell" in an uncomprehending way such nouns as *pin, hat,* and *cup* and a few verbs like *sit, stand,* and *walk.* Why do you think Anne Sullivan started with those particular words? Do you think that Helen's early learning was similar to the way two- and three-year-old children are taught to sing the alphabet song and to learn the names of the letters?
5. What problem did learning to read bring to Frederick Douglass? Why did he say that in some ways he envied the ignorance of fellow slaves?
6. When Frederick Douglass was a young teenager he began looking forward to the time he could escape safely, but first he said he needed to "learn how to write, as I might have occasion to write my own pass." What did he mean by this?
7. What is the tone of Frederick Douglass's piece? He was only twenty-four years old when he wrote it, which means that his memories of being a slave were still fresh. In which paragraphs did Douglass use sarcasm to express his bitterness?
8. What is the tone of Malcolm X's piece? Does it make a difference that Douglass's piece was written in 1841, Helen Keller's in the early 1900s, and Malcolm X's in 1964? If you see a difference in tone, try to figure out if it is a result of the subject matter, the life experiences of the writer, changes in language fashion, or something else.

ACQUIRING LANGUAGE

David Crystal

In an excerpt from *The Cambridge Encyclopedia of Language,* David Crystal writes about the acquisition of speech not from the personal viewpoints that Chris Arthur and Helen Keller used, but from the perspective of linguists who study the acquisition of language. Few things are as thrilling to parents as when their babies begin to talk. Speech is what separates infancy from childhood, and regardless of which side thoughtful people take in academic arguments about how children develop their abilities to comprehend and produce speech, they all agree that children's acquisition of language is miraculous. One other point they agree on is that for children to learn language, they must be in an environment where language is used by real people, who talk to and interact with the learners.

PRODUCTION, COMPREHENSION, IMITATION

1   "Acquiring a language" involves two distinct skills: the ability to produce speech in a spontaneous way; and the ability to understand the speech of others. The former is relatively easy to study: all we have to do is turn a tape recorder on, and analyze what comes out. Research into speech comprehension is far more difficult because we need to take into account not only what is spoken to the child, but the situation in which it is uttered, and the child's prior knowledge of the world. In one study, a 2-year-old child was observed to respond correctly when his mother said, at bedtime, "Go and get your pajamas out of the drawer in your bedroom." But it is not at all clear, without a careful investigation, which parts of this sentence the child had understood— it might simply be that the word *pajamas,* said at bedtime, and coupled with the knowledge of where pajamas are kept, was enough to produce the appropriate action.

2   What is the relationship between production and comprehension when it comes to language learning? There are three possibilities. The traditional, common sense view is that comprehension always precedes production: children need to understand a word or grammatical construction before they use it. However, there is increasing evidence that this simple relationship does not always obtain. Production may precede comprehension, or the two processes may be so intimately connected that they develop in parallel. There is certainly a great deal of evidence to show that children produce a word or

construction without having a full understanding of it. *Doggie,* says one young child, pointing to a cat. *He got hat on,* says another, and then later says, *Take that hat on off*—as if *hat on* were a noun. This kind of thing happens frequently from around age 2—and, indeed, it could be argued that our readiness to use linguistic forms we do not fully understand stays with us throughout life!

3   It has also been recognized that imitation is a distinct skill in language acquisition—many children spend a great deal of time imitating what their parents have just said. This is most noticeable when new sounds or vocabulary are being learned, but it has been shown that imitation may be important in the development of grammar too. Often, children imitate sentence patterns that they are unable to produce spontaneously, and then stop imitating these structures when they start to use them in their speech—suggesting that imitation is a kind of "bridge" between comprehension and spontaneous production.

PLOTTING THE COURSE OF LANGUAGE DEVELOPMENT

4   A popular metaphor in child development is to talk of "milestones"—the age at which a child takes a significant step forward in behavior (such as sitting, crawling, standing). The metaphor does not work so well when it comes to language: too much happens too quickly. There is simultaneous development of sounds, grammar, meaning, and interaction skills; and significant progress can be made on several different fronts in a matter of days. It is thus no easy matter to quantify the amount of language learned by a child within a particular period (as we need to do in deciding what counts as "normal" development, and in plotting departures from this norm).

5   Several attempts have been made to find important single measures of development, within particular linguistic levels—notably the notions of sentence length and vocabulary size, both of which steadily increase as children grow older. Such indices can provide general indications of progress, but they have serious limitations. Two sentences may consist of exactly the same number of words, morphemes, or syllables, and yet be very different in terms of their syntactic complexity: *I see a cat and a dog and a cow* is much simpler than *I see a cat that is next to a dog,* though both are the same length. Similarly, two children may both have vocabularies of 100 words, yet differ in the range of words used and in their meanings: one child may use *cold* to mean only "cold weather," whereas the other may use it to apply to water, food, and grim facial expressions. In these circumstances, a single score, based on one developmental parameter, conceals more than it illuminates: it needs to be supplemented by a wider and more detailed series of measures that take into account the qualitative range of linguistic features used by the child.

6   After several years of acquisition research, in which many measures have been investigated, it is possible to isolate certain broad trends with some con-

fidence. . . . It appears that most children do follow the same general path as they acquire sounds and grammatical structures, and several common trends are evident in the learning of vocabulary and pragmatics also. However, there seems to be considerable variation in rate of development, and there are many individual differences in the order of acquisition of specific features that have to be taken into account. The study of these variations is a major emphasis of current child language research.

IMITATION

7   Language acquisition has long been thought of as a process of imitation and reinforcement. Children learn to speak, in the popular view, by copying the utterances heard around them, and by having their responses strengthened by the repetitions, corrections, and other reactions that adults provide. In recent years, it has become clear that this principle will not explain all the facts of language development. Children do imitate a great deal, especially in learning sounds and vocabulary; but little of their grammatical ability can be explained in this way. Two kinds of evidence are commonly used in support of this criticism—one based on the kind of language children produce, the other on what they do not produce.

8   The first piece of evidence derives from the way children handle irregular grammatical patterns. When they encounter such irregular past-tense forms as *went* and *took,* or such plural forms as *mice* and *sheep,* there is a stage when they replace these by forms based on the regular patterns of the language. They say such things as *wented, taked, mices, mouses,* and *sheeps.* . . .

9   The other kind of evidence is based on the way children seem unable to imitate adult grammatical constructions exactly, even when invited to do so. The best-known demonstration of this principle in action is the dialogue reported by the American psycholinguist, David McNeill, where a child proved unable to use a pattern, even though the parent presented the correct adult model several times:

> *Child:* Nobody don't like me.
>
> *Mother:* No, say "Nobody likes me."
>
> *Child:* Nobody don't like me.
>
> *(Eight repetitions of this dialogue.)*
>
> *Mother:* No, now listen carefully: say *"Nobody likes me."*
>
> *Child:* Oh! Nobody don't likes me.

The child, at this point in its learning of grammar, was clearly not ready to use the "single negative" pattern found in this dialect of English. Such examples suggest that language acquisition is more a matter of maturation than of imitation.

INNATENESS

10   The limitations of an imitation/reinforcement view of acquisition led in the 1960s to an alternative proposal, arising out of the generative account of language. It was argued that children must be born with an innate capacity for language development: the human brain is "ready" for language, in the sense that when children are exposed to speech, certain general principles for discovering or structuring language automatically begin to operate. These principles constitute a child's "language acquisition device" (LAD).

11   The child uses its LAD to make sense of the utterances heard around it, deriving from this "primary linguistic data" hypotheses about the grammar of the language—what the sentences are, and how they are constructed. This knowledge is then used to produce sentences that, after a process of trial and error, correspond to those in adult speech: the child has learned a set of generalizations, or rules, governing the way in which sentences are formed. This sequence of events can be summarized in the following way:

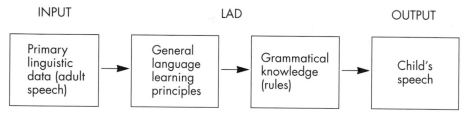

INPUT   LAD   OUTPUT

| Primary linguistic data (adult speech) | → | General language learning principles | → | Grammatical knowledge (rules) | → | Child's speech |

12   There have been many differences of opinion over how best to characterize LAD. Some have argued that LAD provides children with a knowledge of linguistic universals, such as the existence of word order and word classes; others, that it provides only general procedures for discovering how language is to be learned. But all of its supporters are agreed that some such notion is needed in order to explain the remarkable speed with which children learn to speak, and the considerable similarity in the way grammatical patterns are acquired across different children and languages. Adult speech, it is felt, cannot of itself provide a means of enabling children to work out the regularities of language for themselves, because it is too complex and disorganized. However, it has proved difficult to formulate the detailed properties of LAD in an uncontroversial manner, in the light of the changes in generative linguistic theory that have taken place in recent years; and meanwhile, alternative accounts of the acquisition process have evolved.

COGNITION

13   The main alternative account argues that language acquisition must be viewed within the context of a child's intellectual development. Linguistic structures will emerge only if there is an already-established cognitive foundation—for example, before children can use structures of comparison (e.g.,

This car is bigger than that), they need first to have developed the conceptual ability to make relative judgments of size. Several early child language scholars maintained such a relationship exists, but the most influential account stems from the model of cognitive development proposed by the Genevan psychologist Jean Piaget.

14 Several controlled studies have been carried out investigating the link between the stages of cognitive development proposed by Piaget and the emergence of linguistic skills. The links have been most clearly shown for the earliest period of language learning (up to 18 months), relating to the development of what Piaget called "sensori-motor" intelligence, in which children construct a mental picture of a world of objects that have independent existence. For example, during the later part of this period, children develop a sense of object permanence—they will begin to search for objects that they have seen hidden—and some scholars have argued that the ability to name classes of objects (i.e., to give them a comparably "permanent" linguistic status) depends on the prior development of this cognitive ability. However, it is difficult to show precise correlations between specific cognitive behaviors and linguistic features at this early age. The issue is a highly controversial one, which increases in complexity as children become linguistically—and cognitively—more advanced.

INPUT

15 For many years, in the wake of the innateness hypothesis, the importance of the language used by adults (especially mothers) to children was minimized. But studies of "motherese," as it came to be called in the 1970s, showed that maternal input is by no means as complex and fragmentary as proponents of innateness theory claimed it to be. Many parents do not talk to their children in the same way as they talk to other adults. Rather, they seem capable of adapting their language to give the child maximum opportunity to interact and learn. Several of these adaptations have been noted (after C. A. Ferguson, 1977).

■ The utterances are considerably simplified, especially with respect to their grammar and meaning. Sentences are shorter: one study showed that the average length of maternal sentences to 2-year-olds was less than four words—half that found when the mother talked to other adults. There is a more restricted range of sentence patterns, and a frequent use of sentence "frames," such as *Where's _____?* or *That's a _____.* The meanings are predominantly "concrete," relating to the situation in which mother and child are acting.

■ There are several features whose purpose seems to be clarification. Extra information is provided that would be considered unnecessary when talking to other adults. Sentences are expanded and paraphrased and may be repeated several times. The speed of speaking is much slower than that used to other adults.

- There is also an expressive, or affective, element in motherese, shown by the use of special words or sounds. Diminutive or reduplicative words (e.g., *doggie, choo-choo*) are common. English makes particular use of *y/ie* ending, and similar forms have been noted in several other languages, such as Japanese *-ko*, Gilyak *-k/-q*, Berber *-ʃh/ʃht*. Occasionally, totally different words will be used, e.g., *bunny* for "rabbit." There may be special use of individual sounds, such as the use of rounded lips in English, or special palatal sounds in Latvian and Marathi.

  Some of these features also seem to function as ways of holding the child's attention, or of identifying particular words and sounds. This may well be the reason for the very common use of high, wide pitch range in maternal speech. Mothers also devote a great deal of time to obtaining feedback from their children, especially in the first three years. Their speech contains a very high frequency of question forms, and many utterances have a high rising intonation (*yes?, all right?*).

These modifications are evidently important ways of establishing and maintaining meaningful communication with the child, as they can be found in the earliest mother–child interactions. It has even been suggested that these features are universal, but this claim is premature in the absence of empirical studies, and there is already some counter-evidence from other cultures—several of these features are lacking in Samoan and Quiché Mayan, for instance. However, the highly structured character of maternal input is not in doubt, and its possible influence on the course of language acquisition is now taken very seriously.

16   Unfortunately, it is difficult to show correlations between the features of motherese and the subsequent emergence of these features in child speech, and even more problematic to move from talk about correlations to talk about causes. Some studies, searching for such relationships, have found very few; others have found occasional correlations between specific structures, though often with an appreciable gap between the use of a feature by the mother and its subsequent use by the child; yet others argue that input structures are very closely tailored to the needs of the child (the "fine tuning" hypothesis). The use of different research methodologies clouds the picture, but it is now plain that the nature and frequency of linguistic features in maternal input can no longer be neglected in devising theories of language acquisition.

CONCLUSIONS

17   It is not possible, in the present state of knowledge, to choose between these various approaches. The number of definite, general facts known about language acquisition is still very small. In particular, much more information is needed about the way children learn languages other than English. Doubtless imitative skills, a general language-learning-mechanism, cognitive awareness, and structure input all play their part in guiding the course of language

acquisition. Unraveling the interdependence of these factors constitutes the main goal of future child language research.

COMPREHENSION

1. Words to talk about:

   - number of words, *morphemes,* or syllables
   - their *syntactic* complexity
   - one developmental *parameter*
   - A child's *LAD*
   - the *innateness hypothesis*
   - studies of *"motherese"*
   - *diminutive* or *reduplicative* words

2. Why is it harder to study children's comprehension than their production of speech?
3. In relation to children learning grammar, what did Crystal mean when he said that "imitation is a kind of 'bridge' between comprehension and spontaneous production"?

DISCUSSION

1. What indices are commonly used to measure a child's development in acquiring speech? Why should these be viewed as only rough indicators of "normal" development?
2. What does it show about children's linguistic maturity when they say such things as *wented, taked, mices, mouses,* and *sheeps?*
3. Crystal wrote that "indeed, it could be argued that our readiness to use linguistic forms we do not fully understand stays with us throughout life!" Do you agree? Can you give examples? Does this readiness differ among individuals? If so, how might it influence someone's ability to learn a foreign language? To become a poet? To write advertising copy? To write love letters?
4. What are the characteristics of *motherese or caregiver speech* that linguists have identified? Why is it difficult to show whether or not these help children learn to talk? What do you think?
5. Explain what Crystal means by the four contributing factors to language acquisition that he mentions in his conclusion: *imitative skills, a general language-learning-mechanism, cognitive awareness,* and *structure input.*
6. What information does Crystal say we need before we can come to an agreement on how children learn language?

THE MOTHER TONGUE

William F. Allman

If ancestors from long ago hadn't invented language, none of the preceding stories—or in fact, civilization as we know it—would have been possible. The questions of how they did it and how they passed it down to us have long fascinated scholars, as well as ordinary speakers and readers. "The Roots of Language: How Modern Speech Evolved from a Single, Ancient Source" was the featured topic of the November 5, 1990, issue of *U.S. News and World Report*. Reprinted below is the lead story about how linguists are working back from modern speech to re-create the first language of the human race.

1   In 1786, Sir William Jones, an Englishman serving the Crown as a judge in India, turned a series of seeming coincidences into an extraordinary discovery about human nature. A scholar of the Orient by training, Jones had embarked on an effort to learn Sanskrit, the language in which many ancient Indian religious and literary texts are written. To his amazement, Jones found that Sanskrit's grammatical forms and vocabulary bore a striking resemblance to those of Greek and Latin, so much so that "no philologer could examine them all three without believing them to have sprung from some common source." As Charles Darwin was to assert almost a century later about the human body, Jones suggested that a fundamental part of the human psyche—language—had a hidden ancestry of its own.

2   Today, scientists are leading a new revolution in understanding the roots of language. While linguistic pioneer Noam Chomsky and his followers have focused on language as a psychological phenomenon, a small band of renegade scholars is revealing how languages are a product of cultural evolution. Sifting through modern tongues for linguistic "fossils" in the form of common words and grammatical structures, these "linguistic paleoanthropologists," many of whom have worked in obscurity in the Soviet Union, are reconstructing the pathways by which the world's roughly 5,000 languages arose from a handful of ancient "mother" tongues. A few radical linguists have gone even further, claiming they have reconstructed pieces of the mother of them all: The original language spoken at the dawn of the human species.

3   These linguistic findings are a windfall for archaeologists, anthropologists and other social scientists who are trying to piece together the story of the peopling of the earth. "We've come to realize," says Alexis Manaster

Ramer, a researcher at Wayne State University in Detroit, "that a lot of the answers to the big questions lie in something you might call anthro-psycho-socio-linguistics." Language is an integral part of the cultural glue that binds people together and signals their presence. Tracing the evolution of language can reveal how ancient peoples migrated into new lands, for instance, just as reconstructing the vocabularies of lost languages can give researchers clues to what ancient people saw, ate and thought, or how one culture coexisted— or collided—with another. The new linguistic findings also neatly dovetail with conclusions drawn from a very different area of evolutionary research. Comparisons of human genes worldwide have produced a "family tree" of the human race whose branches closely mirror the branching of languages proposed by linguists, leading to the startling suggestion that all people— and perhaps all languages—are descended from a tiny population that lived in Africa some 200,000 years ago.

ENGLISH PEDIGREE

4   The idea that languages are constantly evolving is obvious from looking at English over time: Consider Shakespeare's Elizabethan "Shall I compare thee to a summer's day?"; Chaucer's 14th-century, Middle English "Whan that Aprille with his shourse sote," and the opening line from the eighth-century Old English epic *Beowulf:* "Hwaet! We Gar-Dena, in geardagum."

5   These dramatic sound changes within a single language are possible only because, with the exception of onomatopoeic words like sizzle, the sound of a word has no direct connection to its meaning, says Merritt Ruhlen, a scholar in Palo Alto, Calif., who is tracing the relationships among the world's languages. Like coins, words get their value from the community at large, which must agree on what they represent. The word *dog* may mean a furry creature with four legs and a wagging tail, for instance, but *hippopotamus* or *ziglot* would serve just as well, as long as both speaker and listener agreed on its meaning.

CREAM IN YOUR COFFEE

6   These arbitrary associations between sounds and meanings provide the key to reconstructing the linguistic past, says Ruhlen. Because any number of sounds could be associated with a particular meaning, the presence of similar-sounding words with similar meanings in two different languages suggests that both languages had a common ancestor. For instance, diners might order their coffee *au lait, con leche* or *latte,* depending on whether they are in a French, Spanish or Italian restaurant. Using these similar-sounding "daughter" words for milk and a knowledge of how the sounds of words change as languages

evolve, linguists could come close to reconstructing the Latin form, *lacte,* even if this mother tongue of Romance languages were unknown.

7   Similar comparisons among words are what led Jones to suspect that Latin, along with Greek and Sanskrit, had descended from an even more ancient mother tongue. The word for the number three, for instance is *tres* in Latin, *treis* in Greek and *tryas* in Sanskrit. Over the years, scholars following up on Jones's suggestion have demonstrated that dozens of languages, including English, Swedish, German, Russian, Polish, Hindi, Persian, Welsh and Lithuanian, are all descendants of this same ancient "proto-language." Called Indo-European by linguists, this mother tongue was spoken some 8,000 years ago, before the invention of writing, and is known only by the traces left behind in the vocabularies of its daughter languages.

8   From these remnants, however, linguists have reconstructed a vast lexicon of proto-Indo-European words, providing clues to the origins of the ancient people who spoke the language when they populated nearly all of Europe. According to recent work by two Soviet linguists, Thomas Gamkrelidze and Vyacheslav Ivanov, words for domesticated animals such as cows, sheep and dogs as well as plants such as barley, flax and wheat suggest that the people who spoke proto-Indo-European were farmers. Likewise, the prevalence of words evoking mountains and rapidly flowing rivers suggests the Indo-European people originally lived in a hilly terrain.

9   Using these and other linguistic clues, Soviet researchers have offered new evidence that Indo-European originated in an area known as Anatolia, which is now part of Turkey, and from there spread throughout Europe and the sub-Continent. Linguists had long thought that the Indo-European proto-language had originated in southern Russia and had been spread throughout Europe by hordes of conquering warriors. But Gamkrelidze, Ivanov and other Soviet scholars cite words in proto-Indo-European that appear to have been borrowed from the languages of Mesopotamia and the Near East, suggesting that the speakers of proto-Indo-European lived in close geographical proximity to these cultures. The proto-Indo-European word for wine, for instance, appears to have its ancient roots in the non-Indo-European Semitic word *wanju* and the Egyptian *wns.*

FARMING IN EUROPE

10   The Soviets' linguistic work has found unexpected support in new research by British archaeologist Colin Renfrew, who, unaware of the linguistic studies, independently determined that the Indo-European homeland was in Anatolia, based on a reassessment of the archaeological evidence. Renfrew suggests that it was farmers, not warriors, who were responsible for the spread of the Indo-European language into Europe. He notes that even if a farmer's offspring had moved only 10 miles from the family farm to set up

farms of their own, the resulting wave of agriculture could have swept throughout Europe from Anatolia in about 1,500 years, carrying the Indo-European language with it. Because farming can support a larger number of people than hunting and gathering, the existing inhabitants of Europe were probably pushed out or adapted to farming on their own, says Renfrew.

11   While the existence of proto-Indo-European has been accepted among scholars for years, linguists have now begun to trace the lineage of languages back even further. Linguists studying languages from other areas of the world have identified ancestral mother tongues such as Altic, which gave rise to east Asian languages including Japanese and Korean, and Afro-Asiatic, the ancestor of Semitic. Working backward from reconstructions of Indo-European, Altic, Afro-Asiatic and several others; Soviet scholars have found that these ancestral tongues derived from an even more ancient language. Called "Nostratic," meaning "our language," this ancestral tongue was reconstructed independently by Soviet linguists Vladislav Illich-Svitych and Aharon Dolgopolsky during the 1960s, though their work was not translated into English until recently.

12   To re-create this ancient mother tongue, the Soviet scholars examined words considered by linguists to be the most stable parts of a vocabulary, such as names for body parts, personal pronouns and natural objects such as the sun and moon. Analyzing how the sounds for these words changed among Nostratic's various daughter languages, they were able to reconstruct hundreds of words. The Nostratic word for young man, for instance, is *majra,* which evolved into *merio* in Indo-European and thousand of years later became *mari* in French, meaning husband, and *marry* in English.

13   The reconstructed words of Nostratic vocabulary offer a glimpse of how the people who spoke the language lived, and they suggest a date when the language thrived. The absence of words for domesticated plants suggests the Nostratic speakers were probably hunter-gatherers, says Vitaly Sheveroskin, a former student of Dolgopolsky's who is now at the University of Michigan. Even more intriguing is the word *kuyna,* which can mean either dog or wolf; the "k" evolved into an "h" in Germanic languages, leading to *hound* in English. The ambiguity of meaning in the word suggests that wolves were in the process of becoming domesticated, says Sheveroskin, who notes that the oldest bones of dogs date to 14,000 years ago, giving a time frame when Nostratic was spoken. The speakers of Nostratic were well-traveled: Not only is the lexicon peppered with words that refer to "long journey" but over the next several thousand years, Nostratic split into several major language families as its speakers migrated from the Near East, their suspected homeland, into Europe, Persia and India.

14   The reconstruction of another such "macrofamily" of languages has given new clues to another mass migration, the original settling of the Americas. Joseph Greenberg, a linguist at Stanford University, recently proposed a controversial theory that all the languages spoken by Native Americans can be

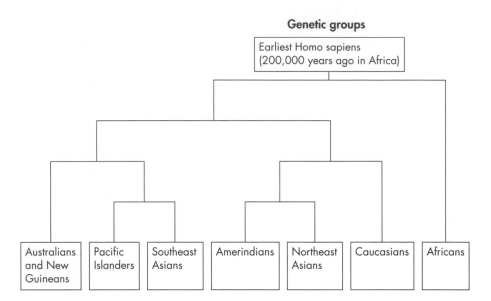

Genetic groups

All in the Family. Comparing genes from people around the world, biologists have created a family tree for the human species. The human race can be divided into seven major groups, each the result of ancient migrations. Strikingly, these genetic groups roughly mirror the major language families reconstructed by historical linguists: Australian and Indo-Pacific, Austric, Dene-Caucasian, Amerind, Nostratic, Khoisan, and Congo-Saharan.

grouped into three families that correspond to three waves of migration from Asia into the New World thousands of years ago. The largest, oldest and most controversial group proposed by Greenberg is a macrofamily that he calls Amerind, which is made up of all the languages in South and Central America as well as many in North America. The other two language groups are Na-Dene, which includes tongues spoken by Native Americans in the Northwest as well as Navajo and Apache, and Eskimo-Aleut, which contains languages spoken mostly in the Arctic; this group was the last to arrive in the New World.

SCHOLARLY FUROR

15   Greenberg's theory has created a furor among linguists, even some of those who champion the deep reconstruction of languages. At a recent conference in Boulder, Colo., linguists attacked Greenberg's admittedly unconventional methodology, in which he compares common-sounding words across many languages rather than attempting to reconstruct the sound shifts that occurred when one tongue diverged from another. Yet Greenberg's defenders cite his

track record: A classification of African languages he made 20 years ago created a similar furor among linguists and is now widely accepted.

16   Greenberg's theory is being given new weight by an upheaval in archaeological thinking about the peopling of the Americas. Archaeologists have long believed that the first migration to the New World occurred some 12,000 years ago—too short a time, some linguists argue, for the hundreds of Indian languages to arise from Greenberg's proposed Amerind mother tongue. But recently, several archaeological sites in the Americas have been shown to be far older than 12,000 years, suggesting that the first migration to the New World may have occurred much earlier—thus allowing more time for languages to diverge. One site, a rock shelter in Pennsylvania, has been dated at 16,000 years and another site in Chile may date back as far as 33,000 years. New studies that compare changes in the genes of Native Americans suggest that the date of the first migration might stretch back as far as 60,000 years.

17   Research on American languages is also throwing light on a longstanding linguistic mystery in Europe—as well as testifying to the remarkable wanderlust of ancient humans. Linguists have long wondered about the origins of Basque, a language spoken in the north of Spain that is one of the few non-Indo-European languages on the Continent. Soviet linguists have uncovered evidence that Basque is related to Na-Dene, and that both languages are part of yet another language macrofamily that includes tongues ranging from Chinese to the ancient Mediterranean tongue Etruscan. Called Dene-Caucasian, this ancient language was reconstructed in large part by Soviet linguist Sergei Starostin, another student of Dolgopolsky's. This wide-ranging tongue, spoken on both sides of the Bering Strait and at both ends of the Eurasian land mass, reflects the vast movements of ancient peoples who took their language with them and in some cases, such as Basque, kept it alive despite their being surrounded by other tongues.

18   The survival of an exotic linguistic island like Basque suggests that language, like genes, can

---

LINEAGE OF A WORD

Kujan
Proto-World

Kuyna
Nostratic

Kuon
Indo-European

Hound
English

LINEAGE OF A WORD

Hita
Proto-World

Hit-
Amerind

-ita
Nostratic

Hed
Indo-European

Edmenai
Greek

Edere
Latin

Ezzan
Old German

Eat
English

sometimes serve as a marker for a distinct group of people. Historical linguistic studies are generating widespread interest among scientists involved in one of the most exciting new developments in science: Tracing the evolutionary history of human genes. "It's quite clear why you have a correlation between genes and language," says Stanford University geneticist Luigi Cavalli-Sforza, a pioneer in the new genetic techniques. "When the human expansion around the earth took place some 50,000 years ago, it caused a number of separations between groups that didn't communicate again, genetically or linguistically. As the genes become different, the languages become different, too."

19   Cavalli-Sforza and his colleagues recently examined genetic markers from 42 different indigenous peoples from around the world and used the divergence among the genes to construct a family tree for the entire human race. The tree shows the human diaspora over tens of thousands of years, as a single population split into several large groups and then into the smaller tribes that exist today.

AFRICAN SPLIT

20   More important, Cavalli-Sforza found that the groupings of the human family based on genetic evidence closely mirrored the language groupings laid out independently by historical linguists. The oldest split occurred between Africans and other world populations, reflecting the migration of Homo sapiens out of Africa. This split is reflected in languages as well: Africa's Khoisan languages, such as that of the !Kung San, which uses a clicking noise denotated by an exclamation point, is only distantly related to other languages in the world. A recent paleoanthropological discovery in the Near East of the oldest fossils of Homo sapiens gives a rough date for when this first split might have occurred: The fossils date back 92,000 years.

21

LINEAGE OF A WORD
Kuni Proto-World
Küni Nostratic
Gwen Indo-European
Queen English

22

Another study that similarly traced the human genetic lineage suggests that all languages may have their roots in a small population that lived some 200,000 years ago. In their famed "Eve" hypothesis, Allan Wilson, Mark Stoneking and Rebecca Cann of the University of California at Berkeley traced genetic material from women around the world and concluded that all humans alive today are descendants of a tiny population of Homo sapiens that lived in Africa.

If the human race did arise from this small group of people, then it is likely they all spoke the same language, contends Sheveroskin. What's more, he says, the same techniques that gave rise to the reconstructions of ancient macrofamilies can also be used to dredge up bits of the original mother tongue of the human race. For example, the Nostratic word for leave, *lapa,* is similar to *tlapa* in Dene-Caucasian and *dap* in Amerind. And the Amerind word for woman, *kuni,* closely resembles the Nostratic word for woman, *küni.* It is from this word that the English word *queen* is derived.

FLEAS AND IN-LAWS

23 Sheversokin and other linguists have reconstructed dozens of words in this original mother tongue, which has been dubbed simply "proto-World." The word for I, for instance is *ngai; nas* means nose. The linguists have also reconstructed proto-World words referring to body parts, fleas, in-laws and a category of words that referred to pairs of objects—reflecting, perhaps, a culture that before the invention of mathematics counted the world in ones, twos and many. *Niwha* and *hwina* refer simultaneously to life, breath and blood, but, strangely, notes Sheveroskin, there appear to be no words in proto-World that refer to human emotions.

24   In the end, discovering the roots of language is inexorably tied to the still unresolved task of defining what language is, and this is where the ultimate impact of the new linguistic research may lie. The deep connections between languages demonstrate that far from a mere communication device, language is the palette from which people color their lives and culture. Intimately connected to the human experience, language oils the gears of social interactions and solidifies the ephemera of the mind into literature, history and collective knowledge. It is the calling card of the human race; announcing the presence not only of those alive today, but, with its deep roots into the past, the ancient ancestors who came before us.

Comprehension

1. Words to talk about:

   - no *philologer* could examine them
   - band of *renegade* scholars
   - these linguistic *paleoanthropologists*
   - the human *diaspora*
   - a *macrofamily*

2. What is the comparison that Allman makes between coins and words? Is it an apt description?

3. What did Allman say was so interesting about the fact that the word *kunya* was used for either dog or wolf?

Discussion

1. Allman wrote that tracing the evolution of language can reveal things about how people lived as well as suggest dates when the language thrived. Explain how this works. Give some specific examples.
2. Much of the linguistic research that Allman wrote about was conducted over the last thirty years by Soviet linguists. Why didn't Americans hear about it before the 1990s?
3. What are the most stable parts of a vocabulary? Why?
4. Allman wrote that with the exception of onomatopoeic words, the sounds of words do not directly connect to their meanings. But even onomatopoeic words differ from language to language because speakers translate sounds from nature into the combinations that already appear in their languages. In America and England, Kellogg's Rice Krispies are advertised as going "Snap! Crackle! Pop!" But as shown in the chart below, this same cereal says something quite different when milk is poured on it in other countries.

Country	Sound
Austria and Switzerland	Piff! Paff! Poff!
Brazil	Crak! Crak! Crok!
Central and South America	Pim! Pum! Pam!
Denmark and Norway	Pif! Paf! Puf!
Finland	Piks! Paks! Poks!
Germany	Schnapp! Krackle! Popp!
Japan	Pitchie! Patchi! Putchi!
Sweden	Piff! Paff! Puff!

Just from looking at these sounds, which languages would you conjecture are the most closely related to English and to each other?
5. Why are the linguists who are proposing these ancient language interrelationships so interested in archaeological evidence about early Native Americans on this continent?
6. Look at Allman's concluding paragraph and note the different metaphors he uses to talk about language. Why does he rely so heavily on metaphorical speech? Which comparison communicated the most to you? Why?

ON LANGUAGE FOSSILIZING

Jack Rosenthal

Much closer to home, both in space and time, is this column written in 1995 by the editor of the *New York Times Magazine.* He begins his article with a reference to the reopening of the dinosaur display at a New York museum, an event which he assumes most of his readers know about. Like Allman, he refers to linguistic fossils or dinosaurs, but his are much younger. They come from the early twentieth century in America when one-third of all Americans lived on farms or in rural communities. As you read the article, consider how his examples illustrate some of the points that William F. Allman made in the previous essay.

1   After three years out of sight, the dinosaurs are back, in splendid new quarters, at the Museum of Natural History in New York. A different kind of fossil meanwhile continues on permanent display, in language.

2   When President Clinton describes someone as dumb as a post or Senators talk about each other as show horses or workhorses, they're giving merely routine examples of Washington political vernacular—but superb illustrations of how a living language changes and churns. Each generation finds ways to reflect new experience. Yet many old expressions remain embedded in the language, long after the experience that prompted them has passed. Just as deep digs in Egypt or Kenya or Yucatán yield up the bones of species long extinct, earthy expressions often yield up language fossils.

3   The barnyard idioms that still salt colloquial speech echo from another America. From 1910 to 1920, when farm population peaked, one-third of all Americans lived on the farm. As recently as 1950, 15 percent of us did so. But now the farm population is less than 2 percent. If people know how high the corn will get, they probably got their information from musical comedy rather than rural reality.

4   Hardly a day goes by that someone in Congress doesn't accuse an opponent of acting pig-headed, without having any first-hand notion of just how pig-headed a pig can be. Officials take errant employees to the woodshed. Anthony Lake, the National Security Adviser, remembers thinking during the Nixon Administration that "woodshed" was a nickname for the White House Situation Room. That, he heard, was where an angry Henry Kissinger was taking the C.I.A.

5   A Philadelphia police captain, referring to protest demonstrators last month, insisted that "they can march until the cows come home." When Oklahoma City bombing case charges were dropped recently against James Nichols, the Michigan farmer was asked whether he would celebrate. "Celebrate?" he responded. "I've got to make hay while the sun shines, so to speak."

6   So to speak. At a recent gathering in northwest Connecticut, a woman visiting for the weekend asked, "What's for dinner?" "Spring chickens," answered the host, who grows poultry as a hobby. She did a double take; it was the first time she had ever heard the term used other than to describe how young some older person is not. In a column last spring about California's Pete Wilson, A. M. Rosenthal of *The Times* challenged the idea that governors have a responsibility to fill out their elected terms, rather than run for President. That's an idea to which "I would say hogwash if I knew exactly what hogwash was." His modesty is not widely shared by other users of the term.

7   Language fossils suffuse ordinary speech: *Silk purse out of a sow's ear. Till the cows come home. Separate the sheep from the goats.* People whose closest contact with horses is with carriages in Central Park nonetheless routinely say *stop horsing around, hold your horses, horse of another color.* Citizens of this hatless society casually drop terms like *old hat, high hat, hat in hand, eat my hat, at the drop of a hat.*

8   Many such expressions are generational and will fade with the passing of a generation that says *we need to get our socks up* or *like salts through an old maid.* Rather than *hold your horses,* young adults today would probably say *chill.* Yet many dated terms live on because they remain useful. Kids who have never seen a rotary phone outside a Lily Tomlin skit still know what it means to *dial* a number. People who have only rarely used carbon paper know what the letters *cc:* and *bcc:* mean at the bottom of a page. There is as yet no other convenient way to let a recipient of a document know that the writer is sending it along blind, without telling the addressee. Until there is, language fossils like this will not allow themselves to be buried.

COMPREHENSION

1. Words to talk about:
   - examples of Washington political *vernacular*
   - *deep digs* in Egypt or Kenya.
   - still salt *colloquial* speech
   - officials take *errant* employees

2. What has happened in real life since 1995 to make Rosenthal's reference to James Nichols obsolete?

3. What reason does Rosenthal give to explain that most of his examples are related to farm life? Does his reasoning make sense to you, or could there be some other reason?

4. Compare Rosenthal's observations to one or two of the linguistic conclusions that William F. Allman cited from usages uncovered from thousands of years ago.

DISCUSSION

1. Do you know that corn is supposed to be "knee high by the fourth of July"? Where do people learn this "fact"? Is it based in reality? If so, whose reality? What about farmers in warm southern states who hope to get two or three crops in a year?
2. Rosenthal presented at least fifteen dead metaphors related to farm life. Find them and explain their origins. Which are the easiest to understand, even if you've never been on a farm? Which ones will be more meaningful if you've experienced them?
3. What non-farm-related terms did Rosenthal include? How did he manage without having them sound out of place?
4. Rosenthal could have included many other examples of farm-related dead metaphors. In the following pairings, which do you think came first? Why?

a tulip bulb   a light bulb
the honking of a car   the honking of a goose
stemware (cocktail glass)   the stem of a rose
a head of cabbage   a head on a person
a drifter (a homeless person)   a snow drift

5. The importance of geese on farms is shown by the fact that people who have never been close to a goose still tell their children Mother Goose rhymes and recite the proverb "What's sauce for the goose is sauce for the gander." They also use the metaphors illustrated in the following phrases. Notice how each one is based on a single salient feature. Explain what that is.

a goose-neck lamp (or hook)
to goose someone
goose step (the marching style for Hitler's soldiers)
goose bumps or goose flesh
to goose an engine
to take a gander (to walk about)
a silly goose
a gosling
a goose egg (a score of zero)

WORKSHOP 2.1

Recycling Each Other's Symbols

One of the reasons that languages have such long histories is that while humans may not be good at recycling the earth's resources, they are amazingly skilled at recycling symbols, including personal names. On the one hand, this kind of recycling lengthens the lives of words and so helps linguists and anthropologists find related references, but on the other hand, when speakers appropriate a word or a symbol they put their own slant on it, often giving it quite a different meaning.

For example, when words are borrowed into another language, their meanings are often changed by the two groups of speakers. For speakers of Spanish, *actual* means "present," *libraria* means "bookstore," *principio* means "beginning," and *molestar* means "to bother," not "to molest." When cultures mix, the newcomers, even if they are officially in charge, realize that they probably aren't going to be able to replace parts of the culture that are firmly established, and so they sometimes adopt an if-you-can't-beat-them-join-them philosophy and conspire to change the group's symbols to match their own.

Early Christians were masters at this. They adopted the pagan holiday celebrating the December solstice and turned it into Christmas. Then they adopted the March Equinox and turned it into a celebration of the resurrection of Jesus. Here they didn't even change the name of the *Easter* festival, which was named after *Eos,* the Greek goddess of the dawn.

A wonderful example of how symbols are appropriated and adapted to changing times is the name *Jiminy Cricket,* which makes most Americans think of the Walt Disney movie *Pinocchio* and the cricket that played the role of Pinocchio's conscience. In the original 1881 Italian story by C. Collodi, there is no mention of a Jiminy Cricket. However, there is a talking cricket, who appears on fewer than a dozen pages out of the 310-page book and in Chapter Four is killed when Pinocchio throws a hammer at him. Somewhere between the original Italian story and the Walt Disney movie, a creative mind thought of appropriating a name from popular culture in order to turn this bit player into a major character.

Jiminy Crickets and *Jiminy Christmas* were "soft" swear words developed out of *Gemini,* which had long been used as a swear word with the implication being that the speaker was swearing double. Gemini is the constellation created when Castor and Pollux, the twin sons of Leda who had been seduced by Zeus, were placed in the sky. Dictionary editor Stuart Flexner has cited a 1660 English printing of *Gemini* as a swear word, which by the 1830s in America was spelled *Jiminy,* by 1848 *Jiminy Crickets,* and by 1905 *Jiminy Christmas.* Based on the similarity in beginning sounds to *Jesus Christ,* the phrase gradually changed from being a swear word referring to the twins of Greek and Roman mythology, to being a euphemistic slang term for *Jesus Christ* used by speakers who felt religiously proscribed from using the actual name.

What could be a better name for a naughty little boy's conscience than a veiled and playful reference to Jesus Christ?

The appropriation of Camelot as a symbol for the Kennedy years provides a different kind of example. During the 1960s, the Kennedy family and *Life* magazine had a symbiotic relationship in which the Kennedys would give the magazine exclusive photography rights while the magazine gave the Kennedys unusual control over editorial content. After President Kennedy's assassination, Mrs. Kennedy requested that T. H. White, author of *The Once and Future King,* a four-volume novel about King Arthur's Camelot, write the obituary article for *Life,* and that he build it around a metaphorical comparison between King Arthur and John F. Kennedy.

On May 26, 1995, the Kennedy library released the interview notes that White had specified not be made public until a year after Mrs. Kennedy's death. The notes revealed the purposeful manner in which Jacqueline Kennedy set about to make a connection in people's minds between King Arthur's reign and her husband's presidency. She did this with the name *Camelot,* which is defined in dictionaries as the site of the legendary King Arthur's court and "A time, place, or atmosphere of idyllic happiness." When Editor Graves of *Life* suggested to White that he had used the word too often and could perhaps delete it from a couple of sentences, White said that he had already tried such a revision, but that Mrs. Kennedy insisted on keeping it as it was. The success of her plan was shown thirty years later by how many times *Camelot* appeared in news stories and headlines about the auctioning of her personal belongings.

A final example shows how instant, world-wide communication encourages appropriation. In 1994 when Norway's most famous piece of art *The Scream,* painted by Edvard Munch, was stolen from the National Gallery in Oslo, antiabortion activist Borre Knudsen capitalized on the coincidence of the painting's name and the name of the controversial antiabortion film *The Silent Scream.* Knudsen hinted that the painting would be returned if the film showing a twelve-week-old fetus being aborted were shown on national television. The film was not shown, and police recovered the painting three months later. There was no connection between the thieves and the abortion protestors.

BRAIN TEASERS

1. In the early days of Christianity, a simplified outline of a fish was used as a secret code of identification. One person would casually make a crescent mark in the dirt. If the other person were a Christian, he would make the same mark turned the other direction to complete the outline. See the picture on page 80 showing

continued

Workshop 2.1

Recycling Each Other's Symbols   continued

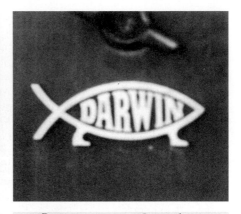

Source: Antismoking ad © 1997 Reister-Robb and Maricopa County Sheriff's Department.

how this fish symbol is used on a church sign. As part of today's commercialized graffiti, the same fish outline, and several variations, are sold to be attached to cars. Explain what is being communicated by the one shown in the picture. If you have seen variations, describe them and what they are communicating.

2. In 1994 the Republic of Abkhazia, formerly part of the Soviet Union, issued a commemorative postage stamp picturing Groucho Marx and John Lennon. What was the joke?

3. In Arizona, Maricopa County Sheriff Joe Arpaio launched a campaign telling merchants they were "dead meat" if they sold cigarettes to teenagers. Whose symbol did he appropriate for his posters?

4. Good things had happened to Augustus Caesar in the final month of summer, so when the Julian calendar (named after his great uncle Julius Caesar) was put into place, Augustus chose to have the eighth month named after himself. He named the previous month after Julius, who had preceded him as Emperor. If you know Latin (or other romance languages), explain the meanings of *September, October, November,* and *December.* How did Augustus Caesar's actions change these meanings?

5. With people in show business, name recognition is especially important, so they often appropriate someone else's name to get a head start in the business of fame. When sixteen-year-old Allan Konigsberg submitted a joke to the *New York Times,* he signed his name "Woody Allen." Whether or not his name was inspired by the cartoon character Woody Woodpecker, "Woody" was a good choice because people already knew the name and associated it with humor. How were the present owners of the following names advantaged in the game of name recognition? Who do the following names remind you of?
   - Singer Marilyn Manson
   - Actress Liv Tyler
   - Singer Madonna
   - Brett Butler, star of *Grace Under Fire*
   - Actress Sandra Bernhard
   - Magician David Copperfield
   - Rapper Snoop Doggy Dog
   - Singer Engelbert Humperdinck

continued

WORKSHOP 2.1

Recycling Each Other's Symbols   continued

6. The alliterative name of the Midas Muffler shops is to remind customers of the old legend about King Midas. To help customers get the image, the *i* is dotted with a stylized crown, and the signs are painted in black on a gold background. What is the story? What well-known maxim makes the story especially appropriate for a muffler shop?
7. *Okay* (or *OK*) is the most famous English word in the world. How does this relate to the Circle-K name and logo?
8. From what did the 7-Eleven corporation appropriate its name? In the early years of these convenience markets, what secondary meaning did the name have?

OTHER THOUGHT QUESTIONS

1. Friday is named after the Norse goddess Freya, the wife of Woden, for whom Wednesday is named. When Christian missionaries from Rome went to Northern Europe they taught that Friday was an unlucky day, especially if it falls on the thirteenth (one number after the number of Jesus' apostles). What might their motivation have been? In what ways did their influence last? In what ways is it being eroded?
2. "As quick as you can say Jack Robinson" has been in the language for nearly two centuries. Various explanations have been given for its origin—none conclusive. But fifty years ago, the fact that it was already part of everyday language probably helped people remember a new baseball player in the major leagues. What was his name?
3. The mascot for Kennesaw State College has long been the Fighting Owls, commonly called the Hooters, after which Hooter Field and the Hooterdome were named. In 1993 school officials announced they were dropping the names because "the term has come to mean something besides Owls." Who appropriated the Kennesaw mascot?
4. People carry on running arguments through slogans and bumper stickers as when "I ♥ [love] my dog" is appropriated and changed to "I ♠ [spayed] my dog"; "Envision World Peace" becomes "Envision Whirled Peas" or "Envision Using Your Turn Signal"; and "My Child Is An Honor Student at _____ Elementary

School," is topped by "My Kid Beat Up Your Honor Student!" Try to figure out the original for these examples of second- or third-generation slogans or proverbs.

- Ask not what your mother can do for you; ask what you can do for your mother.
- Be all you can be; work for peace!
- Save the Humans!
- A Woman's Place Is in the House—And the Senate, Too!
- A Woman's Place Is on the Tennis Court!

What other examples can you think of?

5. Basketball player Kareem Abdul-Jabbar (who before he converted to Islam was known as Lew Alcindor) wasn't especially excited in 1995 when a professional football player decided to change his name so that it sounded exactly the same as Abdul-Jabbar's, but with a slightly different spelling. In 1997, Martina Hingis was ranked the number one women's tennis player in the world. Hingis, who was born in Czechoslovakia, was given the name at birth in 1981 by her tennis-playing mother. She wanted to honor Martina Navratilova and to acknowledge her hopes that her daughter could follow in Navratilova's footsteps. How do these two cases of athletes appropriating other athletes' names differ?

6. When products and their names become universally known, the public sometimes appropriates them into metaphors. For example, press photographers refer to people who hang around celebrities in hopes of being included in pictures as "Velcroids" because it's like they've been attached with Velcro. Identify the product names in the following sentences, and explain the connection between the product and its metaphorical use:

- The Susan B. Anthony dollar is the Edsel of U.S. coinage.
- My brother-in-law is a Mr. Clean.
- It's a BAND-AID approach—too little, too late.
- That no-tax promise is another example of Twinkie economics.
- I'm in the mood for a Kleenex movie.
- We've apparently got another Teflon administration.

7. Read Living Language 2.1, and talk about these contemporary examples of appropriation. Can you think of other examples? Can you point to specific illustrations in your own community?

Living Language 2.1

Contemporary Appropriations

Someone else's symbol is being appropriated whenever graffiti taggers change a rival gang's signature into their own, when college students paint their school's colors on a rival school's mascot, when the general public uses trademarks metaphorically, when companies create parody advertisements, and when the makers of generic-brand products copy package designs from their more expensive counterparts. Here are some more specific examples:

■ Advertisers steal the exciting parts of athletic events when they create commercials based on puns and pay to have announcers insert them at key points. For example, during a basketball game, fans hear the "Sherman-Williams in the Paint" score and "What a Shot! What a Burger!" In football, they might hear the "Blue Cross and Blue Shield Health Report."

■ The biggest toy success of the 1980s was the Teenage Mutant Ninja Turtles whose individual names were Michaelangelo, Donatello, Leonardo, and Raphael. These toys stood out from the mass of children's toys partly because the names were long and difficult to pronounce and spell. President Reagan's Secretary of Education William Bennett used the names in a lead to an article decrying the lack of solid education for America's youth. He had overheard an animated conversation between his son and a friend in which they kept dropping these names. However, he was severely disappointed when he found out that neither his son nor his friend had ever heard of the Italian painter and sculptor Michelangelo (1475–1564), the Florentine sculptor Donatello (1386–1466), the Italian painter, sculptor, engineer, and architect Leonardo da Vinci (1452–1519), or the Italian painter Raphael (1483–1520).

■ Suggested Topics for Writing

1. Write an autobiographical piece telling about your own literary development. Choose to focus either on reading or writing. Describe your earliest memories and how you became aware of the pleasure and the benefits to be gained from literacy. Do you remember people reading to you? Do you remember the first thing you read on your own? Did you

- Babe Ruth (baseball player George Herman Ruth) was so famous that most people think Baby Ruth candy bars were named for him. But in 1921 when the Curtiss Candy Company invented the bars, they named them after the youngest daughter of President Grover Cleveland. As a White House baby, she had been adored by the public in the same way that Caroline and John-John were during the Kennedy years. However, the popularity of the candy bar and the popularity of the baseball player (he died in 1945 at age 50) may have reinforced each other.
- New York Yankee catcher Lawrence Peter Berra, universally known as Yogi Berra, had his name appropriated by cartoon character Yogi Bear, so that a generation grew up more familiar with his namesake than with him.
- Appropriating a place name gives people a leg up in having a memorable name. Rock Hudson started life as Roy Fitzgerald of Winnetka, Illinois. Talent scout Henry Willson explained, "I always gave a green actor the gimmick of a trick name to help him get known. . . . I tried to think of something strong and big. *Rock of Gibraltar.* Hudson came from the Hudson River, for no reason. I knew that was it. Rock Hudson." Other examples are John Denver, River Phoenix, and Chevy Chase. Comedian Chevy Chase took advantage of the fame of Chevy Chase, Maryland, and the nationally known Chevy Chase bank. Janet Reno's father was a newspaper reporter with the last name of Rasmussen, which no one could remember or spell. He looked on a map and found Reno, which a generation later helped his daughter make a name for herself.

have a favorite childhood book? Do you remember learning to write? Did you have to write your name to get a library card or to graduate from kindergarten? As you describe your early experiences and how you progressed to where you are now, be specific so that your story won't sound like everyone else's.

2. Describe an incident in your life that made you think about the power of words. If you are a parent, you might write about your child learning to speak. Or have you ever been overjoyed to hear someone's voice on a telephone or in person? Have you had an epiphany when you found yourself in a foreign country with people who couldn't understand you? Have you come to a slow realization that you've grown to know

and love someone through letters or e-mail? Or maybe you've had a quarrel or have suffered a loss of some kind that could have been prevented if you had been better able to communicate.

3. If you speak or understand a second language, write an essay in which you show how it is related to English or how it differs from English. To keep from being so general that you don't say anything of interest, you should focus on one aspect of the two languages. You might write about confusing the two languages or combining them as when people speak "Spanglish." You could compare metaphors based on animals or on body parts, or you might write about differences in how gender is marked, or the differences in sound patterns. Are there words which are especially hard to pronounce in the language that you learned second? Why?

4. Write an essay about the recycling of symbols. You can begin with some of the examples in Workshop 2.1, but try to extend them or find new illustrations of the principles that are demonstrated. One suggestion is to examine brand names that have been given new meanings, as when someone wants a little reward for good behavior and asks, "Where are the M&Ms?" Tie the information about recycling into the idea of language change as demonstrated in William F. Allman's article, "The Mother Tongue."

INFORMATION SOURCES FOR WRITING

The *Human Language* video series produced by Gene Searchinger and shown on PBS in 1995 (distributed by Ways of Knowing, 200 W. 72nd Street, New York, NY 10023 and available in many university collections), teaches linguistic concepts while introducing dozens of linguists, some of whose essays are in this text. Parts One and Two, "Discovering the Human Language, 'Colorless Green Ideas,' " and "Acquiring the Human Language, 'Playing the Language Game,' " focus on the same subjects as treated in this chapter's essays, while Part Three, "The Human Language Evolves, 'With and Without Words,' " moves on to the topics treated in later chapters. Listed below are the titles of some useful books:

American English, by Albert H. Marckwardt. Oxford Univ. Press, 1958.
Cambridge Encyclopedia of Language, by David Crystal. New York: Cambridge Univ. Press, 1997.
Grow Your Vocabulary by Learning the Roots of English Words, by Robert Schleifer. New York: Random, 1995.

A History of Reading, by Alberto Manguel. New York: Viking, 1996.

I Hear America Talking: An Illustrated Treasury of American Words and Phrases, by Stuart Berg Flexner. New York: Van Nostrand Reinhold, 1976.

The Henry Holt Encyclopedia of Word and Phrase Origins, by Robert Hendrickson. New York: Henry Holt, 1987.

The Language Instinct: How the Mind Creates Language, by Steven Pinker. New York: Morrow, 1994.

Listening with My Heart, by Heather Whitestone and Angela Elwell Hunt. New York: Doubleday, 1997. Heather Whitestone, who has been profoundly deaf since she was eighteen months old, tells the story of her life, including her reign as the first handicapped Miss America. Her reign was controversial in the deaf community because she wears a hearing aid, uses oral speech, and communicates in both American Sign Language and in Signing Exact English.

Speaking of Reading, by Nadine Rosenthal. New York: Heinemann, 1995.

Train Go Sorry: Inside a Deaf World, by Leah Hager Cohen. Boston: Houghton, 1994.

Word Play: What Happens When People Talk, by Peter Farb. New York: Knopf, 1974.

Wordstruck, by Robert MacNeil. New York: Viking Penguin, 1989.

Sch ol Cen

Teen shot in
graffiti war

By Arthur C. Carlton
ASSOCIATED PRESS
NY, New York

AIR SAFETY THREATENED
BY LANGUAGE PROBLEMS

By DE
ASSO
PHIL
Air Tra
allow a
to fly i
at all ti
it is no
interna

Oral laws of Navajos
illustrated to law stud

Students disprove apathy label

Hold everything and th
before it was a simple

lk the talk!
t so easy in
ise filled jo

may have place,
not in class

conditions in these environments are conducive to

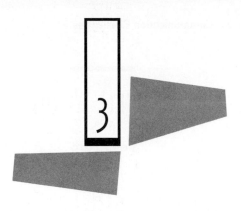

COMMUNICATION CHALLENGES

While we marvel at the wonders of language and how it has enabled humankind to preserve the information gathered by one generation and pass it on to the next, we also need to realize that communication, even face-to-face with people of our own generation, is full of pitfalls. Misunderstandings occur sometimes because words are ambiguous and sometimes because our body language contradicts the words we are saying, and sometimes because we are intentionally misled. In some situations words aren't even possible, forcing speakers to rely on gestures or pictures or some other kind of symbol. And when we try to cross the gender lines or the lines between different ethnic groups, our backgrounds and the expectations that we grew up with may be so different that the common words we share will have different meanings for those who are speaking and for those who are listening. Nowhere is this more evident than in the public conflicts over graffiti and tagging.

This kind of miscommunication often results in calls for censorship, while other calls for censorship are made simply because the people doing the censoring do not like what is being said. Closely allied, but on the opposite side of the coin, are questions related to people's right to privacy. Developments in technology and the mass media, along with changing public attitudes, have resulted in some challenging new questions about protecting individuals (especially children from pedophiles), while also protecting people's privacy.

These are the topics that will be discussed in this chapter. But because they are new and society is in the midst of coming to terms with them, the writers are likely to leave you with more questions than answers.

In Other Words

Peter Farb

While words make up our primary source of communication, in this essay Peter Farb shows that body language and other more subtle forms of communication also enter the picture. He tells about a famous experiment that illustrates what psychologists call the mirror image. People, adults as well as children, look at others for confirmation of their identities. They make themselves fit the image that they see reflected in the eyes of those with whom they associate.

1 Early in this century, a horse named Hans amazed the people of Berlin by his extraordinary ability to perform rapid calculations in mathematics. After a problem was written on a blackboard placed in front of him, he promptly counted out the answer by tapping the low numbers with his right forefoot and multiples of ten with his left. Trickery was ruled out because Hans's owner, unlike owners of other performing animals, did not profit financially—and Hans even performed his feats whether or not the owner was present. The psychologist O. Pfungst witnessed one of these performances and became convinced that there had to be a more logical explanation than the uncanny intelligence of a horse.

2   Because Hans performed only in the presence of an audience that could see the blackboard and therefore knew the correct answer, Pfungst reasoned that the secret lay in observation of the audience rather than of the horse. He finally discovered that as soon as the problem was written on the blackboard, the audience bent forward very slightly in anticipation to watch Hans's forefeet. As slight as that movement was, Hans perceived it and took it as his signal to begin tapping. As his taps approached the correct number, the audience became tense with excitement and made almost imperceptible movements of the head—which signaled Hans to stop counting. The audience, simply by expecting Hans to stop when the correct number was reached, had actually told the animal when to stop. Pfungst clearly demonstrated that Hans's intelligence was nothing but a mechanical response to his audience, which unwittingly communicated the answer by its body language.

3   The "Clever Hans Phenomenon," as it has come to be known, raises an interesting question. If a mere horse can detect unintentional and extraordinarily subtle body signals, might they not also be detected by human beings?

Professional gamblers and con men have long been known for their skill in observing the body-language clues of their victims, but only recently has it been shown scientifically that all speakers constantly detect and interpret such cues also, even though they do not realize it.

4   An examination of television word games several years ago revealed that contestants inadvertently gave their partners body-language signals that led to correct answers. In one such game, contestants had to elicit certain words from their partners, but they were permitted to give only brief verbal clues as to what the words might be. It turned out that sometimes the contestants also gave body signals that were much more informative than the verbal clues. In one case, a contestant was supposed to answer *sad* in response to his partner's verbal clue of *happy*—that is, the correct answer was a word opposite to the verbal clue. The partner giving the *happy* clue unconsciously used his body to indicate to his fellow contestant that an opposite word was needed. He did that by shifting his body and head very slightly to one side as he said happy, then to the other side in expectation of an opposite word.

5   Contestants on a television program are usually unsophisticated about psychology and linguistics, but trained psychological experimenters also unintentionally flash body signals which are sometimes detected by the test subjects—and which may distort the results of experiments. Hidden cameras have revealed that the sex of the experimenter, for example, can influence the responses of subjects. Even though the films showed that both male and female experimenters carried out the experiments in the same way and asked the same questions, the experimenters were very much aware of their own sex in relation to the sex of the subjects. Male experimenters spent 16 percent more time carrying out experiments with female subjects than they did with male subjects; similarly, female experimenters took 13 percent longer to go through experiments with male subjects than they did with female subjects. The cameras also revealed that chivalry is not dead in the psychological experiment; male experimenters smiled about six times as often with female subjects as they did with male subjects.

6   The important question, of course, is whether or not such nonverbal communication influences the results of experiments. The answer is that it often does. Psychologists who have watched films made without the knowledge of either the experimenters or the subjects could predict almost immediately which experimenters would obtain results from their subjects that were in the direction of the experimenters' own biases. Those experimenters who seemed more dominant, personal, and relaxed during the first moments of conversation with their subjects usually obtained the results that they secretly hoped the experiments would yield. And they somehow communicated their secret hopes in a completely visual way, regardless of what they said or their paralanguage when they spoke. That was made clear when these films were shown to two groups, one of which saw the films without hearing the sound track while the other heard only the sound track without seeing the films. The

group that heard only the voices could not accurately predict the experimenters' biases—but those who saw the films without hearing the words immediately sensed whether or not the experimenters were communicating their biases.

7   A person who signals his expectations about a certain kind of behavior is not aware that he is doing so—and usually he is indignant when told that his experiment was biased—but the subjects themselves confirm his bias by their performances. Such bias in experiments has been shown to represent self-fulfilling prophecies. In other words, the experimenters' expectations about the results of the experiment actually result in those expectations coming true. That was demonstrated when each of twelve experimenters was given five rats bred from an identical strain of laboratory animals. Half of the experimenters were told that their rats could be expected to perform brilliantly because they had been bred especially for high intelligence and quickness in running through a maze. The others were told that their rats could be expected to perform very poorly because they had been bred for low intelligence. All the experimenters were then asked to teach their rats to run a maze.

8   Almost as soon as the rats were put into the maze it became clear that those for which the experimenters had high expectations would prove to be the better performers. And the rats which were expected to perform badly did in fact perform very badly, even though they were bred from the identical strain as the excellent performers. Some of these poor performers did not even budge from their starting positions in the maze. The misleading prophecy about the behavior of the two groups of rats was fulfilled—simply because the two groups of experimenters unconsciously communicated their expectations to the animals. Those experimenters who anticipated high performance were friendlier to their animals than those who expected low performance; they handled their animals more, and they did so more gently. Clearly, the predictions of the experimenters were communicated to the rats in subtle and unintended ways—and the rats behaved accordingly.

9   Since animals such as laboratory rats and Clever Hans can detect body-language cues, it is not surprising that human beings are just as perceptive in detecting visual signals about expectations for performance. It is a psychological truth that we are likely to speak to a person whom we expect to be unpleasant in such a way that we force him to act unpleasantly. But it has only recently become apparent that poor children—often black or Spanish-speaking—perform badly in school because that is what their teachers expect of them, and because the teachers manage to convey that expectation by both verbal and nonverbal channels. True to the teachers' prediction, the black and brown children probably will do poorly—not necessarily because children from minority groups are capable only of poor performance, but because poor performance has been expected of them. The first grade may be the place where teachers anticipate poor performances by children of certain racial,

economic, and cultural backgrounds—and where the teachers actually teach these children how to fail.

10   Evidence of the way the "Clever Hans Phenomenon" works in many schools comes from a careful series of experiments by psychologist Robert Rosenthal and his co-workers at Harvard University. They received permission from a school south of San Francisco to give a series of tests to the children in the lower grades. The teachers were blatantly lied to. They were told that the test was a newly developed tool that could predict which children would be "spurters" and achieve high performance in the coming year. Actually, the experimenters administered a new kind of IQ test that the teachers were unlikely to have seen previously. After IQ scores were obtained, the experimenters selected the names of 20 percent of the children completely at random. Some of the selected children scored very high on the IQ test and others scored low, some were from middle-class families and others from lower-class. Then the teachers were lied to again. The experimenters said that the tests singled out this 20 percent as the children who could be expected to make unusual intellectual gains in the coming year. The teachers were also cautioned not to discuss the test results with the pupils or their parents. Since the names of these children had been selected completely at random, any difference between them and the 80 percent not designated as "spurters" was completely in the minds of the teachers.

11   All the children were given IQ tests again during that school year and once more the following year. The 20 percent who had been called to the attention of their teachers did indeed turn in the high performances expected of them—in some cases dramatic increases of 25 points in IQ. The teachers' comments about these children also were revealing. The teachers considered them more happy, curious, and interesting than the other 80 percent—and they predicted that they would be successes in life, a prophecy they had already started to fulfill. The experiment plainly showed that children who are expected to gain intellectually do gain and that their behavior improves as well.

12   The results of the experiment are clear—but the explanation for the results is not. It might be imagined that the teachers simply devoted more time to the children singled out for high expectations, but the study showed that was not so. Instead, the influence of the teachers upon these children apparently was much more subtle. What the teachers said to them, how and when it was said, the facial expressions, gestures, posture, perhaps even touch that accompanied their speech—some or all of these things must have communicated that the teachers expected improved performance from them. And when these children responded correctly, the teachers were quicker to praise them and also more lavish in their praise. Whatever the exact mechanism was, the effect upon the children who had been singled out was dramatic. They changed their ideas about themselves, their behavior, their motivation, and their learning capacities.

13   The lesson of the California experiment is that pupil performance does not depend so much upon a school's audio-visual equipment or new textbooks or enriching trips to museums as it does upon teachers whose body language communicates high expectations for the pupils—even if the teacher thinks she "knows" that a black, a Puerto Rican, a Mexican-American, or any other disadvantaged child is fated to do poorly in school. Apparently, remedial instruction in our schools is misdirected. It is needed more by the middle-class teachers than by the disadvantaged children.

COMPREHENSION

1. Words to talk about:

   - what they said or their *paralanguage*
   - represent *self-fulfilling prophecies*
   - which children would be *"spurters"*

DISCUSSION

1. Explain the success of Hans the horse. Have you had a pet who could read your body language? If so, give some examples.
2. Farb mentions professional gamblers and con-artists as being skilled in "reading" body language, but really most of us learn to do this even before we learn to talk. Give some examples of when and how you read another person's body language. How does body language relate to lie detector tests? How about biofeedback?
3. Can people use body language to lie? Give some examples of body language that deceives in contrast to body language that gives away someone's genuine feelings.
4. Look at the photo of the two football referees on page 95 and explain the difference in their body language. What is it about sports that makes body language so important?
5. In reference to the study that reported on experimenters giving more attention to the opposite sex, can you think of other examples when this happens in everyday life?
6. Did you go to a high school where students were grouped or tracked? What are the implications from Farb's article about such grouping? What does it do to children who are placed in the "gifted program"? In high school, do you think teachers act differently when they are teaching an advanced placement or an honors class than when teaching a basics class?

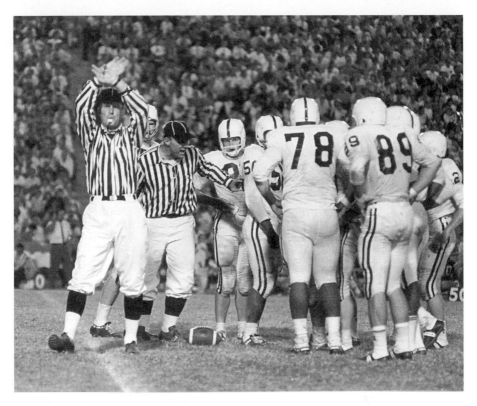

Source: Courtesy of Conley Photography, Inc.

WORKSHOP 3.1

To Tell the Truth

While few would disagree with the commandment, "Thou shalt not lie," most people's lives are filled with incidents illustrating how people tolerate, if not participate in, lying. In the previous essay, Peter Farb explained that the Harvard researchers "blatantly lied" to the teachers who cooperated with them in the research. Some people excuse this kind of lying by saying that the end justifies the means. What do you think? If you were a student working on this research project, would you have gone along with this lying? Are some lies more acceptable than others? Why do you think people react differently to different kinds of lies?

PART I: A QUESTION OF HONESTY

Talk about the situations described here and decide in what ways they are honest and in what ways they are dishonest. Which situation do you think is most acceptable and which is most unacceptable according to your code of ethics? What factors need to be taken into account? Do you expect everyone in the class to agree on the levels of acceptability? Why or why not?

- When a book drive was held for a high school library, an automobile dealer donated a new pickup truck to be given to the student who brought in the most books. To lull their competitors into not working quite so hard, the two leading contenders for the prize waited until the last afternoon of the contest to turn their books in. Between 4:00 and 5:00 P.M., they both arrived with friends and family members to help unload boxes and bags of books from trucks, trailers, vans, and station wagons. The next morning at the ceremony announcing the prize winners, the librarian listed the winner as having brought in 6,342 books while the runner up brought in 4,290 books. Although no one said anything, even a casual observer could see that the books were still in their original boxes and bags, stacked in a mountain in the middle of the library. There was no way they could have been counted.

- An Associated Press story (April 24, 1998) cited evidence gathered by *Rolling Stone* magazine and a TV entertainment show that the fights on Jerry Springer's show are staged. Christopher Sterling, a George Washington University media scholar, said the show "is like wrestling. The whole thing is a put-up job." Suzanne Muir, a Canadian restaurant owner who helped stage a high-profile hoax on the Springer show three years ago, said she wasn't surprised at the reports. Henry Travis, a 28-year-old computer worker was glad to hear the news. He cited such stories as "I'm Sleeping with My Cousin and My Other Cousin," and "My Brother Is the Father of My Baby," and said "It's almost reassuring to find out . . . it's not really happening."

- At one university, each student who successfully defends a master's thesis or a doctoral dissertation must take the finished product, along with the signed approval sheets from the committee members, to the graduate college for the graduate dean's signature. Students bring their documents to the front desk of the graduate college, where a secretary disappears with them for a few minutes and then comes back with the required signature. Anyone who has tried to get an appointment with a dean realizes how unlikely it is that the Dean of the Graduate College is actually sitting in his office from 8:00 A.M. to 5:00 P.M. every day waiting to sign cover sheets on students' graduate projects.

- "Talking Points: Primer for Liars" was the headline on an *Arizona Republic* story (Feb. 1, 1998) abour the White House scandal and the list of ideas that Monica Lewinsky allegedly gave to Linda Tripp to use if she were called to testify before the Ken Starr grand jury. Opinions expressed in national media differed about the document, with some people saying that it was too sophisticated—it had too much legal jargon in it—to have been prepared by Lewinsky, while others said it was not sophisticated enough to have been prepared by a legal team. Still others thought the document had been prepared by Clinton opponents wanting to plant evidence that the White House was illegally coaching a witness.

- Psychiatrist Harvy Roy Greenberg told Glenn Lovell, a reporter for the *San Jose Mercury News* (Feb. 15, 1998), that "people know they're being lied to; they expect to be lied to." Lovell's story seemed to support Greenberg's belief. He cited the popularity of the 1998 political movie *Wag the Dog* in which Dustin Hoffman and Robert De Niro have careers based on lies; the *Seinfeld* sitcom, which finds humor in best friends George, Jerry, and Elaine conning each other; and from real life, such as the case of M. Larry Lawrence lying about his war record so that he could be buried at Arlington Cemetery, Air Force pilot Lt. Kelly Flynn lying about her relationship with a married man, the singing group Mili Vanilli lying about its hit records, and Fran Drescher contriving a story about almost cutting her finger off on Halloween while she was slicing a low-fat muffin. Drescher invented her dramatic story while she was talking to Jay Leno on the *Tonight Show* and the conversation began to lag.

PART II: SCHEMES AND SCAMS

Every year the U.S. Post Office receives over 400,000 complaints about mail fraud. The top five categories are misleading vacation or travel offers, chain letters, land fraud, variations on the pigeon drop (that is, the recipient is asked to put up good-faith money in exchange for profits that will come from helping to straighten out some banking problem), and sweepstakes letters in which people are led to believe they

continued

WORKSHOP 3.1

To Tell the Truth   continued

have won a fabulous prize. On the sweepstakes letters, the fine print always includes an "if you have the winning number" clause, but many people do not notice the disclaimer.

BRAIN TEASERS

1. The first challenge for those who send out fraudulent mail is to get the recipients to open the envelopes. One envelope announcing a sweepstakes offer included the following special messages printed in different colors of ink to look as if they had been attached separately. How are the statements true? How are they false? What is their overall purpose? Could they be put on any piece of mail?
   - (on a piece of tape covering the flap closure) "TAMPER PROOF: If this seal is broken at the time of arrival, please notify local postal authorities."
   - "MONITORED DELIVERY"
   - A bar code with a seventeen-digit number
   - "URGENT NOTICE: Time-Sensitive Registered Documents Enclosed! Failure to respond to this notice will result in the forfeiture of any and all money that may be due you."
   - (visible through the window, along with another bar code and the name and address of the recipient) "Approved for delivery to:"
   - "ATTENTION POSTMASTER: Handle in conformance with postal law and regulations as outlined in section No. GO11.5 of the United States Domestic Mail Manual."

2. Federal law requires that sweepstakes offers inform people of their chances of winning. On the envelope described above, this information was included in small print on the back of the envelope in the middle of a long paragraph. The beginning and ending of the paragraph focused on how the prize could be claimed either in a lump sum or spread out over 20 years. Why did the sweepstakes company choose to present the required information in this particular way?

3. Another sweepstakes letter had a message on the outside saying "Please note: As you may know, we'll be announcing our $10,000,000.00 winner right after the Super Bowl live from the winner's home. Since you are a potential winner, we need to know where to find you on Super Bowl Sunday. There's no need to call if you plan to be home." This was followed by a signature in blue ink and an 800 phone number that people who were going to be away from their homes could call "at any time up until January 24." What was the purpose of this gimmick?

4. See the figure on page 99 for an example of the beginning of a sweepstakes letter. Its real purpose is to entice the recipient to return the form with validation

⌈CLAIM #TS6F8M291⌉ SWEEPSTAKES NOTIFICATION

If you have and return the Grand Prize winning entry in time, we'll confirm that

OUR SWEEPSTAKES RESULTS ARE NOW FINAL:
JOHN B. WEALTHY HAS WON
A CASH PRIZE OF $977,207.00

ATTENTION, JOHN B. WEALTHY: WE NOW HAVE APPROVAL TO PAY THE ENTIRE PRIZE IN A SINGLE CASH PAYMENT!
You are hereby duly notified that funds are now on reserve to issue a bank check in the amount of 977,207.00 as payment for our latest Grand Prize, and that we are prepared to deliver said check via certified mail. Therefore, it is urgent that you validate and return the entry enclosed within 10 days.

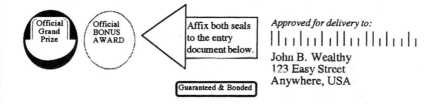

Official Grand Prize

Official BONUS AWARD

Affix both seals to the entry document below.

Guaranteed & Bonded

Approved for delivery to:

John B. Wealthy
123 Easy Street
Anywhere, USA

If you have and return the Grand Prize winning entry in time, we'll confirm that

WE ARE NOW AUTHORIZED TO PAY
$977,207.00 IN CASH TO
JOHN B. WEALTHY

DEAR JOHN B. WEALTHY:

You probably thought it could never happen to you! And even now you probably STILL find it hard to believe that John B. Wealthy of Anywhere, USA, could actually be our $977,207.00 cash prize winner. But it's absolutely true: John B. Wealthy is now positively guaranteed to be awarded $977,207.00--the biggest single cash payment ever made to ANYONE in our sweepstakes--if you have and return the Grand Prize winning entry within 10 days! In fact, the funds have been put on reserve for the express purpose of paying the entire $977,207.00 amount in full. And now that we've been authorized to pay the prize money, the very next time you hear from us, it could well be to inform you that

A BANK CHECK FOR $977,207.00 IS ON
ITS WAY TO 123 EASY STREET!

continued

WORKSHOP 3.1

To Tell the Truth   continued

stickers attached in the appropriate spaces, which would commit the recipient to paying for one or more magazine subscriptions. Does the letter make this clear at the beginning? Why or why not? In the spring of 1998, the State of Florida filed a lawsuit against American Family Publishers and Time Customer Service Inc., along with Dick Clark and Ed McMahon, who are high-profile pitchmen for the largest sweepstakes. Florida Attorney General Bob Butterworth accused the company of trying to defraud the public. The return address on some of the letters had been listed as Tampa, and according to Butterworth, dozens of people, many of them elderly, were not willing to trust the U.S. Mail to make their claim within the prescribed five-day limit, and so they flew to Florida to claim their "winnings." Two Georgetown University Law Center professors had already filed a similar class-action lawsuit in Maryland. Look carefully at this sample letter and list what points you think the Maryland and Florida lawyers will bring up in court. What techniques did the sweepstakes company use to make careless readers think they had won?

5. If possible, bring in examples of sweepstakes envelopes and their contents that you have received at home. Analyze the envelopes for how effectively the sweepstakes companies were in encouraging you to open the envelope. Then analyze the contents to see what techniques were used to encourage you to return the form.

DEAR ANN LANDERS

When there's no one else to ask, people often write to syndicated columnist Ann Landers or to her sister Abigail Van Buren. This particular Ann Landers column, printed in December of 1996, illustrates a kind of body language not nearly as subtle as the type Peter Farb wrote about in the previous essay.

1 A while back, in an effort to promote peace and tranquillity on highways and city streets, a reader in Bethel Park, Pa., suggested that motorists come up with a signal of apology when they goof.

2 I have been inundated with suggestions.

From Fayetteville, Ark.:

3 The driver who made the mistake should lower his head slightly and bonk himself on the forehead with the side of his closed fist. The message is clear: "I'm stupid. I shouldn't have done that."

Valparaiso, Ind.:

4 Make a temple with your hands, as if you were praying. It worked for me back in 1955 when I was driving a semi. It will make people smile.

Kilgore, Texas:

5 Move the index finger of your right hand back and forth across your neck— as if you are cutting your throat. The message is clear.

Monterey Park, Calif.:

6 I'm a retired police officer who has driven several million miles, and I've seen it all. You never know if the person in the next lane has been drinking, has been doing drugs or has a death wish, so be careful. If you make a driving gaffe, flash the well-known peace sign. (A V with index and middle fingers.) It works every time.

Cochran, Ga.:

7 Use your knuckles to knock on the side of your head. Translation: "Oops! That was a no-brainer."

Effingham, Ill.:

8 Place your right hand high on your chest and pat a few times, like a basketball player who drops a pass or a football player who makes a bad throw. It says, "I'll take the blame."

Nescopeck, Pa.:

9 How about using sign language for "I'm sorry"? Place your right fist over the middle of your chest and move it in a circular motion. It's universally understood.

Pompano Beach, Fla.:

10 Open your window and tap the top of your car roof with your hand. It works for me.

Waco, Texas:

11 I suggest the natural gesture children use—place the flat of your hands against your cheeks.

Atlanta, Ga.:

12 I think the universal gesture for surrender, or forgiveness, is to smile and raise both arms, palms outward. Of course, if your car is still moving, you should do this for only a brief second.

Florissant, Mo.:

13 The perfect hand signal to let another driver know you goofed is the military salute. It's simple, everybody knows how to do it and it shows respect for the other driver.

COMPREHENSION

1. Why won't words work in these situations?
2. Try following the directions in each of these suggestions. Are they clear enough that everyone in the class does them exactly the same way? How many of them were familiar to you?
3. News stories have told about belligerent people mistaking someone's wave or other greeting as a gang signal. Which of these signals are most likely to be mistaken for hostile gestures?

DISCUSSION

1. Why do you think there are so many different suggestions?
2. Will these kinds of light-hearted apologies always work? If not, why not?
3. What brings about the communication? The motion of the hands, the facial expression, or a combination?
4. Which of these suggestions for gestures seems the best to you?

5. The American Automobile Association advises against establishing eye contact with other drivers. In light of this advice, what do you plan to do next time you make a mistake in traffic?

6. In the following summaries of news stories, what techniques for communication are being used in place of, or in addition to, words? What advantages do the nonverbal strategies have over plain words?

(a) "Do shoes in a tree at George Washington University constitute a harmless tradition or sexist symbolism?" began a story in the *Chronicle of Higher Education* (Feb. 21, 1997). Apparently, members of the Delta Tau Delta house tie a pair of shoes together and toss them over the branches of a tree near their fraternity house whenever two of them have had sex with the same woman. In answer to feminist complaints that the practice was sexist and offensive, fraternity members said that the custom started as outlined but had turned into just a fun way to get rid of old shoes. Either way, city officials are putting a stop to the practice because it is illegal to hang anything on city-owned trees. The fraternity will be charged $400 for clean-up expenses.

(b) Secretary of State Madeleine Albright has added the wearing of pins to her already impressive array of diplomatic language. When she goes abroad, she wears either a red-white-and-blue eagle or an Uncle Sam top hat as a symbol of American power and glory. For more subtle forms of communication, she wears a bumble bee pin to remind her of Muhammad Ali's motto, "Float like a butterfly, sting like a bee." When she's feeling "up," she wears a jewel-encrusted hot air balloon, and when she met with Iraqi Deputy Prime Minister Tariq Aziz she wore a jeweled snake pin instead of a name tag because she is so often referred to in the Iraqi press as "a serpent" (*Time*, March 24, 1997).

(c) One hundred and eight employees of Insight Company in Tempe, Arizona, agreed to have their heads shaved as a show of solidarity with a co-worker who had lost his hair because of treatments for cancer. The company donated $100 for each shaved head to the American Cancer society (*Arizona Republic*, March 22, 1997).

(d) In late December of 1996, Kraft Foods, Inc., found itself in trouble because their Post Honeycombs cereal boxes showed pictures of Kenan Thompson and Kel Mitchell, the smiling stars of the *Kenan and Kel* comedy show, part of Viacom's Nickelodeon, flashing gang signals. A spokesperson for Post Honeycomb cereal said the picture was provided by the television show Nickelodeon, which was cosponsoring a promotion. When complaints began coming in, the Post company attached blue stickers on "a couple of million boxes," covering up some of the signs, but that didn't keep offended judges and police officers from encouraging a boycott.

7. Talk about other situations where people typically use something be-
    sides or in addition to words to communicate. For instance, if you have
    ever worked in a restaurant, how did you know that a customer hadn't
    yet ordered or that he had finished eating and was ready for the check?
    What is being communicated with the following hand signals? Such
    signals aren't taught in school. How do people learn their meanings,
    and do they mean different things to different people?

GRAFFITI AS SOCIAL DISCOURSE

Anne Winter

Anne Winter was a graduate student at Arizona State University when she began to study graffiti and tagging as part of a linguistics class project. In 1994, when the issue was at its peak in the Phoenix metropolitan area, she wrote an article about her findings for the local newspaper and was surprised when it attracted a record number of letters to the editor, as well as a counter-balancing article from the County Attorney. As a cautionary note, she does not recommend just walking up to taggers and graffiti artists and asking for interviews. Most of her conversations were set up through social agencies or through one person introducing her to another.

1   Mention tagging to most people, and you get rolling eyes and derisive remarks about how it is ugly and everywhere. An understandable response, given that writing graffiti is a criminal act that defaces property, and given that even the best taggers say most of the writing out there is "Toy," or unskilled. In my own case, I sensed that urban graffiti was language, and realized that what annoyed me most about it was simply the fact that I could not read it. Curiosity about what graffiti said, and about the rage that the public feels towards it, led me to search out the graffiti writers to find out more about its meaning both linguistically and culturally.

2   Rhetorically, graffiti has the time-proven honor of being the text of the voiceless and the voice of taboos, ranging from the political to the sexual. We've all seen the anonymous expressions of latrinalia in public rest rooms. When the Berlin Wall came down in 1989, with it came years of written political protests. Although those types of graffiti will not be discussed here, urban graffiti—the ubiquitous scribbling of seemingly meaningless symbols all over America—share the same rhetorical impact.

3   To extract the linguistic and cultural aspects of graffiti, I photographed graffiti-covered walls and buildings in Phoenix, Arizona. Armed with a portfolio of words and pictures, I then interviewed numerous taggers and gang members asking them to talk about their writing. They talked a lot. And the more they talked, the more we extracted the linguistic aspects of graffiti. Through interviews with taggers, gang members, and consultations with others, including police gang squad members and youth workers, I found that urban graffiti

had two distinct genres: tagging and gang graffiti. Both forms, like all languages, are complex mixtures of linguistic rules and (sub-)cultural influences.

4   Unlike a mainstream language, however, graffiti owes its power to the breaking of the rules of the mainstream language, and the rules of the dominant society. People who adhere to rules see graffiti as threatening and criminal. The creators do not necessarily see it as threatening to society; however, they know that society perceives it that way, which is part of the fun.

5   The public finds it easier to hate graffiti than to think about it. Unfortunately, this focus on hating solidifies the public's fear and misunderstanding. While newspaper headlines describe graffiti as a sign of *chaos* and *social collapse*, tagging is not a sign of social collapse as much as it is of social discourse—in other words—language. It is a conversation between society and one of its youth subcultures, but it is a conversation that society did not choose to participate in. Our linguistic intuitions tell us that it has meanings from which we are excluded. This creates an environment of fear and mistrust, as shown by such metaphorical references to graffiti and graffiti writers as *blight, plague, pox,* and *vermin*. Taggers have their own metaphorical lexicon, which puts them in control: *bomb, burn, battle, hit,* and *kill*. Both sets of metaphors reinforce the public's belief that graffiti is to be feared.

6   The refusal to think about differences between tagging and graffiti leads to misconceptions. People compare them both to dogs urinating to mark their territory. Gangs threaten! They violate, and they create chaos. Graffiti is an iconic expression of an enemy taking the public's space.

7   In fact, it should be to everyone's relief that tagging and gang graffiti are two distinct genres. Tagging is the writing of a *tag* or a nickname of the writer, as often and as artistically as possible. The motivation is to *get up,* to put one's name in front of the public. The writer acquires fame through his writing style and the frequency with which he writes. Because fame is predicated on frequency and volume, taggers are not motivated by territory. Writing on trains and buses guarantees that the writer's name will be seen all over the city, and possibly beyond. Prestige is also associated with the difficulty of the placement of the graffiti, which explains the predilection taggers have for freeway signs and other tall structures.

8   Unlike gang members, taggers either work alone, with a friend, or in loosely knit crews. In Phoenix, crew names reflect the same metaphors as used to describe graffiti: CSK = Can't Stop Killing, MTC = Mexicans Taking Control, OBN = One Brown Nation, and OTBK = Out To Bomb Killers.

9   Although the metaphors used by taggers reflect a violent lifestyle, taggers are typically non-violent. They may have fierce rivalries with other crews, but the type of violence associated with gangs is usually not condoned in the tagging community. An exception is a relatively small number of *tagbangers,* groups who tag like taggers, but also get involved in violent rivalries that include shooting at rival taggers.

10   The tagger's search for fame draws the public into the discourse exemplifying the relationship between language and power. These youths have successfully manipulated the public into raging rhetoric by simply recording their existence—a tag is their name, nothing more.

11   Gang graffiti, on the other hand, is written by members of generally tightly knit groups of youths. The audience for their writing is the gang subculture itself. Gangs seldom write on publicly viewed spaces as taggers do; they prefer alleys and neighborhood walls because gang graffiti is a conversation among gangs. We are not supposed to be able to read it because we are not part of that social group. It's what linguists call an *anti-language*.

12   Anti-languages are created by criminal subcultures to reinforce their identity as distinct from society. This isn't too different from the way mainstream

speakers use professional jargon to show what groups they identify with. Because gang graffiti is an anti-language that communicates messages, it has a more complex linguistic system. While taggers typically limit their expressions to their tag, crew name, and an occasional show of disrespect, gang graffiti describes the social networks of the gang. The most common type of gang graffiti is the gang name with or without the name of the writer. Expressions to reinforce the in-group and out-group relationships of the gang include affirmations of gang life and solidarity among certain gangs, cultural identifications, memorials to dead members of a gang, and roll calls of gang members.

13   The most common out-group expression is to cross out the name of a rival gang; however, verbal threats, boasts, and expressions of disrespect are also found. Gang members told me the worst *dis* is when a rival gang member incorporates the first gang's writing into his own. Gang members also incorporate symbols of the dominant culture as when they use *187* as a term for murder based on the penal code in California. This is an example of the relexification found in anti-languages, where communicators use someone else's code so others won't know what is being written. Another characteristic of anti-languages is *overlexification*- -using many terms for one representation as when gangs write their street name in numerous ways: *nineteen, 19, XIX, X9,* and *9teen.* Bilingual gangs have even more possibilities.

14   Both gang members and taggers purposely write so that the public will feel left out. Even if the messages aren't literally threatening, our ignorance of what they say makes us feel a loss of power. One way they do this is to deviate from standard spelling as when they spell *crew* as *kroo* and *tomorrow* as *2morrow.* Although this is common wordplay (much like that used on vanity license plates), when the situation is already threatening the deviant spelling makes people feel that those who flaunt spelling rules have different values.

15   Graffiti should not be feared as a symbol of impending chaos created by those with values different from ours, but merely as young people thumbing their noses at society. They have figured out how to use the language intuitions we all share to thumb their noses at us.

16   As with all young people beginning to assert their identity, taggers want to feel they have some power and control. Public spaces and businesses are perfect targets, because they represent the power in society. Taggers' values aren't different from ours; in fact the majority quit when they assimilate in societal roles of employee, spouse, and college student. As one writer told me, "One thing I know I can tell my kids when I grow up is, 'I was a good tagger.'"

17   I've asked several writers what they think would stop tagging. As with the rest of us, they all have different opinions. The more candid ones say that probably no enforced measure, including "legal walls," will work. The most consistent response I've heard is that tagging in the Phoenix metropolitan area is mostly a fad and will die out of its own accord. In the case of gang graffiti, asking this question is like asking how to stop language.

18   As tagging exploded in Phoenix in 1994, many aggressive measures were taken to stop it before it got the upper hand as it has in other cities such as Los Angeles, Chicago, and New York: Richard Romley, the County Attorney for Maricopa County, began a "zero tolerance" campaign against graffiti. He asked for stiffer sentences for tagging. A law was passed banning sale of spray paint to minors. The Phoenix Police Department created a hotline for reporting graffiti; a local Ford dealership began a costly paintout campaign at its own expense; community groups and blockwatches painted over graffiti in their neighborhoods weekly. Although initially these measures created a cat-and-mouse game between taggers and authorities, over the last three years tagging has become nearly nonexistent in Phoenix. Where there were once over 100 tagging crews, there are now only ten. This has been hailed as a victory for a combination of tougher laws and vigorous community action. Perhaps so, but I believe the greatest deterrent is what every tagger told me he hated most—spending time writing only to have it painted over the next day. In other words, someone else has the last word.

19   Hating graffiti will always be easier than understanding it. However, once understanding is there it becomes obvious that graffiti writers are using their language intuitions to create a language that provokes thought. That is the power of graffiti. It has been the anonymous voice of social provocation from early times. Recognizing this does not mitigate the criminal aspects of graffiti writing; however, it helps us understand our world a little better, and perhaps to fear it a little less.

COMPREHENSION

1. Words to talk about:

   - anonymous expressions of *latrinalia*
   - an *anti-language*
   - *relexification* found in anti-language
   - a characteristic is *overlexification*
   - the worst *dis* is
   - *mitigate* the criminal aspects

2. What basic difference did Winter find between tagging and gang graffiti?

DISCUSSION

1. Why does the general public fear graffiti? Describe two or three contributing factors.
2. What kinds of messages do gangs put in their graffiti?

3. What factors contributed to slowing down graffiti in Phoenix?
4. When people found graffiti painted on their property, they could call the car dealer who was sponsoring the paintout. Within a day or two, workers would be sent to paint over the offending message. What public relations benefit did the car dealer get from this project?
5. Did this article make you feel any differently toward tagging and graffiti?

CRIME AND PUNISHMENT: SHAME GAINS POPULARITY

Jan Hoffman

In contradiction to the old nursery rhyme about sticks and stones breaking bones but names not hurting, Americans have launched into a new kind of punishment that relies for its effectiveness on name calling and social disapproval. This article by Jan Hoffman was published in November 1996 in the *New York Times*. It centers around the case of an Illinois farmer who was ordered to identify himself as "a violent felon" by posting a sign with letters eight inches high. It was to be on display for thirty months, but midway through his punishment he protested by taking the case to the Illinois Supreme Court. An April 17, 1997, decision allowed the man to remove the sign, while his case was sent back to Circuit Court for new sentencing. The judge observed, "The authority to define and fix punishment is a matter for the legislature," and Illinois laws do not stipulate shaming punishments. However, this does not mean that shaming punishments will no longer be used because different states have different laws and shaming punishments are frequently a matter of plea bargaining in which the convicted individual agrees to the conditions.

1   In the gray winter light, the views along the road into this small town [of Pittsfield] in western Illinois are severe but serene: stretches of brown, stubbled cornfields interrupted only by the occasional farmhouse. Abruptly, a driver's reverie is jolted by the green plywood and white-lettered sign at the end of Glenn Meyer's driveway. "Warning," it reads. "A violent felon lives here. Travel at your own risk."

2   The sign is a condition of the probation sentence given to Meyer, a 62-year-old farmer, for having bashed another farmer in the face with a truck fuel pump. The judge intended the sign to alert people about Meyer's dangerous streak and to shame him into behaving. But Meyer is unrepentant. Last week, he went before the Illinois Supreme Court to challenge the imposition of the sign.

3   Judicially created public humiliations like this are being introduced in courtrooms across the country, usually as alternatives to incarceration. Known as shaming penalties— after the punishments like the stocks favored by 17th-century Puritans—they usually take the form of a mea culpa message to the community.

4   Drunken drivers have to put special license plates on their cars. Convicted shoplifters must take out advertisements in their local newspapers, running

their photographs and announcing their crimes. And men in cities around the country who are convicted of soliciting prostitutes are identified in newspapers, on radio shows and on billboards.

5   In November, a judge in Port St. Lucie, Fla., ordered a woman to place an advertisement in her local paper saying she had bought drugs in front of her children. This summer, at the behest of a judge in Houston, a man who pleaded guilty to domestic violence stood on the steps of City Hall, facing lunchtime workers, reporters, and battered-women's advocates, and apologized for hitting his estranged wife.

6   Proponents of shaming penalties say they address the needs of a public weary of crime, frustrated by the failures of the criminal-justice system and yet unwilling to pay for prison expansion.

7   "The penalties can satisfy the public's need for dramatic moral condemnation in a way that's effective and just," said Professor Dan Kahan of the University of Chicago law school. "And they result in the outcome you want: less imprisonment."

8   Critics say that the penalties have a circuslike quality that blunts whatever rehabilitative function they may have, and that they often cross the line into ridicule. Judith Libby, the lawyer who argued Meyer's case this week, offered her bottom line critique.

9   "Mostly," Libby said, "they're just mean."

10   When it came time to sentence Meyer, whom a jury convicted of aggravated battery in June 1995, Judge Thomas Brownfield had a difficult decision. Meyer had a previous conviction for aggravated battery for stomping an insurance adjuster on his farm and an acquittal for scuffling with a collection agent.

11   In the 1995 episode, Gary Mason, a farmer from nearby Beardstown, had tried to return a truck fuel pump to Meyer, who runs a modest salvage yard. In the ensuing argument, Meyer swung the metal-encased pump at Mason, smashing his nose and eye socket.

12   The state's attorney urged incarceration. By law, Meyer could have received a sentence ranging from two to 10 years. But many in Pittsfield, with a population of 4,500, saw Meyer as a good-hearted, thoughtful neighbor. Dozens wrote letters to the judge on his behalf.

13   "He's as mild a mannered man you'd ever want to meet," said Bruce Lightle, the former chairman of the Pike County board. "We've been friends for more than 40 years, and I've never seen him angry."

14   A social worker testified at a hearing that Meyer, who was taking antidepressant medication, seemed capable of controlling his temper.

15   Still, Brownfield said that, if Meyer had not had an elderly mother at home, he would have sentenced him to the maximum. In trying to balance retribution with compassion, the judge gave Meyer probation but confined him to his home for a year, allowing him to leave only to keep doctors' appointments and to attend church.

16   In addition, he had to pay a $7,500 fine and Mason's medical bills, which reached nearly $10,000. And Meyer had to make and post the warning sign for 30 months, of which about 16 remain.

17   "I try to take rehabilitation into consideration as well as protecting the public," the judge said. "I certainly feel more comfortable knowing that someone who may not know Meyer will have some warning."

18   The judge added that since the sign went up, there have been no other incidents of violence.

19   If the setting for a modern shaming penalty could approximate that of the early American colonists, Pittsfield might qualify. With something of the intimacy of 17th-century rural towns like Salem, Mass., Pittsfield is a churchgoing farming community with a village green and coffee-shop waitresses who serve the regulars scrambled eggs with a side of fresh gossip.

20   But Colonial towns were bound even more tightly than Pittsfield: An offender would be put in stocks in front of neighbors who shared a church, a leader and iron-clad values. The most frequently prosecuted offense was fornication.

21   At that time, jail as punishment was relatively unknown in America. "A penalty was intentionally exacted in full view of the community, which represented an ideal of behavior that the shamed one should emulate.

22   "The point of punishment was to teach them a lesson and also make it possible to reintegrate themselves into the community," said Lawrence Friedman, a Stanford University law professor.

23   By the 19th century, public punishment was looked down upon as undignified spectacle. The community was no longer a paragon of morality and was understood to have corrupting influences as well. Prisons were established, and offenders were sent there for their own good.

24   In modern times, Americans no longer associate prison with rehabilitation; its purpose is strictly punitive. Still, the public complains about defendants serving short sentences in prisons that offer television, weight rooms and the opportunity to learn advanced criminal skills.

25   The return to shaming penalties, which began in the 1980s with mortified Wall Street traders appearing on the nightly news in handcuffs, is to some extent a nostalgic longing for an era when a community and its principles were so uniform that people could police themselves.

26   "The penalties bring the community back into sentencing and punishing policies," said Robert Teir of the American Alliance for Rights and Responsibilities, a public-interest group that filed a brief supporting Meyer's warning sign. "And they give the community a sense of empowerment that jailing or letting someone go without a punishment does not do."

27   Local judges, many of whom are elected, have seized on shaming penalties as an alternative to prison. Judges in Arkansas and Wisconsin have ordered shoplifters to parade in front of the stores they have robbed, carrying placards admitting their guilt. A Memphis, Tenn., judge has given thieves pro-

bation if they permit victims to pluck something from the thief's home. An Ohio judge ordered a man convicted of harassing his ex-wife to let her spit in his face.

28   Even those skeptical of the penalties, the effectiveness of which never has been studied, concede that they have value in cohesive communities. Bar organizations publish lists of lawyers who have been sanctioned because peers consider publicity a humiliating deterrent. The Amish and some American Indian tribes use a form of shaming known as shunning.

29   "But it's understood in these communities that there is something the shamed one can do to get back in," said Toni Massaro, a law professor at the University of Arizona.

30   By contrast, Massaro added, most penalties by local judges are whimsical, coarsely drafted and do not have restorative components.

31   "They are merely expressions of disgust," she said. "We can get behind it, but it's not likely to stop the behavior."

32   Here in Pittsfield, Meyer's warning sign has met with strong but mixed reactions. Friends of the family say it is too harsh. Some people who have tasted his temper say he got off easy. Mason, the farmer who caught the fuel

pump in his eye, said he was simply relieved that others were being cautioned about Meyer.

33   Vicki Thayer, a waitress at the Red Dome Inn, said that she did not think that the sign was unjust but that it was unfair.

34   "Half the town beats up their wives," Thayer said, "and gets off with a slap on the wrist."

35   Lightle, the former county board chairman, said his friend was angry and embarrassed by the sign. The family resented it deeply, he said; Meyer's wife moved out.

36   Whether the sign will change Meyer's behavior remains to be seen. He failed to report to probation several times and missed some restitution payments, court records show.

37   Libby, who spoke on her client's behalf, said he did not feel ashamed about the dust-up that led to the punishment. On the contrary.

38   "Mr. Meyer says he feels that the sign is illegal and that the court knows it's illegal," she said.

39   "He has always professed his innocence, and he still does."

COMPREHENSION

1. Words to talk about:

   - a driver's *reverie*
   - alternatives to *incarceration*
   - the form of a *mea culpa* message
   - at the *behest* of a judge
   - blunts whatever *rehabilitative function*
   - convicted of *aggravated battery*
   - purpose is strictly *punitive*
   - lawyers who have been *sanctioned*
   - consider publicity a *humiliating deterrent*
   - do not have *restorative components*

DISCUSSION

1. List some of the differences between community life today and community life in the seventeenth century. How might these differences affect shaming penalties?
2. Who benefits from today's shaming penalties? In what ways?

3. Who gets punished with shaming penalties? Note that Meyer's wife moved out. The article didn't say whether he has children or grandchildren, but if so how do you think the sign would have affected them?

4. Hoffman said that today's shaming penalties began in the 1980s with mortified Wall Street traders appearing on the nightly news in handcuffs. Can you think of other incidents in the news that contributed to people's approval of such penalties?

5. Hoffman mentioned several other examples of shaming penalties. Find at least six of these and decide which ones are justifiable as genuine warnings needed by the public, and which ones are, in the words of Meyer's lawyer, "just mean."

6. Look at the incidents described in Living Language 3.1, "Privacy and Your Good Name." Which of them relate to public shaming? Which are, in fact, based on the opposing idea that publicity will normalize events and take away the "shame"?

LIVING LANGUAGE 3.1
Privacy and Your Good Name

The meaning of "my good name" was known long before Shakespeare wrote, "He who steals my good name enriches not himself and leaves me poor indeed," but social and technological developments in the intervening four hundred years have created endless new ways through which people can lose their good names.

■ In the early 1990s, the issue of whether or not the name of a rape victim should be made public was brought to national attention when newspapers in Florida broke a state law by naming the woman who had accused William Kennedy Smith of rape (she had already been named by reporters whose states did not have such laws). At about the same time, the *Des Moines Register* won a Pulitzer Prize for a series of articles in which a rape victim agreed to be named and interviewed. In a poll of 313 women conducted by *USA Today*, 68 percent of the respondents said they did not think rape victims' humiliation would lessen if their names were routinely made public, and almost half said they would be less likely to report a rape if they thought they would be named by a newspaper.

■ In 1991 a health activist group in Boise, Idaho, went against the custom of keeping medical malpractice information confidential by publicly naming eight Idaho physicians subjected to disciplinary action by the state medical board. In the mid-1990s, the federal government released state-by-state the names of medical practitioners who had not repaid their federally guaranteed education loans.

■ In what they called *outing*, homosexual activists in the 1990s publicly identified several high profile individuals who had chosen to keep their homosexuality secret. The stated purpose was to educate the public.

■ Medical societies in New York brought a suit asking that AIDS be named a communicable disease. The court rejected the suit, which if it had been successful would have allowed doctors to publicly name infected patients.

■ A school teacher who "borrowed" a blank check and identification materials from another teacher's purse was then filmed by the bank's automatic video as she cashed the check for $2,000. She was suspended at a public meeting of her school board. Because recent laws in some states have limited employers to sharing only "public" information in letters of recommendation, the school attorney advised the board to make the matter public.

■ In 1994 legislators in New Jersey enacted "Megan's Law," named after seven-year-old Megan Kanka who was raped and murdered by a paroled sex offender who had moved into her neighborhood without anyone knowing his background. The law, which by 1997 had been adopted by 41 states, requires that police warn people about sex offenders living in their midst. Officers in Placentia, California, found that the law was easier to devise than to enact. Their use of Explorer Scouts to distribute 1,000 fliers bearing the name, description, and a photograph of a recently released "serious sex offender" resulted in near-riots, the loss of the man's job, and his eviction from two apartments. When his attorney filed suit, the Chief of Police said, "We'd rather fight a lawsuit by his attorney than a lawsuit by a victim if we had done nothing and he committed another offense." (*Washington Post*, April 6, 1997)

Anti-Gay Policy Hinders Classroom Talk

In early Rome, two government magistrates had the job of taking the census. One of them had the additional job of inspecting and assessing morals and conduct, hence the meaning of censor to refer to someone who examines materials in order to suppress or delete anything considered objectionable. Today in the United States, probably as a reaction to the loss of privacy and the invasion of the mass media into areas of life that used to be considered private, there has been an increase in censorship, especially as parents try to protect their children. This Associated Press story, from Merrimack, New Hampshire, and dated March 4, 1996, describes one such effort.

1   Ask Tom Gotsill, an English teacher for 30 years, how Walt Whitman's homosexuality affected his poetry.

2   "I can't discuss that," Gotsill says.

3   James Roy, a math teacher for 21 years, surely can explain a newspaper article citing AIDS statistics.

4   "I apologize. I just can't talk about that," Roy responds lowering his head as color rises in his face.

5   Until this school year, both teachers would have answered these questions. Today, they back away for fear of violating a school district ban on teachers discussing homosexuality as a part of life and living.

6   "For the first time in my life, I feel I have to look over my shoulder every time I say something," says Roy, who has joined parents and others suing Merrimack schools in federal court on grounds the policy prohibits freedom of speech.

7   The policy, titled the "Prohibition of Alternative Lifestyle Instruction," has pitted neighbor against neighbor in this town of 22,450.

8   The school board's conservative majority is standing firm, insisting the policy protects children. Hundreds of students, however, are wearing black arm bands or pink triangle pins in protest. Meanwhile, teachers have altered how they teach such classics as *Moby-Dick, Of Mice and Men, A Raisin in the Sun, The Glass Menagerie* and William Shakespeare's *A Midsummer Night's Dream* and *As You Like It* to avoid any discussion of homosexuality, either in plot or authorship.

9   Under the policy, enacted on a 3–2 vote last August, teachers are not allowed to pass out materials, instruct or offer counseling portraying homosexuality as an acceptable way of life.

10   School board chairman Chris Ager, who proposed the policy, has said violations would be regarded as insubordination—grounds for firing. Ager

won't specify what he would consider a violation, so teachers say they are in the dark.

11   "I will say that as of today, not a single teacher has been disciplined as a result of this policy," Ager says.

12   That's because teachers are taking every precaution to protect their jobs, says Sue Ruggeri, president of the Merrimack Teachers' Association, one of the plaintiffs in the U.S. District Court lawsuit.

13   According to the suit, classes no longer address AIDS prevention and suicide among gay teens.

14   Roy says he altered plans to have math students clip newspaper stories citing statistics because he was afraid someone would bring in an article on AIDS or homosexuality.

Gotsill says he stopped using a video about Walt Whitman because it
15   mentions the poet was gay.

"If you build a class around discussion, as we do in literature, then you oftentimes don't know in what direction conversations might go. For fear it might end in discussions of prejudice or bigotry against homosexuals, you
16   shy away from it," Gotsill says. "As a result, our discussions have been stifled. Education has been hampered."

17   Lymon Mower, a 15-year-old freshman at Merrimack High School, has worn a black arm band to school all year. He says the policy cheats students out of a full education.

18   "A lot of times we'll have class discussions and the teacher will feel they can't go on because of fear of violating the policy," Mower says. "My friend was taking a social problems class, where the whole point is to talk. One day they were talking about AIDS and, of course, you have to talk about homosexuality. The teacher said, 'Sorry, we can't talk about this anymore.' "

19   Mower now attends the volatile monthly school board meetings and urges other students to wear arm bands and gay rights buttons. He says he's lost regard for teachers who abide by the policy.

20   "There isn't really a single teacher in this district who supports that policy, but they're practicing it," Mower says. "I really have to say I don't have a lot of respect for anyone who can do that. What's a job if you are forced to be the agent of injustice?"

Comprehension

1. Words to talk about:
   - one of the *plaintiffs*
   - *volatile* monthly school board meetings

2. What is specifically banned by the school district's policy?
3. Give three examples of how the policy has affected the teaching of academic subjects usually not thought to be related to health or sex education.

DISCUSSION

1. In reference to this story, how does the statistic that one out of ten people is gay or lesbian tie in with the idea that in a democracy "the majority rules"? What else in a democracy would cause such a story as this one to be considered news?
2. Only within the last few years have policies about gays and lesbians been implemented in high schools. Why are such policies being enacted today when they weren't twenty years ago?
3. The following reasons have been given for increases in the number of censorship challenges experienced by public schools and libraries. If there have recently been school or library conflicts in your local area, talk about them in relation to the following hypotheses. Then rank these hypotheses in relation to censorship in general. Which do you think are the strongest contributing factors?
   (a) As science and technology have become more complicated, people are faced with more things they do not understand. Out of self-defense and nostalgia for simpler times, they reject such concepts as evolution and ask that their children be taught creationism.
   (b) As society has become more permissive, and popular culture messages have become more suggestive and scatological, parents fear losing control over their children's attitudes and behaviors. While they feel powerless to control rock musicians or the violence on television, they can do their part by going to the local school and asking that a book be taken off the library shelves.
   (c) Women and minorities who used to be the butt of the joke without complaining are now more aggressive in asking for fair play. When they find educational materials that are consistently insulting or exclusionary, they protest. There is a spiraling effect (see Chapter 4 on labeling) as more and more groups demand to be portrayed in positive ways.
   (d) Because textbooks are so expensive to produce, publishers suffer major financial losses if their books are censored or rejected by selection committees. Therefore, prior to publication, apprehensive editors remove anything they judge to be potentially offensive.

(e) Political groups from both the right and the left have found that they can gain access to school curricular decisions and to the courts and the media by asking for bans on particular books. A serendipitous effect is that the criticism of schools and books serves as a way of opening discussions and recruiting individuals who initially might not be interested in the organization's overall goals.

LIVING LANGUAGE 3.2

Censorship: Variations on a Theme

While further complications will be discussed in later chapters, these news summaries show that even without considering children's access to the Internet, cable television, and pornographic videos, the questions of who is entitled to "free speech" and what the term means are increasingly difficult to answer.

■ On February 14, 1989, when the Ayatollah Khomeini named Salman Rushdie an enemy of Islam for having written *The Satanic Verses,* he openly commanded that Rushdie be assassinated through a *fatwa,* or religious decree. Khomeini died four months after the event, but rather than improving the situation for Rushdie, who is in hiding under the protection of the British government, it further complicated matters because of the belief that a *fatwa* is a holy pronouncement that can be revoked only by the person who issued it.

■ In June 1997, delegates to the Southern Baptist Convention voted to boycott the Disney Company, which owns movie studios, theme parks, television companies (including ABC), a publishing house, a radio network, sports teams, and retail outlets. The boycott was a protest against Ellen DeGeneres's coming out as a lesbian on the TV sitcom *Ellen* and the fact that Disney provides full benefits for the partners of gay and lesbian employees. Shortly after the boycott was declared, Disney "recalled an estimated 100,000 copies of a new, obscenity-laced hip-hop album from store shelves." Officials said that the album "The Great Milenko," by the group Insane Clown Posse, "slipped through the company's review system and that the recall had nothing to do with the boycott." Rev. Wiley S. Drake, who originally proposed the boycott, disagreed and announced, "In reference to the battle between Disney and Southern Baptist, it's Southern Baptist one, Disney zip." (*Arizona Republic,* June 27, 1997)

■ "Murder is the Ultimate Censor" read the headline on a November 1996 Associated Press story about 164 journalists in North and South America being murdered between 1988 and 1996. Responsibility for sixty-two of the deaths was claimed by drug dealers in Colombia. Seven of the deaths occurred in the United States.

4. Read the censorship incidents described in Living Language 3.2, and decide whether the motivation behind each one is primarily one of the following factors, a combination, or something else:
   (a) Political (protection of adult group interests)
   (b) Moral or educational (protection of young people's innocence)
   (c) Financial (protection of a company's selling power and income)

■ In a letter to the editor of *English Journal* (April 1997), high school teacher John Oster told about reading Ray Bradbury's anticensorship book *Farenheit 451* with his junior high students, who had a paperback edition while he had a hardback. "When we came to a passage with *damn* in it, the student did not say the word. I assumed he felt uncomfortable swearing, so I said nothing." After the same thing happened again, the teacher took a turn reading. His passage contained *damn, hell,* and *bastard.* A student asked, "Mr. Oster, where are you getting these words? They aren't in our book." When he looked at the students' books, "sure enough, they had been omitted." After he got over his embarrassment about the students thinking he had inserted the swear words "to enliven the text," he explained what must have happened at the publishing house and told them if they ever forgot the meaning of irony, they could "just think back to this situation."

■ When showing the Oscar-winning movie *Rain Man,* fifteen airlines excised a crucial scene. In the movie two brothers, played by actors Dustin Hoffman and Tom Cruise, go to an airport for a cross-country flight. The autistic-savant brother refuses to fly because his brain is full of statistics, including facts about 30 crashes with 211 fatalities. The only airline he will consider is Qantas because it has never had a crash (Qantas showed the film uncut). A United Airlines representative explained that it was company "policy to remove portions of feature films as they relate to violence, nudity, obscenities or anything that could create discomfort for passengers about being on airplanes." (Associated Press, June 29, 1989)

■ In a 1988 decision, *Hazelwood School District* v. *Kuhlmeier,* the Supreme Court declared that the content of newspapers at public high schools could be censored by a school's administration. In spite of a footnote stating, "We need not now decide whether the same degree of deference is appropriate with respect to school-sponsored activities at the college and university level," a lawyer in the Office of the General Counsel for the university system in Texas has interpreted the ruling as applicable to the college press as well. Already, the student editor at the University of Texas-Pan American resigned in protest when the

continued

Living Language 3.2

Censorship: Variations on a Theme
continued

faculty advisor removed an article and replaced it with an ad. The disagreement in Texas is of national interest because if *Hazelwood* is applied to college newspapers in Texas, there will probably be a ripple effect to other states. (*Chronicle of Higher Education,* March 28, 1997)

■ The Ackerley Outdoor Advertising company, which owns two-thirds of the 250 billboards in Tacoma, Washington, rejected an antismoking advertisement, which was part of a "Same Names" series. The rejected ad, prepared by the Tobacco Free Coalition, came from an eighty-year-old retired attorney who happens to have the name of R. J. Reynolds. The controversial message read "R. J. Reynolds says: 'Smoking Kills. Don't buy cigarettes.' " (*Arizona Republic,* Sept. 9, 1996)

■ In the United States, Wal-Mart stores are the single largest seller of pop music, and because the discount chain will not stock albums with "objectionable" lyrics or cover art, studios "design new covers and booklets, drop songs from their albums, electronically mask objectionable words and even change lyrics in order to gain a place on Wal-Mart's shelves." The adapted versions are sold in shrink-wrapped packages with such markings as "edited," "clean," and "sanitized for your protection." Other family stores such as KMart and Blockbuster Video request the same kinds of changes for movies. "A new form of censorship," complained Oliver Stone, when his version of *Natural Born Killers* was banned by Blockbuster, KMart, and Wal-Mart (*New York Times,* Nov. 17, 1996). Singer Sheryl Crow did more than complain. She created a song "Love Is a Good Thing," which implied that children could buy guns at Wal-Mart and subsequently use them to kill each other. Wal-Mart chose not to carry that album at all.

■ In the fall of 1996, the federal Department of Health and Human Services wrote to HMO's (Health Maintenance Organizations) telling them to put a stop to "gag clauses" or "gag orders" as practiced by some HMO's, which discouraged doctors from telling patients about possible treatment options. Such practices helped HMO's keep costs down, but speaking particularly for Medicare patients, the letter said they were entitled to a full range of benefits and one of those benefits is advice from doctors on "treatment options."

"Put Down That Paper and Talk to Me!": Rapport-Talk and Report-Talk

Deborah Tannen

Linguist Deborah Tannen has been a pioneer in illustrating that many communication problems are caused by the different expectations that men and woman have when they talk. Matt Williams, one of the most successful writers of television comedy (*The Cosby Show*, the early *Roseanne*, and *Home Improvement*), said in a *New York Times* interview (June 8, 1996) that Deborah Tannen's book *You Just Don't Understand: Women and Men in Conversation*, from which the following essay is taken, was a major influence on his development of the sitcom *Home Improvement*. "The underlying premise of the show is that men and women should never live together, but they do, so how can they do it?" As you read this excerpt from Tannen's book, look for ways in which the differences she writes about underlie the misunderstandings.

1   I was sitting in a suburban living room, speaking to a women's group that had invited men to join them for the occasion of my talk about communication between women and men. During the discussion, one man was particularly talkative, full of lengthy comments and explanations. When I made the observation that women often complain that their husbands don't talk to them enough, this man volunteered that he heartily agreed. He gestured toward his wife, who had sat silently beside him on the couch throughout the evening, and said, "She's the talker in our family."

2   Everyone in the room burst into laughter. The man look puzzled and hurt. "It's true," he explained. "When I come home from work, I usually have nothing to say, but she never runs out. If it weren't for her, we'd spend the whole evening in silence." Another woman expressed a similar paradox about her husband: "When we go out, he's the life of the party. If I happen to be in another room, I can always hear his voice above the others. But when we're home, he doesn't have that much to say. I do most of the talking."

3   Who talks more, women or men? According to the stereotype, women talk too much. Linguist Jennifer Coates notes some proverbs:

A woman's tongue wags like a lamb's tail.
Foxes are all tail and women are all tongue.
The North Sea will sooner be found wanting in water than a woman be at a
    loss for a word.

Throughout history, women have been punished for talking too much or in the wrong way. Linguist Connie Eble lists a variety of physical punishments used in Colonial America: Women were strapped to ducking stools and held underwater until they nearly drowned, put into the stocks with signs pinned to them, gagged, and silenced by a cleft stick applied to their tongues.

4   Though such institutionalized corporal punishments have given way to informal, often psychological ones, modern stereotypes are not much different from those expressed in the old proverbs. Women are believed to talk too much. Yet study after study finds that it is men who talk more—at meetings, in mixed-group discussions, and in classrooms where girls or young women sit next to boys or young men. For example, communications researchers Barbara and Gene Eakins tape-recorded and studied seven university faculty meetings. They found that, with one exception, men spoke more often and, without exception, spoke for a longer time. The men's turns ranged from 10.66 to 17.07 seconds, while the women's turns ranged from 3 to 10 seconds. In other words, the women's longest turns were still shorter than the men's shortest turns.

5   When a public lecture is followed by questions from the floor, or a talk show host opens the phones, the first voice to be heard is almost always a man's. And when they ask questions or offer comments from the audience, men tend to talk longer. Linguist Marjorie Swacker recorded question-and-answer sessions at academic conferences. Women were highly visible as speakers at the conferences studied; they presented 40.7 percent of the papers and made up 42 percent of the audiences. But when it came to volunteering and being called on to ask questions, women contributed only 27.4 percent. Furthermore, the women's questions, on the average, took less than half as much time as the men's. (The mean was 23.1 seconds for women, 52.7 for men.) This happened, Swacker shows, because men (but not women) tended to preface their questions with statements, ask more than one question, and follow up the speaker's answer with another question or comment.

6   I have observed this pattern at my own lectures, which concern issues of direct relevance to women. Regardless of the proportion of women and men in the audience, men almost invariably ask the first question, more questions, and longer questions. In these situations, women often feel that men are talking too much. I recall one discussion period following a lecture I gave to a group assembled in a bookstore. The group was composed mostly of women, but most of the discussion was being conducted by men in the audience. At one point, a man sitting in the middle was talking at such great length that several women in the front rows began shifting in their seats and rolling their eyes at me. Ironically, what he was going on about was how frustrated he feels when he has to listen to women going on and on about topics he finds boring and unimportant.

RAPPORT-TALK AND REPORT-TALK

7   Who talks more, then, women or men? The seemingly contradictory evidence is reconciled by the difference between what I call *public* and *private speaking*. More men feel comfortable doing "public speaking," while more women feel comfortable doing "private" speaking. Another way of capturing these differences is by using the terms *report-talk* and *rapport-talk*.

8   For most women, the language of conversation is primarily a language of rapport: a way of establishing connections and negotiating relationships. Emphasis is placed on displaying similarities and matching experiences. From childhood, girls criticize peers who try to stand out or appear better than others. People feel their closest connections at home, or in settings where they *feel* at home—with one or a few people they feel close to and comfortable with—in other words, during private speaking. But even the most public situations can be approached like private speaking.

9   For most men, talk is primarily a means to preserve independence and negotiate and maintain status in a hierarchical social order. This is done by exhibiting knowledge and skill, and by holding center stage through verbal performance such as storytelling, joking, or imparting information. From childhood, men learn to use talking as a way to get and keep attention. So they are more comfortable speaking in larger groups made up of people they know less well—in the broadest sense, "public speaking." But even the most private situations can be approached like public speaking, more like giving a report than establishing rapport.

PRIVATE SPEAKING: THE WORDY WOMAN AND THE MUTE MAN

10   What is the source of the stereotype that women talk a lot? Dale Spender suggests that most people feel instinctively (if not consciously) that women, like children, should be seen and not heard, so any amount of talk from them seems like too much. Studies have shown that if women and men talk equally in a group, people think the women talked more. So there is truth to Spender's view. But another explanation is that men think women talk a lot because they hear women talking in situations where men would not: on the telephone; or in social situations with friends, when they are not discussing topics that men find inherently interesting; or, like the couple at the women's group, at home alone—in other words, in private speaking.

11   Home is the setting for an American icon that features the silent man and the talkative woman. And this icon, which grows out of the different goals and habits I have been describing, explains why the complaint most often voiced by women about the men with whom they are intimate is "He doesn't talk to me"—and the second most frequent is "He doesn't listen to me."

12   A woman who wrote to Ann Landers is typical:

> My husband never speaks to me when he comes home from work. When I
> ask, "How did everything go today?" he says, "Rough . . . " or "It's a jungle
> out there." (We live in Jersey and he works in New York City.)
>   It's a different story when we have guests or go visiting. Paul is the
> gabbiest guy in the crowd—a real spellbinder. He comes up with the most
> interesting stories. People hang on to every word. I think to myself, "Why
> doesn't he ever tell *me* these things?"
>   This has been going on for 38 years. Paul started to go quiet on me af-
> ter 10 years of marriage. I could never figure out why. Can you solve the
> mystery?
>
> —The Invisible Woman

Ann Landers suggests that the husband may not want to talk because he is
tired when he comes home from work. Yet women who work come home
tired too, and they are nonetheless eager to tell their partners or friends everything that happened to them during the day and what these fleeting, daily
dramas made them think and feel.

13   Sources as lofty as studies conducted by psychologists, as down to earth
as letters written to advice columnists, and as sophisticated as movies and
plays come up with the same insight: Men's silence at home is a disappointment to women. Again and again, women complain, "He seems to have
everything to say to everyone else, and nothing to say to me."

14   The film *Divorce American Style* opens with a conversation in which Debbie Reynolds is claiming that she and Dick Van Dyke don't communicate, and
he is protesting that he tells her everything that's on his mind. The doorbell
interrupts their quarrel, and husband and wife compose themselves before
opening the door to greet their guests with cheerful smiles.

15   Behind closed doors, many couples are having conversations like this.
Like the character played by Debbie Reynolds, women feel men don't communicate. Like the husband played by Dick Van Dyke, men feel wrongly accused. How can she be convinced that he doesn't tell her anything, while he
is equally convinced he tells her everything that's on his mind? How can
women and men have such different ideas about the same conversations?

16   When something goes wrong, people look around for a source to blame:
either the person they are trying to communicate with ("You're demanding,
stubborn, self-centered") or the group that the other person belongs to ("All
women are demanding"; "All men are self-centered"). Some generous-
minded people blame the relationship ("We just can't communicate"). But underneath, or overlaid on these types of blame cast outward, most people
believe that something is wrong with them.

17   If individual people or particular relationships were to blame, there
wouldn't be so many different people having the same problems. The real
problem is conversational style. Women and men have different ways of talking. Even with the best intentions, trying to settle the problem through talk

can only make things worse if it is ways of talking that are causing trouble in the first place.

COMPREHENSION

1. Words to talk about:

   - expressed a similar *paradox*
   - silenced by a *cleft stick*
   - institutionalized *corporal* punishments
   - maintain status in a *hierarchical* social order
   - setting for an American *icon*

2. What does Tannen mean by *public* versus *private speech*? How can private situations be approached like public speaking and vice-versa?
3. What ideas does Tannen put forth to explain popular culture notions that women talk more than men?

DISCUSSION

1. Tannen says that institutionalized corporal punishments for women talking too much have given way to "informal, often psychological ones." Can you think of contemporary examples of women being "punished" for talking?
2. Can you think of a Biblical scripture or of proverbs or famous quotes that express the idea that women should remain silent in public places?
3. Tannen quite rightly observes that when things go wrong, people look around for a source to blame. When a man and a woman fail to communicate, what are some of the sources that get blamed?
4. Look at a television sitcom where some of the humor comes about because of communication problems between males and females. Do some of the incidents support Tannen's observations? If so, in what ways?
5. Find *Dave Barry's Complete Guide to Guys* (Random House, 1995) and read Chapter 4, "Tips for Women: How to Have a Relationship with a Guy." What are some of Tannen's points that Barry illustrates through exaggeration and humor?
6. Some people are philosophically opposed to the kind of research and writing that Tannen does because they think it exacerbates the problem and teaches males and females to communicate differently. If communication differences between male and female are not innate (which has not been proven one way or another), what are some of the social factors that contribute to encouraging such differences?

NOTES ON THE EBONICS CONTROVERSY

Suzette Haden Elgin

In December 1996, the Oakland (California) School Board announced a policy stating that African Americans speak a language distinct from English. They were referring to such regularized forms as using an unconjugated *be* and the dropping of a final consonant, as in "I be goin' "; different pronunciations, as with *aks* for *ask*; different stress patterns, as in *PO-lice*; the marking of plurals only once, as in "*Three boy do it*"; simplified consonant clusters, especially at the end of words, as in *desk* becoming *des* and then *desses* for the plural; and an inversion of the agreement rule so that -s signals plural on the verb as well as on the noun, as in "*The boys goes*" and "*The boy go.*"

While not saying that all African Americans follow these patterns, nor that they are exactly the same from one community to another, the board claimed that African-American speech is different enough from the English of the wider community that students need special help. They called the language Ebonics (from "ebony" and "phonics"), a word that immediately captured headlines and inspired hundreds, if not thousands, of writers, cartoonists, talk show hosts, and joke makers to offer opinions. Jokes on the Internet made sly references to Hebonics (speaking with a Yiddish accent or Yiddish sentence patterns) and described kids as being "Hooked on Ebonics." The problem was that different publics interpreted the word differently.

Suzette Haden Elgin, a linguist and writer of science fiction, who lives in Huntsville, Arkansas, publishes a "Linguistics and Science Fiction" newsletter. "When the Ebonics flap began," she was buried in mail, more than she had received on any one subject during the sixteen years she had published her newsletter. Subscribers asked her, "Please to put something in the newsletter that would straighten out the confusion." Following is the piece that she wrote in response.

1   Most of your letters on the subject of Ebonics have contained some version of this question: "WHY don't you linguists straighten out this mess?" (I know from the lengthy e-mail discussion on the Linguist List—including the complete texts of all the documents from Oakland—that I'm not the only linguist who got asked.) There are really two questions in your question. First: "What is the explanation for the mess?" And second: "Why don't linguists clean it up?" The thought of trying to answer either one at less than book length makes me want to flee into the wilderness; nevertheless, I will do my best, with apologies in advance for what is certain to be an unsatisfactory result, and the warning that you're not likely to like what I say. And I will preface

my answers with this statement: The inner-city kids involved in this controversy have excellent excuses for their ignorance about language and grammar
and linguistics; the bevy of adults pontificating in the media about Ebonics
recently have none. The depth of ignorance that has been demonstrated, and
the arrogance with which it has been set forth, are simply unacceptable.

2   Now . . . Do linguists have the information necessary to put things in order? They *should* have; it's very basic stuff. The problem is that there are no
"bar exams" for being a linguist, no licensing boards, not even a requirement
for continuing education. I made myself hugely unpopular with my colleagues long ago by campaigning *for* some sort of minimal standards. I believed then, and still believe, that linguists should be "certified" in some way;
but I seem to be alone in that. So, any qualified linguist has the information
needed, but not all linguists are qualified. Sadly, the more qualified they are,
the less likely it is that they are interacting with teachers and other educators.

3   Next, assuming we're talking about *qualified* linguists, why don't they
straighten this out? I know no quicker way to explain than to bring my mother
into this. She was an elementary school teacher, with a degree; she was educated and sophisticated; she was a voracious reader all her life, and she read
"literature." She did not read science fiction, not even that written by her
daughter; she read Good Books. And about once a month, from the time I
turned up with a Ph.D. in linguistics, she fired up a discussion about "the awful way people talk" and demanded that I do something about it. Her position was the usual one: Decent people speak Standard English, the failure to
do so is proof that the speaker is not only ignorant but lazy, and something
should be done about it—NOW.

4   With my mother, I had the opportunity to explain in detail and at length,
over hundreds and hundreds of hours. I could explore every last scrap of the
issue with her, and I did. And it had no more effect than if I'd recited nursery
rhymes. Furthermore, she was never willing to go along with my pleas that
we simply agree to disagree and drop the whole thing. She was *determined* to
hear me say, "Mother, you're right, and I'm sorry it took me so long to see
that."

5   And this is, almost without exception, what happens when we linguists
try to explain this particular matter. Because our educational system has made
the mythical "Standard English" a matter of morality. English uses that set of
words that includes "wrong" for both factual errors *and* moral errors, introducing great confusion and many opportunities for abuse. Adults in schools
couldn't get away with saying to kids, "Don't say 'ain't'; it's a sin!" But they
can say that it's *wrong* as much as they like, quite safely; the children understand that "morally wrong" is what's meant. Then, after hearing all day that
the way they talk is wrong, they are expected to go home and be respectful to
the adults in their family—who talk the same way they do—and to continue
to respect themselves in the midst of it all. *This* is what the teachers in Oakland, to their great credit, are so worried about. They are absolutely right, and

it is very wrong—morally wrong—that they haven't been given the tools and training to do something about the problem without becoming laughing-stocks.

6   The term "Standard English" refers to a myth. It's a label of convenience to save trees and time. There is no such thing as Standard English. Even if we expand the term to something a bit closer to the real world—Standard American English—there's no such thing. If anything remotely close to a Standard exists, it exists only as *written* English. Nobody speaks it, no matter how many degrees he or she has—and even for written English it is impossible to get all the teachers and pundits to agree on what the rules are.

7   Everyone speaks at least one dialect; every last one of those dialects is nonstandard. (*Non*standard—not *sub*standard.) The President [Clinton] speaks nonstandard English, George Bush speaks nonstandard English . . . we all speak nonstandard English. The closest thing we have to a spoken Standard, in my opinion, is the "performed" English of Peter Jennings and Diane Sawyer when they're speaking on television; nevertheless, their English is nonstandard. Which nonstandard dialects are looked down upon and which are admired is not a matter of logic or learning but of fashion.

8   *Why* Black English (BE), only one nonstandard dialect of many, is the way it is is not the issue here. Consider just one of the characteristics that draws criticism from people who mistakenly believe that they themselves speak Standard English. (I hope all of you heard Paul Gigot, expert and pundit, on the news recently talking solemnly about "the passive tense of English"? And all the senators talking about matters that are "as important than" other matters?) Many BE speakers say things like "He a carpenter" and "She tired." Language pundits use this as evidence to call BE (like my own native dialect) "inadequate for the expression of logical thought." It is a failure of our educational system that these hypereducated adults are unaware that a large percentage of the world's languages use precisely that "She tired" pattern, with no sacrifice of quality or elegance. Whether Black English uses it because of the influence of African languages isn't the issue (although it's an interesting question); the issue is *why this feature of BE is alleged to matter.* No speaker of English, hearing "He a teacher," understands it to mean anything other than "He is a teacher." "He a teacher" is not "wrong," just very unfashionable.

9   Many people have stressed a claim that kids have to learn to speak SE because without it they can't possibly succeed in this country. That's clearly nonsense, since *nobody* speaks it. The truth behind this usually very well-intended claim is that in order to succeed in most kinds of work (not all, but most) you have to be able to speak *without a set of linguistic items and structures that are looked down upon by the majority of those who have already succeeded.* That is: It's not a matter of "acquiring" the mythical Standard at all, but of getting *out* of your speech that set of unfashionable items. The set is small. It contains such things as "ain't" and the "double negative" and some nonstandard (but totally logical) verb forms like "knowed" and "growed." It contains items that

have nothing to do with grammar but are part of *usage*, like "irregardless." And it contains the set of English obscenities stronger than "damn." If you take a group of kids and teach them not to use those stigmatized items they will then be perceived as speaking SE; often, getting rid of just the top half dozen items is enough. And this is true for the sounds of the language as well as for the words, although I don't have space to go into that here. (For example, you can teach Latino speakers of English to eliminate the Anglo perception that they "have an accent" by teaching them to put the tip of their tongue just behind their upper teeth when they pronounce "t, d, l, and n"; that one change will often make them sound "Standard" enough.) It would be useful and honest to teach these things, just as it's useful and honest to teach people that they shouldn't go to work in their pajamas; it has nothing at all to do with logic or morality. It would also be honest and useful to show kids how to use the technique of simultaneous modeling— speaking *along with* tapes of speakers of Fashionable English—a method that has, in my opinion, been proved to work well for all types of "accent" learning.

10   But it is dishonest, and largely useless, to try to "teach kids to speak Standard English," with the meaning that line ordinarily has. Tens of thousands of kids speaking even the *most* unfashionable dialects spend as much as six hours a day listening to "more Standard" varieties of English on television, without that having any effect on their speech. Why would daily lessons at school about speaking SE make a difference? Children here in the Ozarks don't speak the English they hear hour after hour on TV; they speak the English their families and peers speak, as do the teachers who torment them about "talking right." Teachers stand and drill the kids in the "pen/pin distinction"; when you ask them why, they tell you it's so the kids will learn to speak correct "Inglish." They don't do that because they're wicked; they do it because they don't hear the difference between "Inglish" and "English" unless you stand over them and drill them the way they drill the kids.

11   I don't know what to do about this. The conviction that English other than Fashionable English is "wrong" and must be stamped out isn't an educational matter, it's an emotional one. People have an enormous emotional investment in all the scraps of the "Standard English" myth they've been forced to learn. The education/textbook/testing industries have an enormous financial investment in maintaining the current mess just as it is. Changing all this would literally threaten the U.S. economy; admitting that we let that keep us from doing it would threaten our image of ourselves as good and intelligent people who "believe in" education. When I go through this discussion, even with friends, people get very angry; they say, "Well, I don't know about other people, but I *do* speak Standard English!" Where it will all end I do not know. *Maybe* Noam Chomsky has clout enough (with the public) to state the basics and make them stick; but Chomsky is dedicated to turning the world around by pulling the strings dangling off politics. He doesn't do the kind of basics I do, and I don't have his clout.

12   There you are, as promised; don't yell at me, please. Perhaps I have at least demonstrated to you three crucial things. (1) This is more complicated—linguistically, emotionally, and economically —than you might think. (2) The misunderstandings and distortions are overwhelming. (3) The way the teachers in Oakland have been and are being treated is wrong. In the moral sense of the word as well as the actual.

COMPREHENSION

1. Words to talk about:
   - *bevy* of adults *pontificating*
   - the *mythical* "Standard English"
   - without becoming *laughingstocks*
   - teachers and *pundits*
   - not to use those *stigmatized* items

2. What was her point in citing "Paul Gigot, expert and pundit, on the news recently talking solemnly about 'the passive tense of English' " and "all the senators talking about matters that are 'as important than' other matters"?
3. Who is Noam Chomsky?

DISCUSSION

1. Notice that, with the exception of her title, Elgin does not use the word *Ebonics.* What does she use instead? What effect on the controversy did the newly created word have?
2. Elgin said that the more qualified linguists are, the less likely it is that they will be interacting with teachers and other educators. What factors might contribute to this situation?
3. What complications does Elgin ascribe to the fact that English uses the same word (*wrong*) for a factual error and a moral error?
4. Why does Elgin stress that *non*standard is not *sub*standard?
5. Conjecture on some of the ways that education, textbook, and testing industries benefit from maintaining the "Standard English" myth.

If Black English Isn't a Language, Then Tell Me, What Is?

James Baldwin

In 1979, nearly twenty years before the Ebonics controversy, James Baldwin wrote this piece for the *New York Times*. This essay from a highly respected and articulate African-American writer lends perspective to the recent debate.

1   The argument concerning the use, or the status, or the reality, of black English is rooted in American history and has absolutely nothing to do with the question the argument supposes itself to be posing. The argument has nothing to do with language itself but with the role of language. Language, incontestably, reveals the speaker. Language, also, far more dubiously, is meant to define the other—and, in this case, the other is refusing to be defined by a language that has never been able to recognize him.

2   People evolve a language in order to describe and thus control their circumstances or in order not to be submerged by a situation that they cannot articulate. (And if they cannot articulate it, they are submerged.) A Frenchman living in Paris speaks a subtly and crucially different language from that of the man living in Marseilles; neither sounds very much like a man living in Quebec; and they would all have great difficulty in apprehending what the man from Guadeloupe, or Martinique, is saying, to say nothing of the man from Senegal—although the "common" language of all these areas is French. But each has paid, and is paying, a different price for this "common" language, in which, as it turns out, they are not saying, and cannot be saying, the same things: They each have very different realities to articulate, or control.

3   What joins all in languages, and all men, is the necessity to confront life, in order, not inconceivably, to outwit death: The price for this is the acceptance, and achievement, of one's temporal identity. So that, for example, though it is not taught in the schools (and this has the potential of becoming a political issue) the south of France still clings to its ancient and musical Provençal, which resists being described as a "dialect." And much of the tension in the Basque countries, and in Wales, is due to the Basque and Welsh determination not to allow their languages to be destroyed. This determination also feeds the flames in Ireland for among the many indignities the Irish have

been forced to undergo at English hands is the English contempt for their language.

4   It goes without saying, then, that language is also a political instrument, means, and proof of power. It is the most vivid and crucial key to identity: It reveals the private identity, and connects one with, or divorces one from, the larger, public, or communal identity. There have been, and are, times and places, when to speak a certain language could be dangerous, even fatal. Or, one may speak the same language, but in such a way that one's antecedents are revealed, or (one hopes) hidden. This is true in France, and is absolutely true in England: The range (and reign) of accents on that damp little island make England coherent for the English and totally incomprehensible for everyone else. To open your mouth in England is (if I may use black English) to "put your business in the street." You have confessed your parents, your youth, your school, your salary, your self-esteem, and, alas, your future.

5   Now, I do not know what white Americans would sound like if there had never been any black people in the United States, but they would not sound the way they sound. *Jazz*, for example, is a very specific sexual term, as in *Jazz me, baby*, but white people purified it into the Jazz Age. *Sock it to me*, which means, roughly, the same thing, has been adopted by Nathaniel Hawthorne's descendants with no qualms or hesitations at all, along with *let it all hang out* and *right on*! *Beat to his socks*, which was once the black's most total and despairing image of poverty, was transformed into a thing called the Beat Generation, which phenomenon was, largely, composed of *uptight*, middle-class white people, imitating poverty, trying to *get down*, to get *with it*, doing their *thing*, doing their despairing best to be *funky*, which we, the blacks, never dreamed of doing—we were funky, baby, like *funk* was going out of style.

6   Now, no one can eat his cake, and have it, too, and it is late in the day to attempt to penalize black people for having created a language that permits the nation its only glimpse of reality, a language without which the nation would be even more *whipped* than it is.

7   I say that the present skirmish is rooted in American history, and it is. Black English is the creation of the black diaspora. Blacks came to the United States chained to each other, but from different tribes. Neither could speak the other's language. If two black people, at that bitter hour of the world's history, had been able to speak to each other, the institution of chattel slavery could never have lasted as long as it did. Subsequently, the slave was given, under the eye, and the gun, of his master, Congo Square, and the Bible—or, in other words and under those conditions, the slave began the formation of the black church, and it is within this unprecedented tabernacle that black English began to be formed. This was not, merely, as in the European example, the adoption of a foreign tongue, but an alchemy that transformed ancient elements into a new language. A *language comes into existence by means of brutal necessity, and the rules of the language are dictated by what the language must convey.*

8   There was a moment, in time, and in this place, when my brother, or my mother, or my father, or my sister, had to convey to me, for example, the dan-

ger in which I was standing from the white man standing just behind me, and to convey this with a speed and in a language, that the white man could not possibly understand, and that, indeed, he cannot understand, until today. He cannot afford to understand it. This understanding would reveal to him too much about himself and smash that mirror before which he has been frozen for so long.

9   Now, if this passion, this skill, this (to quote Toni Morrison) "sheer intelligence," this incredible music, the mighty achievement of having brought a people utterly unknown to, or despised by "history"—to have brought this people to their present, troubled, troubling, and unassailable and unanswerable place—if this absolutely unprecedented journey does not indicate that black English is a language, I am curious to know what definition of language is to be trusted.

10   A people at the center of the western world, and in the midst of so hostile a population, has not endured and transcended by means of what is patronizingly called a "dialect." We, the blacks, are in trouble, certainly, but we are not inarticulate because we are not compelled to defend a morality that we know to be a lie.

11   The brutal truth is that the bulk of the white people in America never had any interest in educating black people, except as this could serve white purposes. It is not the black child's language that is despised. It is his experience. A child cannot be taught by anyone who despises him, and a child cannot afford to be fooled. A child cannot be taught by anyone whose demand, essentially, is that the child repudiate his experience, and all that gives him sustenance, and enter a limbo in which he will no longer be black, and in which he knows that he can never become white. Black people have lost too many black children that way.

12   And, after all, finally, in a country with standards so untrustworthy, a country that makes heroes of so many criminal mediocrities, a country unable to face why so many of the nonwhite are in prison, or on the needle, or standing futureless, in the streets—it may very well be that both the child, and his elder, have concluded that they have nothing whatever to learn from the people of a country that has managed to learn so little.

COMPREHENSION

1. Words to talk about:

- a situation that they cannot *articulate*
- one's *antecedents* are revealed
- make England *coherent* for the English
- creation of the black *diaspora*
- the institution of *chattel* slavery

- this *unprecedented tabernacle*
- but an *alchemy* that transformed

2. Where and what are the areas (cities, countries, provinces) that Baldwin mentioned as illustrations of how French speakers differ, not only in how they speak but in what they say? Where do Basque speakers live? What is the history of Welsh speakers?

DISCUSSION

1. What is the effect on the reader of Baldwin beginning his essay talking about various kinds of French and then Basque and Welsh before moving on to England and the United States?
2. What did Baldwin mean when he said, "To open your mouth in England is to 'put your business in the street.' " Was he implying that this is more true for England than for the United States? If so, why would this be the case?
3. Baldwin says, "There have been, and are, times and places, when to speak a certain language could be dangerous, even fatal." Explain his meaning. Can you think of examples?
4. Baldwin said that black people were brought to this country chained to other black people who spoke different languages. Why was this done? What was the effect? How did religion enter the picture?
5. Talk a little about the following excerpts from Baldwin's essay. Then read the sample of news excerpts from recent stories about the Ebonics controversy, and discuss how they relate to one or more of Baldwin's statements
    (a) "It is not the black child's language that is despised. It is his experience. A child cannot be taught by anyone who despises him, and a child cannot afford to be fooled."
    (b) "The present skirmish is rooted in American history. . . . He [the white man] cannot afford to understand it. This understanding would reveal to him too much about himself and smash that mirror before which he has been frozen for so long."
    (c) "The brutal truth is that the bulk of the white people in America never had any interest in educating black people, except as this could serve white purposes."
    (d) "There was a moment, in time, and in this place, when my brother, or my mother, or my father, or my sister, had to convey to me, for example, the danger in which I was standing from the white man standing just behind me, and to convey this with a speed and in a language, that the white man could not possibly understand. . . . "

(e) "A child cannot be taught by anyone whose demand, essentially, is that the child repudiate his experience, and all that gives him sustenance, and enter a limbo in which he will no longer be black, and in which he knows that he can never become white."

NEWS EXCERPTS

(i) "To prepare teachers to use black English in the classroom, this oral language would have to be *reduced* to writing. Reducing the language to writing would take control of the language away from those who create and speak it and give control to bourgeois bureaucrats for whom it is a foreign language. By the time the materials for teachers had been written, edited, printed, distributed, and read, they would be obsolete. The language in question would have evolved away from its bureaucratized mutation." (Robert Hinton, Director of African and African-American Studies at Kenyon College in a letter to the *Chronicle of Higher Education,* March, 7, 1997)

(ii) "Educational history is replete with examples of broad-minded psychologists, eager-to-please administrators and unqualified public-school teachers desperately seeking a magical new method to educate feral ghetto kids when, to me, the answer is as simple as reaching up and touching your nose: respect and discipline. Those two standards always have been at the core of educating people, whether the setting was the mud and grime of a military boot camp or the ivy-covered walls of a prestigious medical school." (Ken Hamblin, *New York Times* columnist, Jan. 8, 1997)

(iii) "The contempt for Ebonics before any investigation has been remarkable. Even *The Bell Curve,* a book based on research not nearly as sound as the work on which Ebonics is based, was taken more seriously. *The Bell Curve* said black people were genetically inferior, and it got serious discussion. Ebonics offers a method for bringing heretofore forgotten black children into the mainstream of American life, and it gets laughed at. I guess we believe what we want to believe." (Language consultant Mary R. Hoover, quoted by Courtland Milloy, *Washington Post,* Dec. 29, 1996)

(iv) "Growing up black in Montreal, is quite different from growing up in a metropolitan U.S. city. A commonality is the racism to which people of African descent are exposed. The manner in which this is perpetrated may vary but the net effect is the same: keeping us down as a people. My parents permitted us to speak only 'the Queen's English,' i.e., standard English, at home, though we could speak whatever we wanted to in the street. Their rationale was simple: 'As blacks, we have enough strikes against us. You will not add to them by not being able to speak and write properly.' " (Diane C. Jacobs, doctoral student at Arizona State University, writing for the *State Press,* Jan. 27, 1997)

(v) "This is my third visit to the controversy now raging over what has come to be called Ebonics. . . . If the idea is that making Ebonics (or 'African Language Systems' or 'Pan-African Communications Behaviors' as the Oakland school board also described what used to be known as black English) an 'official' language will keep teachers from disrespecting the children who speak it, isn't that just a bit naive?" (Columnist William Raspberry, *Washington Post*, Jan. 3, 1996)

SUGGESTED TOPICS FOR WRITING

1. Write a paper about the Ebonics controversy. Pick out the different ideas that impressed you from the essays and the news summaries. Experiment by putting them together until you have one cohesive thesis you can develop. For example:

   ■ African Americans need to feel their language is respected.
   ■ The challenge is to teach standard English while not insulting students' home language.
   ■ Teachers who understand that African-American dialects are just as structured as standard English will be better prepared to teach.
   ■ Students who don't learn standard English will be disadvantaged.

2. Write a paper on the idea of public shaming. Can words really replace prison bars? Read and think about the issue long enough to develop a point of view more refined than "Yes, I'm in favor of it" or "No, I don't think it's good." Besides the incidents cited in this chapter, you can probably find additional examples through talking with people and through a computer-assisted search of recent news stories. If you wish to focus on the role of the mass media, then you could group the incidents according to how information is disseminated. If you are focusing on how the individual being punished will be affected, then you might rank the various kinds of punishment on a continuum according to whether they are designed to ostracize the person or help him or her get back into the community. If you are focusing on issues of criminal justice, then you might classify the incidents according to whether they are designed for the benefit of the community, the benefit of the individual, or the benefit of the judge.

3. Write about differences you have observed between the ways males and females communicate. Ask yourself such questions as whether or not the differences Tannen describes "always," "mostly," or "sometimes" hold true. Could it be that many of the differences relate to the roles people play? For example, does a man working as a flight attendant speak differently to the passengers than does a woman? Does a female attorney argue a case differently from a male attorney? Explore the idea of whether or not people are so predictable that we can divide communication patterns into two opposite camps. What are the complicating factors? Could such divisions become self-fulfilling prophecies?

4. Write a paper in which you explore body language. You might start by making a list of all the kinds of body language you can think of. Become a people watcher to get additional ideas. Possibilities for classification include body language that has agreed upon meanings such as hand shaking and waving; body language a person is aware of but isn't necessarily meant as communication such as smiling and jiggling one's leg; and body language that occurs without people being aware they are communicating such as the facial expressions that give away the fact that someone is lying.

5. Write a paper about lying. You might start with the incidents discussed in relation to Peter Farb's essay, but go on from there to examine your own experiences. Collect examples of habitual lies that you, your family, and your friends tell. Add examples from national news such as the story of Susan Smith, who went on television begging for a kidnapper to return the two sons she had drowned, and Mark Fuhrman, who testified at the O. J. Simpson trial that he had not used "the N word" in the past ten years. You might focus on the intent of the speakers, or you might focus on "good" lies versus "bad" lies, or on the impact of lies on people's lives and on history.

6. Write a paper about variations in the way people in the United States speak English. In a language, a marked form is any usage that stands out as different. Elgin's and Baldwin's essays were about various marked forms. As a class, talk about usages you have heard that were marked—that is, they sounded so strange you took notice of how something was being said as opposed to what was being said. If you have people in class from different parts of the country, you may find dialectal differences for what you call carbonated drinks, large sandwiches, drinking fountains, or various actions. For example, one student reported that, when in the car, her family always said, "*Screw* up the window," while everyone else's family said, "*Roll* up the window." If each person in the class can think of one or two examples—different grammar, different pronunciation, work-related jargon, words adapted into English from other languages, new slang, and so on—then you will

have a sizable body of samples of marked language. Experiment with various methods of classification to see what ideas you can come up with. For example, you might decide to write on the pros and cons of bilingualism; the logic of nonstandard English; the snob value of standard English; the influence of television on general speaking patterns; or the importance of being able to code-switch, that is, to move quickly from one dialect or one level of formality to another.

INFORMATION SOURCES FOR WRITING

Anguished English: An Anthology of Accidental Assaults upon Our Language, by Richard Lederer. New York: Dell, 1989. Lederer writes a newspaper column and has several other books including *The Miracle of Language* (New York: Pocket Books, 1991), *More Anguished English* (Dell, 1992), *Fractured English* (Pocket Books, 1996), and *Crazy English* (Pocket Books, 1989).

Banned in the U.S.A.: A Reference Guide to Book Censorship in Schools and Public Libraries, by Herbert N. Foerstel. Westport, Connecticut: Greenwood, 1994.

Censorship: A Threat to Reading, Learning, Thinking, edited by John S. Simmons. Newark, Delaware: International Reading Association, 1994.

Hunger of Memory, by Richard Rodriguez. Boston: Godine, 1982.

Language and Woman's Place, by Robin Lakoff. New York: HarperCollins, 1975.

Management of the Absurd, by Richard Farson. New York: Simon & Schuster, 1996.

Newsletter on Intellectual Freedom, published by the American Library Association Intellectual Freedom Committee. Most libraries will have copies of this newsletter published six times a year with both feature articles and accounts of current censorship cases in school and public libraries.

The Right to Privacy, by Ellen Alderman and Caroline Kennedy. New York: Knopf, 1995.

Savage Inequalities: Children in America's Schools, by Jonathon Kozol. New York: Crown, 1991.

The State of the Language, edited by Christopher Ricks and Leonard Michaels. Berkeley: Univ. of California Press, 1990.

Talking from 9 to 5: How Women's and Men's Conversations Affect Who Gets Heard, Who Gets Credit, and What Gets Done, by Deborah Tannen. New York: Morrow, 1994. A related video recording, "Talking 9 to 5: Women and Men in the Workplace," is available from International Learning Corporation, Burnsville, MN. Tannen's *You Just Don't Understand: Women and Men in Conversation* (Morrow, 1990) also has a related video recording, "Men and Women: Talking Together," presented by New York Open Center and available from Mystic Fire Video, Inc.

Watching My Language: Adventures in the Word Trade, by William Safire. New York: Random, 1997. William Safire writes an "On Language" column for the *New York Times Magazine* and has several books relating to various aspects of language.

What Johnny Shouldn't Read: Textbook Censorship in America, by Joan Delfattore. New Haven: Yale Univ. Press, 1992.

Who Can Speak? Authority and Critical Identity, edited by Judith Roof and Robyn Wiegman. Urbana, Illinois: Univ. of Illinois Press, 1995.

Woe Is I: The Grammarphobe's Guide to Better English in Plain English, by Patricia T. O'Connor. New York: Grosset Putnam, 1996.

The Family that Protests Togeth

azine ranks top
0 Hispanic colleges

Students vote to
drop Indian name

rl A. Banter
ATED PRESS
nto, CA
all town of Palos Heights, students
cal high school have taken team sports

panel endorses
ng racial prefer

he Senate announced that it will be creating a new
anel to determine whether or not a harmful series
ay actually be harmful, especially in a complex en

CULTURE CLASH

Showing stereotypes

All blacks are lazy. Al
All Mexicans are
All Jews are mo
All Germans are
Englishmen are e
Scots are cheap,
All Irishmen are
Frenchmen are un
are stupid. All Spa

Group Names:

Labels of Primary Potency

This chapter is in some ways a continuation of Chapter 3, but the topic it explores is important enough to rate separate treatment. Philosopher Gordon Allport, in his book *The Nature of Prejudice* (Addison-Wesley, 1954), used the term *labels of primary potency,* to discuss words that affect people's emotions so strongly their minds do not process or remember the other information that is being presented. Labels of primary potency are those words that would make needles jump up and down if any of us heard them while being fastened to a lie detector machine. The tricky part is that, just as with a lie detector test, different words will affect each of us differently depending on our physiology and our experiences.

This is more of a problem today than when Allport wrote his book because in today's world, where so many of us live in urban areas and work mostly with crowds of strangers, we try to get a handle on our surroundings by grouping and labeling people. As Allport explains, "In the empirical world of human beings there are some two-and-a-half billion grains of sand corresponding to our category 'the human race.' We cannot possibly deal with so many separate entities in our thought, nor can we individualize even among the hundreds whom we encounter in our daily rounds. We must group them, form clusters. We welcome, therefore, the names that help us to perform the clustering."

To do this clustering and labeling, we rely on what we think we see and on whatever stereotypical knowledge we have picked up over our lifetimes. Labeling others makes us feel in control because the label says the "others" are different and it's okay to move them to the outer circles of consideration. But for all of those who find themselves labeled and moved aside, their feelings of insecurity and insignificance are increased. It is little wonder that groups of people who have been marginalized are protesting the kinds of labeling and stereotyping that makes them feel like outsiders. This chapter explores various kinds of labeling and how people are working to combat the labels that make them feel marginalized.

THREE NEWS STORIES ON THE SEARCH FOR GROUP NAMES

These three articles about groups trying to name themselves illustrate some of the complexities of such a task, as there are groups within groups, people who don't all think the same way, and many individuals who don't belong to just one group. The differences in these three stories illustrate why it is inaccurate and inappropriate to lump all minority groups together. And while each group is trying to decide on a name for itself, each one is considering very different historical facts.

A PEOPLE IN SEARCH OF THE NAMING POWER

Linda A. Moore

1   Shakespeare asked, "What's in a name?" and for 30 million black Americans—colored people, Negroes, Afro-Americans, African-Americans—it's more than just a rhetorical question.

2   Perhaps changing a rose's name won't change its scent. As Shakespeare asked, would a rose not smell as sweet if it were called something else?

3   However, it's not that simple with people.

4   A name draws a picture: Colored, Negro, black, Afro-American, African-American, or African all call forth an image of the people to whom they are attached.

5   During this month, *The Tennessean* is focusing on the black image, its current status, history and future.

6   What image does a name create?

7   Early on in the American slave trade, blacks were called Africans by themselves and [by] whites, said Raymond Winbush, director of the Black Cultural Center at Vanderbilt University.

8   Eventually, blacks wanted to disassociate themselves with the name because of the negative image Africa had.

9   "The image of Africa was of the dark continent, and we wanted to get away from that image," Winbush said.

10   Then blacks accepted the other labels that were given to them, colored and Negro.

11   "It wasn't until the 20th century that we started naming ourselves," said Andrew Jackson, a sociology professor at Tennessee State University.

12   "We didn't argue about whether to call ourselves colored or Negro," he said.

13   The debate was whether to use capital letters when the words were written.

14   "That was nonsensical because of the fact that we were neither colored or Negroes," he said. While some may argue that the names themselves are not important, one question is where the names should come from.

15   "That's what the name changing is all about. It's about cultural self-determination.

16   "The cultural nationalist would say that free men name themselves; slaves and animals are named by their masters."

17   Negro may have hinted at dignity, but the name, which is Spanish for black, still denied people the right to name themselves. It also goes back even further, to the Greek word *necro,* which means dead, Jackson said.

18   It was not until the black power movement of the 1960s that *black* became popular, Jackson said.

19   The word had always had negative connotations—blackmail, the black sheep and bad guys in black hats—so by embracing the term and making it their own, black people felt they were creating a positive image from a negative one.

20   "We started using phrases like 'The blacker the berry, the sweeter the juice,' " Jackson said.

21   "So we're reversing the psychology. The psychology that they used to make us feel inferior by giving black a stigma, now we're making it into a positive attribute rather than a negative one."

22   *Black* is now the most widely accepted term, and *colored* and *Negro* have gained rather negative connotations.

23   However, organizations such as the National Association for the Advancement of Colored People and the United Negro College Fund have chosen to maintain the names they have had since they were founded.

24   "Having been in business since 1909, the NAACP is perhaps among the most recognized names in the country," said Jim Williams, head of public relations at the organization's Baltimore headquarters.

25   "If we were to change every time we went through a change in the way people wanted to be referred to, we would destroy our own identity."

26   The organization will hold its national convention in Nashville this summer, and at this time there are no plans to put a name change to a vote, Williams said.

27   The same is true for the United Negro College Fund, according to a prepared statement submitted by spokesman Mark Stubis.

28   "The name our founders selected in 1944, the United Negro College Fund, has held us in good stead through the years," Stubis' statement said. "This name is our trademark, recognized nationally and internationally."

29   That organization did put the word *Negro* to a vote, and the presidents of its 41 historically black colleges and universities chose to keep the word.

30   According to Jackson, the reluctance to change is not surprising because blacks throughout the country are in debate over the use of African-American vs. black.

Papago Just Won't Go Away

Joseph Garcia

1   Play Tohono O'odham Bingo.

2   Sound funny?

3   With frequent television, radio and newspaper advertising, "Papago Bingo" does have a more familiar ring to it.

4   Perhaps that's why the tribe has left the name intact despite its decision four years ago to officially change its name from Papago to Tohono O'odham.

5   *Papago* is a Spanish word meaning "bean eater," and some in the tribe believe that term is derogatory. Tohono O'odham means "desert people" in the tribe's language.

6   But in Sells, the business district of the 2.8-million-acre reservation west of Tucson, Papago won't go away.

7   There's the First Papago Baptist Church, the Papago Trading Post, Papago Legal Services, the *Papago Runner* newspaper and the Bureau of Indian Affairs Papago Agency.

8   After the January 1986 decision, the reservation's most popular eatery did not suddenly become the Tohono O'odham Cafe. It's still called the Papago Cafe.

9   "It's too much trouble to change it," said owner Suzie Lopez, whose business-sign letters are made from ocotillo [cactus] ribs. "I wanted to change it at one time, but my husband said it was too much trouble."

10   Lopez said the word *Papago* isn't offensive to her or to too many people she knows.

11   "It doesn't bother me. I think the Papagos eat a lot of beans," she said, referring to the accuracy of the Spanish word. The Indian taco with beans is a favorite of lunchtime customers.

12   With tribal leadership battles brewing, use of Tohono O'odham vs. Papago isn't the great debate of the desert these days. But while some care very little what they're called, others have chosen sides.

13   "I refer to myself as Tohono O'odham," said Debra Cachora, 18, a sales clerk at Margaret's Indian Arts and Crafts in the Sells Shopping Center.

14   "The tribe doesn't really want to be known as Papago anymore and I'm more or less helping them," she said, explaining her self-identification preference.

15   But just next door, at O'odham Video, clerk Kenneth Hendricks is a Papago.

16   "For myself, I know I'm a Papago, and I don't care what anybody calls me," said Hendricks, 31.

17   "We've been known as Papago all these years, and the rest of the United States know us as Papago, and I feel like I'm a Papago. That's the way I've always been known and would like it to continue that way."

18   His boss, store owner Andrew Patricio, is a tribal legislator who backs the name change—hence, O'odham Video. But Patricio also is board chairman of the Papago Tribal Utility Authority, O'odham Water and Power.

19   It's that sort of schizophrenic name reference that has some younger residents scratching their heads, Hendricks said.

20   "I think a lot of them may be wondering, are we O'odham or Papago? What do we call ourselves? The younger ones, they'll probably go with what the tribe says," said Hendricks.

21   But the older generation, particularly those in remote areas and Mexico, will probably stick with Papago, as will those who did not vote for the change, he said.

22   Papago baskets—intricately woven beargrass and yucca—are famous throughout the world. Cahora said people from as far away as Japan, the - Soviet Union, Germany and England come into her store in search of baskets.

23   "They ask, 'Is a Papago basket different than a Tohono O'odham basket?' I tell them there really is no difference but in name," she said.

24   Others ask if Tohono O'odham and Papago are two different tribes. Tohono O'odham—difficult for some to pronounce—sounds so mysterious, they say. They'd never heard of it.

25   "A lot of people protested," former legislator Rosemary Lopez recalled of the name change to Tohono O'odham. "They were worried that a lot of people, including the city of Tucson, wouldn't be able to pronounce it. We said, 'That's their problem.' But they've learned it. They've learned it."

26   Lopez, who served 12 years through 1987 as a representative of the Chukut-Kuk district, said both terms are used on the reservation.

27   "It depends on where the individual is coming from. When you talk in English, it's 'Papago.' When you talk in the (native) language, it's 'O'odham,'" said Lopez, supervisor of disease prevention services for the Tohono O'odham Health Department.

28   But she said many of the tribe's young don't speak the native language and therefore use Papago.

29   Lopez, who was chairwoman of the tribe's constitution committee, said the name change to Tohono O'odham was part of the tribe's effort at self-determination.

30   "That was the argument, that (Papago) was a name given to us, not one we chose," she said.

31   O'odham simply means "people." And Lopez believes eventually the term will be the people's choice. But for now, people choose between the two names and often use both.

32   "Everybody still uses what they want—Tohono O'odham or Papago—whatever they feel like at the time," said local BIA Superintendent James A. Barber.

33   Although his district is still officially known as the Papago Agency, Barber prefers the Tohono O'odham term. "Desert people—to me, that sounds a heck of a lot better than bean eaters," he said.

34   But with no more than 2,100 of the 15,000 residents on the reservation voting for the name change as part of its new constitution, Barber said it's likely many were unaware of the decision.

35   "When the people voted on this, some people way out there probably didn't even know there was a vote going on for this," he said.

36   When the new tribal constitution—and subsequently the use of Tohono O'odham—passed, the BIA was ready to change its letterhead stationery to reflect the change. But Barber said it turned out such a move was not automatic.

37   His district remains the Papago Agency today because the tribe has yet to request an official name change with the assistant secretary of Indian affairs, he said.

38   "That hasn't been done, and until that happens we're still the Papago Agency, even though they've officially changed their name," Barber said. "I don't know why it hasn't been done."

39   Tribal officials declined comment.

40   But on official BIA documents and maps, the term *Tohono O'odham* is popping up, followed by "formerly Papago" in parenthesis.

Term Limits: Hispanic? Latino? A National Debate Proves No One Name Pleases Everyone

Mark McDonald

1   Use Domingo Garcia as the appropriate metaphor.

2   "When I was a kid growing up I was 'Spanish-surnamed,' says the Dallas City Council member.

3   "Then I was Latin-American, then Chicano, then Mexican-American, then Hispanic.

4   "And now," he says, "I'm Latino."

5   Such has been the progression of the debate, a debate still percolating, over the collective, politically correct term for more than 22 million people in the United States.

6   Are they Hispanic? Or are they Latino?

7   And should one-fourth of the people in Texas be called Chicanos? Or is Mexican-American the better term?

8   The debate can get complicated, but one thing is clear: In the 1990 census, 22.4 million people said they were of "Spanish/Hispanic origin." What to call them—as a group—has intrigued and exasperated any number of academics, activists, demographers, linguists and historians.

9   Although Hispanic was used in the '90 census, not everyone whom the government considered to be part of this amorphous group spoke Spanish. Nor did they all have Spanish surnames.

10   The word *Hispanic* was chosen by default. "It really came right out of the dictionary," says one census official.

11   The word doesn't please everyone, of course, and it doesn't even exist in the Spanish language. Further, it conjures up images of colonial domination by Spain and Portugal while denying the people's Indian and African heritages.

12   "Latino" is gaining currency as an umbrella term, especially on the East and West coasts, although some still find it too limiting.

13   "The word Hispanic got its play among the middle class, but it's really a relic of the Reagan era," says Mr. Garcia. "Latino is more inclusive now. I use it when I speak in national terms, and you hear Henry Cisneros using Latino now.

14   "In reference to Americans of Mexican descent, I prefer Chicano. Locally, I say 'Chicano community,' or *'Mejicano.'* "

15   The word *Chicano* apparently comes from the shortening of a colloquial pronunciation of "Mexicano," in which the first syllable sounds like "Metch."

16   In modern usage, "Chicano" has come to mean American citizens or residents with Mexican heritage. It has been most widely used in California and Texas, although some Mexican-Americans, especially the elderly, still find the word crude and offensive.

17   "Chicano" also has political connotations left over from the '60s, when it was the term of choice among left-wing activists.

18   "Chicano has always been the most predominant word here, especially in the barrios," says Mr. Garcia. "Go to a high school or into the community—especially among those 35 and older, the word is Chicano. Or among the older crowd, Mejicano."

19   So the debate goes—locally, nationally, politically, academically—and the opinions can be as challenging as they are diverse.

"PROCESSED MILK"

20   Although Martha Cotera publishes the *Austin Hispanic Directory*, she doesn't care too much for the adjective.

21   "*Hispanic* is a generic term that doesn't express a national heritage or any ethnic pride," she says. "It tends to homogenize us, like processed milk. It's sanitized. It only acknowledges our European roots and denies our Indian roots. A more apt term might be *Indo-Hispanic.*

22   "I don't know where this argument for *Latino* comes from. It's false, especially for Texans. The word goes back to the Latin conquest of Spain and Portugal. It is so remotely connected to us.

23   "*Hispanic* blends us into mush. And *Latino*—it's such an old term—just makes us into an *older* mush.

24   "Neither *Latino* nor *Hispanic* are satisfactory terms, although I might use them publicly. I always use *Mexican-American* in official documents. There is very seldom the choice of *Chicano*, but my gut reaction would be to mark *Chicana* if they had it.

25   "In Texas we're very practical. *Latino, Chicano, Hispanic*—we don't give a damn what we're called, just as long as we're doing okay."

GEOPOLITICS

26   The National Council of La Raza uses "Hispanic" and "Latino" interchangeably. "It's a very fluid situation," says Lisa Navarrete, an NCLR spokesperson. "It depends a lot on where you are."

27   "Latino hasn't caught on in Texas, but it's the preferred term in Chicago, New York and California. It's a bad thing to say 'Hispanic' in California.

28   "The exception (to Latino) is the Southwest and Florida. The Cuban-American community feels less connection with national Hispanic groups. They see themselves as an exile community, and they have more tenuous ties.

29   "We deal so much with census data we use 'Hispanic' a lot. But the direction seems to be toward 'Latino.' It's the more progressive movement. We don't trash people who use one or the other. It's clearly something people are thinking about."

"SLAVE NAME"

30   Sandra Cisneros, 38, is the author of *Woman Hollering Creek, The House on Mango Street* and *My Wicked, Wicked Ways.* She grew up in a Mexican-American family in Chicago, now owns a home in San Antonio and has described herself as "a Chicana feminist."

31   Ms. Cisneros, no relation to the former San Antonio mayor, does not allow her work to be included in anthologies or collections that use the word *Hispanic,* a term she says is "a repulsive slave name." " 'Hispanic' is English for a person of Latino origin who wants to be accepted by the white status quo," she said recently in an interview in *The New York Times.*

32   "*Latino* is the word we have always used for ourselves. . . . To say 'Latino' is to say you come to my culture in a manner of respect."

"BENITO JUAREZ FACES"

33   Guillermo Galindo is a Spanish-English interpreter, a longtime political activist and a member of the Dallas Park Board.

34   "To most gringos, I'll say I'm Chicano. If it's a Mexican-American, maybe an older person or conservative, I'll say I'm Mexican-American. It's more comfortable for them.

35   "*Hispanic* is a term that identifies us with Spain. But up until the last century, Spain and Portugal were two of the most backward countries in the world. Nothing in the entire history of Spain makes me proud. Why would I want to claim or belong to a country that created the Inquisition?

36   "Some people say, 'The Spanish gave us culture and language.' They didn't give us anything. They *imposed* it on us.

37   "As Mexicans we are a conquered people. I speak a conquered language. As Roman Catholics we practice a conquered religion. We have an imposed culture.

38   "And Latinos—they all want to be descended from the motherland, from Spain. If you call yourself Latino, you're trying to escape from the existential reality as to what you really are.

39   "Mexican-Americans are always denying our Indian heritage. You can have 20 Mexican-Americans sitting around talking about 'Hispanics' and they all have these Indian Benito Juarez faces. It's a joke."

NUANCE AND INSULT

40   Author Earl Shorris titled his new book *Latinos: A Biography of the People.* "To many Latinos, drawing the distinctions among the nationalities constitutes a kind of game, like a quiz program," he writes. "Everyone has a theory about everyone else. Some are amusing, all are accurate, and every nuance is important."

41   Mr. Shorris grew up in El Paso, became a novelist, and for the last 20 years has been a contributing editor at *Harper's* magazine.

42   Laborers and the very poor in Mexico were known as Chicanos, he says, and although the word was derogatory, "it was the mildest of insults."

43   "Nevertheless, many older people continue to be appalled at the use of the term. . . . The Chicano generation began in the late 1960s and lasted about six or eight years. Some people call themselves Chicanos but the definition is vague and the word has lost its fire."

"DISTINCT POPULATIONS"

44   Dr. Rodolfo de la Garza had some ideas about what he and his colleagues might find in their now widely quoted Latino National Political Survey. Not all those ideas worked out, however.

45   "One thing that was surprising to us: We thought 'Latino' was more popular. It's absolutely not. More people call themselves American than Latino.

46   People don't come here with a Latino identity," says Dr. de la Garza, the Mike Hogg professor of community affairs at the University of Texas. "They come as Bolivians, Venezuelans, Colombians. They might *become* Latino or Hispanic in the United States, but they don't have that sort of identity when they arrive."

47   The survey also showed a sort of hierarchy of terms that people prefer when describing themselves.

48   "The first labels are national origin, such as 'Mexican' or 'Mexican-American,' 'Puerto Rican' or 'Cuban.' Then depending on the national origin, people prefer pan-ethnic terms such as *Hispanic, Latino, Spanish,* or *Hispano.* Then comes the nonethnic label which is American."

49   Dr. de la Garza knows well the objections to Hispanic. "Some say that Hispanic eliminates the indigenous people and I used to make that left-wing radical position myself. I used to participate in this debate on the side of Latino. No more. *Mea culpa.* I've gone back to being Mexican."

COMPREHENSION

1. Words to talk about:

   - it's about *cultural self-determination . . . cultural nationalist*
   - that sort of *schizophrenic* name reference
   - academics, activists, *demographers,* linguists
   - images of *colonial domination*
   - every *nuance* is important

2. Explain these metaphors, which Mark McDonald used:

   - a debate still *percolating*
   - an *umbrella* term
   - tends to *homogenize* us
   - we don't *trash* people

3. In the story about the Papago/Tohono O'odham, Kenneth Hendricks predicts that younger people will probably use the new name of Tohono O'odham, while Suzie Lopez predicts that young people will probably stick with Papago. On what different bases did the two informants make their predictions?

4. Have you heard the word *gringo* before? What is its meaning? Does the tone influence how it is interpreted?

5. Guillermo Galindo was quoted in the article on Hispanic names as saying that Mexican-Americans deny their Indian heritage: "You can have 20 Mexican-Americans sitting around talking about 'Hispanics' and they all have these Indian Benito Juarez faces. It's a joke." Who was Benito Juarez?

DISCUSSION

1. Linda Moore builds the lead to her story around the Shakespeare quotation: "What's in a name? That which we call a rose/By any other word would smell as sweet." This line comes from *Romeo and Juliet,* and is the question Juliet asks when she discovers Romeo belongs to the Montague family, a family hated by her own. The line is often quoted with the implication being that it is the substance not the name of something that is important. While that may be Juliet's hope, does the play support the theory?

2. Two processes through which words change meanings are *amelioration* and *pejoration.* When a word is ameliorated, it acquires positive conno-

tations; it may even become opposite in meaning as when teenagers use *pfat* as a positive term. When a word undergoes *pejoration,* it acquires negative connotations. A complication is that these two processes do not happen at the same time with all speakers. How does this relate to the problems of choosing pan-ethnic names?

3. The introduction to these three stories mentions "groups within groups." What evidence can you find to support the observation that this concept presents a challenge? Which of the news stories best illustrated the challenge?

4. None of these articles provide absolute answers to the question of what names should be used for these three groups. What then was their value? What did you learn?

5. Read Living Language 4.1 and compare the incidents to the articles about groups trying to come to consensus on their names. How do these stories differ?

Living Language 4.1

Exonyms

The word *exonym,* coined from the Latin morphemes for "outside" and "name," refers to the common practice of people giving names or labels to groups they do not belong to; for example, in the 1990s it was not teenagers but middle-age journalists who began calling young adults GenXers or Generation X.

- Not only were American Indians misnamed by Columbus when he thought he had reached the Indies, they suffered further insult when in many cases whites picked up exonyms instead of the tribe's own names. For example, rather than *Innuit,* which means "the people" or "the human beings," Europeans picked up the Algonquin term *Eskimo,* which means "eaters of raw fish."
- Sixteenth-century Englanders thought that the itinerant people now known as gypsies came from Egypt (they actually came from northwest India), and so they called them Egyptians, later shortened to Gypsies. Their name most likely inspired the verb *gyp.*
- Nonbelievers gave the name of Quaker to members of the Society of Friends as a way of deriding their teaching that people should "quake and tremble at the word of the Lord." Members accepted the name as a mark of humility. Two hundred years later, members of the Unification Church, founded by Korean evangelist Sun Myung Moon, probably aren't as happy to be called Moonies.
- Members of the Church of Jesus Christ of Latter Day Saints, founded by Joseph Smith in 1830, were distressed when the world at large began calling them Mormons, based on their *Book of Mormon* scriptures. Although they have doctrinal reasons for retaining the official name, today most church members go along with the efficiency of such terms as *Mormon missionary, Mormon temple, Mormon history,* and *Mormonism,* especially in Israel where their official name would be a label of primary potency.
- Condoms have long been called "French letters," except in France where they were called "English caps." In most countries, syphillis was known as the French disease; while the French called it the Naples or Italian disease; Poles referred to it as the German sickness, Dutch as the Spanish Pox, and Asians as the Portuguese disease.
- People living in what the world calls "Wales" have long resented the name because it means "strangers" or "foreigners." When the Anglos, the Saxons, and the Jutes came into England they pushed the inhabitants further and further into the western hills and used their name in insulting ways: To *welsh* on a deal is to cheat; a *Welsh comb* is running your fingers through your hair; a *Welsh carpet* is a painted floor; and a *Welsh rabbit* (now changed to *Welsh rarebit*) is a cheap substitute, as when cheese is poured over toast and called a "rabbit."
- Nineteenth-century Americans viewed China as a faraway and exotic place and so used Chinese to mean "different or unusual," as in Chinese Checkers. But as Chinese immigrants were forced to take low-paying jobs, Chinese took on pejorative meanings of cheap, as in a *Chinese home run* (the ball barely makes it over the fence), or stupid, as in a *Chinese fire drill* (practiced by teenagers who jump out of a car at a stoplight, run around it, and jump back in).

FROM IN WHOSE HONOR? AMERICAN INDIAN MASCOTS IN SPORTS*

Jay Rosenstein

Jay Rosenstein wrote, produced, and directed *In Whose Honor?*, which was shown on PBS's *Point of View* series on July 15, 1997. He lives and works in Champaign-Urbana, home of the University of Illinois. He used to be a huge sports fan, always holding season tickets to basketball and football games. When he was studying engineering at the university in the late seventies and early eighties, he went to the games and watched the half-time entertainment provided by the dancing Chief Illiniwek, the university's mascot (now referred to as "honored symbol"). In response to occasional protests, he remembers thinking, "Don't these people have anything better to do?" Years later, when he came across some insulting Indian caricatures in a newspaper, they reminded him of the shock he felt as a kid attending Hebrew School in Chicago, where he saw films about the Holocaust that included exaggerated cartoons of Jews. His thinking about how these caricatures were manipulated and used by the Nazis made him take a new interest in the situation at the University of Illinois that was developing from a one-woman protest by graduate student Charlene Teters. As of 1999, the university was still using Chief Illiniwek as an "honored symbol," but as shown in these pages excerpted from the film script, the matter is far from settled.

1   *On screen text:* It has ever been the way of the white man in his relation to the Indian, first, to sentimentalize him as a monster until he has been killed off . . . and, second to sentimentalize him in retrospect as the noble savage.

—James Gray
"The Illinois," 1940

2   *Charlene Teters (University of Illinois graduate student):* I've never looked for the role of being anything other than a good mother, a good family member. I've never looked for it, in terms of being one of the leaders of a movement, I never looked for that. It's like something that came to me. Our people paid with their very lives to keep what little we have

*This documentary film is available on video from Rosenstein Productions.

left. The fact that we even have anything today speaks to the strength of our ancestors. And that is what I'm protecting.

3   *Title on screen:* "In Whose Honor?"

4   *Charlene Teters:* If I knew ahead of time what was ahead of me, I would not have come here. And I certainly would not have brought my kids here.

5   *Narrator:* It's a fall Saturday at the University of Illinois. Fans come from all around to support the home team, the Fighting Illini. It's a mix of business and pleasure, politics, and local celebrities. And everywhere is the symbol of the University of Illinois, a fictitious American Indian character called Chief Illiniwek.

6   Chief Illiniwek has been part of the University of Illinois for 70 years. Dancing at half-time of home football and basketball games, the chief has become a crowd favorite.

7   *Susan Gravenhorst (University of Illinois trustee):* He's the focal point. He draws the community, the student body, the faculty together.

8   *Rick Winkel (University alumnus and state legislator):* I've seen the performance many, many times and have found it nothing but inspiring.

9   *Lou Liay (Representative of university alumni association):* I don't know that there's any school in the country that has the feeling toward its symbol like the University of Illinois.

10   *Narrator:* Yet little was heard from American Indians about their feelings on the chief. But that all changed one night in 1989, when a Spokane Indian graduate student, and a mother of two, took her children to a basketball game.

11   *Charlene Teters:* I got tickets to the game, and I tried to prepare them ahead of time for what they were going to see there, you know. They have this Indian mascot as you know, they wear paint, some people wear feathers, you know they have war chants, you know I just tried to go through all the things that they would experience there, so, you just have to ignore that, just enjoy the game. But it was when the chief came out, and I'd never seen him, didn't know at all what he looked like, what he wore, I just heard that the chief comes out and does what is billed as an authentic dance. And he came out wearing that buckskin, wearing what looked like real eagle feathers all the way to the ground, and started to do his dance. And of course the fans go into a frenzy. And all around us there were these people standing in their seats yelling "The chief!" "The chief!" . . . and my kids just sank in their seats. I saw my daughter try to become invisible, my son tried to laugh. With me, it's a sadness that still won't leave me. But that sadness turns to anger just like that. And it still makes me really angry because I know they do that, and I know they are hurting other people when they do

that. And I knew that I couldn't be here and not address that issue. My children know who they are. They know they're Indian. They have been taught to respect the person who has earned the right to wear an eagle feather headdress. What I saw in my children was a blow to their self-esteem and it still makes me angry.

12   *Narrator:* Charlene Teters was recruited by the University's art department in 1988 in an effort to increase its diversity. She arrived with her family from Santa Fe, New Mexico, having never seen the campus. What they found when they arrived was not just a university, but an entire community that was deeply attached to the Fighting Illini. . . .

13   But Charlene was from a traditional American Indian community. She was raised near a reservation in Spokane, Washington, and grew up learning traditional Indian culture, ceremony, and religion. She too was trying to pass these on to her children. . . .

14   *Susan Gravenhorst:* I can't imagine that the chief, who deports himself with such dignity, and such solemnity, I can't imagine that that can be perceived as a racial insult or a slur on the Native American community. To me it's a compliment.

15   *Football fan:* And I don't think the people here should cave into a bunch of out-of-state foreigners. (*Off-camera question:* You think the Indian people are foreigners?) If they're from Oklahoma. I'm a taxpayer in Illinois. Are they a taxpayer in Illinois? I pay my taxes in Illinois and I support the U of I. They come in from out of state, and they don't support us. They don't pay any taxes. They shouldn't have any say here.

16   *Charlene Teters:* In the beginning it was really very frightening for me. At that time when I was standing alone outside of the basketball stadium people would spit on me, people would throw things at me. They felt very comfortable coming up to me and ridiculing me and threatening me and it was a very threatening environment. I was very afraid, but I knew I had to be there.

17   *Narrator:* In October of 1989, the current Chief Illiniwek was giving a talk at the student union and Charlene decided to go.

> *WICD TV Reporter (Inserted news package):* Today, Tom Livingston, the university's current chief was scheduled to talk about the history and tradition behind the mascot.
>
> *Tom Livingston:* Chief Illiniwek is designed to be inspirational, majestic, reverent, moving.

18   *Charlene Teters:* We got there a little bit late, and I made it through the crowd to where I could see him, and he was holding up the chief headdress. And when I saw him holding it up like that, you know, it really made me angry. Because he was holding it up like a trophy.

Reporter (Continuation of news insert): Charlene Teters is a Native American who says the only thing authentic about the chief is the costume. And she called the dance, "Pure gymnastics."

Charlene Teters: You keep referring to your dance, your eagle feathers, your outfit or whatever you want to call it, as ceremony, as religion. Why is the university involved with some kind of religious ceremony at half-time?

19   *Charlene Teters:* As that happened the media started to turn their cameras on me and those microphones coming out of everywhere kind of listening to me. So that began a kind of real frenzy within the media. From that point on I had no normal life really. I became this focus of media attention.

20   I see the mascot as a symbolic display of our leadership, that we control you, we own you. Every time that was being paraded around I felt I also had to be there to challenge it.

21   *Narrator:* Chief Illiniwek first appeared in 1926, part of an idea by the assistant band director for a half-time stunt. A student and former boy scout with an interest in Indian history made a homemade Indian costume; on the afternoon of Oct. 30th, he appeared on the field for the first time. . . .

22   As the chief's popularity continued to grow, so did his role and his activities. And the attachment of the fans to their Indian symbol and Indian identity grew as well. Indian caricatures became a part of the University of Illinois landscape.

23   But these were different times in America. While blackface and black caricatures have virtually disappeared, Indian caricatures remain.

24   *Charlene Teters:* These images should have gone by the wayside along with Little Black Sambo and the Frito Bandito. If it was any other religious practice that was being abused we would hear about it. We would certainly hear about it if it was some kind of distortion of a Catholic ceremony or a Jewish ceremony, we would hear about it. But somehow because it is a Native practice and ceremony and religious items and practices it's not respected. . . .

25   *Rick Winkel:* I realize that there probably was no such person as Chief Illiniwek and to some extent it's mythological I suppose. But it's an attempt, I think, of people in Illinois to try to remember a vanished tribe, the Illini tribe, that was annihilated apparently by an opposing Native American tribe around the 1760s. To try to remember their heritage, to do it in a way that's respectful. After all, the Illini tribe is where we get our state's name from.

26   *Narrator:* Yet there is no Illini Indian in Chief Illiniwek. His costume is from the Sioux, and his dance has been made up by the students who

have portrayed the chief. In 1990, in its official literature, the University stopped referring to the chief dance as authentic.

27 *Charlene Teters:* These symbols do nothing to help us remember Indian people. But add another layer of misinformation. We have to continue to peel away all of these layers of misinformation of who we are in order for people to really see us for who we are.

28 *Narrator:* The Indian population in America is relatively small. Yet the popularity of Indian images in sports and on TV affects what many people know—and think about Indians.

29 *Leigh Estabrook (Ph.D. and university dean):* I'm 52 years old. I grew up with cowboys and Indians, black-and-white movies running across the television screen. And because the Native American Indian population is so small, and in fact so segregated from the rest of our populations, the experiences that I have, that most of us have with Native American Indians, is extraordinarily limited. So that it is hard for me to think of Indians as somebody I eat dinner with, as friends of my kids, as somebody one of my children might marry. And if I have Chief Illiniwek dancing around it perpetuates the old 1950s, '40s, '30s cowboy and Indian myths. . . .

30 *Narrator:* In November of 1989, Illinois Senator Paul Simon signed a petition against Chief Illiniwek. It caused a sudden uproar throughout the state.

> *Senator Paul Simon (Inserted news package):* I could have handled it better. Frankly some native American Indian leaders came to me and asked me to sign a petition. I have long felt there are problems with the designations for teams, but I think it would have been better if I said I'll get in touch with the president of the university and set up a meeting to see how we can move in a constructive direction here.

31 *Narrator:* Simon was roundly criticized for making the chief a political issue. In response, Chancellor Morton Weir issued a statement supporting the chief. But with all the attention from the growing controversy Chancellor Weir asked people to stop using Indian caricatures. . . .

32 *Michael Haney (American Indian activist):* Last year when the University of Illinois played Iowa, Iowa had a real aggressive Greek community that hung effigies of the chief all the way down Greek row, and we had American Indians that were going to class, they had to walk past these Indians hanging from trees and they called and said, can you help us because we're playing the University of Illinois, we have to suffer racial slurs all week. And they call themselves the Hawkeyes, it's got nothing to do with Indians. That's how Indians suffer because of the University of Illinois. So you have an effect on people you don't even know because of the racist symbol here of Chief Illiniwek. . . .

33   *Narrator:* In 1990 the Board of Trustees voted to make Chief Illiniwek the official symbol of the University of Illinois.

34   Charlene left the University of Illinois and moved on to continue her fight. The first stop was the big money world of professional football and the Washington Redskins.

35   *Dennis Tibbetts (Ph.D. and Indian counselor):* The irony of the whole thing is here you have Redskins, which is the most blatant racist symbol, term, depiction right in the capitol and everyone's kind of numb to it. They're all Redskin's fans. "Yeah, I'm a Redskins fan!" So they've numbed themselves to that so much that you have these politicians who are supposed to represent all people saying, "I'm a Redskins fan."

36   *Man shouting at Charlene Teters (He is selling Redskins souvenirs and dressed in a cheap Indian costume):* Sure, I love you people. Your blood is the same blood as mine. I don't have nothing against you. I'm not making fun . . . you know what, the dollars is what I'm concerned with, the dollars is what I'm concerning with darling. It comes down to one simple thing, dollars honey. Money. You know it. You know it.

37   *Narrator:* Charlene continued on, staging protests and rallies at other sites. Support from American Indian coalitions and leaders began to grow. . . . But the biggest protest was just ahead, at the Superbowl between the Buffalo Bills and Washington Redskins.

38   It was working. The mainstream media began to pay attention. Some newspapers restricted or banned the use of the word *Redskin.* In Minnesota, the State Board of Education asked schools to stop using American Indian symbols. And some universities were doing the same. Eastern Michigan, Southern Colorado, St. John's, Marquette, and Bradley University all eventually dropped their Indian references.

39   Yet the University of Illinois continued to hold firm. But soon the pressure increased. Three fellow members of the Big Ten conference, the Universities of Wisconsin, Minnesota, and Iowa decided to take a stand against American Indian mascots.

> *KCRG (Inserted news package): Woman:* In other news, you won't see team mascots that represent American Indians at the University of Iowa anymore. In fact, with one exception, the Hawkeyes won't even schedule teams that have American Indian mascots.
>
> *Man #1:* TV 9's Mark Harmon joins us with details of the university's decision. And Mark, that one exception is Iowa's Big Ten opponent, Illinois.
>
> *Man #2:* That's right. Big Ten rules state you have to schedule opponents within the conference, but the University of Iowa's athletic department wants to make sure their message is loud and clear to the University of Illinois as well.

40   *Tom Lamont (University of Illinois Trustee):* Most of my colleagues on the board share that being politically correct to merely appease a minority group of individuals is not in and unto itself an appropriate position to take. Speaking personally, I don't care frankly what some would do at those universities. Because I'm not sure that they are capable of understanding the environment in which we share and enjoy the chief. . . .

41   *Narrator:* In 1994, University Chancellor Michael Aiken appointed a committee to recommend how to make the university a more inclusive place. When their report came out, the first recommendation was that Chief Illiniwek be eliminated. It was the first time an official body appointed by the administration had spoken out against the chief. The recommendation caused a great backlash, especially from university alumni.

42   *James Stukel (University president, answering to an off-camera question, "Why do you think so many people love the chief?"):* I have no idea. It's a tradition that's been here for many decades and I suspect people are very supportive of it because of its long tradition. But thank you very much for coming by today. . . .

43   *Narrator:* The alumni are especially important to the university, contributing millions of dollars to finance scholarships, programs, and new buildings. . . .

44   Contributions poured into the University. The recommendation from the inclusiveness committee was dropped. According to a university spokesperson it was not an academic recommendation.

45   Still, one university alumnus decided to take control. State representative Rick Winkel proposed a law that would guarantee Chief Illiniwek as the official symbol of the University of Illinois. . . .

46   *Durango Mendoza (Native American resident in Rick Winkel's legislative district):* I've met a lot of nice people who have been hurt. And my question to Rick Winkel is, as my wife would say, what part of "ouch" don't you understand? And I would tell him that you need to make sure when you go and try to legalize something that is hurtful, that you have second thoughts about it. And you ask the people—those people who say it hurts and disturbs them. Those are the people you need to listen to.

47   *Rick Winkel:* We have a rich heritage in this country, especially over the past few decades of protecting minority rights. And I think that that's important that we continue to do that. But minority rights aren't always right.

48   *Charlene Teters:* What's at stake for me; my people paid with their blood to have anything left. So I have to guard it and protect it so we have it for those generations yet unborn. And I owe it to those people. I owe it to my children, I owe it to myself.

49   *On screen text:* The Chief Illiniwek Bill passed by an overwhelming majority. Governor Jim Edgar later vetoed the bill.

50   Rick Winkel's attempt to override the veto failed.

51   In 1994, a group of Native Americans from the University of Illinois filed a federal complaint with the Department of Education.

52   Eleven area congressmen, led by Tom Ewing, pressured the department to drop the complaint.

53   A few months later, it was dismissed.

54   In 1996, two more universities dropped their Indian mascots.

55   In 1997, the Cleveland Indians opened the baseball season in Oakland. Charlene Teters was there to protest.

56   She currently lives in Santa Fe, New Mexico.

COMPREHENSION

1. Words to talk about:

   - *sentimentalize* him as a monster
   - sentimentalize him *in retrospect*
   - a *fictitious* American Indian character
   - University of Illinois *trustee*
   - *Off-camera* question
   - inserted *news package*
   - along with *Little Black Sambo* and *Frito Bandito*
   - the Illini tribe, that was *annihilated*
   - *Greek community* that hung *effigies*

2. How long has Chief Illiniwek been used as a symbol at the University of Illinois?
3. How authentic is the representation of Chief Illiniwek?
4. How did state politics enter the picture?
5. Is the matter bigger than the University of Illinois? If so, how?

DISCUSSION

1. Going back to the concept of "Labels of Primary Potency," as explained in the introduction to this chapter, find three or four examples in the film that illustrate how people on each side of the issue react to Chief Illiniwek as a label of primary potency. What emotions does he arouse

for the alums who are most in favor of keeping him? What emotions does he arouse for those protesting against him?

2. Make a list of the points coming from those arguing that Chief Illiniwek honors American Indians and from those arguing that he damages American Indians. Can you see evidence of a mismatch when people try to use logic and historical fact to argue about something that is mainly an emotional issue?

3. Find a couple of places where money enters the picture. Explain how arguments are made more complicated when one group is arguing on financial grounds and another group is arguing on emotional grounds. Try to think of other examples.

4. If you are able to view the video, talk about the differences between reading these excerpted comments from the film and seeing them in the context of the documentary. What parts of the film were especially memorable? Even for the sentences printed on the screen, how was the impact different from when you read them in this excerpt?

WORKSHOP 4.1

Public Naming and Labels of Primary Potency

PART I: LABELS OF PRIMARY POTENCY

Choosing the names for public entities, whether for sports mascots, highways, buildings, towns, or even historical events, is troublesome because the public can't agree on who or what should be honored. For example, in 1996, Governor Christine Whitman of New Jersey took a lot of ribbing for keeping her campaign promise to shock-jock Howard Stern. When she was on his show, she jokingly agreed that if she were elected, she would name a highway rest area after him.

BRAIN TEASERS

Here are descriptions of other controversies relating to symbols and naming. For each incident, identify the group or the individuals emotionally affected by something in the name. What is it that serves as a label of primary potency? How do the situations compare to the Chief Illiniwek controversy?

1. In 1995 a group of Native American activists from the Minnesota-Dakota region released a poster showing a Washington Redskins banner, along with newly created banners for such imaginary teams as the New York Fighting Jews, Chicago Blacks, San Antonio Latinos, San Francisco Orientals, and St. Paul Caucasians. The poster's message: "Racism and Stereotyping Hurt All of Us. Native Americans Know That. Now You Do Too." Actually, the Boston Celtics are named after the Irish who settled Boston, while the New York Knicks (from knickerbockers) are named after the Dutch who settled New York. What is the difference? Why are people protesting against the Washington Redskins and the Atlanta Braves but not against the Boston Celtics or the New York Knicks?

2. In the 1970s, the townspeople of Pekin, Illinois changed their high school nickname of Chinks to Dragons. The name had been created by early settlers who conjectured that Pekin, Illinois, was directly opposite on the globe from Pekin(g), China, and so the town adopted Chinese motifs and names. At the time, and with these particular people, the name had no implication of ill will.

3. The Tomb of the Unknown Soldier in Arlington National Cemetery is now referred to as the Tomb of the Unknowns. Who do you think asked for the change?

4. In an example of what was called being "geographically correct," the Australian government announced that it would call the fiftieth anniversary of the end of World War II Victory-Pacific or V-P Day instead of the traditional Victory-Japan or V-J Day. Who do you think favored the change? Who do you think opposed it?

5. Most Bob's Big Boy restaurants have changed their name to J. B.'s and dropped their logo of an overweight boy in coveralls. The Kentucky Fried Chicken chain now avoids the word Fried by using its initials KFC. They have also excised a reminder of "greasy" by dropping their "Finger lickin' good" slogan.

6. The citizens of Sioux City, Iowa, chose the name Sioux City Explorers (named for the Lewis and Clark expedition) for its new professional baseball team instead of the previous team name of Sioux City Soos, which had as its mascot Lonesome Polecat, a grinning cartoon-style Indian wearing a loincloth and waving a hatchet.

7. In 1989, the Colgate company paid all the expenses for its Far East partners to relabel and repackage the most famous (or infamous) toothpaste sold throughout Asia. Darkie toothpaste became Darlie toothpaste, and the toothy, black-face minstrel figure was changed to a man in a top hat with no markings of ethnicity.

8. When in 1993 the Federal Center for Disease Control in Atlanta, Georgia, announced that it was naming a newly discovered disease Four Corners Hantavirus "in honor" of the area of its discovery on the Navajo reservation, protests were both timely and effective. The Center then announced the name would be Muerto Canyon Hantavirus, but again the name was found offensive because the nearby Muerto (Spanish for "the dead") Canyon had been the site of a Navajo massacre. In June of 1994, the center said it would use the name Hantavirus Pulmonary syndrome for the disease, which by then had killed 42 people in 18 states. The hantavirus family of diseases is named for the Hantaan River in South Korea, where the first strain was discovered when it infected 3,000 American soldiers during the Korean War. Why were there protests to Four Corners and Muerto Canyon, but not to Hantavirus, which is also geographical?

9. On Veteran's Day in November of 1992, descendants of the Sioux, Cheyenne, and Arapaho warriors, who in 1876 defeated the U.S. Seventh Calvary under the direction of Lt. Col. George Armstrong Custer, met at the historic cite to celebrate the renaming of Custer National Battlefield to Little Bighorn National Battlefield. The event was the climax of years of congressional lobbying, which resulted in the new name as well as the building of an additional monument to honor the one hundred Native Americans who were killed in the battle.

10. At the height of Charles Lindbergh's popularity, dozens, if not hundreds, of American towns had streets named for him. But just prior to World War II, when Lindbergh appeared to be a Nazi sympathizer and was given a medal by Adolph Hitler, communities rushed to drop his name from public places. The Lindbergh Beacon, atop a Chicago skyscraper, was renamed the Palmolive Beacon, while in the Colorado Rockies Lindbergh Peak was changed to the less obvious Lone Eagle Peak.

11. In 1993, Mark Twain's name was suggested for a new college in his home town of Hartford, Connecticut. The college was being created from combining the Greater Hartford Community College and the Hartford State Technical College. After a controversy arose, the college was eventually named the Capital Community Technical College. Who didn't like Mark Twain's name?

continued

WORKSHOP 4.1

Public Naming and Labels of Primary Potency   continued

PART II: MAKING COMPROMISES

As development efforts (a euphemism for "fund raising") have increased at colleges, many schools are trading naming honors for donations. Prices mentioned in recent news stories included $50,000 for naming the Dominion Energy Reference Library, a small collection within a department at West Virginia University; $5 million for naming the Coors Events Center at the University of Colorado; $15 million for naming the University of Utah business school after David Eccles; and $100 million for changing State College in New Jersey to Rowan College of New Jersey. Thanks to a donation from Henry Rowan, this latter change went forward in spite of a law suit from a disgruntled graduate who didn't like the idea of his Alma Mater "disappearing."

In 1988, the Oklahoma legislature devised a solution to the problem of who should get top billing when they named a bridge on Oklahoma 99 in honor of Representative Lonny Abbott and Senator Kelly Haney. To be fair, southbound travelers read Haney's name first while northbound travelers read Abbott's name first.

In *Art Buchwald's Paris* (Little, Brown, 1954), Buchwald explains how the French manage to "give honor where honor is due":

> They select an intersection and make a square of it. Hector Berlioz has one of these makeshift squares at the foot of Montmarte, but because conditions are so crowded he has to share it with Adolphe Max, who figured as the heroic burgomaster of Brussels during World War I.
>
> For Max it's called a place and for Berlioz it's called a square, but the intersection is identical.
>
> Another solution that has driven Parisians mad for years is the system of chopping up streets and giving each section a different name. The poet Guillaume Apollinaire was recently honored with a snip of the rue de l'Abbaye. In some faraway districts of the city as many as three men to a street have been honored. A five-hundred-yard thoroughfare in southern Paris bears the names of Ernest Reyes, a composer, Dr. Lannelongue, a once-prominent surgeon, and Paul Appell, who wrote *The Principles of the Theory of Ellyptic Functions* and other important mathematical texts. Each gentleman has a block to his credit.

Here are some recent news stories about public naming controversies. Having the advantage of hindsight, plus not being emotionally involved with the concerned individuals, talk about each event and see if you can think of a way that the controversy might have been avoided or softened.

1. At Iowa State University, $100 bricks were sold to raise money for renovating a building to be named after Carrie Chapman Catt. After the building was in place, statements Catt had made when talking about the voting rights of white women compared to those of black men were uncovered and publicized. Some donors asked that Catt's name be removed from the building because they would not have contributed had they known about her racist statements.

Putting someone's name on a public landmark is bound to be controversial if the change involves removing someone else's name. Because of this, more and more groups are following the French solution that Buchwald describes of keeping the original name while adding the new honoree's name to some smaller part, as shown in the photographs of Arizona State University's Sun Devil Stadium, which since 1996 has contained "Frank Kush Field." *Source:* Photo of Frank Kush Field courtesy of Conley Photography, Inc.

continued

WORKSHOP 4.1

Public Naming and Labels of Primary Potency   continued

2. After Cesar Chavez died, a 340-acre park in Phoenix, Arizona, which was origi-
    nally named after donor Gilbert Alvord, was renamed to honor the revered cru-
    sader for better treatment of farm laborers. In emotional public hearings, the
    change engendered charges of political exploitation and a brawl between two
    Hispanic leaders. (*Arizona Republic,* March 9, 1994)
3. Florida officials were surprised when 103-year-old Marjorie Stoneman Douglas,
    the matriarch credited with saving the Everglades, asked that her name be re-
    moved from a state law that was supposed to save the ecological gem she made
    famous. She wrote Governor Lawton Chiles, "This piece of law was created and
    named without consulting me and without my permission. I disapprove of it
    wholeheartedly." (*Cox News Service,* March 5, 1994)
4. A Phoenix suburban school district acquired land in 1976 but did not build the
    school until 1992. In the meantime, the board traded the 1976 piece of land for
    a piece with a better traffic pattern. When the board solicited name suggestions
    for the new school, a member of the family that had sold the original piece of
    land to the board in 1976 came forward to tell about a "handshake agreement"
    between the then-superintendent and the family. Although the School Board could
    find no records and only one member of the 1976 board was still serving (she
    remembered nothing of the matter), the board reluctantly agreed to use the fam-
    ily's name. (*Arizona Republic,* Aug. 10, 1992)
5. In 1990, the name of Leomar Parkway in Miami, Florida, was quickly changed
    to West 132nd Avenue when Leonel Martinez, the real estate developer whose
    two names were blended into the street name, pleaded guilty to running a drug
    ring over the past ten years.

PART III: LOCAL GUIDELINES

Try to find local policies or guidelines for such community-chosen names as schools,
parks, buildings, athletic teams, churches, and street names. If you do this as a class
project, you might divide up local sources so as not to be an undue burden on those
who would have the information. The most likely sources to get information would be
mayors' offices, departments of parks and recreation, library boards, school boards,
and provost's offices. If there is no written policy, try to interview an official who can
tell you how decisions are made. If the matter is handled behind the scenes, what are
decisions based on? Have there been any public controversies? Your teacher might
want you to write a report on your findings or to bring them back to class for a discussion. In either case, pay particular attention to the definitions that are included in a
policy or in the information you receive.

SEXISM IN ENGLISH: EMBODIMENT AND LANGUAGE

Alleen Pace Nilsen

Speakers are prone to use the division of male and female as a metaphor for many other aspects of life. The differences in language describing and attributed to males and females illustrates the swirling effects of culture on language and language on culture. As you read this piece, think of the many ways that the language you speak has been shaped by the fact that virtually all living creatures are either male or female.

1   During the late 1960s, I lived with my husband and three young children in Kabul, Afghanistan. This was before the Russian invasion, the Afghan civil war, and the eventual taking over of the country by the Taleban Islamic movement and its resolve to return the country to a strict Islamic dynasty, in which females are not allowed to attend school or work outside their homes.

2   But even when we were there and the country was considered moderate rather than extremist, I was shocked to observe how different were the roles assigned to males and females. The Afghan version of the *chaderi* prescribed for Moslem women was particularly confining. Women in religious families were required to wear it whenever they were outside their family home, with the result being that most of them didn't venture outside.

        The household help we hired were made up of men, because women
3   could not be employed by foreigners. Afghan folk stories and jokes were blatantly sexist, as in this proverb: "If you see an old man, sit down and take a lesson; if you see an old woman, throw a stone."

4   But it wasn't only the native culture that made me question women's roles, it was also the American community within Afghanistan.

5   Most of the American women were like myself—wives and mothers whose husbands were either career diplomats, employees of USAID, or college professors who had been recruited to work on various contract teams. We were suddenly bereft of our traditional roles. The local economy provided few jobs for women and certainly none for foreigners; we were isolated from former friends and the social goals we had grown up with. Some of us became alcoholics, others got very good at bridge, while still others searched desperately for ways to contribute either to our families or to the Afghans.

6   When we returned in the fall of 1969 to the University of Michigan in Ann Arbor, I was surprised to find that many other women were also questioning

The Afghan chaderi is particularly confining. The fact that women must put one on whenever they are outside of their homes discourages them from venturing forth.

the expectations they had grown up with. Since I had been an English major when I was in college, I decided that for my part in the feminist movement I would study the English language and see what it could tell me about sexism. I started reading a desk dictionary and making note cards on every entry that seemed to tell something different about male and female. I soon had a dog-eared dictionary, along with a collection of note cards filling two shoe boxes.

7   The first thing I learned was that I couldn't study the language without getting involved in social issues. Language and society are as intertwined as a chicken and an egg. The language a culture uses is telltale evidence of the values and beliefs of that culture. And because there is a lag in how fast a language changes—new words can easily be introduced, but it takes a long time for old words and usages to disappear—a careful look at English will reveal the attitudes that our ancestors held and that we as a culture are therefore pre-

disposed to hold. My note cards revealed three main points. While friends have offered the opinion that I didn't need to read a dictionary to learn such obvious facts, the linguistic evidence lends credibility to the sociological observations.

1. WOMEN ARE SEXY; MEN ARE SUCCESSFUL

8   First, in American culture a woman is valued for the attractiveness and sexiness of her body, while a man is valued for his physical strength and accomplishments. A woman is sexy. A man is successful.

9   A persuasive piece of evidence supporting this view are the eponyms—words that have come from someone's name—found in English. I had a two-and-a-half-inch stack of cards taken from men's names but less than a half-inch stack from women's names, and most of those came from Greek mythology. In the words that came into American English since we separated from Britain, there are many eponyms based on the names of famous American men: Bartlett pear, boysenberry, Franklin stove, Ferris wheel, Gatling gun, mason jar, sideburns, sousaphone, Schick test, and Winchester rifle. The only common eponyms that I found taken from American women's names are Alice blue (after Alice Roosevelt Longworth), bloomers (after Amelia Jenks Bloomer), and Mae West jacket (after the buxom actress). Two out of the three feminine eponyms relate closely to a woman's physical anatomy, while the masculine eponyms (except for "sideburns" after General Burnsides) have nothing to do with the namesake's body, but, instead, honor the man for an accomplishment of some kind.

10   In Greek mythology women played a bigger role than they did in the biblical stories of the Judeo-Christian cultures, and so the names of goddesses are accepted parts of the language in such place names as Pomona, from the goddess of fruit, and Athens, from Athena, and in such common words as *cereal* from Ceres, *psychology* from Psyche, and *arachnoid* from Arachne. However, there is the same tendency to think of women in relation to sexuality as shown through the eponyms "aphrodisiac" from Aphrodite, the Greek name for the goddess of love and beauty, and "venereal disease" from Venus, the Roman name for Aphrodite.

11   Another interesting word from Greek mythology is *Amazon*. According to Greek folk etymology, the *a-* means "without," as in *atypical* or *amoral,* while *-mazon* comes from "mazos," meaning "breast," as still seen in *mastectomy.* In the Greek legend, Amazon women cut off their right breasts so they could better shoot their bows. Apparently, the storytellers had a feeling that for women to play the active, "masculine" role the Amazons adopted for themselves, they had to trade in part of their femininity.

12   This preoccupation with women's breasts is not limited to the Greeks; it's what inspired the definition and the name for "mammals" (from Indo-Euro-

pean "mammae" for "breasts"). As a volunteer for the University of Wisconsin's *Dictionary of American Regional English* (*DARE*), I read a western trapper's diary from the 1830s. I was to make notes of any unusual usages or language patterns. My most interesting finding was that the trapper referred to a range of mountains as "The Teats," a metaphor based on the similarity between the shapes of the mountains and women's breasts. Because today we use the French wording "The Grand Tetons," the metaphor isn't as obvious, but I wrote to mapmakers and found the following listings: Nipple Top and Little Nipple Top near Mount Marcy in the Adirondacks; Nipple Mountain in Archuleta County, Colorado; Nipple Peak in Coke County, Texas; Nipple Butte in Pennington, South Dakota; Squaw Peak in Placer County, California (and many other locations); Maiden's Peak and Squaw Tit (they're the same mountain) in the Cascade Range in Oregon; Mary's Nipple near Salt Lake City, Utah; and Jane Russell Peaks near Stark, New Hampshire.

13   Except for the movie star Jane Russell, the women being referred to are anonymous—it's only a sexual part of their body that is mentioned. When topographical features are named after men, it's probably not going to be to draw attention to a sexual part of their bodies but instead to honor individuals for an accomplishment.

14   Going back to what I learned from my dictionary cards, I was surprised to realize how many pairs of words we have in which the feminine word has acquired sexual connotations while the masculine word retains a serious businesslike aura. For example, a callboy is the person who calls actors when it is time for them to go on stage, but a callgirl is a prostitute. Compare sir and madam. *Sir* is a term of respect, while *madam* has acquired the specialized meaning of a brothel manager. Something similar has happened to master and mistress. Would you rather have a painting "by an old master" or "by an old mistress"?

15   It's because the word *woman* had sexual connotations, as in "She's his woman," that people began avoiding its use, hence such terminology as ladies' room, lady of the house, and girl's school or school for young ladies. Those of us who in the 1970s began asking that speakers use the term *woman* rather than *girl* or *lady* were rejecting the idea that *woman* is primarily a sexual term.

16   I found two-hundred pairs of words with masculine and feminine forms; for example, *heir-heiress, hero-heroine, steward/stewardess, usher/usherette.* In nearly all such pairs, the masculine word is considered the base, with some kind of a feminine suffix being added. The masculine form is the one from which compounds are made; for example, from king/queen comes kingdom but not queendom, from sportsman/sportslady comes sportsmanship but not sportsladyship. There is one—and only one—semantic area in which the masculine word is not the base or more powerful word. This is in the area dealing with sex, marriage, and motherhood. When someone refers to a virgin, a listener will probably think of a female unless the speaker specifies male or uses a masculine pronoun. The same is true for prostitute.

17   In relation to marriage, linguistic evidence shows that weddings are more important to women than to men. A woman cherishes the wedding and is considered a bride for a whole year, but a man is referred to as a groom only on the day of the wedding. The word *bride* appears in *bridal attendant, bridal gown, bridesmaid, bridal shower* , and even *bridegroom*. *Groom* comes from the Middle English *grom,* meaning "man," and in that sense is seldom used outside of the wedding. With most pairs of male/female words, people habitually put the masculine word first: *Mr. and Mrs., his and hers, boys and girls, men and women, kings and queens, brothers and sisters, guys and dolls,* and *host and hostess*. But it is the bride and groom who are talked about, not the groom and bride.

18   The importance of marriage to a woman is also shown by the fact that when a marriage ends in death, the woman gets the title of widow. A man gets the derived title of widower. This term is not used in other phrases or contexts, but widow is seen in widowhood, widow's peak, and widow's walk. A widow in a card game is an extra hand of cards, while in typesetting it is a leftover line of type.

19   Changing cultural ideas bring changes to language, and since I did my dictionary study three decades ago the word *singles* has largely replaced such gender-specific and value-laden terms as *bachelor, old maid, spinster, divorcee, widow,* and *widower.* In 1970 I wrote that when people hear a man called "a professional," they usually think of him as a doctor or a lawyer, but when people hear a woman referred to as "a professional," they are likely to think of her as a prostitute. That's not as true today because so many women have become doctors and lawyers, it's no longer incongruous to think of women in those professional roles.

20   Another change that has taken place is in wedding announcements. They used to be sent out from the bride's parents and did not even give the name of the groom's parents. Today, most couples choose to list either all or none of the parents' names. Also it is now much more likely that both the bride and groom's picture will be in the newspaper, while twenty years ago only the bride's picture was published on the "Women's" or the "Society" page. In the weddings I have recently attended, the official has pronounced the couple "husband and wife" instead of the traditional "man and wife," and the bride has been asked if she promises to "love, honor, and cherish," instead of to "love, honor, and obey."

2. WOMEN ARE PASSIVE; MEN ARE ACTIVE

21 However, other wording in the wedding ceremony relates to a second point that my cards showed, which is that women are expected to play a passive or weak role while men plan an active or strong role. In the traditional ceremony, the official asks, "Who gives the bride away?" and the father answers, "I do."

Some fathers answer, "Her mother and I do," but that doesn't solve the problem inherent in the question. The idea that a bride is something to be handed over from one man to another bothers people because it goes back to the days when a man's servants, his children, and his wife were all considered to be his property. They were known by his name because they belonged to him, and he was responsible for their actions and their debts.

22   The grammar used in talking or writing about weddings as well as other sexual relationships shows the expectation of men playing the active role. Men *wed* women while women *become* brides of men. A man *possesses* a woman; he *deflowers* her; he *performs*; he *scores*; he *takes away* her virginity. Although a woman can *seduce* a man, she cannot offer him her virginity. When talking about virginity, the only way to make the woman the actor in the sentence is to say that "she lost her virginity," but people lose things by accident rather than by purposeful actions, and so she's only the grammatical, not the real-life, actor.

23   The reason that women brought the term *Ms.* into the language to replace *Miss* and *Mrs.* relates to this point. Many married women resent being identified in the "Mrs. Husband" form. The dictionary cards showed what appeared to be an attitude on the part of the editors that it was almost indecent to let a respectable woman's name march unaccompanied across the pages of a dictionary. Women were listed with male names whether or not the male contributed to the woman's reason for being in the dictionary or whether or not in his own right he was as famous as the woman. For example:

Charlotte Brontë = Mrs. Arthur B. Nicholls

Amelia Earhart = Mrs. George Palmer Putnam

Helen Hayes = Mrs. Charles MacArthur

Jenny Lind = Mme. Otto Goldschmit

Cornelia Otis Skinner = daughter of Otis

Harriet Beecher Stowe = sister of Henry Ward Beecher

Dame Edith Sitwell = sister of Osbert and Sacheverell

Only a small number of rebels and crusaders got into the dictionary without the benefit of a masculine escort: temperance leaders Frances Elizabeth Caroline Willard and Carry Nation, women's rights leaders Carrie Chapman Catt and Elizabeth Cady Stanton, birth control educator Margaret Sanger, religious leader Mary Baker Eddy, and slaves Harriet Tubman and Phillis Wheatley.

24   Etiquette books used to teach that if a woman had Mrs. in front of her name, then the husband's name should follow because Mrs. is an abbreviated form of Mistress and a woman couldn't be a mistress of herself. As with many arguments about "correct" language usage, this isn't very logical because Miss is also an abbreviation of Mistress. Feminists hoped to simplify matters by introducing Ms. as an alternative to both Mrs. and Miss, but what

happened is that Ms. largely replaced Miss to become a catch-all business title for women. Many married women still prefer the title Mrs., and some even
resent being addressed with the term Ms. As one frustrated newspaper reporter complained, "Before I can write about a woman I have to know not
only her marital status but also her political philosophy." The result of such
complications may contribute to the demise of titles, which are already being
ignored by many writers who find it more efficient to simply use names; for
example, in a business letter: "Dear Joan Garcia," instead of "Dear Mrs. Joan
Garcia," "Dear Ms. Garcia," or "Dear Mrs. Louis Garcia."

25   Titles given to royalty show how males can be disadvantaged by the assumption that they always play the more powerful role. In British royalty,
when a male holds a title, his wife is automatically given the feminine equivalent. But the reverse is not true. For example, a count is a high political officer with a countess being his wife. The same pattern holds true for a duke and
a duchess and a king and a queen. But when a female holds the royal title, the
man she marries does not automatically acquire the matching title. For example, Queen Elizabeth's husband has the title of prince rather than king, but
when Prince Charles married Diana, she became Princess Diana. If they had
stayed married and he had ascended to the throne, then she would have become Queen Diana. The reasoning appears to be that since masculine words
are stronger, they are reserved for true heirs and withheld from males coming into the royal family by marriage. If Prince Phillip were called "King
Phillip," British subjects might forget who had inherited the right to rule.

26   The names that people give their children show the hopes and dreams
they have for them, and when we look at the differences between male and
female names in a culture, we can see the cumulative expectations of that culture. In our culture girls often have names taken from small, aesthetically
pleasing items; for example, Ruby, Jewel, and Pearl. Esther and Stella mean
"star," and Ada means "ornament." One of the few women's names that refers
to strength is Mildred, and it means "mild strength." Boys often have names
with meanings of power and strength; for example, Neil means "champion";
Martin is from Mars, the God of war; Raymond means "wise protection";
Harold means "chief of the army"; Ira means "vigilant"; Rex means "king";
and Richard means "strong king."

27   We see similar differences in food metaphors. Food is a passive substance
just sitting there waiting to be eaten. Many people have recognized this and
so no longer feel comfortable describing women as "delectable morsels."
However, when I was a teenager, it was considered a compliment to refer to
a girl (we didn't call anyone a "woman" until she was middle-aged) as a cute
tomato, a peach, a dish, a cookie, honey, sugar, or sweetie-pie. When being af-
fectionate, women will occasionally call a man honey or sweetie, but in general, food metaphors are used much less often with men than with women. If
a man is called "a fruit," his masculinity is being questioned. But it's perfectly
acceptable to use a food metaphor if the food is heavier and more substantive

than that used for women. For example, pin-up pictures of women have long been known as "cheesecake," but when Burt Reynolds posed for a nude centerfold the picture was immediately dubbed "beefcake," that is, a hunk of meat. That such sexual references to men have come into the language is another reflection of how society is beginning to lessen the differences between their attitudes toward men and women.

28   Something similar to the fruit metaphor happens with references to plants. We insult a man by calling him a "pansy," but it wasn't considered particularly insulting to talk about a girl being a wallflower, a clinging vine, or a shrinking violet, or to give girls such names as Ivy, Rose, Lily, Iris, Daisy, Camelia, Heather, and Flora. A positive plant metaphor can be used with a man only if the plant is big and strong; for example, Andrew Jackson's nickname of Old Hickory. Also, the phrases *blooming idiots* and *budding geniuses* can be used with either sex, but notice how they are based on the most active thing a plant can do, which is to bloom or bud.

29   Animal metaphors also illustrate the different expectations for males and females. Men are referred to as studs, bucks, and wolves, while women are referred to with such metaphors as kitten, bunny, beaver, bird, chick, and lamb. In the 1950s we said that boys went "tom catting," but today it's just "catting around," and both boys and girls do it. When the term foxy, meaning that someone was sexy, first became popular it was used only for females, but now someone of either sex can be described as a fox. Some animal metaphors that are used predominantly with men have negative connotations based on the size and/or strength of the animals; for example, beast, bullheaded, jackass, rat, loanshark, and vulture. Negative metaphors used with women are based on smaller animals; for example, social butterfly, mousey, catty, and vixen. The feminine terms connote action, but not the same kind of large scale action as with the masculine terms.

3. WOMEN ARE CONNECTED WITH NEGATIVE CONNOTATIONS; MEN WITH POSITIVE CONNOTATIONS

30   The final point that my note cards illustrated was how many positive connotations are associated with the concept of masculinity, while there are either trivial or negative connotations connected with the corresponding feminine concept. An example from the animal metaphors makes a good illustration. The word *shrew* taken from the name of a small but especially vicious animal was defined in my dictionary as "an ill-tempered scolding woman," but the word *shrewd* taken from the same root was defined as "marked by clever, discerning awareness" and was illustrated with the phrase "a shrewd businessman."

31   Early in life, children are conditioned to the superiority of the masculine role. As child psychologists point out, little girls have much more freedom to

experiment with sex roles than do little boys. If a little girl acts like a tomboy, most parents have mixed feelings, being at least partially proud. But if their little boy acts like a sissy (derived from *sister*), they call a psychologist. It's perfectly acceptable for a little girl to sleep in the crib that was purchased for her brother, to wear his hand-me-down jeans and shirts, and to ride the bicycle that he has outgrown. But few parents would put a boy baby in a white-and-gold crib decorated with frills and lace, and virtually no parents would have their little boy wear his sister's hand-me-down dresses, nor would they have their son ride a girl's pink bicycle with a flower-bedecked basket. The proper names given to girls and boys show this same attitude. Girls can have "boy" names—Cris, Craig, Jo, Kelly, Shawn, Teri, Toni, and Sam—but it doesn't work the other way around. A couple of generations ago, Beverly, Frances, Hazel, Marion, and Shirley were common boys' names. As parents gave these names to more and more girls, they fell into disuse for males, and some older men who have these names prefer to go by their initials or by such abbreviated forms as Haze or Shirl.

32   When a little girl is told to be a lady, she is being told to sit with her knees together and to be quiet and dainty. But when a little boy is told to be a man, he is being told to be noble, strong, and virtuous—to have all the qualities that the speaker looks on as desirable. The concept of manliness has such positive connotations that it used to be a compliment to call someone a he-man, to say that he was doubly a man. Today many people are more ambivalent about this term and respond to it much as they do to the word *macho*. But calling someone a manly man or a virile man is nearly always meant as a compliment. Virile comes from the Indo-European *vir,* meaning "man," which is also the basis of *virtuous*. Consider the positive connotations of both virile and virtuous with the negative connotations of hysterical. The Greeks took this latter word from their name for uterus (as still seen in *hysterectomy*). They thought that women were the only ones who experienced uncontrolled emotional outbursts, and so the condition must have something to do with a part of the body that only women have. But how word meanings change is regularly shown at athletic events where thousands of *virtuous* women sit quietly beside their *hysterical* husbands.

33   Differences in the connotations between positive male and negative female connotations can be seen in several pairs of words that differ denotatively only in the matter of sex. Bachelor as compared to spinster or old maid has such positive connotations that women try to adopt it by using the term *bachelor-girl* or *bachelorette*. Old maid is so negative that it's the basis for metaphors: pretentious and fussy old men are called "old maids," as are the leftover kernels of unpopped popcorn and the last card in a popular children's card game.

34   Patron and matron (Middle English for "father" and "mother") have such different levels of prestige that women try to borrow the more positive masculine connotations with the word *patroness,* literally "female father." Such a

peculiar term came about because of the high prestige attached to patron in such phrases as *a patron of the arts* or *a patron saint.* Matron is more apt to be used in talking about a woman in charge of a jail or a public restroom.

35   When men are doing jobs that women often do, we apparently try to pay the men extra by giving them fancy titles. For example, a male cook is more likely to be called a "chef" while a male seamstress will get the title of "tailor." The armed forces have a special problem in that they recruit under such slogans as "The Marine Corps builds men!" and "Join the Army! Become a Man." Once the recruits are enlisted, they find themselves doing much of the work that has been traditionally thought of as "women's work." The solution to getting the work done and not insulting anyone's masculinity was to change the titles as shown below:

waitress = orderly

nurse = medic or corpsman

secretary = clerk-typist

assistant = adjutant

dishwasher = KP (kitchen police) or kitchen helper

36   Compare *brave* and *squaw.* Early settlers in America truly admired Indian men and hence named them with a word that carried connotations of youth, vigor, and courage. But for Indian women they used an Algonquin slang term with negative sexual connotations that are almost opposite to those of brave. Wizard and witch contrast almost as much. The masculine *wizard* implies skill and wisdom combined with magic, while the feminine *witch* implies evil intentions combined with magic. When witch is used for men, as in witch-doctor, many mainstream speakers feel some carry-over of the negative connotations.

37   Part of the unattractiveness of both witch and squaw is that they have been used so often to refer to old women, something with which our culture is particularly uncomfortable, just as the Afghans were. Imagine my surprise when I ran across the phrases *grandfatherly advice* and *old wives' tales* and realized that the underlying implication is the same as the Afghan proverb about old men being worth listening to while old women talk only foolishness.

38   Other terms that show how negatively we view old women as compared to young women are *old nag* as compared to *filly, old crow* or *old bat* as compared to *bird,* and being *catty* as compared to being *kittenish.* There is no matching set of metaphors for men. The chicken metaphor tells the whole story of a woman's life. In her youth she is a chick. Then she marries and begins feathering her nest. Soon she begins feeling cooped up, so she goes to hen parties where she cackles with her friends. Then she has her brood, begins to henpeck her husband, and finally turns into an old biddy.

39 I embarked on my study of the dictionary not with the intentions of prescribing language change but simply to see what the language would tell me about

sexism. Nevertheless, I have been both surprised and pleased as I've watched the changes that have occurred over the past three decades. I'm one of those linguists who believes that new language customs will cause a new generation of speakers to grow up with different expectations. This is why I'm happy about people's efforts to use inclusive languages, to say "he or she" or "they" when speaking about individuals whose names they do not know. I'm glad that leading publishers have developed guidelines to help writers use language that is fair to both sexes. I'm glad that most newspapers and magazines list women by their own names instead of only by their husbands' names. And I'm so glad that educated and thoughtful people no longer begin their business letters with "Dear Sir" or "Gentlemen," but instead use a memo form or begin with such salutations as "Dear Colleagues," "Dear Reader," or "Dear Committee Members." I'm also glad that such words as *poetess, authoress, conductress,* and *aviatrix* now sound quaint and old-fashioned and that *chairman* is giving way to *chair* or *head, mailman* to *mail carrier, clergyman* to *clergy,* and *stewardess* to *flight attendant.* I was also pleased when the National Oceanic and Atmospheric Administration bowed to feminist complaints and in the late 1970s began to alternate men's and women's names for hurricanes. However, I wasn't so pleased to discover that the change did not immediately erase sexist thoughts from everyone's mind, as shown by a headline about Hurricane David in a 1979 New York tabloid, "David Rapes Virgin Islands." More recently a similar metaphor appeared in a headline in the *Arizona Republic* about

40 Hurricane Charlie, "Charlie Quits Carolinas, Flirts with Virginia."

What these incidents show is that sexism is not something existing independently in American English or in the particular dictionary that I happened to read. Rather, it exists in people's minds. Language is like an X-ray in providing visible evidence of invisible thoughts. The best thing about people being interested in and discussing sexist language is that as they make conscious decisions about what pronouns they will use, what jokes they will tell or laugh at, how they will write their names, or how they will begin their letters, they are forced to think about the underlying issue of sexism. This is good because as a problem that begins in people's assumptions and expectations, it's a problem that will be solved only when a great many people have given it a great deal of thought.

Comprehension

1. Words to talk about:

    ■ the *Taleban Islamic* movement
    ■ The Afghan version of the *chaderi*
    ■ suddenly *bereft* of our traditional roles
    ■ when *topographical* features are named

2.   In what ways are males disadvantaged in relation to royal titles?
3.   What three main points did the dictionary study reveal? What was the purpose of the information that did not fall into these three points?

DISCUSSION

1.   Did you play "Old Maid" when you were a child? What was the point of the game? A couple of generations ago, it was the most popular game for children. What connotations does the term have for you? Do you remember when you first heard the term or how you acquired your

LIVING LANGUAGE 4.2

Gender Reflections

Besides bringing new words into English, the feminist movement is bringing changes to language customs, naming patterns, and even basic English grammar.

■   When the Minnesota legislature ordered the removal of gender-specific language from state statutes, over 20,000 pronouns were removed (only 301 of them were feminine). Less ambitious lawmakers have resorted to inserting a sentence in documents saying that pronouns are not to be used for legal implications except in relation to paternity and maternity issues.

■   Of the 43,800 students enrolled in Seattle, Washington, public schools in 1993, 829 had hyphenated surnames. That this naming pattern is becoming increasingly popular was shown by the fact that there were only 26 such names in grade 12, but 111 in kindergarten. (*Arizona Republic,* May 18, 1993)

■   The La-Z-Boy furniture company counters the implications of its name by advertising "his and her" chairs. Manpower Temporary Services communicates that it provides secretarial services by including long-stemmed roses and a beautifully manicured hand in its display ads. The Kelly Girl company changed its name to Kelly Temporary Services dropping the word *girl,* which most women consider best left to children. They also wanted to show that it supplies more than secretarial help.

■   In 1994, an ABC television news story showed workers sanding the artwork from nose cones of planes because of a new United States Air Force policy outlawing gender-specific names and art work on military aircraft. If the policy had been in effect in 1945, there would have been no Enola Gay (named after the mother of the pilot) and no Little Fat Boy atomic bomb. Nor would there have been such World War II airplane names as Lady in Dis-Dress, Slick Dick, Miss Hap, Kansas Farmer, Gravel Gertie, and Satan's Sister.

attitudes toward it? Compare your experiences with the term *old maid* to your experiences with the term *bachelor.*

2. Tell one or two stories from Greek or Roman mythology about each of the mythological characters who are mentioned. Why would people feel more comfortable in naming their towns after Pomona and Athena than after Mars or Poseidon?

3. Do you think the way the language and the media portray males and females as being opposites affects children's expectations of how they should act? For example, do girls try to make their bodies little, while boys try to make theirs big? Do girls sit back and expect boys to take the lead, and do girls spend more time and money on making themselves look sexy than do boys?

- "No more Bearcats and Bearkittens at Northwest Missouri State" read a sports-page story about colleges dropping team names marked for gender. The University of Rhode Island now uses just Rams instead of calling the women's team Wrams. At Wagner on Staten Island the Shehawks have given way to the Seahawks; while at Northern Arizona there are no more Ladyjacks, just two kinds of Lumberjacks. But still, a *USA Today* poll found that of the twenty-five top women's college teams, about half were officially called "Lady," as in Lady Techsters, Lady Tigers, and Lady Tar Heels.

- Researchers Carol Lee Johnson and Helen Petrie reported that one-fourth of the college women they studied in Britain were using a unisex or cross-sexual nickname such as Lee, Robin, Terry, Ashley, or Leslie. Only one in ten men go by names that might be considered cross-sexual, and none of them chose such definitely female names as Sue or Ellen. The researchers found a woman named Jacqueline, who goes by Jack, and a woman named Stephanie, who goes by Steve. She was the first woman to be elected president of a British computer society. (*San Diego Union Tribune,* Dec. 30, 1994)

- In 1996, a primogeniture bill was brought before the House of Lords to change the laws of succession so that the British throne would pass to the firstborn, regardless of gender. The bill's sponsor, Lord Jeffrey Archer, says the bill has the "general approval of the British public," and Queen Elizabeth is known to be in favor of modernizing the image of the monarchy. However, there will probably be no real effect for seventy years because Prince Charles and Prince William are next in line. (*Chicago Tribune,* Nov. 24, 1996)

Workshop 4.2

Evaluating Illustrative Material

No matter what your goal is in writing a paper, chances are that you will use a variety of techniques for explaining and illustrating your point. The authors whose essays were reprinted in this chapter relied on their personal observations, but they backed them up with stories and anecdotes, facts, historical details, news stories, expert opinions, and both short and extended examples. The more controversial the issue or the newer the idea that a writer is trying to develop, the greater is the need for a careful selection of supporting material. Especially today when it's so easy to get material off the Internet and when there are so many "junk" news sources, it's probably possible to gather supporting material for absolutely any point a writer wants to make. To succeed as an honest and effective writer, you need to become a discerning judge of source material.

BRAIN TEASERS

To give you practice in evaluating material and in deciding how you might incorporate various items into an essay some raw data, all related to the word *squaw,* is presented below. Whether you choose to write on this particular topic or to choose one of the other suggestions, it would be good for you to work with this data. By going through it, you may get ideas on how to collect an equivalent set of data for whatever topic you choose to write about.

As a first step, read through the material and then come back and analyze it. It is currently organized according to where the material came from; first, a public event is reported on; next, definitions from various dictionaries are cited, followed by excerpts from related news stories, a history of the word from a single source, and finally a discussion of the word's connotations. As you work with the data, you might get insights from reclassifying it along different lines; for example, historical information versus current information; anecdotal information versus factual information, or positive usages versus negative usages. What parts do you find hard to believe? What parts are particularly interesting? This is important because writers always do a better job if they are working with something they personally relate to. Does the data make assertions that aren't proven or that aren't provable? How can you distinguish between "guesses" and solid information? Where else might you go for further information?

By the time you have become familiar enough with the material to answer these questions, you will probably have thought of an approach; that is, a tentative thesis, which you could set out to develop if you were to write a paper on the word *squaw.*

PART I: AN ACCOUNT OF A PUBLIC EVENT

On December 6, 1996, members of the American Indian Movement (AIM) held a protest rally in Phoenix, Arizona. At Squaw Peak Park and a new freeway named

Squaw Peak Park is the most popular park in Phoenix, Arizona. Every day over a thousand people use the climbing trails to hike up the mountain. Locally, the name became controversial in the mid-1990s when a newly built freeway leading to the park was named Squaw Peak Parkway.

Squaw Peak Parkway, they set out 500 signs containing the word *squaw* overlaid with a red circle and a slash. The purpose of the rally was to ask for the removal of the word *squaw* from geographical sites.

In reference to the protest, this two-sentence letter-to-the-editor appeared in a local newspaper:

> Webster's Dictionary defines *squaw* as an American woman; among Indians, any woman; a female. Did anyone bother to look it up?

continued

WORKSHOP 4.2

Evaluating Illustrative Material   continued

The man who wrote this letter did not understand that looking up a word in one dictionary does not answer all the questions there might be about that word. Look at his letter in relation to the data given below and try to figure out:

1.   What's missing from the intellectual side of the story?
2.   What's missing from the emotional side of the story?

PART II: DEFINITIONS FROM A VARIETY OF DICTIONARIES

- *Webster's New Collegiate Dictionary* (1973) says the word is of Algonquian origin; akin to Natick *squaas* woman. Its first meaning is "an American Indian woman," while the second meaning is "woman, wife—usu. used disparagingly."
- Harold Wentworth and Stuart Berg Flexner's *Dictionary of American Slang* (Crowell, 1975) says the word is colloquial for "wife," and that during World War II it was used to refer to "an ugly prostitute."
- *Merriam Webster's Collegiate Dictionary* (1993) traces the word to 1634 from Massachuset *squa, uddqua,* meaning "woman." Definitions include an American Indian woman or any woman or wife, "usually used disparagingly."
- *Webster's Collegiate Thesaurus* (1976) lists as synonyms wife//ball and chain, lady//little woman,//missus, Mrs.,//old lady,//old woman,//rib, woman.
- *Random House Dictionary of the English Language* (second edition, 1987) says that the word is "often offensive" when used to refer to a North American Indian woman, especially a wife. When used as slang for a wife or for any woman or girl it is "disparaging and offensive."
- Esther and Robert E. Lewin's *Thesaurus of Slang* (1994) lists as synonyms *prostitute, harlot, hussy,* and *floozy.*

PART III: EXCERPTS FROM RELATED NEWS STORIES

- In a letter to the editor, two Native American women wrote:

  The word *squaw* derived from the Mohawk word *genesqua* meaning "female genitals." Early European fur traders shortened the word to *squaw* and its usage implied the crudest sexual connotations. The common use of the term spread across the United States with the settlement of European Americans. Although the word became accepted as part of the English language, through education we have come to understand the word's inappropriate and derogatory origin. Because of this knowledge we propose the adoption of the English translation of the original Akimel O'odham (Pima) name for the mountain: Iron Mountain.

- In an earlier discussion of the matter, some Arizonans defended the mystique and romance of Arizona's place names, which include Tortilla Flat, Whiskey Row, Apache Leap, and Hell's Hole. Others pointed to the magnitude of the task of revising the state's names to lessen offense. The *National Gazetteer,* a publication of the U.S. Geological Survey, identifies seventy-three Arizona locations beginning with the word squaw. Among them are ten Squaw Peaks, four Squaw Tits, three Squaw Buttes, and one Squaw Coxcomb.
- In Minnesota, the legislature in 1995 ordered eleven county boards to rechristen nineteen locations that had the word in their names. The 1995 law against using squaw in the names of public places was passed after two students in an Indian-culture class at a Minnesota high school traced the word *squaw* to a French corruption of an Indian word for female genitalia. Squaw Lake became Nature's Lake, for example, and fifteen other locations have been renamed. However, members of two county boards refused to comply. One county board registered its protest by renaming Squaw Creek and Squaw Bay, near the Canadian border, Politically Correct Creek and Politically Correct Bay. Minnesota's Department of Natural Resources, which administers the new law, said the names were not acceptable.

PART IV: HISTORY OF THE WORD

The *Dictionary of Americanisms,* published in 1951 by the University of Chicago Press, gives these sample sentences to show how the word has been used in written English:

- 1634: "If her husband come to seeke for his Squaw and beginne to bluster the English woman betakes her to her armes which are the warlike Ladle, and the scalding liquores."
- 1642: "When they [Indians] see any of our English women sewing with their needles, or working coifes, or such things, they will cry out, Lazie *squaes!*"
- 1704: "After further examination of the said Squaw they kill'd her also."
- 1831: "The poor Indian died of his scalding, after enduring for a few days the taunts of his companions, for being defeated by an 'Englishman's squaw.' "
- 1808: "I directed my interpreter to ask how many scalps they had taken, they replied 'none;' he added they were all squaws."
- 1879: "He spoke of Mrs. Price and Josephine Meeker heap brave squaws."
- 1950: "Indian women bitterly resent being called 'squaws.' "

continued

WORKSHOP 4.2

Evaluating Illustrative Material   continued

PART V: CONNOTATIONS OF THE WORD

■ The *squa* cluster is fairly uncommon in English. Although not everyone agrees that sounds have intrinsic positive or negative connotations, there nevertheless seems to be a correlation between some sounds and negativity. What other words start with *squa*? Are they mostly positive, negative, or neutral in connotation? Do you think these other words might be relevant to people's feelings toward *squaw*?

■ Oliver LaFarge, author of *Laughing Boy,* which won a Pulitzer Prize in 1929 but is now considered racist and condescending, dedicated his book to "The only beautiful squaw I have ever seen in all my life, whose name I have forgotten."

■ In "The Pocahontas Perplex: the Image of Indian Women in American Culture" (*Massachusetts Review,* 164 [1975], 698–714) Rayna Green showed how European immigrants viewed Indian females as either virgins or whores. She described numerous references from the popular culture showing how young, slender women were viewed as maidens and princesses living in beautiful forest glens. In sharp contrast, other Native American women were viewed as darker and fatter squaws "with cruder, more 'Indian' features," living "in shacks on the edge of town rather than in a woodland paradise."

■ Also contributing to the connotations of a word are the combinations that have been made from it. What is your feeling about these combination words listed in *Webster's Third* (the unabridged dictionary published in 1967 that is used as the basis for many later dictionaries): squawberry, squawbush, squaw cabbage, squaw carpet, squaw corn, squaw currant, squaw dance, squaw drops, squaw duck, squaw fish, squawflower, squawgrass, squaw hitch, squaw huckleberry, squaw lettuce, squaw man, squaw mint, squaw root, squaw side, squaw vine, squaw winter?

■ The most common use of the word in modern English is as a name for a mountain that supposedly resembles the shape of a woman's breast, as is the case with Squaw Peak in Phoenix, Arizona. How has this usage affected people's feelings toward the word? Would you expect its effect to be different on different people?

SUGGESTED TOPICS FOR WRITING

1.   At Arizona State University, women students who served as hosts for high school and junior college football and basketball recruits belonged

to a group named Devils' Darlings, after the Sun Devils mascot. After an incident of sexual harassment in 1992 involving one of the members and a campus visitor, the ASU *State Press* did a story about similar groups at other schools. Reporters found several groups of Mat Maids (working with wrestling teams), as well as the 'Bama Belles at the University of Alabama, the Catamount Kittens at Western Carolina, the Crimson-and-Cream at the University of Oklahoma, Gator Getters at the University of Florida, Hurricane Honeys at the University of Miami, and the Boilerettes at Purdue. An already defunct group at the University of Washington had been named Huskies Honeys. If your school has such a group, see if you can find enough information to write an interesting paper. What is its history? Does it have both male and female members? Does it have a "sexy" name? What is its purpose? Do you get different answers depending on whether you ask group members, your school's Director of Athletics, members of the team being supported, or other students? Over the last two decades, what changes have come about in college sports that make people take a second look at these kinds of support groups?

2. Write about an experience you have had with a label of primary potency. The usual problem with such labels is that people, even those with good will, do not always know that a term is going to have an emotional impact on someone else. A student at Arizona State University, who is married to a woman half as tall as he is, told how, when the couple was first dating, the woman cautioned him to never use "the *m* word." He thought she meant *marriage.* This delayed his courtship for several months until he happened to find out that the *m* word was *midget.*

3. Once we label someone, we have a tendency not to think about the person's other attributes. To give yourself practice in thinking beyond a label, choose two people who could both fit one of these labels: absent-minded professor, computer jock, frat rat, future CEO, Gen Xer, left-wing loonie, religious fanatic, returning student, soccer mom (or another label). Write an essay describing the two individuals. Show how they both fit the label, and then show how they differ.

4. Write an essay on the controversies surrounding the use of sports mascots and team names related to American Indians. Try to tie it into your own geographical area or to experiences you have had.

5. Choose a source to use as data and look at it in relation to the three main points from the essay on sexism and language. For example, find a standard book of quotations (not one specialized for the feminist movement), a book that lists the meanings of names, a book of American folklore, the advertisements in a general purpose magazine, the lyrics of songs from your favorite group, or the jokes in a published collection. As you read a randomly chosen sample, mark any that relate to different attitudes about males and females. See if what you find

supports or counters the ideas that women are valued for being sexy while men are valued for being successful, that women play a passive role as compared to men's active role, and that women are likely to be viewed more negatively than are men. Present the results of your research in a paper.

6. Write an extended definition of a term related to this chapter; for example, activist, feminist, label of primary potency, political correctness, liberal, conservative, and so on. The first step in defining a word is to fit it into a class, then into increasingly smaller classes that will distinguish it from similar items. Descriptions, stories, examples, comparisons, illustrations, and explanations are all useful in helping to show how one concept is different from another.

7. Write an essay on the naming of buildings or streets or some other set of names in your area. Who is honored by the names? What values are reflected? An alternative is to choose one particular name and to write about its history and its present connotations.

INFORMATION SOURCES FOR WRITING

The American Language, by H. L. Mencken, abridged with a new introduction by Raven I. McDavid and David W. Maure. New York: Knopf, 1995. This is a new edition of a classic written by the famous Baltimore journalist. The book, which tells as much about American attitudes and history as about language, was first printed in 1919. By 1936, Mencken had expanded it to a three-volume set, which by 1970 was in its eighteenth printing.

Asian America: Chinese & Japanese in the United States Since 1850, by Roger Daniels. Seattle: Univ. of Washington Press, 1988.

Backlash: The Undeclared War Against American Women, by Susan Faludi. New York: Crown, 1991

The Big Aiiieeeee! An Anthology of Chinese American and Japanese American Literature, edited (with commentary) by Jeffery Paul Chan, Frank Chin, Lawson Fusao Inada, and Shawn Wong. New York: Meridia/Penguin, 1991.

Black Talk from the Hood to the Amen Corner, by Geneva Smitherman-Donaldson. Boston: Houghton Mifflin, 1994.

Culture Wars: The Struggle to Define America, by James Hunter. New York: Basic, 1991.

The Dictionary of Bias-Free Usage: A Guide to Nondiscriminatory Language, by Rosalie Maggio. Phoenix, Arizona: Oryx, 1991.

Discourse and Discrimination, edited by Geneva Smitherman-Donaldson and Teun A. van Dijk. Detroit: Wayne State Univ. Press, 1988.

Ethnic Humor around the World, by Christie Davies. Bloomington: Univ. of Indiana Press, 1990.

Talking Leaves: Contemporary Native American Short Stories, edited and introduced by Craig Lesley. New York: Dell/Laurel, 1991.

Wicked Words: A Treasury of Curses, Insults, Put-Downs and Other Formerly Unprintable Terms from Anglo-Saxon Times to the Present, by Hugh Rawson. New York: Crown, 1988.

A Woman's Place: Quotations about Women, edited by Anne Stibbs. New York: Avon, 1992.

Author motivates with fun

A new tech
of teaching a
children is on
currently for c

More college stud
ecognize three s
han three candic

DENVER- (AP)- In arecent survey conducted by the Bureau of the Int
determined at various areas throughou

ntera' reaches
v heights

, AZ. (AP)—Pantera is being
d off. Repeatedly.
this case, it's street sign, not
opular rock band that bears
me name.
on as we put them up, they'd
hem again."

Sick humor is fun

I would like to take a minute out of my bus

ssage with humor

ge signs execution
er with happy face

Richard Bramley
SOCIATED PRESS

Did you hear
he one about?

NGTON (AP)—There once was a man who decided it would be ben
but you've probably heard it all already before

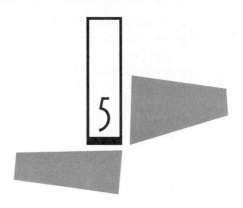

Language for Fun: Humor in America

While humor plays a surprisingly large part in American culture, its characteristics and uses are seldom studied. One of the reasons is that humor is so ubiquitous and so varied. We laugh all the time—not uproarious, knee-slapping belly laughs, but soft little chuckles that are the social lubricant needed to keep the worlds of work, school, family, and love spinning harmoniously. Businesses are finding that happy workers perform better; they're more creative in solving problems, and if they enjoy their jobs they come on time and have fewer sick days. Hospitals are welcoming clowns to patient's rooms, creating humor rooms, and filling humor carts with videos, jokes, books, puppets, and toys. Historians, sociologists, and anthropologists use humor as evidence to corroborate their observations about cultural values and attitudes. Advertisers use humor to attract the attention of potential customers, while politicians use it to divert attention away from their own flaws and onto the flaws of their competitors.

But as with any other powerful communication tool, humor can also be used for negative purposes. E. B. and Katherine White compared joking to playing with the hot fire of truth. Hurtful aspects of humor are often in the news today because modern technology blurs the boundaries between who's telling and who's listening to jokes. Mean-spirited people give humor a bad name by disguising hate speech as riddles or jokes and putting them on the Internet. Others pretend to be using humor when they make sexual or hostile advances and then back off with, "Just kidding! Where's your sense of humor?"

Well-meaning individuals and groups have over-reacted by trying to censor humor, at least the humor that relates to gender and ethnicity, but as this chapter shows humor is much too complicated for such a simplistic solution. It isn't enough to look just at the subject matter of a joke; you also need to look at the attitude of the joke teller, who the intended audience is, and the situation out of which the joke develops, which includes the frame of mind of both the teller and the listeners. Because of such complications, the essays in this chapter were chosen as good examples to study in relation to analysis and evaluation.

WHEN DEMOCRATS NEED TO LIGHTEN UP, HE HAS LAUGH LINES

Dana Milbank

Dana Milbank, a staff reporter for *The Wall Street Journal,* wrote this story in December of 1995, which was about the time that Republican candidates for the next presidential election were shifting into high gear in their criticisms of the Clintons. Have you ever known a "class clown" (perhaps even yourself) who could conceivably do what Mark Katz does?

1   Democrats are leaving the Party. Republicans are having their way in Congress. The country, the president said, is in a funk.

2   There can be only one solution for the Democrats. Send Mark Katz on a congressional joke-finding mission.

3   Paid humor consultant to the Democratic National Committee and a modern-day court jester to the White House, Mr. Katz arrives from New York by train and begins to sniff around Capitol Hill. He talks to staffers, watches C-SPAN and scans the political horizon for setups.

4   Newt Gingrich? "It's too bad he decided not to run for president. He only needed another 10,000 frequent-flier miles for an upgrade to first class on Air Force One."

5   Budget cuts? "The proposed Medicare and Medicaid cuts are the work of the Congressional Ways to Be Mean Committee. Remember the good old days when the Republican Party just ignored the poor?"

6   Abortion? "Now that Pete Wilson and Arlen Specter have quit the campaign, all the pro-choice Republicans in the race have terminated in the first trimester."

7   This isn't Mr. Katz's first brush with fame. In 1984, as a student at Cornell, he appeared on "Late Night With David Letterman" with a poodle that played piano. These days, he teaches tricks to the top dogs. The impish, 31-year-old son of an orthodontist writes zingers for the president, vice president, first lady and Democratic congressmen.

8   He certainly helped Al Gore get in touch with his funny inner child. Until last year, the vice president was stereotyped as stiff or wooden. But after a few sessions with Mr. Katz, Mr. Gore was doing after-dinner routines worthy

of Jay Leno. Mr. Gore had himself wheeled in on a hand truck at one affair and then he launched into self-deprecating one-liners about himself: "He's so boring his Secret Service code name is Al Gore," and "He is an inspiration to the millions of Americans who suffer from Dutch elm disease."

9   The *Washington Post*'s judgment on the performance: "Al Gore, bore no more."

10   A week later, the vice president met Mr. Katz at a reception and gave him a bear-hug that lifted him off the ground—causing Mr. Katz to spill his wine on both of them. ("The Secret Service guy jumped in to take the stain," Mr. Katz says.)

THE PRESIDENT'S GRATITUDE

11 Mr. Katz runs the Soundbite Institute, which is really his one-bedroom apartment on Manhattan's Upper West Side. He is the "resident scholar" and sole employee. On one wall hangs a collection of photos of him and President Clinton, with witty inscriptions.

12   "The egg timer was great," says one. (To lampoon his lengthy State of the Union speech, the president used the timer at a comic dinner, resetting it repeatedly.) Another autograph reads: "Thanks to the spork, there is a Third Way." (Mr. Clinton, courtesy of Mr. Katz, had joked in a speech that the school-lunch program could be streamlined by merging forks and spoons as one utensil.)

13   Mr. Katz's task is to counteract the nightly savaging of President Clinton by Messrs. Leno and Letterman and their huge teams of writers. "They've got cannons on their side," he says, "I'm one small derringer."

14   Mr. Katz's White House role is limited mostly to the four comic dinners of Washington's "silly season," which begins next month. But a performance at the spring dinner of the Gridiron Club—a main event of the Washington journalistic and political establishment—can make or break a career. "Unfortunately, humor is being taken too seriously," says Landon Parvin, who writes jokes for the Republicans.

15   The jitters have a lot to do with what is called "the line." Cross the line and a Washington crowd will gasp. The next day, your staff will be issuing apologies. Ethnic references are very dangerous: New York's Republican Sen. Al D'Amato got into terrible trouble for mocking Judge Lance Ito with a Japanese accent on the nationally syndicated radio show "Imus in the Morning."

16   Also dangerous is humor that is funny but too mean—such as Bob Dole's remark at a 1983 Gridiron dinner calling Presidents Carter, Ford and Nixon "see no evil, hear no evil and evil."

17   Democrats for some reason have been in the comedy wilderness ever since President Kennedy. Would-be jokers, particularly earnest Democrats,

Humor used for political criticism has a long history. The practice of a comedian speaking through one or more dummies goes back to the middle-ages, when the king's fools carried blown-up pigs' bladders as though they were mock scepters. When these clowns or fools wanted to say something especially scathing, they would hide behind their mock scepters. Shown here is Texas ventriloquist Timothy Jones, who uses his dummies in the same way that medieval clowns used pigs' bladders. He shocks people and makes them laugh by the caustic observations he has his dummies say. But today, the success of stand-up comedians and humorous writers proves that we no longer require critics to hide behind a dummy. As political columnist Art Buchwald has observed, "It's wonderful to live in a country where one can grow rich by criticizing the powers that be."

18   are spooked by everything but mild, self-deprecating humor. "Too many liberals have had their funny bones removed," says Paul Begala, a sometime Clinton strategist. "Katz has dragged a lot of liberals back in the operating room." Mr. Katz, however, says he can't make the dull droll. "A page of random one-liners will fit them like a mail-order toupee," he says.

19   Humor plays a therapeutic role, too. When Mr. Katz read some of his lines to Mr. Clinton in an Oval Office meeting, "the president broke out into absolute, uncontrollable, unstoppable, red-in-the-face, unable-to-breathe laughter," recalls White House adviser George Stephanopoulos.

20   Weaned on Watergate and Woody Allen, Mr. Katz started out as a class clown, delivering telegrams in his spare time, dressed as a gorilla. When the president met Mr. Katz's parents, Mr. Clinton praised his wit. His mother responded to the commander in chief: "You know, you just complimented Mark for the same things I used to spank him for."

21   As a gofer for the Michael Dukakis campaign in 1988, Mr. Katz gained status among Democrats with a series of one-liners for Mr. Dukakis, including one applause line for a debate with George Bush: "George, if I had a dollar for every time you used the word liberal, I'd qualify for one of your tax breaks for the rich." Mr. Dukakis, however, was not easily amusing. "Writing humor for the Dukakis campaign was like being staff photographer for *The Wall Street Journal*," he observes.

22   Mr. Katz formed the Soundbite Institute three years ago after losing his job at the ad agency McCann-Erickson. His fees range from $500 for a few wisecracks to $7,000 for an after-dinner speech. He is also completing a book of never-uttered quotations, such as Queen Isabella's remark during the Spanish Inquisition: "I want a crueler, more gentile nation."

23   Mr. Katz's first gig with the White House came in 1993. By now he has a hand in almost all goofy moments, including the Clinton speech at which the president showed up with camera and press badge to take pictures of the photographers. He wrote Hillary Clinton's explanation of her short haircut ("When the president called for sacrifice and asked everybody at the White House to give him a 25% cut, I decided to go for 50%"). She wrote Mr. Katz a sweet thank-you note.

COMPREHENSION

1. Words to talk about:

    - *court jester* to the White House
    - He talks to *staffers*
    - They've got cannons . . . I'm one small *derringer*
    - Humor plays a *therapeutic role* too
    - As a *gofer* for the Michael Dukakis campaign
    - Mr. Katz's first *gig* with the White House
    - "Thanks to the *spork*, there is a Third Way."

2. What brought Mr. Katz to the attention of the Democratic party?
3. What language process was at work when Mark Katz named his company the Soundbite Institute and described himself as the "resident scholar"?

4. Milbank began the third, fourth, and fifth paragraphs with "Newt Gingrich?" "Budget cuts?" and "Abortion?" What was the effect of such abbreviated beginnings?

DISCUSSION

1. Milbank wrote that when Mr. Katz arrives by train in Washington from New York, he begins to "sniff around Capitol Hill" as he "scans the political horizon for setups." Communicate this same information without relying on these metaphors.
2. Why did the reporter choose to quote Mr. Katz's line about "Writing humor for the Dukakis campaign was like being staff photographer for *The Wall Street Journal*"? Why could Milbank assume readers would find this amusing?
3. According to the script model theory of humor, when people are listening to a joke, their mind envisions a pattern or writes a script of what the characters will do. The surprise or humor comes when the teller upsets the listener's expectations by a reference that makes the listener think of a different script. This means that to catch on to jokes, the listener has to know enough about the world to be able to switch to the unexpected script. What do readers or listeners need to know to be amused by Katz's references to:

   ■ Newt Gingrich "needing another 10,000 frequent-flier miles for an upgrade to first class on Air Force One"?
   ■ the Congressional "Ways to Be Mean Committee"?
   ■ Pete Wilson and Arlen Specter terminating their candidacies "in the first trimester"?

4. What did people need to know to catch on to Bob Dole's remark about Presidents Carter, Ford, and Nixon as being "see no evil, hear no evil, and evil"? Even though this was witty, Milbank said it did not succeed. Why not?
5. In the book that Katz is compiling of "never-uttered quotations," what are the two scripts, one historical and one contemporary, that readers have to know to catch on to Queen Isabella's remark during the Spanish Inquisition: "I want a crueler, more gentile nation"?

WORKSHOP 5.1

What Makes Us Smile?

Philosophers, psychologists, linguists, writers, and comedians have all tried to figure out what makes people smile and what makes people laugh. No one has come up with a guaranteed answer, but here are ten of the features that often correlate with what people find funny. And although they can be separately listed and discussed, in actual humor the features are intertwined, working together to contribute to the pleasure that comes with surprise.

1. **Surprise or shock:** The one steady requirement for humor is that people have to be surprised. Sometimes the surprise is of the slipping-on-a-banana-peel type, while other times it relates to hearing talk about a forbidden subject such as a disaster, or hearing a joke teller "dis" authority. Not every surprise is funny, but everything that is funny has an element of surprise.

2. **Superiority:** Even kindergartners laugh at "Little Moron Jokes" because they know they are too smart to do the dumb things he does. In an article asking why there were so many "redneck" jokes on the Internet, the editors of the *New York Times Magazine* (Sept. 4, 1994) explained, "Cruelty and humor are old pals. Secretly, almost everyone relishes making fun of the less fortunate. So as the pool of acceptable targets shrinks, the humorous impulse seeks out people who . . . are supposed to be *bad*—reactionary and racist—and thus deserving of all they get. And there's an added bonus: So few rednecks have computers."

3. **Hostility:** Expressing hostility is closely allied with feelings of superiority because joke tellers may express hostility in hopes of making themselves feel superior to the joke targets. Children make jokes about their teachers, while adults make jokes about their bosses. Sigmund Freud and a whole host of other philosophers and psychologists have claimed that all humor expresses hostility. While not everyone agrees with the hostility theory, those who do say that even puns are expressions of hostility, because the creators are being hostile to expectations and showing they are clever enough to outwit the language.

4. **A trick or a twist:** Remember being fooled by tongue twisters, knock-knock jokes, and riddles where you would get pinched if you gave the right answer because the joke was about someone named Pinch Me Quick? As people grow up and mature, they find more sophisticated ways to trick their listeners, but the fun still lies in joke tellers proving their superiority by stumping their listeners.

5. **Incongruity and irony:** The stories about the cat in the microwave, the rat tail in the fried chicken, the Doberman that is found choking on a man's finger, and the man who dumped a load of cement in the new car his wife was buying for him are urban legends that exemplify the kinds of ironies that fill modern lives. This feature is tied closely to the superiority theory in that people enjoy urban leg-

ends, along with strange and bizarre news stories, because they think they are too smart to let such misfortunes befall them.

6. **Sudden insight:** We smile when a comic writer gives us insight into our own fears or emotions. This is what's at the root of self-deprecating humor and all those confessional monologues, where comedians talk about their personal worries. Such writers as Dave Barry, John Updike, Garrison Keillor, and Nora Ephron are funny because they are so often "right on" as they describe human relationships and emotions.

7. **Exaggeration:** Exaggeration is a useful technique to give people insights because once they have seen an exaggerated portrayal of characters with tendencies like their own, then they will get an image of how they might appear to an outsider. James Thurber's "The Secret Life of Walter Mitty" (1942) is a wonderful exaggeration of a day dreamer. People who are in pain or trouble often tell exaggerated jokes to help themselves feel better about their real situations.

8. **Succinct word play:** The best creators of word play are the ones who hone every sentence down to the bare necessities. One of the reasons they succeed is that they beat their audience to the punchline. There's no surprise left for the comedian who dawdles so that listeners have already figured out the joke.

9. **Ambiguity:** We enjoy the ambiguity of humor because it forces our minds to interact. Joke tellers are notorious for leading us down the garden path by dropping false clues. Our minds have to go to work to figure out and weigh both the false meaning and the surprise of the joke, which is where the pleasure occurs.

10. **Situation:** Jokes told in isolation are never as funny as those created on the spot to relate to real life or to the pseudo real life provided by television sitcoms. We've all heard the half-apology for a lame joke, "You had to have been there." This isn't so much an apology as a statement of fact. The situation and the relationship among those sharing a joke is crucial to many jokes. The surprise and the pleasure comes from seeing someone's mind work so fast as to make a quip or a put-down exactly fit a situation that no one could have foreseen.

BRAIN TEASERS

PART I: IDENTIFYING THE FEATURES OF HUMOR

Here are some examples of jokes or amusing statements. Decide which of the above ten features are primarily responsible for the humor in each one. This exercise is not asking you to put each joke in a definite category. Instead, it is asking you to read a joke and then look at the ten features and decide which one(s) the joke teller used to

continued

WORKSHOP 5.1

What Makes Us Smile?   continued

add to the humor. Chances are that most of the jokes will include two or three if not more of the described features.

(a)   Nurse Patty Wooten, president of the American Association of Therapeutic Humor, collects stories from nurses. In one, a precocious four-year-old was brought to an emergency room with a bad cough. The nurse, who reported the incident, wrote, "She kept up a nonstop conversation while I was trying to assess her lung sounds. Finally, I said, 'Shhh, I have to see if Barney is in there.' The child looked at me and calmly stated, 'I have Jesus in my heart. Barney is on my underwear.'"

(b)   A *Wall Street Journal* article about the new trend of professional child comedians quoted eleven-year-old Claire Friedman, who was on stage at the Knitting Factory in Manhattan. In one of her routines, she told about a classmate she calls Tiffany: "During lunch, Tiffany was staring at her carton of orange juice. I asked why. She said, 'The box says concentrate.' . . . Tiffany is so dumb she'd get fired from an M&M factory for throwing away all the W's."

(c)   During the 1960s, one of the truly elegant and educated women in American politics was Senator Margaret Chase Smith from Maine. There was talk of nominating her for president of the United States. A newscaster stuck out his microphone and asked, "Mrs. Smith, what would you do if you should wake up some morning and find yourself in the White House?" Without batting an eye, this elegant woman responded, "I would go to the president's wife, apologize, and leave immediately."

(d)   David Letterman's first job in broadcasting was at Ball State University's classical music radio station, WBST. He was a constant trial to Tom Watson, the manager, who in exasperation fired him after he introduced the song "Clair de Lune" with "You know the de Lune sisters; there was Claire; there was Mabel. . . ."

(e)   Winston Churchill and George Bernard Shaw had a running duel of wits between them. In one incident, Shaw sent Churchill opening night tickets for one of his plays. He penned a note, "Here is a ticket for you and a friend—if you have one." Churchill sent back the message that he couldn't attend the first night, but "would love to go to the second performance—if you have one."

(f) In *Alice in Wonderland,* the Mock Turtle explains to Alice that he "only took the regular course." "What was that?" inquired Alice. "Reeling and Writhing, of course, to begin with, and then the different branches of Arithmetic—Ambition, Distraction, Uglification, and Derision."

(g) A good man dies and goes to heaven. When St. Peter asks him if there's anything he can do for him, the man explains that he would love to talk to Mary, the mother of Jesus. St. Peter is happy to set up such a meeting. After a few polite formalities, the man tells Mary the purpose of his request. He has always wanted to ask her something. When she encourages him to go ahead, he says, "I've wondered why in all your pictures, you look so sad. Please tell me what it is." Mary sighs, and then with a little wistful smile confesses, "I always wanted a daughter."

(h) Will Rogers solemnly declared, "They have an unwritten law in the Senate that a new member is not allowed to say anything when he first gets in, and another unwritten law that whatever he says afterward is not to amount to anything."

PART II: ANALYZING AN AUTHOR'S STYLE

Read aloud, or listen to classmates reading, Erma Bombeck's "Four Dialogues," starting on p. 206. Briefly describe at least four of the techniques that she uses to make readers smile.

PART III: IDENTIFYING MORE FEATURES OF HUMOR

Read the news stories about humor-related incidents described in Living Language 5.1. starting on p. 210. Each of them contains aspects of superiority and hostility. Identify what else contributes to the humor.

Four Dialogues

Erma Bombeck

These four dialogues about parents teaching their children to drive were published in 1967 in Erma Bombeck's *At Wit's End*. Russell Baker chose to include the piece in his 1993 *Book of American Humor*.

1   [Dialogue between a mother who was told having a daughter drive would be a blessing and a daughter who up until now believed everything a mother did she did out of love]

2   *Mother:* I'm not a well woman, Debbie. You know that. After the last baby, fifteen years ago, the doctor said I would experience periods of tension and depression. I am tense and depressed now. What are you doing?

3   *Debbie:* Putting the key in the switch.

4   *Mother:* DON'T TOUCH A THING IN THIS CAR UNTIL I TELL YOU TO. First, I want you to relax. You cannot drive a car when your hands are gripped around the door handle and the whites of the knuckles are showing.

5   *Debbie:* You're the one clutching the door handle.

6   *Mother:* That's what I said. Just relax and put all the anxieties about driving out of your mind. Forget that behind the wheel of this car you are a potential killer. That you are maneuvering a ton of hard, cold steel which you can wrap around a telephone pole just by closing your eyes to sneeze. Are you relaxed?

7   *Debbie:* I think so.

8   *Mother:* All right now. Let's go over the check list. Do you have flares in your trunk for when you get a flat tire?

9   *Debbie:* Yes.

10   *Mother:* Do you have a dime so you can call AAA when the motor stops dead on you?

11   *Debbie:* Yes.

12   *Mother:* Do you have your license so you can show it to the nice officer when he stops you for violating something?

13   *Debbie:* Yes, Mother.

14   *Mother:* All right then. Just turn the key and at the same time step on the accelerator.

15   *Debbie:* Aren't you going to fasten your seat belt?

16   *Mother:* Are you crazy? I may want to leave in a hurry. Let's get on with it. Just gently touch the accelerator.

17   *Debbie:* Like this?

18   *Mother:* HOLD IT! STOP THE CAR! Let us get one thing straight. The radio has to be off. There is not room in this car for Dionne Warwick, you and me. One of us has to go. You're driving. It can't be you. I'm supervising. It can't be me. Dionne is singing. She is expendable. Now, just relax and push on the accelerator. Any idiot can drive. I do it every day. Just ease along, unwind, hang loose and don't think about the drunk over the hill waiting to slam into you. What are you doing?

19   *Debbie:* Stopping the car.

20   *Mother:* What for?

21   *Debbie:* There's a stop sign.

22   *Mother:* Why are you stopping back here? That stop sign is forty feet away, for crying out loud. Pull up. Pull up. Give it a little gas. Go ahead. NO, WAIT! Do you realize you almost sent me sailing through the windshield?

23   *Debbie:* I guess I'm not used to the brakes yet. I'm sorry.

24   *Mother:* I know. So was Sylvia's daughter. Remember I told you about her? Her MOTHER was teaching her how to drive. She took off so fast she gave her mother a whiplash. I think she's out of traction now. Her daughter is wonderful, though. Never complains when she has to drive her mother to the doctor or adjust her braces. Now then, where were we? It looks all right. Just sneak out and . . . YOU'RE TOO CLOSE TO MY SIDE OF THE ROAD. We're all tensed up. Maybe if we pulled over to the curb here and relaxed a bit. You're doing fine. It's just that you lack experience. Like, when you meet a car you have to remember that anything on his side of the line belongs to him. We can't be greedy, can we? Are you relaxed? Good. Just put your hand out and enter the stream of traffic. Not too fast now.

25   *Debbie:* But . . .

26   *Mother:* If they want to go over twenty-five miles an hour, let 'em pass. The cemeteries are full of drivers who passed.

27   *Debbie:* Do you suppose you could show me how to park?

28   *Mother:* To what?

29   *Debbie:* To park.

30   *Mother:* There's nothing to it. You just go to the shopping center and make a small right angle and there you are. When your tires bump the concrete island, stop.

31   *Debbie:* No, I mean parallel park between two other cars. One in front and one in back.

32   *Mother:* Where did you hear talk like that? You're driving ten minutes and already you want to get cute with it. It sounds like a wonderful way to get your fenders dented, missy.

33   *Debbie:* Our Driver's Ed teacher says that's part of the test.

34   *Mother:* So the Driver's Ed teacher is smarter than your mother. Then why isn't he sitting here getting stomach cramps? That's the trouble with teachers today. No guts. I think we're getting tired, Debbie, I have a headache and an acid stomach. Let's head for home. There's a pamphlet I want you to read on "Highway Statistics Compiled on a Labor Day Weekend by the New Jersey Highway Patrol."

35   [Dialogue between a daddy who was instructed to check out the driving ability of his wife's reckless daughter and daddy's little girl]

36   *Debbie:* You don't mind if I play the radio, do you, Daddy?

37   *Daddy:* Ummmmmmmmm.

38   *Debbie:* Want me to go over the check list?

39   *Daddy:* Neh.

40   *Debbie:* Could I also dispense with "Mother, may I?" every time I shift gears?

41   *Daddy:* Sure.

42   *Debbie:* Want to test me on the "Highway Statistics Compiled on a Labor Day Weekend by the New Jersey Highway Patrol?"

43   *Daddy:* No. You're doing fine, dear. Wake me when we get home. Szzzzzzzzzzzzz.

44   [Dialogue between a father who regards his car as a mistress and a son who is moving in on his territory]

45   *Father:* Do you know how long it took me to get a car of my own?

46   *Ralph:* You were twenty-eight years old.

47   *Father:* I was twenty-eight years old, boy, before I sat behind the wheel of my first car. Got my first pair of long trousers that same year. And I apprecia . . . I wish to heavens you'd stop making those noises.

48   *Ralph:* What noises?

49   *Father:* You sound like the sound track from the Indianapolis 500. Sitting around shifting imaginary gears and making those racing sounds. It makes your mother nervous. Now, first off, before we even start the motor I want to familiarize you with the mechanics of the car. (Lifting hood.)

50   *Ralph:* Okay.

51   *Father:* Here's the motor . . . this big thing over here. This gizmo is the cooling system and the big square box over there is the battery. Understand so far?

52   *Ralph:* You got a real doggie here, Dad. Boy, if it were my car I'd put a spoiler in the front and back to hold the car down, and a four-barreled carburetor . . . maybe even a super charger. Then I'd put slicks on the back wheels for a faster getaway and this old buggy would be out of sight. Incidentally, Dad, you could use some work on your points.

53   *Father:* Get in the car, Ralph. And pick that chewing gum wrapper off the floor. Any questions before we get on with the driving?

54   *Ralph:* I hope you're not going to get sore or anything. It's not that I'm too proud to drive a heap around but could you take out the dog in the rear window whose eyeballs light up red and green every time you touch the brakes?

55   *Father:* Now see here, boy, your mother bought me that for my birthday and I have no intention of taking it out of the car. It would break her heart. And what do you mean with that "heap" crack?

56   *Ralph:* My buddy, Steve, has a vet four-speed, tri-power with mag wheels, Fiberglas body and four-wheel disc brakes.

57   *Father:* Well, there's a lot of it going around these days. You'll notice over here is the glove compartment. Know your glove compartment. You'll find everything you need here for emergencies. Here's a map of the state, a cloth for wiping moisture off the inside of the windows, a box of nose tissue, a pencil, a pad and . . . YOUR GLASSES. That's the third time this month. You know it's immaturity like this that makes me doubt whether or not you are old enough to drive a car. And while I'm about it: What are you going to do about your rusty bicycle?

58   *Ralph:* Dad, could we get on with the driving lesson?

59   *Father:* Don't use that tone with me, boy. You probably think you got a pigeon sitting next to you. You're not fooling around with the typically square parent. What would you say if I told you I knew what "laying a patch" meant? Huh? I know what I'm dealing with. The insurance companies know what they're doing when they set the highest rates for young boy drivers.

60   *Ralph:* In a few months I'll have a car of my own. I've been saving for three years.

61   *Father:* How much do you have saved?

62   *Ralph:* $27.12.

63   *Father:* That dog with the traffic light eyeballs in the rear window cost more than that.

64   *Ralph:* All the guys get heaps and fix them up.

65   *Father:* We'll see how well you drive this one.

66   *Ralph:* Okay, Dad, hang on.

67   *Father:* Look, son, this isn't test run for Platformate. Slow down. You're bruising the tires. And watch out for that car. Defensive driving, boy.

Living Language 5.1

Humor: The Good, the Bad, and the Ugly

When we say that a *punchline strikes* us as funny, that we would rather hear a *barbed* than a *pointless joke,* and that we enjoy *biting* satire from a *sharp-tongued* wit, especially if it's *aimed* at a *target* other than ourselves, we are acknowledging humor's double-edge, as do these news stories about both positive and negative aspects of humor.

■   "South Africans Find a Spot in Common: It's the Funny Bone" was a headline on a *Wall Street Journal* article (Oct. 5, 1995) about the "Madam & Eve" comic strip that explores the changing relationship between a white woman and her black maid. It appeals to blacks because "while madams and maids will never be a relationship of equals," the strip says, "it should be a relationship of mutual respect. . . . For whites, 'Madam & Eve' provides comic relief to their own concerns. There's a sort of liberal white guilt which has been given a sense of catharsis by 'Madam & Eve.' "

■   "A Bus Joke That Fell Flat," is how the *New York Times* (March 14, 1996) reported a controversy between the Manhattan Transit Authority and a magazine that wanted to advertise on the sides of the buses. The Transit Authority accepted an ad reading, "Our magazine is a lot like this bus. It covers the city and comes about once a week." But because the Transit authorities "don't like jokes about people being hit by buses," they refused a companion ad that read, "If this bus hit you and your life flashed before your eyes, would you be bored by what you saw?"

■   In 1994, Comedy Central began using radio to advertise its wares in hopes of reaching the 25- to 40-year-old audience who listen to more radio than television. They started with a satire on the Emergency Broadcasting System, which

That's the name of the game. It's the only way anyone can survive on the highways these days. And don't race the motor. Wait until she shifts into drive by herself.

68   *Ralph:* Well, Dad, what do you think?

69   *Father* (LOOKING ASHEN): Take me home. I have never seen such an abuse to a car in my life. And slow down. You're driving a lady, boy, and don't you forget it.

70   [Dialogue between a mother and her misunderstood driver son]

71   *Mother:* You remembered to open the door for your mother.

72   *Ralph:* It's nothing.

73   *Mother:* Remember, young man, nothing fancy.

---

ended with "while you're preparing for nuclear war, watch reruns of *Saturday Night Live.*" It was pulled when listeners found "nothing funny about the possibility of nuclear devastation." A more successful commercial played with voice mail and calls to a suicide hotline. It would seem to be equally grim, but it worked because the focus wasn't on suicide but on "the frustration of being placed on hold and not getting to speak to a human being." (*Wall Street Journal,* April 27, 1994)

- A sixth-grade teacher in a Tucson, Arizona, elementary school supplemented the regular end-of-school awards assembly by passing out joke awards to her fifteen students. The father of a boy who spent part of his time in special education classes was not amused when his son received a Pigsty Award, a Procrastinator's Award, and a World's Worst Athlete Award. The father sued and won. (*Arizona Republic,* Dec. 4, 1993)
- The April 3, 1994, *New York Times* included a story on the tens of thousands gathered in Odessa, Ukraine, for Humorina, an annual celebration of comedy. "It may be tempting to wonder what there is left to laugh at in this city of 1.2 million, whose Jews gave rise to the bleak, solopsistic humor that New Yorkers often think they invented. But to the true Odessite, for whom pain is a way of life, bad times make great humor. A typical joke at the festival:

  "Happy New Year."
  "It's not New Year's, you moron, it's April first. What are you talking about?"
  "Well I don't know about you, but I just got my December salary and my landlord turned on the heat yesterday for the first time in six months. So it must be January."

74   *Ralph:* Don't worry. You're not nervous and high strung like Dad. Hey, look at the Daytona 500 and behind it the Duster 340.

75   *Mother:* Where? Where?

76   *Ralph:* Over there. Waiting for the light to change.

77   *Mother:* Oh.

78   *Ralph:* A fella at school has a new TT 500 and another one a GTX. Dad wouldn't understand any of this. He thinks a goat is an animal with whiskers.

79   *Mother:* Isn't he a scream?

80   *Ralph:* Mom, do you suppose you could get Dad to take that miserable dog that lights up out of the rear window?

81   *Mother:* Of course. I can't imagine where he got such a corny thing in the first place. Probably something he got with a lube job.

82   *Ralph:* You're groovy, Mom.

83   *Mother:* It's nothing. Drive.

COMPREHENSION

1. Words to talk about:
   - gently touch the *accelerator*
   - She is *expendable*
   - out of *traction* now
   - I'd put a *spoiler* in the front and back
   - I'd put *slicks* on the back wheels
   - *tri-power* with *mag* wheels

2. Chart the four conversations here. What is the key to their differences?

DISCUSSION

1. Some readers have criticized Erma Bombeck for perpetuating stereo-types about males and females. Do you think these dialogues do that, or do you think they are questioning such differences by making fun of them?
2. Bombeck wrote this piece over thirty years ago. Can you find evidence of its age?
3. What other parenting tasks are comparable to teaching a child to drive?
4. Did your parents teach you to drive? If so, were there any similarities to the exaggerated events that Bombeck describes?

OUR PRIVATE LAUGHTER: AMERICAN CYNICISM AND OPTIMISM

Joseph Boskin

Joseph Boskin teaches history and directs the Urban Studies and Public Policy Program at Boston University. He has recently published a book, *Rebellious Laughter*, with Syracuse University Press. He is an unusual historian in that he collects folk humor and analyzes it for evidence of national concerns. He believes that people make jokes about things that bother them. As you read his article, think about the difference between the way Boskin has written about American history in the last half of the twentieth century and what you might expect from a more typical historian.

1   "Whatever else an American believes or disbelieves about himself," observed the perceptive E. B. White, "he is absolutely sure he has a sense of humor." By humor I am not referring to the endless outpourings of stand-up comics, sit-down talk show hosts, television sit-coms, or comedy films and dramas. While all of these can, and often do, reflect the culture writ large, I refer instead to a national seismograph that registers the slightest shifts of society's most intimate moods: namely, the private laughter of people.

2   Within the cubicles of our culture—in the gym, dining hall, and classroom; in buses, subways, and car pools; in stores, secretarial pools, and managerial offices; over telephones, faxes, and duplicating machines; between friends, businessmen, and relatives—there can be heard the disillusioned laughter of folk from every walk of life, region, and ethnic background. Folk humor responds to large events and small happenings. It encourages a laughter that has always existed in American society and that sounds the distress rising up from the national soul.

THE FIFTIES: AMERICAN DREAMS AND THE HOSTILE FAMILY

3   Sick humor took its cue from severe problems afflicting the American family. Powerful socioeconomic changes had occurred after World War II. Intriguingly, sick humor arose at a time of economic and material expansion, buttressed by superficial optimism. Riddle and joke subject matter exposed a

cynicism toward the very changes that were heralded as realizing the American dream. The extreme emphasis on personal striving and sacrifice, the implicit extolling of social Darwinism as the philosophical beacon—in short, the insistence on individual needs over communal requirements—dented familial and religious institutions.

4   The postwar joke cycle mirrored wrenched relationships. Frequently, the drive to attain "a place in the American sun" produced, among its many consequences, an absentee father or two working parents, separate rooms for each child, acceptance of mobility as a mode of existence, numerous residential moves, an accent on material culture, and at the same time, an increase in marital separation and divorce.

5   Sick (or cruel) jokes and riddles centered on the child and revolved around family life. Their humor touched on matters of intimacy, role models, and hypocrisy. Jokes highlighted parental actions as the source of "unlove" and violence that undermined the family, the nation's primary social unit. Sick humor highlighted parental antagonisms and a hostile family environment. Clearly a throwback to the sentiments of an earlier period of family relations, when "a child should be seen but not heard," the opening phrase of the sick riddle is instructive. To logical questions posed by the child comes the harsh parental answer, "Shut up."

> "Hey, Mom, why does Dad always lose his head?"
> "Shut up and sharpen the axe."

> "Mommy, Mommy. Where's Daddy?"
> "Shut up and keep digging."

> Grandparents also were part of the scenario:

> "Mommy, Grandma is starting to breathe again."
> "Shut up, and get that pillow back in place."

> "Mommy, can we play with Grandpa?"
> "No, shut up. You've dug him up enough already."

6   Adult behavior was scorned as being hypocritical, a criticism that made its way into the ideology of the counterculture in the following decade with the phrase "Don't trust anyone over thirty":

> "Mommy, I want milk."
> "Shut up and drink your beer."

> "Daddy, why is it wrong to gamble?"
> "Shut up, kid, and deal the cards."

7   Undergirding the child-centered jokes was the child's own sense of rejection, the intense fear of being ridiculed as ugly and unwanted:

> "Mommy, what's a werewolf?"
> "Shut up and comb your face."

"Mother, why do I have warts on me?"
"Because you are a toad, honey."

"Dad, it's dark down here."
"Shut up, or I'll flush it again."

8   The jokes, however, extended beyond the immediate family to the concept of the nation as family and excoriated parental symbols writ large. Directed at political and religious leaders, the humor suggested that the national community itself was imperiled:

"How did your husband like the play, Mrs. Lincoln?"

"Did your husband get his polio shots yet, Mrs. Roosevelt?"

"Happy Father's Day, Mr. Lindbergh."

"I don't care if your name is Santa Claus, get your hand out of my stocking."

9   Celebrities who had achieved success during the period but who possessed some ethical, moral, or quirky flaw were not spared. The doll joke focused on the perceived shortcomings of specific personalities (for example, entertainers and politicians):

The Elizabeth Taylor doll: Wind it up and it wrecks two marriages.

The Mort Sahl doll: Wind it up and it attacks an administration.

The Frank Sinatra doll: Wind it up and it chases another doll.

The Eisenhower doll: Wind it up and it doesn't do anything.

The Nixon doll: Wind it up and it goes through a crisis.

THE SIXTIES AND SEVENTIES: GRAFFITI AND A GENERATION OF HOPE

10   Suddenly it was over. In 1960 a young and witty president, John F. Kennedy, was elected. A new group of young and witty stand-up comics arose, and the protests and visions of the hippie generation were expounded. Fifties cynicism was replaced by an idealistic buoyancy almost unprecedented in twentieth-century America. A burst of optimistic energy swept through and challenged society. Across the land, a generation wrote its thoughts and feelings on every public space.

11   Anonymous spoofs and jokes skewering American institutions appeared on handouts, pamphlets, and walls. So extensive was the graffiti that in the early 1970s, the city of Boston placed a large, blank board at each of the four corners of Boston Common, inviting anyone who wished to leave a message, protest, cosmic statement, or whatever. Meanwhile, on the West Coast, a bathroom stall at the University of California in Irvine was completely covered

with student scribblings about politics, sex, teachers, the university, God, and, in short, all the pertinent issues of the day. Eventually, someone wrote, "This wall will appear in paperback in the fall."

12   A heady idealism and activism permeated the "Now" generation. The humor of the young focused on political satire, social arrangements, sexual customs, black jiving, female retaliation, and cosmic pronouncements. Subjects considered off limits during the repressive McCarthy era emerged, as did issues that had been too fearful to expose during more recent years. Taken *en toto*, all this laughter expressed a desire to reform if not revolutionize the national landscape.

13   Graffiti was the in language. Either directly or ironically, such comments as these pointed the way to change:

On the Vietnam War:
"Escalate minds, not war."
"Support peace, or I'll kill you."

On drugs:
"With booze, you lose, With dope, you hope."
"Legalize a Spiritual Discovery." [LSD]

On sexual behavior:
"Chaste makes waste."
"Be creative: Invent a sexual perversion."

On smoking:
"Cancer cures smoking."
"Smoke—Choke—Croak."

On gender politics:
"A woman without a man is like a fish without a bicycle."
"Have pill, will."

On the bomb:
"Ban the Bomb: Save the world for conventional warfare."

On social welfare policies:
"Support mental health, or I'll kill you."

14   But the idealistic hope of creating a new world based on abundance and cooperation could not be realized. The energy crisis of the early seventies was followed by a fierce recession. To this sense of precariousness was added a frightening scandal. Watergate seriously impaired the American sense of trust in government. The social compact was clearly disintegrating. Yet few noticed: The workaholism of the Carter years gave way to the management and marketplace mentality of the yuppie generation of the Reagan era, the ideological victory over communism, and the hopeful "vision thing" of the Bush administration.

"THERE ARE ESSENTIALLY FOUR BASIC FORMS FOR A JOKE— THE CONCEALING OF KNOWLEDGE LATER REVEALED, THE SUBSTITUTION OF ONE CONCEPT FOR ANOTHER, AN UNEXPECTED CONCLUSION TO A LOGICAL PROGRESSION, AND SLIPPING ON A BANANA PEEL."

Source: Courtesy of Sidney Harris.

15   Yet the economic boom, the low unemployment figures, the apparent cornucopia of the eighties were flawed and partially deceptive. Careful observers noticed growing numbers of homeless on the streets, the wrenching of lives by corporate takeovers, and an increasing number of technological disasters. The themes of our humor and popular culture moved in response.

THE EIGHTIES: A FRANKENSTEIN IN OUR MIDST

16   Slowly and perceptibly, a series of technological failures, coupled with industrial pollution of the environment, evoked the image of a Frankenstein (a technological creation destroying its scientific creator) in our midst. There was every reason to be alarmed. The list of technological disasters is more horrifying reading than a gothic novel: the near meltdown at Three Mile Island in Pennsylvania; the radioactive explosion at Chernobyl in the Soviet Union; the unsafe disposal of toxic waste disrupting an entire community at Love Canal, New York; the explosion of the spaceship Challenger and subsequent NASA space launch failures; Union Carbide's massive chemical leak at Bhopal, India; innumerable oil spills symbolized by the Exxon Valdez in Alaska; the extensive famines in Ethiopia and other parts of the globe; the erosion of the ozone layer; the poisoning of water supplies and foods; the sudden appearance of a dreadful new disease, AIDS; the rusted collapse of bridges and highways and portions of cities; the crash of airliners here and abroad; and the mounting number of deaths caused by handguns.

17   Catastrophic events of such major proportions were at variance with the rose-colored pronouncements of our politicians. Society was overwhelmed, and a major joke cycle made its appearance: *disaster,* or in Freud's terminology, *gallows,* humor. Clearly, tragedy has its limits, and humankind learns to cope. Eventually, pain must give way not to unrestrained laughter but to humor: Laughter is the primary way of developing a distance that eventually yields to perspective and connection.

18   Even preceding disaster humor, however, certain jokes could be heard that portended a mounting anxiety. No sooner had the decade gotten under way than a hypothetical question pointed to our growing apprehension. The answer reflected a myriad of concerns:

"What are the four biggest lies of the 1980s?"
1. My mortgage is assumable;
2. My Mercedes is paid for;
3. I'm here from the government to help you;
4. It's only a cold sore.

19   By mid-decade, this pessimism had deepened. Now the riddle totally fused economic matters with sexual practices:

"Which one of the following items doesn't fit? AIDS, herpes, gonorrhea, or a condominium in Florida?"
"Gonorrhea—the other three you can't get rid of."

20   The speed with which the new joke cycle and humor made the rounds indicated that anxiety and apprehension were truly nationwide. The jokes often were cited with embarrassment, and some regarded them as being in bad taste. But as Walter Goodman aptly observed in the *New York Times*, "Tastelessness has a firm place in the history of American humor, from the frontier to the big city." Indeed, as he put it, "tastelessness is no disqualification for funniness."

21   The jokes that follow clearly demonstrate an underlying anxiety and anger:

> A new sign at McDonald's reads sixteen billion served, twenty-one injured, five killed.

> "What's the name of the new Russian coin?"
> "The rubble."

> "Do you know what Exxon executives are drinking these days?"
> "Tanqueray on the rocks."

22   Moreover, a discernible *meanness* coursed through the nation. In urban areas, signs proliferated telling people to be careful or suffer the consequences:

> Park your car in this space and I'll break both your legs.

> Shoplifters will be stomped on, kicked, beaten, bounced off the walls. Survivors will be prosecuted.

> Beware of Owner. (A menacing gun pointed at the intruder)

23   And those yellow, diamond-shaped warnings dangling in the rear of automobiles: "Husband in trunk."

24   Persisting throughout the decade was an unwillingness to believe that things were indeed disintegrating. Reflecting this unwillingness, yet also attesting to a certain ambivalence, was this story of the late eighties:

> A man went to the doctor for a checkup. After a series of tests was taken, the doctor ordered him to follow a strict regime: restricted diet, no milk products, no liquor, no smoking, and no sex.
>   The man was aghast at all these prohibitions and asked the doctor, "Will I live longer if I follow your advice?"
>   "No," replied the doctor. "But it will seem that way."

A LANGUAGE THAT ALL EMPLOY

25   The French philosopher Henri Bergson was keen on the connection between the community and laughter. "Our humor is always the humor of a group," he observed. "You would hardly appreciate the comic if you felt yourself isolated from others. Laughter appears in need of an echo." Bergson offered an

illustration: A man was asked why he did not weep at a sermon when everyone else was shedding tears. He replied: "I don't belong to the parish."

26   What the parish has been saying in humor, in its jokes, quips, anecdotes,
and stories, deserves careful attention from those who want to check the country's pulse.

27   Humor reflects the inner workings of society. Every group defines for itself what is—and is not—laughable. Every group attempts to make sense of
desperate or absurd events. Humor reflects what historian Carl Becker, in attempting to capture the prevailing sense of an era, described as a nonquan-
tifiable measure contained in the phrase *climate of opinion.*

28   What, then, is the climate of opinion at the close of the century? It would
appear that the national mood conveys opposing comedic strains, one expressing frustration and disenchantment, the other espousing an upbeat and
cheerful posture. A symbolic good news/bad news joke symbolized disenchantment with public policy:

> Did you hear the good news/bad news about drinking water in the year
> 2000? The bad news is that in the year 2000 the only water left to drink will
> be recycled sewage. The good news is that there won't be enough to go
> around.

29   Worse, a graphic flyer of a bowing clown tipping his hat carries a cynical
message:

THIS LIFE IS A TEST
IT IS ONLY A TEST.
HAD THIS BEEN AN ACTUAL LIFE
YOU WOULD HAVE BEEN GIVEN FURTHER
INSTRUCTIONS ON WHERE TO GO
AND WHAT TO DO.

30   Yes, despite its gallows mode, a graffito imparts the unshakable optimism
that still remains at the core of American culture:

> What do you call a guy who has syphilis, herpes, AIDS, and gonorrhea?
> A hopeless romantic!

31   The people's jokes, as usual, say it all.

Comprehension

1. Words to talk about:

   - the culture *writ large*
   - a national *seismograph*
   - the explicit extolling of *social Darwinism*

- *buttressed* by superficial optimism
- mirrored *wrenched* relationships
- *Tanqueray* on the rocks

2. Boskin uses metaphors to explain some of his points. Find several examples. Try to reword them in "straight language." What's the difference?
3. Jokes are efficient because they leave out information that the listener or reader must provide. What are some of the references you need to know to catch on to Boskin's celebrity jokes of the 1950s and his disaster jokes of the 1980s?
4. Figure out the process of development for these italicized words. Were they borrowed from another language or created through onomotopoeia, through combining or blending old words, or through *metonomy* (being named for something the item is associated with)? Can you think of other words developed through similar processes?

- the source of *unlove*
- taken *en toto*, all this laughter
- the ideology of the *counterculture*
- *Watergate* seriously impaired
- the *workaholism* of the Carter years
- the *yuppie* generation
- the hopeful *"vision thing"* promises

DISCUSSION

1. There are so many jokes told every year that a good writer could probably pick out selected examples and prove almost any point. What evidence besides the jokes does Boskin present to support his observations about the decades?
2. Boskin says that folk humor has been deemed insignificant because of the status of comics in clubs, films, and television shows. Do you agree? Might there be a circular effect with folk humor influencing professionally prepared humor and vice-versa? Can you think of any examples?
3. The creators of successful graffiti messages, along with those who continue to repeat and smooth them out, rely on such poetic devices as rhyme, contradiction, incongruity or surprise, irony, and alliteration. Look at the graffiti he quotes from the 1970s and explain which of these devices is used for each one.
4. Think about jokes that have recently been popular with you and your friends. Do any of them relate to each other? If so, do they fit into Boskin's belief that people joke about things that bother them? Write an essay about a set of jokes in which you explain their significance.

5. Near the end of the essay, Boskin says, "Only in our music does humor meet its match as a conveyor of values and attitudes." Use popular music as evidence for writing an essay about the concerns of a particular period of history.

6. Daniel Harris wrote an article for the *New York Times Magazine* (March 23, 1997), somewhat similar to Boskin's. However, in his title, he asked the question, "How Many Light-Bulb Jokes Does It Take to Chart an Era?" He wrote that the light-bulb joke "mirrors our ambivalent attitudes toward technology," while at the same time being "the epitaph for an obsolete class of household slaves and the patriotic battle hymn of the bedraggled housewife and the diligent handyman." He started with the old joke of the 1950s:

How many Polacks does it take to screw in a light bulb?
Five—one to stand on a table and hold the bulb in the socket and four to rotate the table.

After this example (which earned him a protest letter), he went on to the sixties with the joke about "How many psychiatrists . . . ? Only one, but the light bulb has to really *want* to change." From the seventies, "How many feminists . . . ? One, and that's not funny!" From the eighties, "How many Reagan aides . . . ? None—they like to keep him in the dark." His concluding jokes from the 1990s were: "How many computer hardware engineers . . . ? Thirty—but of course just five years ago all it took was a couple of kids in a garage in Palo Alto," and "How many Dolly clones . . . ? As many as you'd like. As many as you'd like."

Harris observed, "The fact that a single joke is used to belittle the supposed deficiencies of minorities and the esoteric skills of the intelligentsia suggests that, in some sense, we equate the tensions caused by ethnic conflicts with the tensions caused by the new hierarchies of knowledge."

How do you think Harris's article compared to Boskin's? By restricting his evidence to one kind of joke, Harris had the advantage of simplicity. Did they make some similar points? If so, which ones?

STRIP TEASING: "DILBERT" PRINCIPLE: BARING CORPORATE SOUL FOR LAUGHS

William Porter

In May of 1996, *Business Week* reported that Scott Adams's latest book *The Dilbert Principle* was at the top of their best-seller list, "a roster customarily dominated by such titles as *The Death of Competition*." They described the book as "part comic collection, part management-book parody, and all antiboss." William Porter interviewed Scott Adams and wrote this newspaper article in 1995 when the *Dilbert* strip was appearing in 850 papers. A year later it was appearing in more than 1,000 newspapers and on a Web site receiving 1.6 million hits a day. Adams began drawing *Dilbert* every morning between 5:00 and 6:00 before he went to work as an applications engineer for Pacific Bell telephone company in San Ramon, California, but he now devotes full time to his cartoon and book business.

1   He toils in the cubicle of a high-tech company, his polyester necktie has a mind of its own and all the pocket protectors in the world can't shield him from incompetent bosses and unfathomable interoffice memos.

2   His name is Dilbert, and he's the star of what is arguably the country's hottest comic strip. It runs in 800 newspapers, has spawned six books and was the first syndicated cartoon wired to the Internet. Panels are taped to office walls, computer terminals, bulletin boards and file cabinets everywhere.

3   For Dilbert—a portly, put-upon engineer—is Everyworker.

4   "I'm not trying to change the world," says creator Scott Adams, 38. "I do have a guiding philosophy in the strip, which is that everyone is an idiot, in one way or another, and some more than others."

5   Adams just happens to find most of the idiots and idiocies in the workplace. *Dilbert* chronicles all manner of corporate shenanigans, from the shameful to the outright weird. Compared with this world, *Blondie*'s Dagwood Bumstead has it lucky.

6   Along with such traditional fodder as power lunches and washroom gamesmanship, the strip skewers modern officespeak—*quality vectors, mission-critical functions, dignity enhancement programs* and similar terms are heaped with scorn.

DOGBERT'S LAUGHTER GUIDE

THE AMOUNT OF ENERGY SPENT LAUGHING AT A JOKE SHOULD BE DIRECTLY PROPORTIONAL TO THE HIERARCHICAL STATUS OF THE JOKE TELLER.

LAUGHING AT YOUR BOSS'S JOKE

HEE HEE! I'LL HAVE TO REMEMBER THAT.

YOUR BOSS'S BOSS'S JOKE.

HA HA HA !! I'LL HAVE TO WRITE THAT ONE DOWN.

YOUR BOSS'S BOSS'S BOSS'S JOKE

HA HA HA I'LL HAVE TO TATTOO THAT ON MY BACK !!!

Source: *Dilbert* reprinted by permission of United Feature Syndicate, Inc.

7   A bit of typical *Dilbert* think: "Sick days are vacation days with sound effects."

8   Sound familiar? Probably.

9   And that's the key to the strip's mushrooming popularity. Dilbert is powerless, subject to the whims of faceless authorities perched higher on the corporate food chain. Nearly everyone can identify with that, and those who can't are vacationing in Aruba or St. Moritz, ignoring faxes from underlings.

10   Adams' guiding philosophy on business is a cynical spinoff from the Peter Principle. That theory, made popular in the early 1970s, broached the notion that successful workers are promoted until they reach their level of incompetence. Adams postulates the Dilbert Principle.

11   "What's different is that these days, people are getting promoted without ever having been competent at the jobs they are in," marvels Adams, a former Pacific Bell employee who lives near San Francisco. "There are jobs where no technical competence is required at all. It's a reverse of the old master-apprentice approach.

12   "It's a strange time in history when the employees know more than the boss."

13   Adams swears he isn't preaching. "I go out of my way not to educate or teach lessons," he says. "I'm trying to get a laugh. If you ask me if I have any recipes for fixing things, I don't, except around the margins.

14   "And there's probably nothing I lampoon that wouldn't work in some situations. It's just overapplying them that makes them wacky."

15   Adams says his exit from Pacific Bell had nothing to do with corporate spite. It was all very '90s, very *Dilbert.*

16   "I'd let my boss know that I'd leave if they asked," he says. "There was a restructuring, and they wanted to put resources in other areas."

17   His absence from the workplace hasn't halted the flow of ideas. Loyal readers see to that. The first cartoonist to go online, Adams reckons he gets about 3,500 messages each week.

18   "Most of them are suggestions from people who've had some hideous experience during the day," he says. "About one in 100 are turned into a cartoon, but they all have some impact on the way I understand human emotions."

19   A particularly choice anecdote came his way a few weeks ago. Seems a major nationwide bank is buying life insurance on employees.

20   "It's the first case I know of where a company can get a financial benefit from working an employee to death," Adams says. "It's a real reversal from the 1980s, when they were putting in health clubs and gyms."

21   Readers will draw no comfort to learn that some of the most frequent contributors to Adam's idea bank are hospital workers, military personnel and clergy.

22   *Dilbert* is drawn with a simplicity that makes Ernie Bushmiller's old *Nancy* strip a model of artistic ambition.

23   Adams is the first to concede his lack of formal training. At age 11, the Famous Artists School rejected his application because he was too young. He took a lone drafting class in college. He made the lowest grade.

24   His cartooning future was assured by a mundane event: Adams graduated from college and entered the workforce. That was 1979.

25   Adams, who holds degrees in economics and business administration, says it wasn't long before he discovered corporate life bore no resemblance to what he was taught in college biz courses.

26   "That realization took about 15 minutes," he says. "I'm a quick learner."

27   He worked for a bank, then was hired by Pacific Bell. He was assigned to the Integral Service Digital Network laboratory, where "fast digital phone lines" were designed. Ah, cubicle, sweet cubicle.

28   But he doodled at home, and corporate life became the great theme in his cartoons. He submitted a few to *Playboy* and *The New Yorker,* garnering nothing but rejection letters. In 1988, Adams sent his drawings to United Media. They promptly mailed him a contract.

29   Until he left Pacific Bell in September, Adams rose early to pen his strip. These days, he spends 20 hours a week drawing. Not that he's a gentleman of leisure. The comic is a multimillion-dollar corporation. *Dilbert* books, licensing agreements, newsletters—and, yes, interviews—all demand his attention.

30   "Unfortunately, I've started getting up at 6 A.M. and working until midnight seven days a week," he says.

31   Other than the money and fame, his life seems to have remained the same.

32   "I still have the same digs, the same car, the same girlfriend and the same cats," Adams says.

33   His advice to young people leaping into the corporate maw: Learn and experience as much as possible early in your career, preferably through multiple jobs.

34   "Your own skills and ability to sell yourself is your only real asset over the next 50 years," he says. "You certainly can't rely on a company to take care of you."

35   One other thing: "Work hard, make money, go home early. That's my motto."

COMPREHENSION

1. Words to talk about:

   - chronicles all manner of *corporate shenanigans*
   - nothing I *lampoon* that wouldn't work
   - I still have the same *digs*
   - leaping into the *corporate maw*

2. Explain the following allusions. What academic field does each one come from?

   - For Dilbert—a portly, put-upon engineer—is *everyworker.*
   - Along with such traditional *fodder* as *power lunches* and *washroom gamesmanship*
   - A bit of typical *Dilbert think*

- Dilbert is powerless, subject to the whims of faceless authorities *perched higher on the corporate food chain.*
- A cynical spinoff from *The Peter Principle.*

3. Adams skewers modern officespeak: *quality vectors, mission-critical* functions, and *dignity enhancement programs.* Translate these bits of jargon into everyday language. What's the difference in connotation?
4. What is the difference in connotation when Adams refers to college biz courses instead of college business courses.

DISCUSSION

1. Scott Adams says that corporate life bore no resemblance to what he was taught in college business classes. If he had gone to art school, do you think what he is doing now would be more similar to what he learned in school? Why is there often a mismatch between formal education and work in a particular field?
2. Although Adams creates his cartoons about corporate America, why do many of his e-mail contributors come from such nonprofit segments of society as hospital personnel and people in the military and the clergy?
3. At the 1995 annual meeting of the Association of American Editorial Cartoonists, Rob Rogers presented a "Play by the Rules" cartoon that expressed the frustration felt by many of the group's members. An artist is pondering a sign, "No swearing, No nudity, No Religious icons, No ethnic caricatures, No racial stereotypes, No sexism, No non-PC humor, No horseplay," and mutters, "Well . . . that leaves weather cartoons." From his editor's office comes a voice, "Careful not to offend God!" Scott Adams doesn't seem to be bothered by these kinds of restriction. Why not?
4. Porter says that "*Dilbert* is drawn with a simplicity that makes Ernie Bushmiller's old *Nancy* strip a model of artistic ambition." Look at the cartoon on page 224 and talk about how Adams's streamlined approach comes across to you. Most newspapers would give less space to this cartoon.
5. Dilbert's name became a "household word" in a surprisingly short space of time. What makes the name a good choice?
6. Explain the allusion in "Compared with this world, *Blondie*'s Dagwood Bumstead has it lucky."
7. Explain Adams's guiding philosophy "which is that everyone is an idiot, in one way or another, and some more than others."
8. What does Adams mean when he says that one of the contributing factors to worker frustration is that we are in a "reverse of the old master-apprentice approach"?

LIVING LANGUAGE 5.2

Funny Business

This sample of news stories shows that ambitious and hard working people, who also have a good sense of humor, can laugh all the way to the bank.

- "Comic strips pay the bills for syndication companies, because comics can be developed into other properties," explained Lee Salem of Universal Press Syndicate. His company carries *Doonesbury, Cathy,* and *Garfield,* along with such columnists and authors as William F. Buckley, Jr., and Abigail Van Buren, but as he says, "Nobody ever bought a lunch box with a Bill Buckley column on it. . . . One best-selling calendar will make more money than all of the papers pay for the comic in a year." (*New York Times,* Oct. 28, 1996)

- According to *Forbes* magazine, over the past two years television comedian Jerry Seinfeld has pulled in earnings of $59 million and has played a crucial role "in making comedy big money again." His influence even spread to the book publishing world where the success of *Seinlanguage* encouraged publishers to make book deals with such other television comedians as Paul Reiser (from *Mad About You*), Ellen DeGeneres (from *These Friends of Mine* retitled to *Ellen*), and Brett Butler (from *Grace Under Fire*). Television comedies are relatively cheap to produce and can bring huge returns. *Seinfeld, Friends,* and *Roseanne* cost about $1 million an episode but can pull in two to three times that amount in ad revenues while dramatic shows such as *ER* cost 50 percent more to make and usually sell for less because they don't fit as well into the crucial 6 P.M. to 8 P.M. time slot. (September 23, 1996)

- For the 11th time since 1966, the *Harvard Lampoon* group parodied a major magazine and distributed 500,000 copies to news stands. This time they did *Entertainment Weekly.* Their all-time success was in parodying *Cosmo,* "which sold 1.2 million copies with such tantalizing sell-lines as '10 Ways to Decorate Your Uterine Wall,' 'Myth of the Male Orgasm' and a nude centerfold of Henry Kissinger," which Johnny Carson held up on TV. In looking to the future he said that they would "like to do *Rolling Stone* because it has a strong personality and takes on airs. *Rolling Stone* thinks of itself as the record of rock 'n' roll in this country, and a parody should show them that they're taking themselves too seriously. Seriousness is the essence of good parody." (*Folio,* January 15, 1995)

- In 1995 the Polaroid Corporation began selling a camera designed to get smiles with its three professionally recorded jokes and a chip that will allow the photographer to record an original one-liner (8-second maximum). The camera cost $40.00 as compared to its nontalking counterpart at $30.00. Comedian Sinbad participated in a $9 million U.S. ad campaign.

- Veteran advertising copywriter George Rike advised writers of humorous advertisements not to describe their work for clients "as funny or humorous. They're spending huge sums of big serious money and, to them, funny may well mean zany or strange or bizarre or even eccentric. Just say you've tried to make it light-hearted and entertaining, and let them discover for themselves that it is truly side splitting and hilarious." (*Advertising Age,* May 16, 1994)

FROG PRINCES AND FISH AS BUSINESS EXECUTIVES: "YOU HAVE 7 SECONDS TO MAKE SOMEONE LAUGH"

Zoë Ingalls

One of the reasons for including this article, which was published in the *Chronicle of Higher Education,* is to illustrate the complexities of the humor business. For every famous writer, cartoonist, and performer, there are dozens of other people working behind the scenes. Harald Bakken, the subject of this piece, is a history teacher who has an enjoyable hobby for which he gets paid—he writes jokes for other cartoonists to illustrate.

1   Occasionally, ver-r-r-y occasionally, Harald Bakken comes across a situation in which he can't find humor. Mr. Bakken, an associate professor of history at the University of Massachusetts at Lowell, is a ghost writer for cartoonists, providing ideas to help them over the dry spells. Although some cartoonists generate all of their own ideas, most rely on gag writers like Mr. Bakken at least some of the time.

2   Normally, he can turn out about 25 humorous ideas an hour; no problem. "But occasionally I hit something I can't write for at all," Mr. Bakken says. "Like once somebody asked me to do 29 gags that would be funny for turkey growers. I must say I worked at it, but it never did come. So I gave up on it," he recalls.

3   In most cases, however, Mr. Bakken works quickly and seemingly without effort, delivering a spirited, rat-a-tat string of punch lines with the dexterity of a verbal one-man band. Circus seals, paper shredders, and Little Red Riding Hood—almost any topic.

4   Turning to the shelves that line the wall behind his desk in a modest gray house just a few blocks from Harvard Square, Mr. Bakken retrieves a green, three-ring notebook, fat with photocopies of his *New Yorker* cartoons. Although he's written for some 500 magazines, he now works exclusively with cartoonists for *The New Yorker.*

5   One drawing shows a statue of a man. The inscription reads "Soldier, statesman, author, patriot, but still a disappointment to his mother."

6   In another, two angels with harps stand among the clouds. One says to the other: "Do you ever have days when you wish you had a saxophone?"

7   Mr. Bakken has been writing gags since 1974. Whether he's writing for *The New Yorker* or *Ladies Home Journal*, the process is the same: He forwards the ideas to cartoonists, who illustrate the ones they like and assume all responsibility for marketing them to the magazines.

8   Over the years, Mr. Bakken estimates that he's come up with more than 40,000 funny ideas. Even so, "I don't think of myself as a funny guy—certainly not the life-of-the-party type," he says.

9   "I used to tell jokes, used to have a large repertoire of jokes. But it's a funny thing. I don't tell jokes since I took up gag writing."

"Could you repeat that last idea in a form more appropriate for those of us who were raised on sound bites?"

Source: Reprinted from *The Chronicle of Higher Education.* By permission of Mischa Richter and Harald Bakken.

10   He is nonetheless entertaining as he alternately sings, plays the piano, and shares his gags from cartoons past. His voice slips easily into character, taking on the croak of a frog or the brisk tones of a private reporting to his company commander. And he has one of those full-bodied laughs that seem to clap you on the shoulder and urge you to join the fun.

11   "I used to write 150 gag ideas a week," Mr. Bakken says. "Then it just got to be too much to peddle them. So now I write about 25 a week or something like that."

12   His gags have appeared in a wide variety of publications, including *Playboy, Reader's Digest,* and *The National Enquirer,* in addition to *The New Yorker.*

13   "*The New Yorker* is the pinnacle of cartoon writing in this country: in financial terms (it pays the best), in terms of the prestige of publishing there, and also in terms of the numbers (they publish 1,000 or so cartoons a year)," he says. "Nobody else comes anywhere near that."

14   Mr. Bakken says he knew from the time he was a teen-ager in Aitkin, Minn., that he wanted to write for *The New Yorker.* Over the course of his junior and senior years at Aitkin High School, he haunted the library, poring over every available back issue. "I fell in love with *New Yorker* cartoons," he says, "because they were a way into another world that seemed to me to be more sophisticated."

15 After graduating from high school in 1953, Mr. Bakken earned his bachelor's degree at the University of Minnesota and then received his Ph.D. from Harvard University in U.S. history in 1976. He has taught at the University of Massachusetts at Lowell since 1967.

16   Gag writing is a hobby, a "pleasant sidelight," Mr. Bakken says, but not something he could make a living at. As a rule of thumb, the gag writer gets 25 percent of the cartoonist's pay for a single cartoon. He gets about $125 for each *New Yorker* cartoon, "and you can't sell them that many," he says adding: "I think I sell them one every three weeks or so. And they're the top market."

17   Mr. Bakken estimates that there are about 200 professional gag writers. To make ends meet, they frequently do other forms of writing as well: for comic-strip cartoonists, stand-up comics, and greeting-card companies, among others. Mr. Bakken says he has "done a little bit of all of that stuff." He also has written textbooks; two children's books; and a stage adaptation, including book, music, and lyrics, of a children's novel called *Tuck Everlasting.*

18   In addition, last month [September 1992] he completed a book on cartooning with Mischa Richter, the cartoonist he most frequently collaborates with at *The New Yorker. The Cartoonist's Muse: A Guide to Generating and Developing Creative Ideas* is scheduled for publication this fall.

19   In the book, Mr. Bakken and Mr. Richter demonstrate how they come up with ideas. "A lot of writing gags is the sense of how to take an idea and twist it into something that works as a cartoon," Mr. Bakken says.

20   "In a cartoon," he continues, "the rule is, you have seven seconds to make someone laugh. Everything has to shoot for that instant recognition. If you're

a stand-up comic, you can do a little buildup. If you're writing for sitcoms, you've got characters that the audience already knows, and they're sort of primed to laugh at.

21   "But with a cartoon you've got that seven seconds, and if you don't make them laugh they'll turn the page."

22   The "seven-second rule" explains why so many cartoonists rely on clichés, Mr. Bakken says. "In every other form of writing you want to stay away from clichés. In cartooning you absolutely should embrace them. Because if you can twist a cliché, you've got an almost guaranteed audience.

23   "There's one cartoon I did, I showed fish as business executives, all wearing neckties. The chairman of the board says, 'Well, gentlemen, we're about to go belly up.' "

24   Fairy tales also work—"everybody recognizes the premise," Mr. Bakken says. He uses the tale of the frog prince to show how he gets his ideas. His mind and the conversation jump into a sort of free-association joy ride.

25   "So, the princess and the frog: The first thing I did was to start with the frog," he says. "How does he feel about this? Maybe he doesn't like princesses. So he's on the psychiatrist's couch, and he says, 'I have a phobia about princesses.'

26   "Or he has friends who've had their own experience kissing princesses, and they didn't like it. Or they're radical populists, and they can't stand the idea of monarchy.

27   "And then you can do a whole set of things off his family. Of course they're all frogs. And his mother really wants him to be a doctor, not a prince—my frog the doctor—so she's not happy with that.

28   "Then okay, you take the event. He kisses her. She kisses him. What happens? Suppose he doesn't turn into a prince. Suppose he turns into something else. I can think of 20 premises.

29   "He turns into a vampire. He turns into an IRS auditor. He turns into a bigger frog. There's an endless variety of things that can go wrong with this."

30   Mr. Bakken shifts in his chair, then revs up the narrative. "Okay, assuming the kiss goes the way it's supposed to, and that he turns into a prince, so then what happens? Well, you begin to think forward in time. They get married. All his relatives are frogs. So one side of the church has all frogs and one side has all royalty, and so on.

31   "There's a famous *New Yorker* cartoon—it wasn't mine—there's this frog entering a church for a wedding and he says to the usher, 'Friend of the groom.'

32   "Who marries them? Is there a frog minister and a human minister? What about the wedding reception?

33   "I had a cartoon—the king comes up to the queen and says, 'I don't have anything against frogs, but it's damn hard to make small talk with them.' And so on. So then you can do endless things about the wedding. . . ."

34   Mr. Bakken says that once, in a "flash of youthful bravado," he sat down and in an hour wrote 30 frog-prince gags.

35   "Coming up with ideas is like trolling," he says. "You have to know where to put the line down and, most important, you have to know when something's out there, and you pull it up."

36   Frog-prince jokes will probably always sell, but over the years there are ideas that have become passé. Mr. Bakken says: for example, chorus girls looking for rich tycoons—formerly "stock-in-trade for *The New Yorker,*" he says—and, more recently, jokes about bums.

37   Other ideas "phase in and out," Mr. Bakken says. Jokes about the economy, for instance. "All you have to do is save all your economic-crunch gags and wait till the next one comes around," he says.

38   "I've been recycling these gags from the 1975 recession this last year."

39   Asked to give an example, he blanks out. There's a brief pause while he makes up a new one. "Okay, okay. There are. . . . You put two guys on a desert island. One is reading a message from a bottle, 'The President expects an upturn before the election.' "

40   "Cartooning is the most demanding, I think, of humorous art forms, and I love it for that reason," Mr. Bakken says. "You know when you've gotten through at a sort of visceral level. You know that you've really done it, that it really works."

Comprehension

1. Words to talk about:

   - Mr. Bakken is a *ghost writer* for cartoonists
   - a spirited, *rat-a-tat* string of punch lines
   - a large *repertoire* of jokes
   - *The New Yorker* is the *pinnacle*
   - a sort of *free-association joy ride*
   - a *phobia* about princesses
   - a flash of youthful *bravado*
   - coming up with ideas is like *trolling*
   - a sort of *visceral* level

2. How did Ingalls show that she talked personally to Bakken? Why was this important to the story?
3. How much money does *The New Yorker* pay for each cartoon?
4. What basis is he using when he says that *The New Yorker* is the pinnacle of cartoon writing? What does this reveal about point of view?
5. What jobs, besides cartoons, are open to the 200 professional gag writers in the United States?

Discussion

1. Can you see a difference in the style and focus of Ingalls's article about Harald Bakken compared to Porter's article about Scott Adams? The *Chronicle of Higher Education* is read mostly by college administrators and faculty, while the *Arizona Republic* is the largest, general-audience newspaper in Arizona.

2. Harald Bakken made the statement: "In every other form of writing you want to stay away from clichés. In cartooning you absolutely should embrace them." Why? Give some examples of Bakken's clichés and explain how they relate to his "7-second rule."

3. Bakken doesn't seem as bothered by changing social expectations as do such cartoonists as Scott Adams and John Callahan (see p. 241). What evidence supports this observation? Why is he less bothered about restrictions than some cartoonists?

4. Look at the cartoon on p. 230 created by Bakken and his partner Mischa Richter. From whose viewpoint is it? How does it reflect Bakken's "other job"?

5. Divide into small groups with each group taking an old folktale and playing with it as Bakken did with "The Princess and the Frog." Outline the various parts of the story and then see what might happen if you throw in an unexpected element at various stages. How many cartoon possibilities can you generate? Choose the three best ideas to report to the rest of the class. Stories that are familiar enough to work for most groups include "Sleeping Beauty," "The Three Little Pigs," "Goldilocks and the Three Bears," "Jack and the Beanstalk," "Cinderella," and "The Three Billy Goats Gruff." Don't be disappointed if you don't get as many ideas as Bakken got. He's been practicing for twenty years.

In Celebration of the Bad Girl

Regina Barreca

Regina Barreca is an English professor at the University of Connecticut, who specializes in studying humor and how people respond differently to the humor created by males and females. This article, which was published on two full pages of the *New York Times* with numerous photographs, is excerpted from her book *They Used to Call Me Snow White . . . but I Drifted: Women's Strategic Use of Humor* (Viking, 1991).

1   Television, these days, is full of them. Where did they come from, these fast-talking, wisecracking, brilliantly satiric, funny women? They all seem to be a generic mid-30's to mid-40's and have repealed the restrictions that proclaim Good Girls cannot be funny, a rule as tight and unnatural as a girdle, and far more difficult to shed.

2   At what point was Good Girl Annette Funicello replaced by Madonna? (I keep a close eye on both, these two being the only Italian-American women I remember seeing on the small screen.) Both Annette Funicello and Madonna have the same general shape, but Madonna encases her breasts in steel.

3   How did our culture come to accept a woman who could snap back an answer as well as snap her gum? Good Girl Donna Reed has been replaced by Roseanne Barr Arnold, Mrs. Brady has been eclipsed by Mrs. Bundy. Like the new breed of female comics, this new flock of wayward-women characters refuses to hand over the mike without securing the last laugh. What has allowed us to forsake the Good Girl and celebrate the Bad?

4   While growing up, I noticed that only certain kinds of people were allowed to be funny on *The Dating Game* and *The Newlywed Game*. On *The Dating Game* answers could be sort of dirty, and on *The Newlywed Game* answers could be really dirty, because the couples were married. The idea was to make people in the audience shriek with laughter when the contestants got something wrong: "What does your spouse miss most about his bachelor days?" Her answer: "Playing baseball." His answer, "Playing the field." If he also said baseball, nobody laughed.

5   *The Dating Game* was slightly different. The job of the show's bachelorette was to ask questions that sounded innocent enough but could be answered by lines heavy with innuendo. The audience was given permission to

understand the double meaning and laugh in appreciation of the guy's world-liness and wit, but the female contestant could not, under any circumstances, show that she understood. If she laughed, it gave away a terrible secret about her: she was not a Good Girl.

6   Who and what are Good Girls? Melanie from *Gone with the Wind* was the paradigmatic Good Girl. Mary Tyler Moore's character Mary Richards was Good, at least in public and often despite herself. *That Girl* (Marlo Thomas) was a Good Girl. The "good cousin," Cathy, on *The Patty Duke Show* was a Good Girl with an affected English accent. Good Girls did not brazenly draw attention to themselves or their ideas. They looked around to see what the other people in the audience were doing before they let themselves smile or cry because they had learned not to trust their instincts. Good Girls laughed with their mouths shut, if they laughed at all.

7   One observant viewer of early 60's movies, the comedy writer Anne Beatts, notes that Annette Funicello, the original Good Girl, never laughed. Instead, Annette "just put her hands on her hips and got mad at Ricky or Tommy or Eddie or whoever was carrying her surfboard, so that they could tell her how cute she was when she was mad."

8   The "vocational school" girls on the other hand—with their scary hair-dos, heavy eye makeup and spiked heels—joked with the boys, chewed gum, laughed with their heads thrown back, had the last word and came to a Bad End. But even a Bad Girl's last word rarely crippled her opponent. In part, this is due to what the feminist scholar Emily Toth has called "the humane humor rule." Ms. Toth argues that women tend not to make fun of handicaps or phys-ical appearance, things people cannot change.

9   Women, therefore, are more likely to make fun of those in high or invul-nerable positions than their male counterparts. The bosses on *Roseanne* and *Murphy Brown* are treated as inferior human beings. Rather than laugh at the insecure mail clerk who always drops his papers, a "woman's show" will turn its humorous lens on the Brahmins.

10   In *Designing Women* the heroines challenge repressive institutions, such as nonunionized workplaces and the National Rifle Association by making fun of rules that keep such institutions strong. When Suzanne Sugarbaker wanted to protect her prize pig from pignappers, the show turned its humor on the fact that she was permitted to have a gun in her house. If Suzanne, hys-terically selfish and unreasonable as she was, could own and misuse firearms, the argument ran, gun laws needed work.

11   When we watch a woman initiating humor, we are watching a woman who breaks the rules; it is invigorating and inspiring. Here is a woman who speaks her mind and says aloud what we might think but dare not utter for fear of being considered disgraceful.

12   Although the splitting of a woman into an angel or a whore is not partic-ular to contemporary culture (every book from the Bible to *Jane Eyre* seems to

hold the patent to this formula), it has saturated 20 years of television, manifesting itself in bizarre ways.

13   Remember the immortal words from *The Patty Duke Show*: "You can lose your mind/When cousins are two of a kind"? It's a wonder we didn't lose our minds, given the outrageous premise of a program that promised Identical Cousins. In this program, Patty was the Bad Girl, and her twin cousin was the Good Girl. Cathy adored a minuet and crêpes suzette while Patty liked to "rock-and-roll, and a hot dog made her lose control." Cathy smiled. Patty laughed.

14   The Identical Cousin Syndrome is the working out of the Good Girl–Bad Girl split, which presupposes that any one woman cannot be both sweet and wicked. We know that traditional heroes can be both mean and melting: the character Douglas Brackman on *L.A. Law* is considered attractive even though he's stern, balding and subject to flatulence during intimate moments; Bruce Willis's character David on *Moonlighting* looked as if he had just come off heavy medication, but that didn't stop him from being attractive to Maddie.

15   Our heroes often have feminine, vulnerable sides. The Good Girl–Bad Girl split is the division of woman into two parts that seem never to meet. Heroines are not allowed to show any emotional cleavage.

16   Good Girl Cathy typically looked out from underneath her eyelashes while listening to someone else speak; Bad Girl Patty looked straight up and snapped her gum while she spoke. Cathy listened to Beethoven, and Patty's father sighed and said, "I hope some of Cathy's good taste rubs off on Patty," because Patty liked raunchy rock music by the likes of, oh, Chad and Jeremy. Cathy's response to anything Patty did was to sigh and say, "I shouldn't let her do this, but I know how easy it is to get carried away." Ha!

17   Cathy was the perfect Good Girl. From today's perspective Patty didn't behave too badly (put it this way: she came home late, but never encased her breasts in steel). On the other hand, she was as close as 60's television could get to the Bad Girl. Patty would not only laugh out loud, she would laugh at her own jokes. If her boyfriend, Richard, said something stupid, she would whack him on the forearm. Patty and Richard were destined to be the losing couple on *The Newlywed Game.*

18   The plot pivoted around Patty protesting against what she considered unjust: often "injustice" was limited to a plain girlfriend not being invited to a party. Patty would devise a scheme to right the wrong, and she would follow her own enthusiastic but misguided initiative. Then she would fail because she got carried away—Patty's strong emotions or ideas would trip her up. Cathy, the eternal moderate, would eventually be called in like a member of Miss Manners' cavalry to rescue her cousin. Cathy never lost control, not over a hot dog, not over anything.

19   It is Bad Girls who overdo things, make messes and are reluctant to control themselves. Good Girls, you see, are never supposed to be too much of any one thing.

20   Lucy Ricardo was always too much. Almost all episodes of *I Love Lucy* deal with Lucy's excess—excess ambition (to be in the chorus at Ricky's club), excess desire for attention (to play the lead in the charity pageant) or longing or envy. Lucy always tried and failed; she was more Patty than Cathy.

21   What, after all, was so funny about the show? Well, Lucy wanted to do things—she wasn't content only to play house with big and Little Ricky, keep the apartment clean and cook balanced meals. Each show took Lucy through ambition and deposited her safely back into domesticity—until next time.

22   Control is the quality most explicitly associated with Good Girls. Immune to temptation, the Good Girl can be counted on to have a sobering influence on any group by her very presence. Good Girls don't swear, sweat, succumb, or, most significantly, satirize. We can deduce from this catalogue of characteristics that there are, in fact, no Good Girls in real life. Everybody sweats.

23   Despair though we might at the thought of Madonna or Roseanne as heroines, we must applaud the way they have blurred the line between acceptable and unacceptable behavior for women. And, if we're lucky, the progressive blurring of these lines might, in time, erase them. A recent study has shown that, while in 1947 high-school girls identified almost exclusively with Melanie Wilkes from *Gone with the Wind*, within the last few years virtually all girls identified with Scarlett O'Hara.

24   We are free, in other words, to hope that women are moving away from the insidious grip of the ghost of the Good Girl. Yet even when we are no longer schoolgirls, we often carry around with us an idea about what this Good Girl is meant to be, and this image torments us without giving us help. It's like having a Barbie doll for a role model: attractive but sexless. Decorous but mute. And (echoes of *Pretty Woman?*), easy to position and dress, but basically boring. Nobody—no body—looks like a Barbie. We all laugh out loud. And nobody is always a Good Girl.

COMPREHENSION

1. Words to talk about:

   ■   the job of the show's *bachelorette*
   ■   lines heavy with *innuendo*
   ■   the "*vocational school*" girls
   ■   turn its humorous lens on the *Brahmins*
   ■   deposited her safely back into *domesticity*

2. Look closely at the way Barreca builds her paragraphs. Find two or three paragraphs that build nicely to a concluding sentence that "says it all."

Discussion

1. Find some good comparisons (either metaphors or similes) in Barreca's piece. Why are they effective?
2. Humor scholars are often criticized for writing about other people's humor in a deadly, boring fashion. Barreca does not get criticized for this. Why not? Find a few lines to show that she too has a sense of humor and the ability to communicate it. She is especially good at creating succinct but balanced sentences. Find two or three examples.
3. Expound a bit on Barreca's statement that the Good Girl image is "like having a Barbie doll for a role model." Why do you think the Barbie doll has become such an icon?
4. What is "the humane humor rule"? Do you think the use of this "rule" is determined by gender? Could there be other factors?
5. Only a very few animals have species names that make them sound female. The two most common of such names are ladybug and black widow spider. There are both male and female ladybugs and black widow spiders. Why did these two species names make people think of females? What connection does their naming have with Barreca's statement that "every book from the Bible to *Jane Eyre* seems to hold the patent" on the formula of "the splitting of a woman into an angel or a whore"?
6. As sidebars to Barreca's piece, the *New York Times* listed present and past Cathys (so named for the "good" cousin on *The Patty Duke Show*) and present and past Pattys (so named for the wild cousin).

   The Cathys are "sweet, never lose control and neither sweat nor swear." Cathys of the Past include:

Krystle Carrington	Annette Funicello	Donna Reed
Doris Day	Gidget	Mary Richards
Mamie Eisenhower	The Madonna	Snow White
Chris Evert	Miss Marple	Melanie Wilkes
Jane Eyre	Mary Tyler Moore	

Cathys of Today include:

Any Miss America (except Vanessa Williams)	Ann Landers	Sally Ride
Ariel, the Little Mermaid	Princess Leia	Dr. Ruth
Barbara Bush	Lisa, Bart Simpson's little sister	Martha Stewart
Katie Couric	Penny Marshall	Amy Tan
Jane Fonda, as exercise guru to the nation	Yoko Ono, as a widow	Ivana Trump, post-divorce
Amy Grant	Jane Pauley	

Pattys "overdo things, make messes and are reluctant to control them-selves." Pattys of the Past include:

Morticia Addams
Betty Boop
Lucrezia Borgia
Catwoman
Alexis Colby
Cruella DeVil

Jane Fonda, from Barbarella to Hanoi Jane
Janis Joplin
Natassia Kinski
Scarlett O'Hara

Yoko Ono, as the woman who "broke up" the Beatles
Lucy Ricardo
Suzanne Sugarbaker
Mae West

Pattys of Today include:

Roseanne Barr Arnold
Sandra Bernhard
Elayne Boosler
Murphy Brown
Delta Burke
Carla (*Cheers*)
Duchess of York

Linda Ellerbee
Leona Helmsley
Kitty Kelley
C. J. Lamb (*L.A. Law*)
Fran Lebowitz
Madonna
Bette Midler

Jessica Rabbit
Joan Rivers
Judy Tenuta
Thelma and Louise
V. I. Warshawski

Who are these women? On what basis were the groupings made? Do you agree with them? Can you think of others to add? What does the fact that we know most of these women tell us about the mass media and our worship of celebrities?

7. Barreca wrote about things that most of us have seen all our lives. Did she make you think differently about them? A good critic is one who gives you new insights or provides you with new ways of looking at old things. Did Barreca do this? If so, in what ways?

DEFIANTLY INCORRECT: THE HUMOR OF JOHN CALLAHAN

Timothy Egan

Even though humor has come under suspicion in these politically correct times, cartoonist John Callahan isn't convinced that banishing laughter is a 100 percent positive thing to do. He is a recovering alcoholic with a severed spine, and in 1996 when he ran for the Oregon state legislature, he announced his candidacy by saying he wanted to be Oregon's first "openly quadriplegic" state legislator. The New York Times offered the opinion that "Mr. Callahan's biggest problem could be his paper trail." But Callahan says he is ready for critics. His girlfriend is a strong feminist who beats him "over the head with her Birkenstocks whenever she gets mad." As you read this article, think about the difficulties of creating cartoons that will surprise but not offend the millions of individuals likely to see a nationally syndicated cartoon.

1   The parade of personality disorders, all the men who hate women and the women who love them, marches on in the talk shows of America. Each day brings new revelations, darker and more embarrassing than the previous ones, the kind of details that were once confined to an analyst's couch but now fuel the self-confession racket practiced by Oprah, Geraldo, Donahue and a half-dozen others. John Callahan sits in his small basement apartment in Portland, Ore., his television tuned to the so-called reality shows, and he is inspired.

2   He draws a small, streetside restaurant, the door shut, no one inside. And in the window, he puts a sign: "The Anorexic Cafe, Now Closed 24 Hours a Day."

3   Another day, another image comes to mind. Callahan sketches a blind man and his Seeing Eye dog, walking on an airport Tarmac toward a plane, escorted by a flight attendant. "We've arranged a window seat for your dog so you can enjoy the view," the stewardess says to the blind man.

4   Callahan imagines a twist on a classic story, and draws four small islands, each with a person sitting on it frowning. He labels the cartoon "The Dysfunctional Family Robinson."

5   Finally, he turns on the medium itself. A condemned man sits tied to an electric chair, awaiting the end. Next to him, behind a desk, is a talk-show host. "So," the host asks, "where do you go from here?"

" NOW, CLASS, IS THIS MAN LYING OR LAYING IN THE GUTTER?"

Source: John Callahan cartoon from his collection of cartoons, *Do What He Says! He's Crazy!*

6   Anorexia, blindness, dysfunctional families and the death penalty—in a good week, all of those topics can find their way into the cartoons of John Callahan. Reality, as presented in the tell-all talk shows, provides a steady flow of ideas. He drew a cartoon in March, showing Geraldo Rivera on his knees saying his bedtime prayers. "Thank you, God, for all the tragedy, wretchedness and perversion in the world," Geraldo says.

7   But for his ongoing source of inspiration, Callahan does not need television; for that, he has himself. Abandoned at birth by his mother, he was educated by Roman Catholic nuns of the old-style school of guilt and harsh discipline, became an alcoholic by the age of 12 and then was paralyzed in an auto accident shortly after his 21st birthday. On any given day, Callahan may call on his family isolation, his religion, his alcoholism or the view from his wheelchair to bring life to a blank sheet of paper.

8   At age 41, he finds himself at the center of a debate raging in editorial offices across the country over how far to push the edge of humor in the venerable American craft of cartooning. His 1989 autobiography, *Don't Worry, He Won't Get Far on Foot,* published by William Morrow, was a critical and commercial hit, introducing a voice that had rarely been heard among the volumes of stories about people overcoming physical disasters. It was inspirational, the critics said, but not in the traditional sense of such works. When the actor

William Hurt purchased the rights to make a movie about Callahan's life, based on the book, the cartoonist had one reservation, "Just don't call it 'Children of a Lesser Quad,' " he said.

9   Two books of cartoons, "Do Not Disturb Any Further" and "Digesting the Child Within," and weekly syndication in more than 40 newspapers have helped to establish Callahan among the new breed of quirky sketch-and-gag artists like Gary Larson, creator of the phenomenally popular "Far Side," and Berke Breathed, who won a Pulitzer Prize in 1987 for "Bloom County," a strip he has since discontinued in favor of a new cartoon. "Doonsbury" may trouble editors for its political satire, but Callahan is often accused of doing something that many readers consider more sinister: making fun of invalids and animals.

10   Callahan has yet to achieve the sort of mass-market fame of his friend Larson, who lives in Seattle, or that of another cartoonist and former Portland resident, Matt Groening, the creator of "The Simpsons" on Fox Broadcasting and "Life in Hell," a syndicated strip.

11   In all likelihood, his drawings will never end up on every other coffee cup because they are so polarizing. He is either brilliant and savagely honest, as many fans, in and out of wheelchairs, have told him in letters and phone calls. Or he is sick, making fun of the most vulnerable people in society, as some organizations that represent the disabled have told him.

12   This year [1992] is a landmark for the 43 million Americans whom the Government classifies as physically or mentally impaired. The Americans with Disabilities Act, some of which went into effect in January, forbids bias in hiring and requires businesses and public offices to accommodate the disabled. It has been called the most sweeping anti-discrimination law since the Civil Rights Act of 1964. For all the liberating intent of the new law, Callahan would add another dimension, one that defies legislation: the freedom of the disabled to laugh at themselves.

13   Not that being crippled, blind or diseased is inherently funny. Obviously it is not. But, says Callahan that does not mean pity should monopolize all feelings for or about the disabled.

14   "I'm sick and tired of people who presume to speak for the disabled," says Callahan, wheeling down the street in Portland, where he is a celebrity. "The question of what is off-limits should not be defined by some special interest group. The audience, the readers, should decide."

15   Just as Lenny Bruce broke the rules of stand-up comedy in the early 1960s, Callahan sees himself as a rebel force against politically correct views and people who are trying to narrow the boundaries of appropriate humor. The last thing he wants is to be called by one of the new euphemisms for people with disabilities, terms like "vertically challenged" for dwarfs or "otherly abled" for someone in a wheelchair.

16   "Call me a gimp, call me a cripple, call me paralyzed for life, but just don't call me something that I'm not," he says. "I'm not differently abled. I can't

walk. But I also hate it when people say 'wheelchair-bound.' People who can walk are not car-bound."

17   Callahan's words, which can seem bitter and harsh at times, are softened by the way he talks. He drops one-liners, throwaway jokes and self-deprecatory remarks about himself in between barbs aimed at his critics. On an otherwise gloomy, recent visit to the doctor, he says, "Why couldn't I have walking pneumonia?"

18   He has a mop of fading red hair, a ruddy complexion scarred by adolescent acne and a large body, 6 foot 3, that seems uncomfortably tied into his wheelchair. He struggles with his weight. A cartoon of his reflects the strain of trying to exercise. The drawing shows an aerobics class for quadriplegics. The instructor says, "O. K., let's get those eyeballs moving."

19   The tools of his artistry are simple, pen and sketch pad, but the mechanics are not. Unable to move all his fingers, he draws by clutching a pen in his right hand and then guiding it slowly across the page with his left. He produces 3 to 10 cartoons a week.

20   A few years ago, just as Callahan's cartoons were starting to catch on nationally, he found himself in trouble over one particular drawing. It showed a dark-skinned beggar in the street, wearing a sign that read: "Please help me. I am blind and black, but not musical."

21   Letters poured in to some of the papers that carry Callahan, most of which are on the West Coast. How dare he make fun of blind people, or blacks, or both, the letter writers insisted. Callahan was a bit taken aback by the critics, some of whom accused him of racism. In the midst of the controversy, Callahan says a black man approached him in a restaurant.

22   "Did you draw that black and blind strip?" the man asked, according to Callahan's recollection. The cartoonist nodded. Then, he said, the man shook his hand and thanked him.

23   A similar situation arose over a cartoon about a double amputee. The drawing showed a bartender refusing to pour another drink for a man who had two prosthetic hooks in place of hands. "Sorry Sam," says the bartender, "you can't hold your liquor." Callahan says he was at a concert shortly after the panel appeared, when a man who had lost his hands in Vietnam approached him and thanked him profusely.

24   "My only compass for whether I've gone too far is the reaction I get from people in wheelchairs, or with hooks for hands," says Callahan. "Like me, they are fed up with people who presume to speak for the disabled. All the pity and patronizing. That's what is truly detestable."

25   When pressed by critics, Callahan will rarely defend himself with drawn-out explanations or appeals to reason. Instead, he falls back on a simple answer: "It's funny."

26   Of late, other people have been doing the defending for him. The American Civil Liberties Union of Oregon last year gave Callahan its Free Expression Award. He was cited for a "history of facing challenge to artistic

and intellectual freedom." Last fall, he was honored by the Media Access Office in Los Angeles, a disability information center for the entertainment industry.

27   "From my experience, I would say about 90 percent of the people who find John's work questionable are able-bodied," says Royce Hamrick, a paraplegic who is president of the San Diego chapter of the National Spinal Cord Injury Association. "In the disabled community, we make a lot of jokes that stay within that community. What John is doing is bringing those out to everyone else."

28   But for every compliment and accolade, there is a fresh controversy. Last year, Callahan drew a cartoon called "The Alzheimer Hoedown," which showed confused couples at a square dance. They were scratching their heads, unable to follow the instructions to "return to the girl that you just left." In an angry letter to Callahan, Kathleen Higley, executive director of the St. Louis chapter of the Alzheimer's Association, said the drawing had deeply upset some of her members.

29   "Four million Americans suffer from this mind-robbing disease," Higley wrote in the letter. The victims, she said, "should be treated with dignity and compassion, not ridicule."

30   A paper in California, *The Coast Weekly* of Carmel, canceled Callahan after a storm of protest over one cartoon. It showed a dog, lying on its back, with a windowpane imbedded inside its chest. A passer-by asks, "How much is that window in the doggie?" The cartoon has proved to be one of Callahan's most popular, and he has since adapted it into an animated short film.

31   "A lot of people thought the cartoon was just a bit too distasteful," says Bradley Zeve, editor and publisher of *The Coast Weekly*. "Of course, the editors thought it was hilarious."

32   Callahan says there is a double standard for humor in this country. Virtually within hours of the space shuttle accident five years ago, he says people were making jokes. But when Callahan takes the same impulse that drives street humor about popular events and puts it into print he's vilified.

33   "There is humor in all parts of life, families suffering from Alzheimer's or cancer, have their own private jokes as a way of coping with the pain," he says. "So why is it a crime to share the joke in print?" But applying that same standard to, say, racial humor, would likely put Callahan on shaky ground with fans who are otherwise more tolerant. The question with all gallows humor is whether it dehumanizes its subject or helps to cover pain and break down false pretense.

34   Callahan's best weapon with his critics, of course, is his own disability. He can say things that others may be thinking, and usually get away with it, precisely because he is quadriplegic. "People always say, 'How can he make fun of the handicapped?' " Callahan says. "And then an editor will usually write back and say that I'm in a wheelchair. Their attitude changes immediately."

35   While Callahan's defenders have used his disability to defuse critics, he says he does not want special treatment because he is in a wheelchair. His cartoons, he points out, do not carry a note to readers that the artist is crippled.

36   "Being in a wheelchair has nothing to do with why he can do the things he does," says Sam Gross, a veteran cartoonist whose drawings appear regularly in *The New Yorker, The National Lampoon* and other publications. "He is in the vein of sick humor—but sick humor that's funny. He's intelligent and witty—that is why he gets away with it." . . .

37   By the mid-80's, magazines like *Penthouse* were running Callahan, as was *The Williamette Week,* an alternative weekly in Portland that was also one of the first papers to run Matt Groening and Lynda Barry. Many of Callahan's cartoons went right after the liberal readers of the Portland papers. One drawing, titled "The Politically Appropriate Brain," shows a pie chart inside a man's head. Guilt makes up 40 percent, whales 10 percent, rain forests 10 percent, apartheid 10 percent and comfortable sandals 30 percent. It is the favorite cartoon of Bud Clark, Portland's Mayor.

38   "John is very politically incorrect," says Mark Zusman, editor and co-owner of *The Williamette Week.* "But over the years, everybody has gotten used to him. I remember being taken aback by his answering machine. You'd call and his voice would say, 'Hi, this is John. I'm really depressed right now so I can't come to the phone. Please leave a message after the gunshot.' "

39   Callahan developed a style in which he would take a cliché and turn it on its head. An early cartoon, for example, showed two cowboys getting ready to draw their guns. One of the men is without arms. The other says, "Don't be a fool, Billy."

40   Deborah Levin, a California talent manager who had helped to launch both Groening and Barry into syndication, heard about Callahan while on a Portland visit six years ago. She was responsible for his national syndication, but only after long explanations to the editors of different papers. Readers in south Florida, where Callahan is run in *The Miami Herald,* recently voted him more popular than Dave Barry, the Miami humor columnist.

41   Two of Callahan's longer cartoons, a narrative labeled "The Lighter Side of Being Paralyzed for Life" and a later one called "How to Relate to Handicapped People," have been widely reprinted in magazines and circulars used by the disabled. He wrote in the latter panel that people overcompensate when they meet someone in a wheelchair, usually acting overfriendly or patronizing or directing questions to a friend of the handicapped person. Access Living, a United Way organization in Chicago, has issued a poster of Callahan's satires on attitudes toward the disabled, and the city government of Milpitas, California, wants to use some of his work in educational presentations.

42   Callahan's work has also recently caught on in gift shops of recovery centers, according to Levin. She has also sold his cartoons for T-shirts and postcards. When asked if this spurt of marketing could take away Callahan's edge, Levin says: "It hasn't changed him yet. But he's maturing."

43   Even with new income from books and commercial sales, Callahan lives a spartan life in the Portland studio apartment. He draws from bed, with straps and cables hanging overhead, a cat nearby and the television usually on. The costs of a full-time attendant and medical care have drained much of his earnings, he says.

44   Despite his dismissive remarks, Callahan, who has had a series of girl-friends over the last 20 years, would like to get married and have a family. Some day. But even when speaking in rare solemn tones about his dreams for the future, he cannot resist a self-cutting line: "I think it would be fun to hear the whir of little wheels around the house."

COMPREHENSION

1. Words to talk about:
   - the *self-confession racket* practiced by
   - walking on an airport *tarmac*
   - the *venerable* American craft of cartooning
   - for every compliment and *accolade*
   - puts it into print he's *vilified*
   - lives a *spartan* life

2. What philosophical disagreement separates Callahan from some of those who are offended by his cartoons?

DISCUSSION

1. When John Callahan was interviewed on CBS's *Sixty Minutes*, he com-pared himself to Cinderella because during the day he is free to roam through Portland enjoying a kind of celebrity status, but at night his at-tendant tucks him in bed and leaves him imprisoned until the next morning when he arrives for the two-hour workout of bathing, dress-ing, eating, and getting strapped into a wheelchair for another day of life as Callahan knows it. What did Callahan's comparison do for the millions of viewers who watch *Sixty Minutes*?

2. One of the ways that a cartoonist manages to tell a story in only one frame is to tap into the stories that readers already have in their heads. What are some of the old stories or clichés that Callahan expected his listeners to know? What new twists did he provide?

3. Egan says that John Callahan will probably never achieve the kind of fame enjoyed by Gary Larson with *Far Side* and Berke Breathed with *Bloom County*. Do you agree? Why or why not?

4. Callahan complains about a double standard. Right after any major disaster, creative people are recycling old disaster jokes into new formats and telling them on the street and on the Internet as well as through e-mail, fax, and long distance telephones. But when Callahan puts a similar kind of black humor into a cartoon, he is criticized. What contributes to this double standard?

5. Callahan hates such phrases as *vertically challenged, otherly abled,* and *wheelchair-bound.* He would rather be called a *gimp* or a *cripple.* Can we assume that everyone in Callahan's position feels the same? Or even that at different points in Callahan's recovery, he felt the same? What does this illustrate about how important it is to know individuals and to find out from each of them what they prefer?

6. Of the many examples of Callahan's jokes cited in this essay, which ones do you think come the closest to the "hot fire of truth" that E. B. and Katharine White have mentioned?

SUGGESTED TOPICS FOR WRITING

For each of the suggested topics, some information is presented as an impetus to your thinking. If you have time in class, you might want to discuss these topics because humor is something that has been a part of your whole life even if you've never studied it formally. You may be surprised at how much you know about it. Begin by reacting to what is provided, or take one of the topics and pursue it in an entirely different direction. If you get discouraged because humor is such a slippery topic, remember that even the brightest and most experienced scholars are often frustrated because humor is inherently unpredictable, there are so many different kinds, and people's reactions to it are so individualized.

1. **Analyze the language of stand-up comics in American life:** Two or three generations ago, only a small percentage of Americans went to burlesque theaters; but today television brings stand-up comedy directly into most people's living rooms. In the early 1970s, there were fewer than 200 performers in the United States earning their living as stand-up comics whereas the 1995 *Comedy USA* directory listed 4,800, which fits with George Carlin's observation that "America can be counted on to take any good idea, or any bad idea, and absolutely run it

into the ground." According to the *New York Times*, in the 1996 presidential election, one-fourth of the voting-age population got some of their information about the candidates from listening to the opening monologues of such TV comedians as Jay Leno, David Letterman, and Conan O'Brien. Clifford D. May, associate editor of the *Rocky Mountain News*, wrote, "Throughout American history, there have been mythologized characters who hold sway over the culture and over the public imagination. Examples of these archetypes might include the rugged cowboy, the eccentric inventor, the rags-to-riches entrepreneur, the hell-bent soldier, the suffering artist and the daring astronaut. So who is the ascendant icon of the current era? It's the stand-up comic. I kid you not." What evidence can you gather to analyze the truth of May's statement?

Actually, television ratings for straight comedy shows are down, and in many cities comedy clubs have closed or gone to weekends only. Did this happen in your geographical area? If so, why? Could part of the problem be that as comedians search for new jokes they rely too much on obscenity and nervous laughter? Do the best comedians move to the greater security offered in TV sitcoms? Or could it be that people don't want to pay money to go to a club when they can watch comedy for free on television?

2. **Analyze differences between male and female stand-up comics:** "There's positive humor and there's negative humor," and the latter is mostly a male phenomenon claimed a "News & Trends" feature in *Psychology Today* (Sept./Oct. 1993). The editors cited Andrew Dice Clay for having built a "lucrative career on woman-bashing," Joan Rivers for breaking the "male monopoly on humor" but with mostly self-deprecating jokes that kept women as the butt, Roseanne for a "let's get hostile ourselves" negative comedy, and Lily Tomlin and Rita Rudner as exemplifying a new kind of women's humor that is sympathetic and full of insight on the human condition. One example from Tomlin is "How come when you talk to God you're praying, but when God talks to you you're schizophrenic?" while one from Rudner is "I love to sleep. Do you? Isn't it great? It really is the best of both worlds. You get to be alive and unconscious." To analyze this generalization about differences in male and female comedians, be careful to collect your evidence from the same arena. For example, rather than comparing the performance of a late-night, television program featuring male comedians with a daytime talk show featuring women, you should watch a show that has both men and women presenting to the same audience under the same format.

3. **Analyze how the media affects comic strips:** Some 86 million adults and 27 million kids claim to be regular readers of the comics strips that are an American invention. Sometime during 1895, *The Yellow Kid* (yellow was the only color of ink that would hold to cheap newsprint)

debuted in Joseph Pulitzer's New York daily newspaper, *The World*. Two years later, *The Katzenjammer Kids*, which is still running, was created as competition by William Randolph Hearst. Old time comic strips still running include *Bringing Up Father* from 1913, *Little Orphan Annie* from 1924, and *Mary Worth, Prince Valiant*, and *Blondie* from the 1930s. The last one is still among the five most widely published, which in 1995, according to the *New York Times*, included *Peanuts, Garfield, Calvin and Hobbes, Haggar the Horrible*. Today the Internet is making it possible for artists to publish their own cartoons and comic strips. Some of them do it just to reach out to others, while some sell advertising space and hope to be noticed by a publisher. Dan Perkins, who draws *This Modern World*, syndicated in 80 papers and also on the Internet, says, "The truly great thing about publishing electronically is e-mail," which allows readers to respond directly to him with criticism and also ideas. Scott Adams, who draws *Dilbert*, says he gets about a hundred ideas a day through e-mail.

4. **Analyze the targeting of jokes:** Is it okay to tell jokes about disadvantaged people as long as we take turns in being "equal opportunity" insulters? Or is it best to stick to joking only about ourselves or our own group? How about lawyers and politicians since they are usually privileged? In 1992, Harvey Safferstein, the president of the California Bar Association, held a news conference and announced that he was "calling today on all Americans . . . to stop the lawyer-bashing . . . that sometimes can incite violence and aggression toward lawyers." His announcement followed the awful event of a man going into a San Francisco law firm where he killed eight people and wounded six others before turning the gun on himself. While Safferstein did not draw a definite cause-and-effect between Ferri's actions and lawyer-bashing jokes, he said that for "a fringe person" such jokes could be "the straw that breaks the camel's back." An alternate opinion is that had the man made jokes about the lawyers he blamed for his business failure, then perhaps he wouldn't have felt the kind of hostility that resulted in the tragedy. The question to ponder is whether telling jokes relieves or contributes to the building up of tensions and hostility. The reason this hasn't been definitively answered is that every situation is different and humor is affected by such subtle matters as the twinkle in the eyes or the tone in a joke teller's voice. Think and write about your own experiences in relation to joking and teasing. Do you tease people you really hate or people you basically like but have mild disagreements with? For this topic, you need to realize that there is a difference between jokes and between hate speech, which is sometimes disguised as humor in the form of a riddle or other simple joke pattern.

5. **Analyze what makes something funny:** Look at a book of cartoons or read a half-dozen or so short pieces of humor by the same author and

then write an essay in which you discuss and illustrate the author's most effective techniques (for example, exaggeration, word play, unusual dialogue, funny names, sharp observations, effective characterization, revelations of human emotions, etc.). What are the similarities among the pieces? What parts did you enjoy the most? Did some references seem dated, while other parts were as funny today as when they were written? Why? Good books to choose from would be these that were recommended by the New York Public Library in conjunction with a display, "The Complete Charles Addams." Most of the books are made up of separate short pieces.

Robert Benchley's *The Benchley Roundup: A Selection by Nathaniel Benchley of His Favorites,* Univ. of Chicago Press, 1983.

Sandra Bernhard's *Love, Love & Love,* HarperCollins, 1993.

Erma Bombeck's *A Marriage Made in Heaven—or, Too Tired for an Affair,* HarperCollins, 1993.

Bill Cosby's *Childhood,* Berkley, 1992.

Garrison Keillor's *The Book of Guys,* Viking, 1993.

Ring Lardner's *The Best Short Stories,* Viking, 1993.

Fran Lebowitz's *Metropolitan Life,* NAL/Dutton, 1988.

John Leguizamo's *Mambo Mouth,* Bantam, 1993.

Ogden Nash's *Verses from 1929 On,* Little Brown & Co., 1959.

Dorothy Parker's *The Portable Dorothy Parker,* Viking Penguin, 1978.

S. J. Perelman's *Baby, It's Cold Inside,* Viking Penguin, 1987.

James Thurber's *A Thurber Carnival,* Random House, 1994.

Calvin Trillin's *Travels with Alice,* Avon, 1990.

Judith Viorst's *Forever 50 and Other Negotiations,* Simon & Simon, 1989.

6. **Analyze the teaching role of humor:** Write a paper on how humor teaches people what kind of behavior is to be expected. In the 1920s, philosopher Henri Bergson made the point that humor is the great social corrective. One of the reasons we tell jokes is to make people think. Telling jokes about the behavior (as opposed to physical attributes that cannot be changed) of one's own group is setting off a tiny revolution in which the joke teller chides friends and family to change. This differs from making a joke about the behavior of people in another group where, rather than enlarging the sphere of group behavior, the effect is to tighten the noose by further stereotyping. For example, a cartoon that appeared in the Brigham Young University newspaper showed a bloodied and battered student arising from a pile of stones and saying to the campus policemen who had just arrived, "All I said was 'Let he

who is without sin cast the first stone.' " This was a joke designed to encourage the Mormon students at BYU to ask themselves if they were guilty of self-righteousness. But if the cartoon had appeared in the University of Utah paper where Mormon students are in the minority, then its effect would have been not to change behavior but to further solidify an old stereotype. Can you find other examples of this type? Can you think of jokes that have influenced the way you behave or the way you perceive others to behave? When you were a child did teasing help you learn not to be a "crybaby," or did getting called "four-eyes" make you ask your parents for contact lenses? How many of your attitudes toward sexual matters have been influenced by jokes you've heard?

7. **Analyze the reasons behind disaster jokes:** Write a paper exploring some aspect of disaster jokes. When there is a tragedy such as the Challenger explosion, the Mexico City earthquake, an airplane crash, or the murder of someone prominent, why do people create and tell jokes? One explanation is that the jokes help people gain an emotional connection to, or a feeling of control over, a terrible misfortune that is being repeatedly shown on television at the same time that it is written about in newspapers and magazines and talked about in neighborhoods, offices, and schools. What do you think is at the root of disaster humor? How do you and your friends react to such jokes? Do they help you distance yourself from the tragedy? Do you feel refreshed, or guilty, from breaking a taboo? Do you sometimes laugh more from shock than from amusement?

INFORMATION SOURCES FOR WRITING

The books listed here are about humor, but you might also go to the humor section of a bookstore or a library and look for collections that you could analyze: for example, *Dave Barry in Cyberspace* (New York: Ballantine, 1996), *Forever Erma* by Erma Bombeck (Kansas City: Andrews McMeel, 1996), and *Russell Baker's Book of American Humor* (New York: W. W. Norton, 1993).

Anatomy of an Illness as Perceived by the Patient, by Norman Cousins. New York: W. W. Norton, 1979.
Comedy Writing Secrets, by Melvin Helitzer. Cincinnati, Ohio: Writer's Digest, 1987.
Cracking Jokes: Studies of Sick Humor and Stereotypes, by Alan Dundes. Berkeley, California: Ten Speed, 1987.
Do What He Says! He's Crazy!, by John Callahan. New York: Quill, 1992.

Handbook of Humor Research, edited by Paul E. McGhee and Jefferey H. Goldstein. New York: Springer-Verlag, 1983.

Humor and Laughter: An Anthropological Approach, by Mahadev L. Apte. Ithaca, New York: Cornell Univ. Press, 1985.

Jewish Wry: Essays on Jewish Humor, edited by Sarah Blacher Cohen. Bloomington: Indiana Univ. Press (hardbound); Detroit: Wayne State Univ. Press (paperback), both 1987.

The Oxford Dictionary of Humorous Quotations, edited by Ned Sherrin. New York: Oxford Univ. Press, 1995.

The Philosophy of Laughter and Humor, edited by John Morreall. Albany, New York: State Univ. of New York Press, 1987.

Political Humor from Aristophanes to Sam Ervin, edited by Charles E. Schutz. Cranbury, New Jersey: Fairleigh Dickinson Univ. Press, 1977.

They Used to Call Me Snow White . . . But I Drifted: Women's Strategic Use of Humor, by Regina Barreca. Viking, 1991. Barreca has also edited *New Perspectives on Women and Comedy* (Philadelphia: Gordon and Breach, 1992).

Too Funny to Be President, by Morris K. Udall. New York: Henry Holt, 1988.

How far should se

BY S

In a p
intervi
how it
relates
in the
actual
time f
thoug

Ads going on school b

BURLINGTON (AP) — The school district of Burlington announced
today that it will support a comprehensive program of advertising

Clinton Assails Talk Radi

WASHINGTON D.C. (AP) - In a statement issued today by Pr

Post office lists
top 10 rip-offs

Companies need
memorable nam

been ripped off by a mailing or flyer? Mil
s have filed complaints abou
fraud in the past

Advertisements hinder
progress in equality

BY Antonin Jobim
GENEVA (AP) — Although we see them every day,

lived La-Z-Boy
died La-Z-Boy

nold R. Beckmann
ARY (AP) — Relaxation for some is more important than
hers. In the case of Walter S. Crilter
was found i

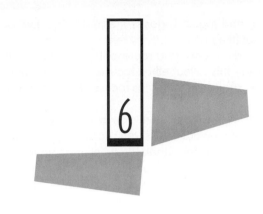

Language to Persuade

There's no end to the techniques that people use to persuade others; nor is there an end to the goals of those doing the persuading. In this chapter, we will look basically at three aspects of persuasion: purpose, intensity, and type of evidence. Like other powerful tools, techniques of persuasion can be used for both good and evil, and for many things in between. For example, depending on who is doing the judging, euphemisms (related to *euphonious*, meaning "good sounds") might be considered close to the "good" end of a spectrum because they are used to smooth social relations and to soften some of life's harsh realities. Doublespeak, on the other hand, is more likely to be viewed as falling near the "evil" end of a scale because it is purposely designed to mislead. However, the people who are creating the doublespeak may view it as "good" under the rationale that the end justifies the means. They are using doublespeak "for the good of the public," "to protect someone's reputation," or to bring about some desired financial goal.

It is a little easier to chart the intensity of a persuasion technique along a continuum running from soft-sell to hard-sell. One example is the difference between the soft-sell approach taken by the sponsors of most programming on public television stations compared to the hard-sell approach that the stations take when fund-raising time comes around and they are advertising for themselves. Another example is the difference between the soft-sell of a disk jockey who calmly invites listeners to call in and request records, as compared to the host of a call-in show who invites hate talk.

A third approach when studying persuasive speech is to look at the kinds of evidence that the persuader presents. Aristotle described three basic types as *ethos, pathos,* and *logos.* Logos is the most objective or logical. Pathos is the most emotional (the *pathetic fallacy* refers to being overly sentimental). Ethos relates to ethics and customs, and represents the author's opinions and beliefs. Another way to say this is that ethos focuses on the author's point of view, logos focuses on the subject, and pathos focuses on creating emotional responses in the listener.

The articles in this chapter give you a chance to study persuasion techniques from different viewpoints. As you read the essays and work with the exercises, you should have two goals: first, protect yourself from political and commercial propaganda; second, understand the techniques and develop the kinds of skills that will allow you to be persuasive when you have a case to present.

Two Persuasive Newspaper Columns

On August 13, 1997, Mary Rose Wilcox, a member of the Maricopa County Board of Supervisors in Phoenix, Arizona, was shot in the pelvis as she was leaving the weekly board meeting. Wilcox's life was probably saved by a security guard, who noticed a man removing something from a brown paper bag. The guard grabbed the man just as he was shooting, which threw off his aim. The fact that Wilcox had been the target of hate talk on a local radio station was immediately brought up for public discussion. A couple of days after the shooting, when it was clear that Wilcox would recover, the following contradictory views about the relationship between the shooting and radio hate talk appeared in the *Arizona Republic* (Aug. 17, 1997). Both writers are regular columnists, with E. J. Montini doing a variety of human interest stories, while Keven Willey concentrates on political matters. Jerry Colangelo, who is mentioned in both columns, is the owner of the Phoenix Suns basketball team and the driving force behind the new Diamondbacks baseball team. At the time of the shooting, a new ballpark was three-fourths completed. The ballpark opened for play in the spring of 1998, and on May 4, 1998, Wilcox's assailant, Larry Naman, was found guilty of attempted first-degree murder.

Hate Talk? You Make the Call

E. J. Montini

1   First, you have to understand we're gutless. This goes for just about everybody who works in television, radio, and newspapers. It explains what happened last week after Mary Rose Wilcox got shot.

2   Here was a politician who'd been ridiculed on a local talk radio station day after day after day. She also took her lumps in the local papers. Then, a guy with a gun goes to a Maricopa County supervisors meeting and shoots her, and the first thing we said was, "It's not our fault."

3   The response didn't come only from people working on talk radio, but all of us. "We can't be blamed for the actions of a crazy man," we said. "A person is responsible for his own behavior."

4   This from a bunch of finger-pointers who are incapable of bending their wrists toward themselves due to a genetic defect called spinelessness.

POWER OF THE WORD

5   Mary Rose Wilcox was verbally attacked over and over again. Then, she was physically attacked. And we're trying to say the words used against her played NO part.

6   None at all.

7   If that were true, if words didn't influence people, talk radio wouldn't exist. And neither would television. And neither would newspapers.

8   For the past couple of years, talk-show hosts have been taking credit for the so-called Republican Revolution of 1994. And they should. Newspaper and TV stations take credit whenever the audience helps out the sick kid or destitute family they've profiled.

9   Why do you think newspapers write endorsements for political candidates?

10   If words didn't work you wouldn't know what company I'm talking about when I said, "Just do it."

11   If words didn't have the power to influence people, there would be no churches. No preachers. No Bible.

12   According to Gospel, "In the beginning was the Word, and the word was with God, and the Word was God."

13   The gospel according to radio station KFYI declared Mary Rose Wilcox a "liar," "intellectually impaired" and "evil."

14   On this same station, hosts suggested that handgun-control activist Sarah Brady be "put down like a dog" and that the innocent men and women blown to bits in Oklahoma City were "not victims."

15   Words are like pills. They can cure and they can have dangrous side effects. Either way, the person who writes the prescription is partly responsible.

16   Only the gutless deny it.

ASSAILANT'S REASONING

17   Here is Larry Naman, the man arrested for wounding Wilcox, speaking from the county jail:

> "I shot Supervisor Mary Rose Wilcox to try to put a stop to the political dictatorship of Jerry Colangelo, the Maricopa County Board of Supervisors, and the Arizona state Legislature in pushing the baseball stadium tax. And to try to force them to demolish the Bank One Ballpark so that it will restore the vote of the people as the bottom line and to restore the public's

faith in their democratic election system and to restore democracy on the non-candidate side of the ballot in Maricopa County."

Here is KFYI-AM radio host Bob Mohan speaking (months before the shooting) from the comfort of his studio:

> "Mary Rose Wilcox . . . is totally without conscience, and I believe she is mentally impaired, and I think she is evil. This woman has affected everyone in Maricopa County because she is in the hip pocket of Jerry Colangelo. You must understand that. She is in the hip pocket of Jerry Colangelo and she, without even any thought before or after, felt no pangs of guilt with taking money from you without your permission in the famous—or infamous— quarter-cent sales tax."

18   I agree with those who say it's unfair to claim the gunman and the radio talk-show host have a lot in common. Anyone who reads the comments of the gunman, then reads the comments of the radio host, can tell there are major differences.

19   The gunman is more articulate, for one.

20   And more honest.

WILCOX FACES HER BIGGEST CHALLENGE

Keven Willey

1   It was shocking.

2   I'm talking about the shooting last week of Maricopa County Supervisor Mary Rose Wilcox.

3   But it wasn't political.

4   This tragedy wasn't about hate radio. It wasn't about Jerry Colangelo. It wasn't about baseball. It was about a madman. Literally. Plain and simple.

5   Larry Naman, the man who pulled a .38-caliber revolver out of a brown paper bag on Wednesday and fired at Wilcox, as she exited the supervisors auditorium, has suffered from mental illness for years.

6   We know this because his doctor says so. We know this because Naman abandoned his family, lived on the streets, spent time in an Oregon mental hospital, has boasted about committing murders and likened himself to Charles Manson.

7   The man is irrational.

8   So we can talk all we want about hate talk on radio.

9   We can talk all we want about Jerry Colangelo.

10   We can talk all we want about a taxpayer-subsidized baseball stadium.

11   But this has nothing to do with that.

12   Naman could just as easily have prattled on about a zoning ordinance, barking dogs or global warming.

13   His selection of Wilcox as his target and baseball as his subject was just a fluke. It was shocking, painful, life-threatening. But it was a fluke nonetheless.

14   To try to read political significance into it is like trying to read political significance into an Elvis sighting.

15   There isn't any.

16   The real significance of this tragedy will be how Wilcox responds—personally, as well as politically.

17   It may be the biggest challenge of her life.

18   We can only imagine how frightening it would be to find yourself the victim of such violence. We never *expect* such a thing to happen. Especially not to ourselves.

19   It rattles to the bone.

20   Eventually, though, shock dulls. Reality takes over. Day-to-day life resumes.

21   The shooting will either drive a shattered Wilcox from office or it will steel a courageous Wilcox to overcome.

22   I'm betting on the latter.

23   I hope she and her husband, Earl, grow beyond the shooting, not into it.

24   I hope they leave martyrdom to others.

25   Agree or disagree with her, Mary Rose Wilcox is dedicated to her community and works tirelessly for her constituency. But she and Earl also are political animals. It's no secret that Mary Rose wants to go to Congress. Or that Earl wants Mary Rose to go to Congress.

26   The Wilcoxes will do almost anything to capitalize on a political advantage. It's both the secret to their success and the source of their critics' complaints.

27   But an assassination attempt isn't something to capitalize on. It's not something to be conveniently trotted out to score a political point or to generate carefully orchestrated sympathy.

28   It's a matter, quite simply, of life and death. Something that should bring clarity, not obscurity, to the important things in life.

29   Honesty, integrity, selflessness. Truth.

30   "Mary Rose will be tempted to milk this for all it's worth," confided a longtime Wilcox ally, who asked not to be identified. "Or rather, Earl will be tempted to milk this for all it's worth."

31   The friend continued:

32   "I hope, instead, that she will use this as an opportunity to reflect on life and what's important.

33   "And change things."

COMPREHENSION

1. Words to talk about:

   - activist *Sarah Brady*
   - could have *prattled on* about
   - was just a *fluke*
   - to *capitalize* on a political advantage

2. Why did people draw a connection between hate radio and the shooting of a county supervisor?
3. Were the two writers arguing the exact same point? If not, how did their perspectives differ?

DISCUSSION

1. Whenever this kind of a crime occurs, people want to figure out why it happened so they can prevent its happening again. What kind of evidence do people use? What are some of the complications in trying to draw an absolute cause-and-effect relationship?
2. Which essay was the most convincing to you? Why?
3. In relation to the three kinds of evidence that Aristotle talked about: *ethos* (a citing of ethics and customs), *logos* (an objective appeal to logic), and *pathos* (a play on emotions), find one or two examples of each. Which essay relied the most on *pathos*? Which the most on *logos*?
4. What differences are there between teasing, trash talk, hate speech, and gang threats? Give a likely scenario in which each might appear.
5. What is there about call-in shows or about Internet Listserves that encourage people to say things that they wouldn't say to someone in person?

Propaganda: How Not to Be Bamboozled

Donna Woolfolk Cross

Donna Woolfolk Cross is a former writer of advertising copy, now working as a professor of English at Onondaga Community College in Syracuse, New York. She wrote this article in the hopes of helping consumers understand the most common techniques of persuasion. Although she has provided modern examples in this updated version of her essay, the techniques she discusses have been used for the past 2,500 years at least. The Greek philosopher Aristotle, who lived between 384 and 322 B.C., taught his students some of these same techniques, only instead of talking about "propaganda" and being "bamboozled," he talked about "principles of argument and persuasion" and "logical fallacies."

1   Propaganda. If an opinion poll were taken tomorrow, we can be sure that nearly everyone would be against it because it *sounds* so bad. When we say, "Oh, that's just propaganda," it means, to most people, "That's a pack of lies." But really, propaganda is simply a means of persuasion and so it can be put to work for good causes as well as bad—to persuade people to give to charity, for example, or to love their neighbors, or to stop polluting the environment.

2   For good or evil, propaganda pervades our daily lives, helping to shape our attitudes on a thousand subjects. Propaganda probably determines the brand of toothpaste you use, the movies you see, the candidates you elect when you get to the polls. Propaganda works by tricking us, by momentarily distracting the eye while the rabbit pops out from beneath the cloth. Propaganda works best with an uncritical audience. Joseph Goebbels, propaganda minister in Nazi Germany, once defined his work as "the conquest of the masses." The masses would not have been conquered, however, if they had known how to challenge and to question, how to make distinctions between propaganda and reasonable argument.

3   People are bamboozled mainly because they don't recognize propaganda when they see it. They need to be informed about the various devices that can be used to mislead and deceive—about the propagandist's overflowing bag of tricks. The following, then, are some common pitfalls for the unwary.

4   **1. Name-Calling.**   As its title suggests, this device consists of labeling people or ideas with words of bad connotation, literally, "calling them names."

Here the propagandist tries to arouse our contempt so we will dismiss the "bad name" person or idea without examining its merits.

5   Bad names have played a tremendously important role in the history of the world. They have ruined reputations and ended lives, sent people to prison and to war, and just generally made us mad at each other for centuries.

6   Name-calling can be used against policies, practices, beliefs and ideals, as well as against individuals, groups, races, nations. Name-calling is at work when we hear a candidate for office described as a "foolish idealist" or "a two-faced liar" or when an incumbent's policies are denounced as reckless, reactionary, or just plain stupid. Some of the most effective names a public figure can be called are ones that may not denote anything specific: "Congresswoman Jane Doe is a *bleeding heart!*" (Did she vote for funds to help paraplegics?) or "The senator is a *tool of Washington!*" (Did he happen to agree with the president?) Senator Yakalot uses name-calling when he denounces his opponent's "radical policies" and calls them (and him) *socialist, opportunist* and part of a *heartless plot.* He also uses it when he calls people who oppose his "Decency Act" *secular humanists, ACLU nuts, betrayers of youth,* and *purveyors of pornography.*

7   The point here is that when propagandists use name-calling, they don't want us to think—merely to react, blindly unquestioningly. So the best defense against being taken in by name-calling is to stop and ask, "Forgetting the bad name attached to it, what are the merits of the idea itself? What does this name really mean, anyway?"

8   **2. Glittering Generalities.**   Glittering generalities are really name-calling in reverse. Name-calling uses words with bad connotations; glittering generalities are words with good connotations—"virtue words," as the Institute for Propaganda Analysis has called them. The Institute explains that while name-calling tries to get us to reject and condemn someone or something without examining the evidence, glittering generalities try to get us to accept and agree without examining the evidence.

9   We believe in, fight for, live by "virtue words" which we feel deeply about: *justice, motherhood, the American way,* our *Constitutional rights,* our *Christian heritage.* These sound good, but when we examine them closely, they turn out to have no specific, definable meaning. They just make us feel good. Senator Yakalot uses glittering generalities when he says, "I stand for all that is good in America, for our American way and our American birthright." But what exactly *is* "good for America"? How can we define our "American birthright"? Just what parts of the American society and culture does "our American way" refer to?

10   We often make the mistake of assuming we are personally unaffected by glittering generalities. The next time you find yourself assuming that, listen to a political candidate's speech on TV and see how often the use of glittering generalities elicits cheers and applause. That's the damage of propaganda; it

works. Once again, our defense against it is to ask questions: Forgetting the virtue words attached to it, what are the merits of the idea itself? What does *Americanism* (or *freedom* or *truth*) really *mean* here? . . .

11   Both name-calling and glittering generalities work by stirring our emotions in the hope that this will cloud our thinking. Another approach that propaganda uses is to create a distraction, a "red herring," that will make people forget or ignore the real issues. There are several different kinds of red herrings that can be used to distract attention.

12   **3. Plain Folks Appeal.**   "Plain folks" is the device by which a speaker tries to win our confidence and support by appearing to be a person like ourselves—"just one of the plain folks." The plain-folks appeal is at work when candidates go around shaking hands with factory workers, kissing babies in supermarkets, and sampling pasta with Italians, fried chicken with Southerners, bagels and blintzes with Jews. "Now I'm a businessman like yourselves" is a plain-folks appeal, as is "I've been a farm boy all my life." Senator Yakalot tries the plain-folks appeal when he says, "I'm just a small-town boy like you fine people." The use of such expressions once prompted Lyndon Johnson to quip, "Whenever I hear someone say, 'I'm just an old country lawyer,' the first thing I reach for is my wallet to make sure it's still there."

13   The irrelevancy of the plain-folks appeal is obvious: even if the man *is* "one of us" (which may not be true at all), that doesn't mean that his ideas and programs are sound—or even that he honestly has our best interests at heart. As with glittering generalities, the danger here is that we may mistakenly assume we are immune to this appeal. But propagandists wouldn't use it unless it had been proved to work. You can protect yourself by asking, "Aside from his 'nice guy next door' image, what does this man stand for? Are his ideas and his past record really supportive of my best interest?"

14   **4. Argumentum ad Populum (Stroking).**   *Argumentum ad populum* means "argument to the people" or "telling the people what they want to hear." The colloquial term is "stroking," which conjures up pictures of small animals or children being stroked or soothed with compliments until they come to like the person doing the complimenting—and, by extension, his or her ideas.

15   We all like to hear nice things about ourselves and the group we belong to—we like to be liked—so it stands to reason that we will respond warmly to a person who tells us we are "hard-working taxpayers" or "the most generous, free-spirited nation in the world." Politicians tell farmers they are the "backbone of the American economy" and college students that they are the "leaders and policy makers of tomorrow." Commercial advertisers use stroking more insidiously by asking a question which invites a flattering answer: "What kind of a man reads *Playboy*?" (Does he really drive a Porsche and own $10,000 worth of sound equipment?) Senator Yakalot is stroking his audience when he calls them the "decent law-abiding citizens that are the

great pulsing heart and the life blood of this, our beloved country," and when he repeatedly refers to them as "you fine people," "you wonderful folks."

16   Obviously, the intent here is to sidetrack us from thinking critically about the man and his ideas. Our own good qualities have nothing to do with the issue at hand. Ask yourself, "Apart from the nice things he has to say about me (and my church, my nation, my ethnic group, my neighbors), what does the candidate stand for? Are his or her ideas in my best interests?"

17   **5. Argumentum ad Hominem.**   *Argumentum ad hominem* means "argument to the man" and that's exactly what it is. When propagandists use *argumentum ad hominem*, they want to distract our attention from the issue under consideration with personal attacks on the people involved. For example, when Lincoln issued the Emancipation Proclamation, some people responded by calling him the "baboon." But Lincoln's long arms and awkward carriage had nothing to do with the merits of the Proclamation or the question of whether or not slavery should be abolished.

18   Today *argumentum ad hominem* is still widely used and very effective. You may or may not support proposals to make English the "Official Language" of the United States, but you should be sure your judgment is based on the merits of the idea itself, and not the result of someone's denunciation of those who are opposed to "English-only" laws as *welfare cheaters, illegals, wetbacks,* and *Johnny-Come-Lately's.* Senator Yakalot is using *argumentum ad hominem* when he dismisses the idea of providing schools with money for computers with a negative reference to *nerds* and *computer hackers.* Refuse to be waylaid by *argumentum ad hominem,* and ask, "Do the personal qualities of the people being discussed have anything to do with the issue at hand? Leaving personal references aside, how good is the idea itself?"

19   **6. Transfer (Guilt or Glory by Association).**   In *argumentum ad hominem,* an attempt is made to associate negative aspects of a person's character or personal appearance with an issue or idea he supports. The transfer device uses this same process of association to make us accept or condemn a given person or idea.

20   A better name for the transfer device is guilt (or glory) by association. In glory by association, the propagandist tries to transfer the positive feelings of something we love and respect to the group or idea he wants us to accept. "This bill for a new dam is in the best tradition of this country, the land of Lincoln, Jefferson, and Washington," is glory by association at work. Lincoln, Jefferson, and Washington were great leaders that most of us revere and respect, but they have no logical connection to the proposal under consideration—the bill to build a new dam. Senator Yakalot uses glory by association when he says the right to carry a gun has "always been as American as Mom's apple pie or a Sunday drive in the country."

21   The process works equally well in reverse, when guilt by association is used to transfer our dislike or disapproval of one idea or group to some other

idea or group that the propagandist wants us to reject and condemn. "John Doe says we need to make some changes in the way our government oper- ates; well, that's exactly what the Ku Klux Klan has said, so there's a meeting of great minds!" That's guilt by association for you; there's no logical con- nection between John Doe and the Ku Klux Klan apart from the one the pro- pagandist is trying to create in our minds. He wants to distract our attention from John Doe and get us thinking (and worrying) about the Ku Klux Klan and its politics of violence. (Of course, there are sometimes legitimate associ- ations between the two things; if John Doe had been a *member* of the Ku Klux Klan, it would be reasonable and fair to draw a connection between the man and his group.) Senator Yakalot tries to trick his audience with guilt by asso- ciation when he remarks that "the words *community* and *communism* look an awful lot alike!"

22   How can we learn to spot the transfer device and distinguish between fair and unfair associations? We can teach ourselves to *suspend judgment* until we have answered these questions: "Is there any legitimate connection between the idea under discussion and the thing it is associated with? Leaving the transfer device out of the picture, what are the merits of the idea by itself?"

23   **7. Bandwagon.**   Ever hear of the small, ratlike animal called the lem- ming? Lemmings are arctic rodents with a very odd habit: periodically, for reasons no one entirely knows, they mass together in a large herd and com- mit suicide by rushing into deep water and drowning themselves. They all run in together, blindly, and not one of them ever seems to stop and ask, "*Why am I doing this? Is this really what I want to do?*" and thus save itself from destruction. Obviously, lemmings are driven to perform their strange mass suicide rites by common instinct. People choose to "follow the herd" for more complex reasons, yet we are still all too often the unwitting victims of the bandwagon appeal.

24   Essentially, the bandwagon urges us to support an action or an opinion be- cause it is popular—because "everyone else is doing it." This call to "get on the bandwagon" appeals to the strong desire in most of us to be one of the crowd, not to be left out or alone. Advertising makes extensive use of the band- wagon appeal ("join the Pepsi generation"), but so do politicians ("Let us join together in this great cause"). Senator Yakalot uses the bandwagon appeal when he says that "More and more citizens are rallying to my cause every day," and asks his audience to "join them—and me—in our fight for America."

25   One of the ways we can see the bandwagon appeal at work is in the over- whelming success of various fashions and trends which capture the interest (and the money) of thousands of people for a short time, then disappear sud- denly and completely. For a year or two in the fifties, every boy in North America wanted a coonskin cap so he could be like Davy Crockett; no one wanted to be left out. After that was the hula-hoop craze that helped to dis- locate the hips of thousands of Americans. Then millions of people rushed

out to buy their very own pet rocks. Next came Cabbage Patch dolls, then Tickle-Me Elmos, and now Beanie Babies.

26   The problem here is obvious: just because everyone's doing it doesn't meant that *we* should too. Group approval does not prove that something is true or is worth doing. Large numbers of people have supported actions we now condemn. Just a generation ago, Hitler and Mussolini rose to absolute and catastrophically repressive rule in two of the most sophisticated and cultured countries of Europe. When they came into power they were welled up by massive popular support from millions of people who didn't want to be "left out" at a great historical moment.

27   Once the mass begins to move—on the bandwagon—it becomes harder and harder to perceive the leader *riding* the bandwagon. So don't be a lemming, rushing blindly on to destruction because "everyone else is doing it." Stop and ask, "Where is this bandwagon headed? Never mind about everybody else, is this what is best for *me*? . . .

28   As we have seen, propaganda can appeal to us by arousing our emotions or distracting our attention from the real issues at hand. But there's a third way that propaganda can be put to work against us—by the use of faulty logic. This approach is really more insidious than the other two because it gives the appearance of reasonable, fair argument. It is only when we look more closely that the holes in the logical fiber show up. The following are some of the devices that make use of faulty logic to distort and mislead.

29   **8. Faulty Cause and Effect.**   As the name suggests, this device sets up a cause-and-effect relationship that may not be true. The Latin name for this logical fallacy is *post hoc ergo propter hoc,* which means "after this, therefore because of this." But just because one thing happened after another doesn't mean that one *caused* the other.

30   An example of false cause-and-effect reasoning is offered by the story (probably invented) of the woman aboard the ship *Titanic.* She woke up from a nap and, feeling seasick, looked around for a call button to summon the steward to bring her some medication. She finally located a small button on one of the walls of her cabin and pushed it. A split second later, the *Titanic* grazed an iceberg in the terrible crash that was to send the entire ship to its destruction. The woman screamed and said, "Oh, God what have I done? What have I done?" The humor of that anecdote comes from the absurdity of the woman's assumption that pushing the small red button resulted in the destruction of a ship weighing several hundred tons: "It happened after I pushed it, therefore it must be *because* I pushed it"—*post hoc ergo propter hoc* reasoning. There is, of course, no cause-and-effect relationship there.

31   The false cause-and-effect fallacy is used very often by political candidates. "After I came to office, the rate of inflation dropped to 6 percent." But did the person do anything to cause the lower rate of inflation or was it the result of other conditions? Would the rate of inflation have dropped anyway,

even if he hadn't come to office? Senator Yakalot uses false cause and effect when he says, "Our forefathers who made this country great never had free hot meal handouts! And look what they did for our country!" He does it again when he concludes that "When everyone speaks English, we will all get along together."

32   False cause-and-effect reasoning is terribly persuasive because it seems so logical. Its appeal is apparently to experience. We swallowed X product—and the headache went away. We elected Y official and unemployment went down. Many people think, "There *must* be a connection." But causality is an immensely complex phenomenon; you need a good deal of evidence to prove that an event that follows another in time was "therefore" caused by the first event.

33   Don't be taken in by false cause and effect; be sure to ask, "Is there enough evidence to prove that this cause led to that effect? Could there have been any *other* causes?"

34   **9. False Analogy.**   An analogy is a comparison between two ideas, events, or things. But comparisons can be fairly made only when the things being compared are alike in significant ways. When they are not, false analogy is the result.

35   A famous example of this is the old proverb "Don't change horses in the middle of a stream," often used as an analogy to convince voters not to change administrations in the middle of a war or other crisis. But the analogy is misleading because there are so many differences between the things compared. In what ways is a war or political crisis like a stream? Is the president or head of state really very much like a horse? And is a nation of millions of people comparable to a man trying to get across a stream? Analogy is false and unfair when it compares two things that have little in common and assumes that they are identical. Senator Yakalot tries to hoodwink his listeners with false analogy when he says, "Trying to take guns away from Americans is as undemocratic as trying to deprive them of the right to vote."

36   Of course, analogies can be drawn that are reasonable and fair. It would be reasonable, for example, to compare the closing of a military base in one area with the possible results in another, *if* the areas have the same kind of history, population, and employment patterns. We can decide for ourselves whether an analogy is false or fair by asking, "Are the things being compared truly alike in significant ways? Do the differences between them affect the comparison?"

37   **10. Begging the Question.**   Actually, the name of this device is rather misleading, because it does not appear in the form of a question. Begging the question occurs when, in discussing a questionable or debatable point, a person assumes as already established the very point that he is trying to prove. For example, "No thinking citizen could approve such a completely unacceptable policy as this one." But isn't the question of whether or not the policy *is* acceptable the very point to be established? Senator Yakalot begs the

question when he announces that his opponent's plan won't work "because it is unworkable."

38   We can protect ourselves against this kind of faulty logic by asking, "What is assumed in this statement? Is the assumption reasonable, or does it need more proof?"

39   **11. The Two-Extremes Fallacy (False Dilemma).**   Linguists have long noted that the English language tends to view reality in sets of two extremes or polar opposites. In English, things are either black or white, tall or short, up or down, front or back, left or right, good or bad, guilty or not guilty. We can ask for a "straightforward yes-or-no answer" to a question, the understanding being that we will not accept or consider anything in between. In fact, reality cannot always be dissected along such strict lines. There may be (usually are) *more* than just two possibilities or extremes to consider. We are often told to "listen to both sides of the argument." But who's to say that every argument has only two sides? Can't there be a third—even a fourth or fifth— point of view?

40   The two-extremes fallacy is at work in this statement by Lenin, the great Marxist leader: "You cannot eliminate one basic assumption, one substantial part of this philosophy of Marxism (it is as if it were a block of steel), without abandoning truth, without falling into the arms of bourgeois-reactionary falsehood." In other words, if we don't agree 100 percent with every premise of Marxism, we must be placed at the opposite end of the political-economic spectrum—for Lenin, "bourgeois-reactionary falsehood." If we are not entirely *with* him, we must be against him; those are the only two possibilities open to us. Of course, this is a logical fallacy; in real life there are any number of political positions one can maintain *between* the two extremes of Marxism and capitalism. Senator Yakalot uses the two-extremes fallacy in the same way as Lenin when he tells his audience that "in this world a man's either for private enterprise or he's for socialism."

41   One of the most famous examples of the two-extremes fallacy is the slogan, "America: Love it or leave it," with its implicit suggestion that we either accept everything just as it is in America today without complaint—or get out. Again, it should be obvious that there is a whole range of action and belief between those two extremes.

42   Don't be duped; stop and ask, "Are those really the only two options I can choose from? Are there other alternatives not mentioned that deserve consideration?"

43   **12. Card Stacking.**   Some questions are so multifaceted and complex that no one can make an intelligent decision about them without considering a wide variety of evidence. One selection of facts could make us feel one way and another selection could make us feel just the opposite. Card stacking is a device of propaganda which selects only the facts that support the propagandist's point of view, and ignores all the others. For example, a candidate could be made to look like a legislative dynamo if you say, "Representative

McNerd introduced more new bills than any other member of the Congress,"
and neglect to mention that most of them were so preposterous that they were
laughed off the floor.

44   Senator Yakalot engages in card stacking when he talks against enforcing
environmental protection measures. He talks only about jobs without mentioning the cost to the taxpayers or the very real—though still denied—threat
of depletion of resources. He says he wants to help his countrymen keep their
jobs, but doesn't mention that the corporations that offer the jobs will also
make large profits.

45   The best protection against card stacking is to take the "Yes, but . . . " attitude. This device of propaganda is not untrue, but then again it is not the
whole truth. So ask yourself, "Is this person leaving something out that I
should know about? Is there some other information that should be brought
to bear on this question?"

46   So far, we have considered three approaches that the propagandist can
use to influence our thinking: appealing to our emotions, distracting our attention, and misleading us with logic that may appear to be reasonable but is
in fact faulty and deceiving. But there is a fourth approach that is probably
the most common propaganda trick of them all.

47   **13. Testimonial.**   The testimonial device consists in having some loved
or respected person give a statement of support (testimonial) for a given product or idea. The problem is that the person being quoted may *not* be an expert
in the field; in fact, he may know nothing at all about it. Using the name of a
man who is skilled and famous in one field to give a testimonial for something
in another field is unfair and unreasonable.

48   Testimonial is used extensively in TV ads, where it often appears in such
bizarre forms as Joe Namath's endorsement of a pantyhose brand. Here, of
course, the "authority" giving the testimonial not only is no expert about
pantyhose, but obviously stands to gain something (money!) by making the
testimonial. It is fine for show business celebrities to endorse political candidates, but we should question whether they are in any better position to judge
than we ourselves. Too often we are willing to let others we like or respect
make our decisions *for us,* while we follow along acquiescently. And this is the
purpose of testimonial—to get us to agree and accept *without* stopping to
think. Be sure to ask, "Is there any reason to believe that this person (or organization or publication or whatever) has any more knowledge or information
than I do on this subject? What does the idea amount to on its own merits,
without the benefit of testimonial?"

49   The cornerstone of democratic society is reliance upon an informed and
educated electorate. To be fully effective citizens we need to be able to challenge and to question wisely. A dangerous feeling of indifference toward our
political processes exists today. We often abandon our right, our duty, to criticize and evaluate by dismissing *all* politicians as *crooked,* all new bills and pro-

posals as "just more government bureaucracy." But there are important distinctions to be made, and this kind of apathy can be fatal to democracy.

50   If we are to be led, let us not be led blindly, but critically, intelligently, with our eyes open. If we are to continue to be a government "by the people," let us become informed about the methods and purposes of propaganda, so we can be the masters, not the slaves of our destiny.

COMPREHENSION

1. Words to talk about:

   - *argumentum ad hominem*
   - *argumentum ad populum*
   - *post hoc ergo propter hoc*
   - *two-extremes fallacy*
   - into the arms of *bourgeois-reactionary falsehood*
   - questions are so *multifaceted*
   - we follow along *acquiescently*

2. Cross uses at least one of the propaganda techniques she identifies. Find an example. Why does she do this, and is it effective?
3. Explain Cross's metaphor when she writes "There are several different kinds of *red herrings* that can be used to distract attention."

DISCUSSION

1. Talk a little about each of the thirteen techniques that Cross writes of to see if you can think of examples from your personal experience. If your teacher wants you to, look for printed illustrations to bring in for discussion. Ads are probably the easiest to find, but look also at statements made by political candidates, at letters-to-the-editor, at articles on the opinion pages of newspapers and magazines, and at junk mail. You could also bring examples from your personal experience.
2. Analyze the persuasive techniques in this description of a book written by a young physician who is advocating the use of over-the-counter food supplements as a cure for arthritis. He grew interested in the problem when he had to stop running because his knees hurt. He experimented with various food supplements until his knees improved, and he is now back to running. He says that no one else is promoting the idea of food supplements to regrow cartilage because drug companies

do not want to invest in something that actually cures a disease. Instead, they want the greater profit margin that comes with selling medicines that control or alleviate symptoms over patients' lifetimes. List three reasons why people with arthritis might be tempted to buy the book. Now list three counterbalancing ideas or questions that a careful reader should think about.

3. Charitable organizations frequently use the mail to ask for donations. Identify a persuasive technique used in each of these paraphrased excerpts:

   ■ Thank you, neighbor, for helping us to prove that Americans are the most caring people in the world!
   ■ Over the 21 years that we have been sending out our greeting cards with the statement, "You have no obligation to send money . . . ," the response has been heartwarming and amazing.
   ■ A wheelchair is a lonely place if you think no one cares—but if people are helping, you are bound to make it.
   ■ By the way, the enclosed address labels are a small gift to you, with no strings attached. Please remember _____ as you use one of them.
   ■ Without your help, there will be many more children like Ethan, who in spite of care and love will never have a normal life.

4. When Cross is talking about the Testimonial technique, she gives the example of football player Joe Namath advertising pantyhose and stresses that he is not an authority on pantyhose. That's true, but could the creators of the commercial have had something else in mind? This is practically the only commercial that people still remember and talk about from the 1970s. Why?

THE SPEEDING TICKET

Garrison Keillor

You may wonder why a short story is included in a chapter on persuasive writing. It is here because the word *bamboozle,* which Donna Woolfolk Cross chose for the title of her article (see page 262), is a perfect description of what the man in the green Lincoln does to the townspeople in Keillor's story. Although Keillor's purpose is more to amuse readers than to arm them against a con artist, the story manages to do both. The casual and leisurely style of Keillor's story exemplifies the soft-sell approach. People are lulled into such a trusting mood that they hardly realize they're being sold a bill of goods. As with many of Keillor's other stories, this one is set in the fictitious Minnesota town of Lake Wobegon, "Where all the women are strong and all the men are good-looking and all the children are above average."

1   It has been a quiet week in Lake Wobegon. The only news was that Gary and Leroy gave out a speeding ticket last week, their first in a month or more. If there was a law against pokiness, they could have made a mass arrest of the entire town—people have been feeling low since the Swedish flu struck. It's the usual flu with chills, fever, diarrhea, vomiting, achiness, and personal guilt, but it's accompanied by an overpowering urge to put things in order. Before you collapse into bed, you iron the sheets. Before you vomit, you plan your family's meals for the upcoming week.

2   The Bakkes got back from two weeks in Florida. Jeanette said it was cold and miserable there and they almost went crazy staying with Jack's sister Judy and her husband D.J. and their four kids in their mobile home near Winter Green. D.J. smokes so much Jeanette said it was like she was smoking herself. It made her nervous and she ate more greasy food and gained six pounds and split a seam on her new red Spandex bathing suit. That depressed her, so she gained three more. The food tasted of smoke. She could smell every puff coming from Judy and D.J.'s bedroom at night, and she could hear them fighting like they were in the room with her. So Jack and Jeanette couldn't sleep. Their mattress smelled of smoke too. Judy's oldest boy worked in a supermarket until 3:00 A.M. and the youngest one sleepwalked and was a bedwetter (as Jeanette and Jack discovered one night when he crawled in with them). On the drive home from Minneapolis, they had the bitterest fight of their eighteen-year-marriage over whether it had been a good vacation or not and why,

and it upset her so she started coughing and she could see *smoke* coming out of her mouth, but, she told Dorothy when she got back, that wasn't the worst of it. The worst was that she set off the metal detector in the Miami airport. So it's true what she read, that a faulty can opener makes steel filings that fall in your food. She's had the same opener since 1969. Jack's mother gave it to her, along with a sarcastic remark about cooking. Shards of steel in her tuna fish, creamed corn, mushroom soup, for eighteen years: how was she supposed to know? If you can't trust your can opener, then what? Is your wastebasket going to get you? Your slippers give you a disease? (Deadly Foot & Mouth Virus Traced to Pink Scuffs, Doctors Reveal.)

3   "If you set off the metal detector, how'd you get on the plane?" asked Dorothy. "Oh, when I took off my cinch belt, it didn't buzz anymore, but that cinch belt never used to set off alarms. It's these filings building up that finally pushed me over the limit," Jeanette explained. "Good gosh! How could I eat for all these years and not notice pieces of steel? I must not've been chewing my food good enough."

4   So she ate more potatoes to try to absorb the filings, although the same magazine that warned about can openers also warns about a virus from unclean potato eyes that can cause hair loss, and now Jeanette has gained so much weight she's afraid to climb on a scale.

5   Jack is still mad at her. As Justice of the Peace, he married a couple last Sunday that looked so happy he told Jeanette he wanted to tell them what it was really like. "If they'da stayed around here fifteen minutes, they'da changed their minds about matrimony," he said sardonically. It was an older couple, in their fifties. They drove up during breakfast. Jeanette was still in her bathrobe. She could tell by their embarrassment that they'd come to get married. When she got them a cup of coffee and they said they were from Grand Forks, North Dakota, and she said, "Oh, That's a long way to drive, isn't it. Where'd you spend the night?" they looked down at their shoes, like teenagers. He was heavy, bald as a bowling ball, and perspiring, and she was skinny and had a little mustache, and the backs of her hands were red and flaky. Jack called up Leroy, who lives next door, to come over and witness. He said to the man, "That'll be twenty-five dollars. I always ask for it in advance because, you know, some people are in a hurry to get away. Heh heh heh heh heh." The man turned crimson and fished out the money. Leroy came over. He was sick, he said, so if he had to depart suddenly, that was why. They got married and Jeanette put on a record of Perry Como singing "True Love" and Jack said good luck to them, and out they went, another story that we'll never know the ending of.

6   Leroy was sick, he thought, because of exhaust fumes in the police car, a 1984 Ford. He and Gary sit in it with the engine idling and they get severe headaches. Clint Bunsen checked it and said it was perfectly all right. But Clint himself has been under the weather, so maybe he missed something. Clint is the sort who doesn't get sick until everyone else has had their turn, then if he has a day or two free he'll be sick too but not quite as much.

7   They had just had the car checked and resumed patrol when they gave out the speeding ticket to a green 1987 Lincoln Continental. Leroy said it was going at least sixty-five down Main Street and never even touched its brakes. Myrtle Krebsbach was about to cross the street in front of the Clinic and heard the engine whine and looked up, and a sheet of water hit her amidships. She thought it was a heart attack. Gary and Leroy tore after it, almost running into the rear end of Rollie Hochstetter's manure spreader, and it took them two miles to catch up. They pulled the Lincoln over and walked up alongside and the man rolled down the window and said, "Just a moment. I'll be right with you." He was talking on his car telephone. They had never see one before.

8   They waited. Leroy stood, his arms folded, and Gary leaned down by the window, looking in. The man was about sixty, with silvery hair and blue suit. He was talking in numerals, it was amazing, the figures he had in his head. They couldn't figure out what he was saying. A minute passed and Gary cleared his throat. "Let's go, we don't have all day," he said. But he wasn't quite as angry as he was before.

9   They told him what he'd done and he almost collapsed from horror. "Oh no," he said over and over, "oh my gosh—thank goodness nobody was hurt. I don't know what happened to me. I didn't even see a stop sign. I don't remember seeing stores or anything. House. Schools. I was concentrating on— you see, I have a carton of belostalone I'm supposed to deliver to the University of Chicago tomorrow—that's who I was talking to—but I should've been paying attention. It's my own fault. Take me in, it's all right. I'll get these drugs there some other way. It's my responsibility."

10   Gary rode in the Lincoln, Leroy following in the cruiser. Leroy noticed that Gary and the guy were talking pretty friendly when they arrived at the Chatterbox. They all sat down in a back booth and Leroy called Jack to come. A lynch party had gathered, including Myrtle and Dorothy, but it didn't hang him right away. It asked questions, that was its first mistake. "Who in the hell are you?" said Myrtle.

11   He gave them his card: Dr. Walter W. Ingersoll, Saint Luke's Biomedical Laboratory, Saint Francis, Ontario. *A Canadian!* "That's right," he said.

12   Leroy said, "What do you think you're doing, going sixty-five miles an hour through a town with children? You're a doctor! A doctor ought to have some sense!"

13   "You're absolutely right," he said, "and there is no excuse for what I did. All I can say is that I'm supposed to be at the U of Chicago hospital at eight tomorrow morning with a carton of belostalone. It's an experimental drug that we've been testing in Canada and now they're about to introduce it in America. I don't know how to explain it to you, it's kind of technical for the lay person."

14   Jack and Jeanette had arrived. Jeanette said, "Well, I think you'd better explain, and, you know, we're not as dumb as you might think. We know about medicine."

15   "Well, then, you've probably heard of the experiments with Compazine in Alaska—" Yes, she'd read a little bit about that. "Well, fine, Compazine was a chemotherapeutic drug that showed some effectiveness against myoplasmia, but it made people lose their hair, so belostalone was developed to combat that side effect, and it turned out that not only did people not lose hair, it . . . I don't know how to say this," he said, "but if Chicago knew I was telling you this, I'd lose not only my license to practice medicine but my doctorate in genetic cybernetics as well—so you have to promise . . . " They promised. "Belostalone not only prevented hair loss, it also reversed the effects of aging in every respect."

16   "It makes you younger?" said Jack.

17   "No, sir. I didn't say that. Your chronological age cannot be changed. But you don't have to show it. I'm seventy-two. But you'd think I was sixty-five, wouldn't you?"

18   Actually he looked more like fifty-five.

19   "If anyone got hold of that carton in my trunk, it would have a street value of approximately sixteen million dollars." He looked them straight in the eye. He said, "I know that what I did was terribly wrong, and I don't think I'm going to sleep well for a long time thinking about how I could've killed someone, a child. . . . There's only one way I can make it up to you, and it's wrong too, I suppose, it's stealing, but it's the lesser of two evils. I'll give you each a bottle of belostalone. It's in my trunk."

20   His trunk was full of blank brown cartons and a black bag and boxes marked "Fragile: Pharmaceuticals." It smelled of disinfectant, the kind you find in doctors' offices.

21   "How long did it take to develop this, Walter?" Gary asked, putting a big foot up on the Lincoln's bumper.

22   "It was found utterly accidentally," he said. "The amazing advances all come about that way. They were looking for a simple booster for spring chicks and started with root extract from Jerusalem artichokes and—This is all natural, by the way. . . ." He fished out a box of tiny glass bottles carefully packed in cotton. He handed a bottle to each of them: Gary, Leroy, Jack, Jeanette, Myrtle, Dorothy, and Floyd, Dorothy's son-in-law, who was helping her paint the cafe. Everyone looked embarrassed. "Listen," Gary said, "we can't have you stealing these for us. Let us pay you something." Walter wouldn't hear of it, but they insisted. "At least your cost."

23   "Well," he said, "that's the thing, it's so expensive, medical research, these new drugs are sky-high: just the cost on this is twenty dollars a bottle."

24   To reverse the effects of aging, this seemed like a good deal.

25   They pressed their money into his hand and he gave it back and they handed it to him again but he waved them away and finally they stuck it in his shirt pocket. There it stayed. They stood by the green Lincoln and talked for a while about Canada and good fishing places up there, and finally he drove off. Only then did Leroy realize that he had never actually written Walter the ticket for speeding.

26   When Clarence heard the story from Leroy, he almost lost his balance and fell over. "Reverses the effects of aging!" he said. "Oh that's good. That's just about perfect. I guess we know what his monologue is going to be about this week. You boys ought to copyright this yourselves, so you can charge royalties."

27   Yes, they knew it themselves: they were had, in broad daylight, swindled by a smooth talker into buying twenty dollars' worth of swampwater, and they were ashamed of it, but the odd fact is that they all look better this week. Jeanette feels terrific. No more flu, and she's losing weight, and her skin color is back. Leroy's headaches have stopped. Gary had another problem from sitting too much in the patrol car, and those have cleared up too.

28   Jack called the University of Chicago hospital and they'd never heard of Dr. Ingersoll or belostalone, and neither had anyone in or around Saint Francis, Ontario. Who else could he call? The problem with a fake like Dr. Ingersoll is that when he does you good and you want more medicine, you don't know how to reach him. There is no place to go. A fake takes you to where you start to get well and then leaves you there, on your own.

Comprehension

1. Some critics today make the claim that there is no longer a division between fiction and nonfiction; instead there is just narrative. If, when you started reading this piece, you didn't know that Garrison Keillor wrote fiction, what would have been your first clue that this was a story rather than an essay?
2. What literary techniques does Keillor use to bring a "plain folks" appeal to his story? Give some examples.
3. How does the "Swedish flu" differ from the more typical Asian flu? What does Keillor's little joke reveal about people's attitudes toward ethnicity?

Discussion

1. Give one or more examples of the behavior of the man in the green Lincoln as he practiced these propaganda techniques, as described by Cross (p. 262).

   - *Argumentum ad populum* (stroking)
   - Transfer (glory by association)
   - Bandwagon
   - Testimonial

LIVING LANGUAGE 6.1

Advertising in the News

Because advertising is such a big part of our lives, it often makes its way into the very news that it pays to produce and distribute. The stories cited here are a small sample chosen to illustrate variety rather than to be comprehensive.

- The *New York Times Education Life* devoted its cover and all or part of ten pages to the troublesome question of whether advertisements should be allowed in schools. In November of 1996, the Seattle, Washington, School Board voted to solve a budget crisis by accepting corporate advertising in the city's middle and high schools. They were following the lead of Colorado Springs, where for the past three years students have ridden buses adorned with corporate logos and walked in hallways dotted with advertising billboards. Book jackets, classroom packets and work sheets, assembly programs, and television sets complete with mandatory news and commercials are among the items currently finding their way into schools. (Jan. 5, 1997)
- Shortly after his surprise wedding, John F. Kennedy Jr. spoke at an advertising luncheon in Portland, Oregon. He got a big laugh when he explained, "One evening not so long ago, I was staring out my window, wondering whether I should make a major life decision, and my eyes focused on a billboard that said: 'Just Do It.' " The reference was to the slogan made famous by Nike shoes. (*Arizona Republic*, Oct. 20, 1996)
- The familiar slogan of "Let your fingers do the walking" is being phased out by U.S. West in favor of *Dex*, a detective-like figure peering through a magnifying glass. The 1998 *Dex* phone books were introduced in a multimillion dollar ad campaign featuring the character who is supposed to remind users of a detective turned "directory expert." His name comes from the Latin *dexter*, meaning "right." U.S. West hopes it will make people think of *dexterity* and *index*.
- "United Way Pulls 2 Misleading Ads" was the headline on a story about an advertising campaign featuring photos of eight "needy" people. While six of the people had been photographed at shelters or on city streets, the photographer had used his own son for one picture and a 79-year-old friend for another. The woman's daughter, who lived in a town 200 miles away, was stunned when she opened the newspaper and saw her mother portrayed as a representative of the "homeless, desperate, or downtrodden" street people in Phoenix. (*Arizona Republic*, Sept. 14, 1996)
- Generic advertisements such as the "Milk, Where's Your Mustache?" "Beef is Leaner," and the singing and dancing California Raisins found themselves in trouble when a group of California growers sued the state program that required them to contribute money to the ads. They said there's no proof the ads are successful, they resent having to support their competitors (e.g., growers of yellow grapes have to contribute to the dancing grapes, yet no yellow grapes have ever

been included), and some growers found the sexual connotations in a new set of commercials for "California summer fruits" (peaches, plums, and nectarines) offensive. The case went all the way to the Supreme Court, with the decision going against the growers who wanted out. (*Knight-Ridder Newspapers*, Nov. 24, 1996)

- For the 1997 Super Bowl, advertisers paid $1.3 million each for the chance to reach 140 million people with a 30-second spot. In typical advertising fashion, Madison Avenue claims the Super Bowl is "the most coveted ad position in the world," but in China a wine maker from Shantung just paid $40 million for a 5-second spot right before the 7 P.M. news. He had to bid at an auction, and he gets the spot for the entire year of 1997. The same spot cost him only $8 million in 1996. (*Parade Magazine*, Dec. 19, 1996)

- In reaction to all the publicity about the Walt Disney movie *101 Dalmatians* and the widely publicized warnings from owners and kennel clubs that the dogs are unpredictable and not good with children, humorist Calvin Trillin wrote a column suggesting that the Disney and Dalmatian industry might be "cooperating in a piggyback promotion scheme designed to have both of their products discussed incessantly." He questioned the sincerity of all these people "with beautiful Dalmations at their feet" insisting that "the average person is not up to coping with a Dalmatian." He vowed to skip the movie so as not to fall victim to the "two-step selling strategy in which the customer is tantalized by such warnings and then smitten by the puppies in the movie." (*Time*, Dec. 9, 1996)

- The Federal Trade Commission and Attorney Generals from 23 states announced agreements with auto makers to halt the "ads you love to hate." This includes a Mazda television commercial showing blissful customers clutching giant, floating pennies to promote a "one penny down" car-lease offer, in which the fine print that rolls by so fast people can't read it explains "the customer must, in fact, put down at least $900, which amounts to 89,999 more pennies than advertised." Honda had an ad showing an odometer "merrily rolling backward to $0000 to illustrate its no-money-down deal. Fat chance." Customers actually had to pay about $600 up front. (*Arizona Republic*, Nov. 22, 1996)

- "Every year consumers are invited to spend billions of dollars on products and services that are misrepresented, that undermine good health and that sometimes are downright dangerous," said Iowa Attorney General Tom Miller, who was the guest speaker at an Academy Awards-style ceremony in Washington, D.C., where the Harlan Page Hubbard Lemon awards were given. The awards, which are gleaming figures, each holding aloft a fresh lemon, were given in absentia to major United States companies judged by a coalition of consumer, safety, and health advocacy groups as trying to sell products through "misleading, unfair, and irresponsible" advertising campaigns. The award is named for the nineteenth century

continued

LIVING LANGUAGE 6.1

Advertising in the News   continued

advertiser of Lydia E. Pinkham's Vegetable Compound, which was "guaranteed" to cure everything from cancer to flatulence, headaches, sleeplessness, and low sex drive. The 1997 winners included R. J. Reynolds, the American Egg Board, and Sprint long-distance phone service. (Associated Press, Dec. 5, 1997)

- The Food and Drug Administration is requiring the dairy industry to use more accurate labels on milk products. Processors now must advertise *reduced fat* rather than *low-fat* for 2 percent milk because it actually has two-thirds the fat of whole milk. Milk with no fat will be called *fat-free* instead of *skim*, while 1 percent milk will be labeled *low-fat*. January 1, 1998, was set as the date for compliance. (Associated Press, Dec. 7, 1997)

---

2. What was Keillor doing in the first half of the story when he presented all the information about the characters before the man in the green Lincoln came to town?
3. Both Cross (p. 262) and Keillor are teaching readers about propaganda. Compare their two approaches. How do they complement each other?
4. Con artists and advertisers often pitch their appeals to basic psychological needs. What were the needs to which Dr. Ingersoll played? How did he do it?
5. How do you explain the improved health of the townspeople?
6. Have you heard of the "Lake Wobegon syndrome"? It has become part of the world's educational jargon. From the introduction to the story, try to figure out what it means. How does the name of the town reinforce the term's meaning?

WORD LAW

Dennis Baron

Nothing is more important to the image of a product or a company than its name. It takes only a tenth of a second to speak or read a name, yet the success of a company may depend on that name, and so the choosing and protecting of commercial names has become big business. Consultants earn an average of $50,000 for doing the work involved in creating a company name, and big companies such as McDonald's have spent millions of dollars protecting theirs. Dennis Baron's article illustrates some of the complications.

1   I saw an ad once in the back of a magazine promising that if I sent in some money, I could have a star in the firmament named after me. For the same low price I would receive a certificate and a photograph of the galaxy where my star was located. I might even be able to see that star if I possessed suitable magnifying equipment. I was not tempted by the offer, but it did occur to me that while I would not like to have a star, as a wordsmith I might like to own my own word.

2   Is it possible to own your very own word? The English language may belong to all of us, but some of its words are the property of individuals or, in most cases of lexical ownership, of corporations. I am referring to the registered trademarks and service marks protected under federal law from the infringement of unscrupulous competitors. Now, I am a language professional, not a manufacturer or a lawyer, so if you want competent advice in the latter areas you should supplement the summary of the complex trademark picture that follows.

3   The law of trademarks, which fills more than two volumes of the Annotated U.S. Code in the local law library—the source of the following information—gives us some guidance as to what words can and cannot be staked out as private property and what that notion of privacy really means when it comes to the use of language.

4   For one thing, you cannot simply coin a word and lay claim to it. You must also sell the goods named by your trademark or perform services named by your service mark. In all, a trademark is a name, logotype, design, or any combination thereof adopted and used by a manufacturer to identify its goods

and distinguish them from articles sold by others. A service mark identifies you as a provider of specific services rather than of vendable articles. For example, *Kodak* is a trademark, *Fotomat,* a service mark. Your trademark or service mark may be registered, but you may have rights to the mark even if you have not registered it. The symbol you choose for your mark may be pictorial, as the bearded representation of the Smith Brothers of cough-drop fame, who as some would have it, are named, respectively, Trade and Mark. But a trademark may also be a word or a group of words.

5   Sounds simple, really. You come up with a no-nonsense product designed to remove widgets, patent it, and market it under the straightforward name Widget Terminator. Maybe the Widget Terminator does its job well, finds a niche in the market, and over the years even makes a little money for you. Only now your brother-in-law decides he is going to get into the act and beat your price. Of course he calls his knock-off the WidgetBuster, a much snappier moniker, and he packages the product behind a picture of a widget inside a barred red circle. Since his product works differently from yours, you cannot get him for violating patent law, so you haul him into court and sue the pants off him for infringing on the implied trademark you have established with your Widget Terminator.

6   Keeping it all in the family, you get your cousin Benny, fresh out of law school and eager for work, to argue that the public has come to love and trust the Widget Terminator and that people will be confused and deceived by the similarity of the name of the rival WidgetBuster. As a result of this confusion of products, your reputation will be damaged and your sales hurt. You ask that the WidgetBuster be withdrawn from the market and that your brother-in-law pay you treble damages and that he pay your cousin Benny, as well.

7   Do you think you will win? That depends on how well Benny did in his Intellectual Property Law course. The law recognizes two basic kinds of trademark, though it allows for a measure of degree in their definition: a "strong trademark" is one used only in a fictitious or fanciful manner, while a "weak trademark" is a meaningful word in common usage that doubles as a suggestive or descriptive trademark. Weak trademarks are more difficult to establish, and they are entitled to narrower protection than strong ones. Your brother-in-law's counsel will argue that you have an invention, but its name is not a trademark, because a trademark cannot be an ordinary word, particularly a descriptive one, if that word is used in its ordinary sense. Both *widget* and *terminator* are common English words—a *widget* is a "gadget, or gizmo," in case you did not know—and they literally describe the function of the product, which is to remove pesky widgets, so you cannot claim them as your own or prevent others from using them.

8   Of course, if you have ever talked to a lawyer you know that things are never what they appear when it comes to the law. There have been trade-

marks that were fairly literal, for example, *Coca-Cola*. *Coca-Cola*, which is a trademark of long standing, originally contained both cocaine and an extract from the cola nut. The cocaine went out when it was declared a controlled substance early in this century. Interestingly, the makers of *Coke* (which is also a registered mark) once sought to prohibit the marketing of something called *Tacola-Cola*, as well as any other drink with the word *cola* in its name. But the courts ruled that because *cola* was a common word describing what was in the beverage, any soda containing *cola* derivatives could be called a *cola*. Coke's trademark was upheld against *Chero-Cola*, *Clio-Cola*, *Coca* and *Cola*, and *El-Cola*; ruled to be non-infringing were *Koke*, *Dope*, *Cherry-Cola*, *Roxa-Cola*, and *Dixie-Cola*. As for other sodas, *Moxie* won its case against *Noxie*, but *Pepsi-Cola* lost against *Pep*, as did *Seven-Up* against *Cheer Up*.

9   On the other hand, if the name of your product is a common word which is applied in an arbitrary or fanciful sense, you should be able to claim it as a trademark. The courts have ruled that *Cyclone*, when naming a fence, and *Innocent*, as a brand of hair coloring (suggesting, as the ruling noted, "the very antithesis of innocence") are legitimate trademarks; but while *Yellow Pages* was found to be a trademark although it is clearly descriptive, *raisin bran* and *spearmint* were not granted exclusive status.

10   Manufacturers are fond of deforming the spelling of an ordinary word to make it distinctive, for example *NU* for *new*, *KWIK* for *quick*, or *Bonz* for *bones* (unfortunately, this last, a dog food lacking the so-called silent *e*, is frequently mispronounced). But a clever or phonetic spelling of a normal descriptive word does not entitle you to own it as a trademark. Rather, a common word can become a trademark only if it acquires a "secondary meaning," if, in other words, it is used so long and so exclusively by one producer that it has come to signal to the general public that the product in question is made by that producer, and that producer alone. (The courts have insisted repeatedly that to be a trademark, a word or symbol must call up not the product or service but its source, the producer or provider.)

11   If your brother-in-law can afford to wait, time may be on his side in the battle against widgets. If you stop selling a product for two or more years, you may lose the right to its trademark. The courts frown on manufacturers who pretend to sell a few samples of a product each year just to hold on to the name for future use. But you may be able to withhold the product from the market while you experiment with ways to improve it, and you can change the product significantly and still retain possession of its name, as the makers of *Tabasco* did when they altered the formula of their hot sauce but successfully defended their right to exclusive use of the trademark.

12   Under the former trademark law, *shredded wheat* was considered a generic term and, hence, not registrable. But because the process for making it was patented, no other company could produce it, hence the patent holder had exclusive rights to the name of a unique product. When the patent

expired, new manufacturers simply used *shredded wheat* as a descriptive term. And although dictionary maker Noah Webster was instrumental in passing our first federal copyright laws to protect an author's intellectual property, the name *Webster* ceased to function as an exclusive trademark when the original Webster's copyright ran out. As early as 1904, G. & C. Merriam, of Springfield, Massachusetts, who claimed to be the literal publishing descendants of Noah Webster's lexicographical projects, attempted to restrain the sale of other dictionaries with *Webster* in the title. In a series of decisions—*Merriam v. Ogilvie* (170 F 167), *Merriam v. Saalfield* (190 F 927; 198 F 369)—the U.S. Circuit Court of Appeals ruled partly for Merriam, partly for the competition: Merriam lost its right to the exclusive use of the name *Webster,* but since that company had become known to the public as the publisher of Noah Webster's dictionaries, would-be Websters were ordered to disclaim on their title pages any connection with the original word book. In the early 1940s, World Publishing Company, producer of *Webster's New World* dictionaries, obtained a ruling to quash the disclaimer requirement. In a more recent action, initiated by Merriam in 1981, the Court of Appeals again affirmed the right of other publishers to use *Webster* in dictionary titles and enjoined the defendants from using any variation or combination of the words *world-famous, authentic, original, genuine,* or *renowned* to suggest a connection between their product and the Merriam-Webster line of dictionaries (*Merriam v. Webster Dictionary Co.* (639 F 2d 29). It is clear that for many, *Webster's* has become a generic word. Despite the fact that this synonym is one that the courts have repeatedly upheld, no dictionary is willing to define *Webster's* simply as "dictionary."

13   Normally, a title cannot function as a trademark, which is why different books can have the same title, as long as their contents are different and there is no intent to deceive the public. Two manufacturers may be allowed access to the same trademark if their products are so different that their markets will not overlap and if there is no indication that the public will be confused by the names. Thus Condé-Nast, the publishers of the magazine *Vogue,* which is a trademark, were unsuccessful in a suit to force the owners of the *Vogue School of Fashion Modeling* to change its name. And VERBATIM, the language quarterly, registered as a trademark in 1974, failed in its suit against the manufacturer of *Verbatim* floppy disks, introduced in 1977, though the *Verbatim* (disk) company agreed never to produce anything but blank recording media, while VERBATIM is enjoined only from producing blank media. The owners of the popular 1984 movie title *Ghostbusters* have extended the range of their trademark with a television show, toys, and other licensed products bearing its name and distinctive logo, and VERBATIM, the language quarterly, is free to do likewise.

14   Ironically, success can sometimes weaken your right to a trademark, particularly if your product name has become a generic term. *Cellophane* failed to

protect itself in an infringement suit when the defense attorney asked the *Cellophane* representative for the generic name of the product. Unable to come up with a synonym for cellophane, the manufacturer lost its trademark. *Celluloid* remained a trademark much longer, though it too has now become a generic term.

15   *Thermos* and *Zipper* were both originally trademarks. But both products became so popular that their names began to function as generics in the public mind, and because of that the courts have ruled that other companies could use these words uncapitalized so long as they did not attempt to confuse or deceive the public. However, a design or distinctive style of typography can be a trademark, and the distinctive manner of printing *Thermos* as a symbol remains protected.

16   Federal law regulates only in the broadest sense what words can or cannot serve as trademarks. Prior decisions have little value in trademark claims, and each case must be argued on its own merits. As a result, trademark rulings may seem idiosyncratic or contradictory. The law clearly specifies, though, that a trademark cannot be immoral, deceptive, scandalous, or disparaging. *Glass Wax*, a glass cleaner which contains no wax, successfully defended its trademark against a charge that the name was deceptive, but in the early 1900s the courts refused to recognize *Madonna* as a trademark for wine because it was ruled scandalous. (The soft drink *Old Monk*, which was not perceived to threaten public morality, was permitted.) Tastes change of course, in wines as well as scandals, and though *Old Monk* is gone from the shelves, today's courts seem not to be offended by the brand of wine known as *Blue Nun*.

17   Foreign words can serve as trademarks in the United States, but their legal status is determined the same way as that of English words. Thus Selchow & Righter, makers of the game *Parcheesi*, could not prohibit other manufacturers from selling games under such names as *Pachisi, Parchisi,* or *Parchesi,* variant spellings of the common Hindi word for the old Indian pastime. Similarly, Duncan was unable to retain exclusive rights to the name *yo-yo* because the toy is called that in the Philippines, where it originated, and because it has no synonyms. On the other hand, both *Scrabble* and *Monopoly* are trademarks for games. Despite the fact that both are ordinary English words, they meet the secondary meaning test, being easily recognized as exclusive product names, although the court also upheld the trademark rights of a game called *Anti-Monopoly* over the objection of *Monopoly*-owner, Parker Brothers. That decision remains confused.

18   A trademark can be longer than a word, or even a pair of words. You can lay claim to an entire slogan if it has become widely enough identified with your product, but the courts do not let you monopolize the language. They will limit your power to control sentences similar to yours, just as they stymied Anheuser-Busch, the owners of the slogan, "Where there's life,

there's Bud," who failed in their attempt to prevent use of all slogans beginning, "Where there's life . . . " including, as far as I know, the age-old proverb, "Where there's life, there's hope."

19   At any rate, it seems that when there's a trademark, there's hope for a lawsuit. The Xerox Corporation, recognizing the potential danger of success, has in the past gone out of its way to protect its right to the words it owns. Though I have found no reference to any trademark suits brought by Xerox against other manufacturers, the company has tried to regulate the use of its trademark in ordinary English. For example, some years ago the xerography pioneer took out half-page ads in the *New York Times* to remind us that *Xerox* is a trademark to be used only as a proper noun, as in *Xerox machine,* or a proper adjective, as in *Xerox* copy. In either case, warned the ad, we must capitalize *Xerox.* Despite such entreaties, the word *xerox* seems to have become generic, if not according to the courts, then at least according to current American usage, where it occurs freely as noun, adjective, and even verb, with or without capitalization. *Xerox* persists because unregulated use by others may cause a trademark to be deemed abandoned.

20   Many publishers, either fearing litigation or simply because they are sensitive to questions of ownership of the printed word, prefer to take a cautious approach to trademarks, capitalizing words like *Xerox, Coke,* and *Formica* in print, though at least one major dictionary recognizes the uncapitalized form of *xerox,* and allows it to function as a verb. But no contemporary lexicon, either desk-sized or unabridged, records for *Webster's* the commonly found meaning "an English dictionary, even one not actually attributable to the lexicographer Noah Webster."

21   But back to the hypothetical case of *Widget Remover Mfg. Co. of North America v. WidgetBuster, S. A.* While you may not be able to restrain your brother-in-law's trade, you can hope that his market share will become so large as to draw the attention of the owners of the *Ghostbusters* trademark and that their battery of high-priced studio lawyers might be able to get the injunction that your cousin could not.

22   Clearly, owning a trademark can be worth so much that a manufacturer will object willy-nilly to any and every use of it by another. In one case the court told a manufacturer that there can be no monopoly on *love:* "No one may preempt the field with respect to marks having *love* as a portion thereof and thus exclude all others from the use of any mark composed in part of such word." But owning a word can do little for a writer like me, except perhaps in the ego department, since according to the law, a word can be a trademark only if such status does not deprive others of their right to the normal use of the English language. So if you were planning to give someone a word for his birthday, think again. Words that do not fit cannot be returned. And owning a word is not like owning a ball: even if the game is not going the way you planned, you cannot just pick up your word and go home.

When you use "Xerox" the way you use "aspirin," we get a headache.

X Boy, what a headache! And all because some of you may be using our name in a generic manner. Which could cause it to lose its trademark status the way the name "aspirin" did years ago. So when you do use our name, please use it as an adjective to identify our products and services, e.g., Xerox copiers. Never as a verb: "to Xerox" in place of "to copy", or as a noun: "Xeroxes" in place of "copies". Thank you. Now, could you excuse us, we've got to lie down for a few minutes.

THE
DOCUMENT
COMPANY
XEROX
Worldwide Sponsor

THE DOCUMENT COMPANY
XEROX

This ad appeared in newspapers and magazines in 1996–1997. When American inventor Chester Carlson (1906–1968) invented a process of copying without using fluids, he named it *Xerox*, from the Greek words *Xeros*, meaning "dry," and *oxys* meaning "sharp." In 1952, he sold the name and the process to the Haloid Company in Rochester, New York, which registered Xerox as a trademark and has been working ever since to keep it from becoming generic. One tactic as shown in this ad is to appeal to the public for help, which also has legal implications in proving that the company has been actively protecting its trademark. Another tactic was for the company to introduce a stylized X, which will be difficult for others to reproduce. (*Source:* Ad reprinted with the permission of Xerox Corporation.)

COMPREHENSION

1. Words to talk about:
   - I could have a star in the *firmament*
   - in most cases of *lexical* ownership
   - from the *infringement* of *unscrupulous* competitors
   - rather than of *vendable* articles
   - finds a *niche* in the market
   - Of course he calls his *knock-off*
   - a much snappier *moniker*
   - pay you *treble* damages
   - either fearing *litigation*
   - manufacturer will object *willy-nilly*

2. Baron says, "You can't just coin a word and lay claim to it." What else do you have to do?
3. If you write a book, how much freedom do you have in devising a name?
4. What's the difference between a trademark and a service mark?
5. How can success weaken a company's right to a trademark? Explain the connection between Xerox and aspirin that makes the Xerox ad more than just a plea for help.

DISCUSSION

1. Baron talks about "strong trademarks" and "weak trademarks." Within the last couple of decades, photocopy shops have proliferated, and they all need to have names. Look at such shops around your campus and decide which ones have strong versus weak trademarks. Which of these six is likely to have a hard time protecting its name from being used by someone else?

Alphagraphics	Kinko's
Campus Copy	Kwik Kopy
Instant Copy	Uni-Print

2. Lawyers who specialize in intellectual property are much more common today than they were even a decade ago. Why? Besides working in protecting patents and trademarks, what kinds of things do they do?
3. Here are some news stories about trademark conflicts. Talk a bit about each one and decide which of Baron's "rules" or examples it comes closest to.
   (a) A million dollar law suit evolved out of a plan by Quality Inns International to open two hundred budget motels under the name

McSleep. Only three days after the initial announcement, the Mc-Donald's Corporation sent a letter alleging trademark infringement and demanding that Quality Inns not use the name. The motel chain claimed that the Mc of McDonald's has become a generic morpheme in English, but at a seven-day trial United States District Judge Paul V. Niemeyer ruled against the Quality Inns plan on the grounds that sleeping and eating were closely allied in people's minds and therefore could be confused. (For details of the story, see "*Mc-*: Meaning in the Marketplace" by Genine Lentine and Roger W. Shuy in the winter 1990 issue of *American Speech*. The authors of the article are linguists who served as expert witnesses for the motel chain.)

(b) Because the United States Olympics Committee does not receive government subsidies, it is supported mostly through the heavy fees that sponsors pay for being allowed to use the overlapping ring design and related Olympics symbols. The day following the announcement that Atlanta was the chosen city for the 1996 Summer Olympic Games, the *Atlanta Journal and Constitution* began selling souvenir T-shirts printed with a reproduction of the newspaper's front page, which included the Olympic rings. The Olympic committee objected; the newspaper stopped selling the merchandise and paid the Committee 10 percent of the $500,000 that had already changed hands. According to the *Phoenix Gazette* (Feb. 21, 1994), within the next twelve months the Atlanta committee "chased more than 300 businesses and individuals off its trademark turf," including church groups who wanted to sponsor a Christian Olympics field day and the city of Atlanta who wanted to sponsor a Trees for Olympic Atlanta tree-planting project.

(c) The Princeton Review and the Kaplan Educational Centers compete with each other in the lucrative business of preparing college students for admissions exams to graduate school. According to the *ASU State Press* (Oct. 11, 1994), the Princeton Review signed itself onto the Internet under the name of Kaplan.Com and used the bulletin board to post complaints about the Kaplan company. The Kaplan folks were not amused: "How would you feel if you called up your BMW dealer and were automatically connected to Hyundai?" asked president Jonathan Grayer. An Internet arbitration panel put a stop to the "prank," and predicted that regulating names on the Internet will probably be necessary in the not-too-distant future.

(d) Two graduates of Iona College in New Rochelle, New York started a pizza shop and named it A No. 1 (Iona spelled backwards). According to the *Chronicle of Higher Education* (Dec. 8, 1993), when they also adopted a logo that resembled the college's, the college sued on the grounds of "a misuse of the Iona identity." The judge sided with the graduates and said, "At best, the similarities that do exist can be interpreted as a satirical play on familiar symbolism."

(e) When the nightly show *Politically Incorrect*, hosted by Bill Maher, was just getting started, Comedy Central cable television channel filed a suit in Federal District Court in Manhattan seeking to bar Jackie Mason from calling his new show *Jackie Mason, Politically Incorrect*. According to the *New York Times* (Nov. 3, 1992), Mason successfully defended his claim by explaining, "I have been associated with the phrase politically incorrect for ten years, ever since the expression became popular. . . . My whole attitude was always politically incorrect; it's my expression of independence."

(f) As part of the Library of Congress's bicentennial celebration, a letter by Groucho Marx was read along with letters written by

LIVING LANGUAGE 6.2

Winning Commercial Names

Some of the greatest product names were developed long before there were name consultants and college courses in advertising. Today's naming consultants are now trying to analyze and imitate those names that proved stunningly successful.

■ Zippers, invented in 1893, went through various names including the Universal, the Hookless, and the C-Curity fastener. In 1921, the B. F. Goodrich Company in Akron, Ohio, started manufacturing overshoes with slide fasteners, and in 1923 one of their engineers coined the onomatopoeic name Zipper. By the time the company tried to claim the name as a trademark, it had already become generic, but in its honor athletic teams at the University of Akron are known as the Zips.

■ In 1858, Brooklyn chemist Robert A. Chesebrough went sight-seeing at the first American oil wells in Pennsylvania. He noticed workers using a waxy substance from the pump rods as an ointment. He gathered the oily residue and invented a medicinal product that he named Vaseline from the German *Wasser* ("water") and the Greek *elaion* ("olive oil").

■ In the 1890s, Mary Wait, the wife of the manufacturer of a new sugary, gelatin dessert, coined the term *JELL-O*, which became one of the most successful trademarks of all time.

■ Between 1870 and 1879, Ivory Soap was called The White Soap until manufacturer Harley T. Proctor went to church and let his mind wander to business during the sermon, which included the verse from Psalms 45:8, "All thy garments smell of myrrh and aloes and cassia, out of the ivory palaces whereby they have made thee glad." He promptly renamed his soap Ivory, and devised the "99 and 44/100% pure" slogan.

Thomas Jefferson and Abraham Lincoln. The Marx letter was in response to a warning that had been sent by Warner Brothers demanding that the Marx brothers not infringe on the name *Casablanca* with their forthcoming movie title, *A Night in Casablanca*. Groucho wrote that he was surprised to learn that Warner Brothers owned the city of Casablanca. He also said that if Warner Brothers was planning to rerelease *Casablanca,* he was sure that most movie fans would be able to distinguish between Ingrid Bergman and Harpo Marx. Then he asked whether he would also have to ask permission from Warner Brothers to use the term *brothers* as in the name *Marx Brothers.* And would the Smith Brothers, the Brothers Karamazov, and Dan Brouthers (an outfielder for the Detroit baseball team) also have to get permission from Warner Brothers?

- The name for Hershey Kisses was chosen in 1907 based on the puckering motion of the machine that ejected them. The pleasant connotations are serendipitous.
- In the naming of Scotch Tape, the 3-M Company was lucky to find an ethnic group whose thriftiness was considered a strength. Besides carrying positive connotations of thriftiness, the name is short and virtually impossible to mispronounce. Another plus is how easily it can be reinforced with package designs incorporating Scotch plaids.
- In 1300, English King Edward I declared that all gold and silver must be stamped with marks to indicate its quality. The stamping was done by Goldsmith's Hall in London, hence a hallmark came to be associated with the idea of quality, an image the Hallmark greeting card company pursues vigorously even to the raised mark on each envelope.
- The first name for the bubbly drink now called Seven-Up was Lithiated Lemon-Lime Soda. When the developer, C. L. Grigg, went looking for a new name, one story says he was inspired by a cattle brand composed from a *7* with a *U* above the right side. Changing the *U* to Up acknowledged the rising bubbles. Another story says he settled on 7 because it was a lucky number and he had already rejected six other suggestions.
- On July 12, 1996, the "Eskimo Pie got itself enshrined as a frosty slice of American history." Thousands of ice-cream bars were handed out on the terrace of the National Museum of American History where David Clark, the CEO ("chief eating officer") of the Eskimo Pie Corp. signed over a gift of documents and artifacts including a small machine built seventy-five years ago, which dipped the vanilla ice cream in hot, bitter chocolate and wrapped it in tin foil.

WORKSHOP 6.1

Signs of Our Times

The owners of businesses hoping to attract customers from people driving by must create signs that are both unique and easily recognizable. This is especially true now that many cities have zoning codes that restrict the size and placement of signs. Service stations, restaurants, and convenience stores aim for instant recognition so people can recognize a sign from a distance, slow down, and drive up for business. Other businesses try to attract customers by being clever or unique, while still others choose names and logos that will inspire comforting or pleasant thoughts.

PART I: COMMERCIAL SIGNS

BRAIN TEASERS

1. Look at the four pictures of fast-food restaurant signs shown on page 293 and see if you can figure out the basis for their success. Answering the following questions may help.
   (a) What kind of food does each of these restaurants offer? Did you already know because the restaurant is so famous, or did some reinforcing idea in the sign (besides the name) tell you?
   (b) Of the reinforcing ideas, which do you think is the most clever? Which is the most effective, and why?
   (c) Some of these signs reveal the history of the restaurants. Which ones? What do they tell?
   (d) What other fast-food restaurant signs are equally effective? Conjecture on the reasons behind their success.
2. Why are restaurant chains so particular about each restaurant using an identical logo? How does technology make this more feasible today than it would have been two decades ago?
3. In your neighborhood, look at business signs other than restaurants and list examples of ones you judge to be visually effective. Talk about their overall shape, how streamlined they are, and how the design of the sign reinforces the product. What do different styles of lettering communicate? When dotting the letter *i*, what symbols can be used?

PART II: PUBLIC CUTESPEAK

Dennis Baron, the man who wrote the "Word Law" article, has written a book called *Guide to Home Language Repair* (National Council of Teachers of English, 1994) in which he complained about the bad puns that have become commonplace in establishments catering to the Yuppie generation. He calls such names as Mustard's Last Stand (a hot dog restaurant), Den of Antiquity (an antique shop), Wreck-Amended (an

auto repair shop), and The Wizard of Ooze (a septic tank company) "public cute-speak" and conjectures that enjoying such names is an acquired taste. Business experts advise that a humorous name may help a small company stand out from the competition in a mall or in telephone directories; however, such names will probably have a negative impact on potential investors.

continued

WORKSHOP 6.1

Signs of Our Time   continued

BRAIN TEASERS

1. Look at the four photos on pages 294 and 295 and talk about the strengths of each. They show signs for a computer store, a pet supply store, a restaurant, and a junkyard that sells second-hand auto parts.
   (a) In which ones are the owners playing with words? Explain the word play.
   (b) Business owners like to include "value" words (words with positive connotations) in their names. Each of these signs includes a value word. What are they?
   (c) Which names most clearly identify what is being sold? What other clues about the products are included in the signs?

2. Explore business names in your town. Begin by making a list of names you remember. Try to figure out if the name has stuck in your mind because you are a frequent customer or because there is something about the wording that makes the name memorable.

3. Brainstorm with other students about names in your town that are memorable. The yellow pages of telephone directories are good sources of information. Try to find examples based on the following attention-getting devices:
   - puns
   - allusions
   - exaggerations
   - clippings and blendings
   - unique spellings

4. Select a particular kind of business and analyze what is important in the names for that business. For exaple, if you look at child-care centers, you will probably notice the inclusion of "virtue" words meant to reassure parents that their children will be well taken care of. With hair salons, you might compare the names of barber shops, beauty shops, and those who welcome both sexes. You might also look to see which ones stress convenience and cost and which ones try to inspire romantic daydreams.

continued

WORKSHOP 6.1

Signs of Our Time   continued

PART III: POLITICS ON THE MOVE

There's more to politics than voting on proposed laws and electing local and national leaders. We engage in politics whenever we develop an idea or adopt someone else's idea and then try to convince our neighbors, friends, relatives, and even strangers that the idea is a good one. While election campaigns are restricted to particular seasons, people who offer proverbs, put bumper stickers on their cars, and wear buttons and T-shirts imprinted with messages are advertising their political beliefs on a daily basis.

BRAIN TEASERS

Look at the pictures of bumper stickers below and on page 297 and answer the following questions:

1. Who do you think chose to display each sign? On what basis are you making your judgment?
2. Can you figure out the intended messages? If you were driving by and just caught a glimpse, which ones would be the hardest to comprehend. Why?
3. How do they communicate tone? Which ones are really obvious? Which ones have secondary, almost hidden, meanings? Which ones present an unusual point of view?
4. Reword two or three. Remember that succinctness as well as originality is a high priority.

THE WEST WAS
LOST NOT WON

 it will be a great day when our schools get all the money they need and the air force has to hold a bake sale to buy a bomber

Proud parent of an Honor Student at a
CATHOLIC SCHOOL

YOU CAN HAVE MY GUN
WHEN YOU PRY IT FROM MY PARANOID,
MENTALLY DISTURBED, PHYSICALLY-ABUSIVE,
COLD, DEAD HAND
NORTHERN SUN MERCHANDISING, 2916 EAST LAKE STREET, MPLS, MN 55406-2065 1-800-258-8579

*Source: © 1968 Women's International League for Peace and Freedom, Philadelphia, PA.

†Source: © Northern Sun Merchandising, Minneapolis, MN, 1 (800) 258-8579.

From "The World of Doublespeak"

William Lutz

For fifteen years, William Lutz chaired the Committee on Public Doublespeak for the National Council of Teachers of English. Part of his duties included editing the *Quarterly Review of Doublespeak* and helping to select winners and runners-up for the annual Doublespeak Award, which is given to organizations or individuals who have demonstrated unusual skill, as well as malfeasance, in using language so as to mislead listeners or readers. Lutz, who teaches English at Rutgers University, now has six file cabinets full of news clippings exemplifying various kinds of doublespeak. He shares some of them in this article.

1   Doublespeak is a blanket term for language which pretends to communicate but doesn't, language which makes the bad seem good, the negative appear positive, the unpleasant attractive, or at least tolerable. It is language which avoids, shifts, or denies responsibility, language which is at variance with its real or its purported meaning. It is language which conceals or prevents thought. Basic to doublespeak is incongruity, the incongruity between what is said, or left unsaid, and what really is: between the word and the referent, between seem and be, between the essential function of language, communication, and what doublespeak does—mislead, distort, deceive, inflate, circumvent, obfuscate.

2   When shopping, we are asked to check our packages at the desk "for our convenience," when it's not for our convenience at all but for the store's "program to reduce inventory shrinkage." We see advertisements for "preowned," "experienced," or "previously distinguished" cars, for "genuine imitation leather," "virgin vinyl," or "real counterfeit diamonds." Television offers not reruns but "encore telecasts." There are no slums or ghettos, just the "inner city" or "substandard housing" where the "disadvantaged," "economically nonaffluent," or "fiscal underachievers" live. Nonprofit organizations don't make a profit, they have "negative deficits" or "revenue excesses." In the world of doublespeak dying is "terminal living."

3   We know that a toothbrush is still a toothbrush even if the advertisements on television call it a "home plaque removal instrument," and even that "nutritional avoidance therapy" means a diet. But who would guess that a

"volume-related production schedule" adjustment means closing an entire factory in the doublespeak of General Motors, or that "advanced downward adjustments" means budget cuts in the doublespeak of Caspar Weinberger, or that "energetic disassembly" means an explosion in a nuclear power plant in the doublespeak of the nuclear power industry? . . .

4   The doublespeak of inflated language can have serious consequences. . . . In the doublespeak of the military, the 1983 invasion of Grenada was conducted not by the U.S. Army, Navy, Air Force, and Marines but by the "Caribbean Peace Keeping Forces." But then according to the Pentagon it wasn't an invasion, it was a "predawn vertical insertion."

5   These last examples of doublespeak should make it clear that doublespeak is not the product of careless language or sloppy thinking. Indeed, serious doublespeak is the product of clear thinking and is carefully designed and constructed to appear to communicate but in fact to mislead. Thus, it's not a tax increase but "revenue enhancement," "tax base broadening," or "user fees," so how can you complain about higher taxes? It's not acid rain, it's just "poorly buffered precipitation," so don't worry about all those dead trees. That isn't the Mafia in Atlantic City, those are just "members of a career-offender cartel," so don't worry about the influence of organized crime in the city. The Supreme Court Justice wasn't addicted to the painkilling drug he was taking, it's just that the drug had simply "established an interrelationship with the body, such that if the drug is removed precipitously, there is a reaction," so don't worry that his decisions might have been influenced by his drug addiction. It's not a Titan II nuclear-armed, intercontinental, ballistic missile 630 times more powerful than the atomic bomb dropped on Hiroshima, it's just a "very large, potentially disruptive reentry system," so don't worry about the threat of nuclear destruction. Serious doublespeak is highly strategic, and it breeds suspicion, cynicism, distrust, and, ultimately, hostility.

6   In his famous and now-classic essay "Politics and the English language," which was published in 1946, George Orwell wrote that the "great enemy of clear language is insincerity. When there is a gap between one's real and one's declared aims, one turns as it were instinctively to long words and exhausted idioms, like a cuttlefish squirting out ink." For Orwell, language was an instrument for "expressing and not for concealing or preventing thought." In his most biting comment, Orwell observes that "in our time, political speech and writing are largely the defense of the indefensible. . . . Political Language has to consist largely of euphemism, question-begging and sheer cloudy vagueness. . . . Political language . . . is designed to make lies sound truthful and murder respectable, and to give an appearance of solidity to pure wind."

7   Orwell understood well the power of language as both a tool and a weapon. In the nightmare world of his novel *1984*, he depicted language as one of the most important tools of the totalitarian state. Newspeak, the offi-

cial state language in *1984,* was designed not to extend but to *diminish* the range of human thought, to make only "correct" thought possible and all other modes of thought impossible. It was, in short, a language designed to create a reality which the state wanted.

8   Newspeak had another important function in Orwell's world of *1984.* It provided the means of expression for doublethink, which Orwell described in his novel as "the power of holding two contradictory beliefs in one's mind simultaneously, and accepting both of them." The classic example of double-think in Orwell's novel is the slogan "War is Peace." And lest you think dou-blethink is confined only to Orwell's novel, you need only recall the words of Secretary of State Alexander Haig when he testified before a Congressional Committee in 1982 that a continued weapons build-up by the United States is "absolutely essential to our hopes for meaningful arms reduction." Or the words of Senator Orrin Hatch in 1988: "Capital punishment is our society's recognition of the sanctity of human life."

9   The more sophisticated and powerful uses of doublespeak can at times be difficult to identify. On 27 July 1981, President Ronald Reagan said in a tele-vision speech: "I will not stand by and see those of you who are dependent on Social Security deprived of the benefits you've worked so hard to earn. You will continue to receive your checks in the full amount due you." This speech had been billed as President Reagan's position on Social Security, a subject of much debate at the time. After the speech, public opinion polls recorded the great majority of the public as believing that President Reagan had affirmed his support for Social Security and that he would not support cuts in benefits. Five days after the speech, however, White House spokesperson David Ger-gen was quoted in the press as saying that President Reagan's words had been "carefully chosen." What President Reagan did mean, according to Gergen, was that he was reserving the right to decide who was "dependent" on those benefits, who had "earned" them, and who, therefore, was "due" them.

10   During the 1982 Congressional election campaign, the Republican Na-tional Committee sponsored a television advertisement which pictured an el-derly, folksy postman delivering Social Security checks "with the 7.4 percent cost-of-living raise that President Reagan promised." Looking directly at his audience, the postman then adds that Reagan "promised that raise and he kept his promise, in spite of those sticks-in-the-mud who tried to keep him from doing what we elected him to do."

11   The commercial was deliberately misleading. The cost-of-living increases had been provided automatically by law since 1975, and President Reagan had tried three times to roll them back or delay them but was overruled by congressional opposition. When these discrepancies were pointed out to an official of the Republican National Committee, he called the commercial "in-offensive" and added, "Since when is a commercial supposed to be accurate? Do women really smile when they clean their ovens?"

12   In 1986, with the Challenger tragedy and subsequent investigation, we discovered that doublespeak seemed to be the official language of NASA, the National Aeronautics and Space Administration, and of the contractors engaged in the space shuttle program. The first thing we learned is that the Challenger tragedy wasn't an accident. As Kay Parker of NASA said, experts were "working in the anomaly investigation." The "anomaly" was the explosion of the Challenger.

13   When NASA reported that it was having difficulty determining how or exactly when the Challenger astronauts died, Rear Admiral Richard Truly reported that "whether or not a cabin rupture occurred prior to water impact has not yet been determined by a superficial examination of the recovered components." The "recovered components" were the bodies of the astronauts. Admiral Truly also said that "extremely large forces were imposed on the vehicle as evidenced by the immediate breakup into many pieces." He went on to say that "once these forces have been accurately determined, if in fact they can be, the structural analysts will attempt to estimate the effect on the structural and pressure integrity of the crew module." NASA referred to the coffins of the astronauts as "crew transfer containers."

14   Arnold Aldrich, manager of the national space transportation systems program at Johnson Space Center, said that "the normal process during the countdown is that the countdown proceeds, assuming we are in a go posture, and at various points during the countdown we tag up on the operational loops and face to face in the firing room to ascertain the facts that project elements that are monitoring the data and that are understanding the situation as we proceed are still in the go condition."

15   In testimony before the commission investigating the Challenger accident, Allen McDonald, an engineer for Morton Thiokol (the maker of the rocket), said he had expressed concern about the possible effect of cold weather on the booster rocket's O-ring seals the night before the launch: "I made the comment that lower temperatures are in the direction of badness for both O-rings, because it slows down the timing function."

16   Larry Mulloy, manager of the space shuttle solid rocket booster program at Marshall Space Flight Center, responded to a question assessing whether problems with the O-rings or with the insulation of the liner of the nozzle posed a greater threat to the shuttle by saying, "The criticality in answering your question, sir, it would be a real foot race as to which one would be considered more critical, depending on the particular time that you looked at your experience with that."

17   After several executives of Rockwell International, the main contractor to build the shuttle, had testified that Rockwell had been opposed to launching the shuttle because of the danger posed by ice formation on the launch platform, Martin Cioffoletti, vice president for space transportation at Rockwell, said: "I felt that by telling them we did not have a sufficient data base and

could not analyze the trajectory of the ice, I felt he understood that Rockwell was not giving a positive indication that we were for the launch."

18   Officials at Morton Thiokol, when asked why they reversed earlier decisions not to launch the shuttle, said the reversal was "based on the reevaluation of those discussions." The Presidential commission investigating the accident suggested that this statement could be translated to mean there was pressure from NASA. . . .

19   President Jimmy Carter in 1980 could call the aborted raid to free the American hostages in Tehran an "incomplete success" and really believe that he had made a statement that clearly communicated with the American public. So too could President Ronald Reagan say in 1985 that "ultimately our security and our hopes for success at the arms reduction talks hinge on the determination that we show here to continue our program to rebuild and refortify our defenses" and really believe that greatly increasing the amount of money spent building new weapons will lead to a reduction in the number of weapons in the world. If we really believe that we understand such language and that such language communicates and promotes clear thought, then the world of *1984* with its control of reality through language is upon us.

COMPREHENSION

1. Words to talk about:

    ■   at variance with its real or its *purported* meaning
    ■   doublespeak *obfuscates*
    ■   members of a *cartel*
    ■   means of expression for *doublethink*
    ■   working in the *anomaly* investigation

2. What was Lutz's goal in writing this essay?
3. Why did Lutz use so many words whose meanings he had to explain?

DISCUSSION

1. One kind of doublespeak comes about through "inflated language," which usually entails the addition of "virtue words" that make ordinary items seem better than they are. Find at least six examples of this process in Lutz's essay.

2. Lutz says that "serious doublespeak" is the result of careful manipulation intended to mislead or deceive. Find three or four examples from the essay.

3. Can you think of examples from your own experience either of inflated language or serious doublespeak? If so, tell why they were used.

4. Many of Lutz's examples come from statements people have made in news conferences. What is it about broadcast media that encourages people to use gobbledygook, which is a form of doublespeak? What statements quoted in the essay would you define as gobbledygook?

5. Why did Lutz bring George Orwell's essay, "Politics and the English Language," into his piece? Explain Orwell's comparison of a cuttlefish to speakers who have a gap between their declared aims and their real aims.

6. What was the goal of "newspeak" in Orwell's novel *1984*?

7. How does newspeak relate to doublethink?

8. What examples of political doublethink did Lutz cite? Explain the underlying logic that made it possible for the speakers to believe what they were saying.

9. Give some examples of NASA doublespeak that Lutz cited in relation to the Challenger disaster. Do they differ in intent and in results?

10. In Lutz's 1996 book *The New Doublespeak: Why No One Knows What Anyone's Saying Anymore* (HarperCollins, 1996), he gives the following names and descriptions of various organizations. Identify the virtue words in each name and conjecture on why the organization chose its particular name.

    The Sea Lion Defense Fund = the Alaska fishing industry's main legal and lobbying organization, fighting government attempts to limit the harvest of pollock, a favorite food of sea lions

    The Maine Conservation Rights Institute = opposes protection for wetlands and forests

    Friends of the River in Massachusetts = fought federal designation of the Farmington River as a wild and scenic river

    The Washington Forest Protection Association = a trade group of timber companies that fights restrictions on cutting forests

    Citizens for the Sensible Control of Acid Rain = lobbies against any bill to control acid rain

11. In the concluding chapter of *The New Doublespeak*, Lutz gives several suggestions for what individuals can do to fight doublespeak. While he cautions against making fun of those who use doublespeak, he isn't above making fun of the doublespeak itself. Probably the major reason that doublespeak thrives today is that there's so much information in

the world that none of us can know it all. We are afraid we will appear ignorant or uninformed and so we hesitate to ask someone to repeat or explain what was just said. With written messages we can take more time. Lutz suggests rewriting doublespeak into plain English and then communicating about it, preferably with the writer or the editor. Choose two or three of the bad examples that Lutz quoted in his article and rewrite them in plain English. Compare results. If different people

LIVING LANGUAGE 6.3

Euphemisms: Getting Better and Better

One of the easiest ways to erase bad memories or to ameliorate negative connotations is to give new names to offending items or concepts, as in these examples:

- After the Alaskan oil spill from the Exxon Valdez, the ship's name was almost as infamous as the *Titanic* and the *Andrea Dorea,* and so high on the list of needed repairs was a new name. After reconstruction, the ship was transferred to the Middle East and christened the *Exxon Mediterranean.*
- When in 1928 an advertising copywriter invented the term *athlete's foot,* he borrowed the positive and healthful connotations of sports to improve the aesthetics, and consequenty the sales, of Absorbine Jr., an "anti-ringworm" medication. The 1970s brought a similar success story when jock-itch was coined to refer to a condition caused by the same fungus.
- During the 1940s and 1950s, electric shock therapy was used with thousands of emotionally ill individuals. It sometimes resulted in broken bones and even death and developed such a bad reputation that most people think it is no longer practiced. However, a modified version under the name of ECT (Electroconvulsive Therapy) is administered every year to an estimated 100,000 Americans.
- In 1992, the NASA team searching for intelligent life in space launched a new high-powered system under the name of High Resolution Microwave Survey. Although NASA insisted the new name was chosen for accuracy rather than for public relations, clearly the old name of SETI (Search for Extraterrestrial Intelligence) had negative connotations from its association with science fiction and less-than-credible stories of UFOs (Unidentified Flying Objects).

in the class wrote quite different interpretations, then it is obvious that the original message was unclear.

12. As you read Living Language 6.3, talk about which items you interpret as inflated language, and which you consider doublespeak. Are any of these changes dangerous in the way that some of the Lutz examples were dangerous?

- On college campuses, name inflation is as prevalent as grade inflation. The president of the University of Colorado suggested that faculty sabbatical leaves should be called "sabbatical assignments." According to an article in the *San Jose Mercury News* (May 14, 1991), San Jose State University changed its departments to schools and its schools to colleges "in order to suggest more complexity." Throughout the country as part of "modernizing," departments of Leisure Studies are changing to Recreation Management and Tourism; Physical Education to Exercise Science; and Home Economics to Human Ecology, Family Living, or Family Resources and Human Development.

- A "Marginalia" note in the *Chronicle of Higher Education* (Oct. 7, 1993) ribbed Iowa State University with a "cluck, cluck" for a proposal to change the name of the Poultry Laboratory to the Aerobiology Laboratory. The campus committee in charge of names suggested that perhaps Entomology Laboratory would be better since few people know the meaning of "Aerobiology." No one suggested sticking with the eminently clear Poultry Laboratory.

- "College Board Testing A Words to Replace the Failing *Aptitude*" was the subheading on a *Washington Post* article about a name change for the SAT (Scholastic Aptitude Test) (Feb. 11, 1993). After months of deliberation, made necessary by the filing of legal complaints from parents' groups, the name was changed to Scholastic Assessment Test, which its creators hope will sound less ominous to the 1.5 million high school students who each year take the test as a prediction of their chances for success in college.

WORKSHOP 6.2

Techniques of Advertising

Advertisers are today's poets and bards. They are artists and wordsmiths able to get double or triple value for the words they use. They delight and entertain us by providing images for our daydreams, and when they can't entertain us themselves they pay for someone else to do the job by underwriting the costs of television, newspapers, and magazines. In exchange for affixing their clients' names, they will even pay for stadiums and athletic domes.

But can such a Fairy Godmother be all good? Should we worry that advertisers goad us into buying things we don't need or want, or that constant reminders of "the good life" make it harder for those left out? Do we find ourselves always running toward, but never finding, the pot of gold that glimmers through most advertisements? And are we even aware of how ubiquitous advertising is and how it shapes our attitudes?

PART I: EMOTIONAL APPEALS

Advertisers don't need to work very hard to sell such basic necessities of life as food, electricity, schooling for children, and medical care. Of course companies compete with each other in hopes of showing that one will offer better prices, more dependable service, or a better product. However, a bigger challenge for advertisers is to convince customers to buy something that is not a necessity. In these cases, the advertiser must work hard to convince the potential client that first, what is being offered is needed or will be beneficial, and that second, the company being advertised is the best one to provide it.

BRAIN TEASERS

Look at the following two ads and try to answer these questions:

1. Compare the intended audiences. So as to reach the intended audiences, what kinds of publications do you think they appeared in?
2. Which one is more of a luxury? Do you think that's why the ad for cosmetic surgery was longer? Dr. Austin wrote this ad himself. How might it be different if he had hired an advertising agency to write it?
3. What major emotion does each ad appeal to?
4. Discuss the logic that each writer uses. Look at Cross's essay and see if you can find parts of the writing from either ad that she could have used for examples.

PART II: OF PRACTICAL MATTERS

BRAIN TEASERS

From magazines or newspapers, cut out a couple of advertisements for items that are considered necessities. Compare the sales techniques used in those advertisements with the ones used in the ads on pages 307 and 308 prepared by the credit union and the plastic surgeon.

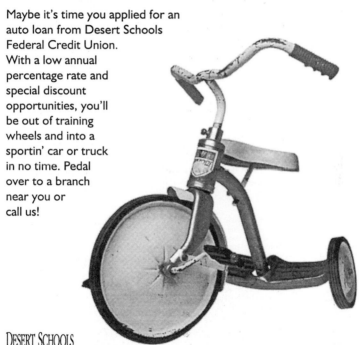

Still riding your bike to school?

Maybe it's time you applied for an auto loan from Desert Schools Federal Credit Union. With a low annual percentage rate and special discount opportunities, you'll be out of training wheels and into a sportin' car or truck in no time. Pedal over to a branch near you or call us!

Desert Schools
Federal Credit Union

433-7000
All ASU students are eligible to join!

* Depending on income and credit history, a co-signer may be required for loan requests.

Source: Property of Desert Schools Federal Credit Union. Copywriter: Amy Leonard. Designer: Chris Marzuola.

continued

BETTER THAN EVER

By Harvey W. Austin, M.D.,
George W. Weston, M.D., and
Robert K. Sigal, M.D.

What Does Your Face Say About You?

OUR FACES ARE FULL OF features. And these features are symbols. Some features, like large eyes, are symbols of attractiveness. Other features, like bags under the eyes, may symbolize unattractiveness. Even though symbols are just symbols, not truth, they still mean something to others ... and to ourselves. A symbol may lie about us, saying we are unattractive when inside, we are beautiful.

When one or more symbols are "off", life seems harder. How painful to see someone frown rather than smile when he first sees our face. Even though the problem lies deeply embedded in our culture of lookism, our pain is intensely personal.

Symbols lie about us

One of our features, say our nose, may be the family gift from our grandfather yet it may symbolize coarseness or masculinity when it shows up on a young woman. A receding chin, memory of a favorite aunt, may be a symbol of weakness. The thin lips or low eyebrows of an uncle may symbolize harshness.

When we look at another person, most of us guess what they are like. If she looks cruel, she probably is, we reason. If he looks tired, he probably is, we think. This thinking goes on automatically and we "buy" our own first impressions. We are wrong as often as not.

Symbols are embedded in our very language: "She looks like she ate something bad." "Don't give me that look!" "He sure looks snooty." "She looks down in the mouth."

We become like the symbols

The problem of symbols is even worse: we become what the symbols say about us. It seems to work like this. The feedback from our mirrors and the feedback from other people act as instructions. So, gradually, without realizing it, our personalities shift to match the symbols. If we look sad, we become sad. If we look angry, we become angry. "It makes me mad when someone says I look mad", she declared.

It's a down-hill spiral. It starts with the feature, the symbol. The symbol results in psychic pain. Then we become what the symbol says. This is more painful. The pain shows on our face, intensifying the symbol. And down the spiral goes.

Cosmetic surgery alters symbols

Cosmetic surgery is about altering the symbols that tell lies about us. Afterwards, our faces and our inner beings become more harmonious and our pain begins to lessen.

Nose : An enlarged nose can overpower your face and even give a sinister look. Plastic surgeons can shorten your long nose, or remove the hump. One woman, five feet two, said, "My nose would look great—if I were six feet two — and male!" Sometimes a nose makes one look a bit silly, not to be taken seriously. We can narrow enlarged nostrils, narrow a bulbous tip.

Before   After
What did her face say about her before? Sherry, a 52 year old woman had a face-neck lift with liposuction, her brow lifted and her upper and lower eyelids done. Cosmetic surgery can alter symbols of tiredness, worry and unhappiness. It removes the mask which hides our real youth and beauty.

Cheeks and Necks : Fat cheeks or a fat neck can say you are overweight, even if you aren't. The heavy-faced can have their cheeks or neck liposuctioned to give them a more sculpted contour. Some thin-faced individuals can achieve the sculpted look of beauty by augmenting the cheekbones with implants or augmenting the sides of the lower jaw to balance a thin lower face.

Chin: The chin is a major facial symbol. When soft, it is a symbol of timidity: when strong a symbol of power. When we view an attractive face from the side, the chin reaches to the "balance point." A weak chin doesn't come out that far. Augmenting the chin is a simple task which does more to increase beauty than almost anything. In addition, one feels more assertive. "I voice my opinion more. I feel stronger."

Other: We can soften masculine features on a woman to have her feel more feminine. Drooping and slow-looking upper eyelids can be brightened. Familial bags-under-the-eyes can be removed. Protruding ears can be brought in closer. Low eyebrows, symbolizing anger, can be raised with a brow lift.

To look more like you: If we all had magic wands, most would wave it at one of our own features. Even though cosmetic surgery has no magic wands, you can find out in a consultation visit what can be done to have your symbols say the right stuff about you. ∎

©1996 Harvey W. Austin, M.D

The

AUSTIN-WESTON
CENTER
for
COSMETIC SURGERY

1776 Old Meadow Rd, McLean, VA 22102
(703) 893-6168 • 1 (800) 385-1011

Source: Courtesy of Austin-Weston Center for Cosmetic Surgery.

Suggested Topics for Writing

Now that you have read about persuasion techniques and have studied examples—both good and bad—try your hand at writing a persuasive essay. Here are some suggested topics relating to the chapter readings and the advertising workshop.

1. Write an essay about hate speech. Possibilities for ideas to develop include:

   - Hate speech is actually beneficial in releasing tensions that might otherwise come out in violent behavior.
   - Hate speech is damaging because it numbs our sense of acceptable behavior.
   - Hate speech encourages violence.
   - We should pay attention to hate speech as evidence of underlying social problems.

2. Write an essay on what it means to be persuasive and, at the same time, honest. Both Cross and Lutz, as well as some of the other writers in this chapter, focus on logical fallacies and on language that is purposely misleading. Turn some of their ideas around and discuss techniques to use when you have a good cause and want to enlist others to your point of view.

3. Write an essay in favor of the kind of advertising creativity that Dennis Baron dismisses as "public cutespeak." Collect supporting evidence from the reactions that you and your friends have to clever names in your geographical area or to humorous ads and commercials. You may get different reactions if you interview people from different generations or from different social groups. What are the benefits? What are the negatives?

4. Cross quoted Joseph Goebbels, propaganda minister in Nazi Germany, as defining his work as "the conquest of the masses." What was her implication in quoting him? Write an essay in which you argue for or against the idea that American commercial advertisers have conquered the masses of today.

5. Illustrate Cross's statement that "propaganda works by tricking us, by momentarily distracting the eye while the rabbit pops out from beneath the cloth."

6. Choose one of these statements to develop:

- The best defense against doublespeak and other misleading language is education of the public.
- The best defense against doublespeak and other misleading language is legislation or some other kind of control as from an advertising council or a governmental body.

7. Write a persuasive paper developing the idea that companies name their products with an eye to influencing consumers on a subconscious level. You might choose to look at the wish fulfilling names on grooming products, the "American" sounding names that have been given to children's shoes manufactured in foreign countries, or the "healthy" names given to food products.
8. Write a paper arguing either for or against the assertion that public opinion is shaped by the messages on bumper stickers. Do such messages mainly reflect or shape public opinion?
9. Investigate the techniques used by companies trying to court long distance phone services. Gather examples of sales techniques used in written form, personal appeals, phone calls, Internet announcements, and whatever else you can find. After you collect your data, analyze the various appeals. Work with the information in a similar fashion to the way Workshop 3.1 on pages 98–100 led you to work with sweepstakes letters.

INFORMATION SOURCES FOR WRITING

Advertising Age is a leading magazine for public relations professionals. Most libraries will have copies; plus, it maintains an active web site with current news about advertising campaigns and innovations.

The American Way of Death, by Jessica Mitford. New York: Simon & Schuster, 1963.

Dictionary of Euphemisms and Other Double Talk, by Hugh Rawson. New York: Crown, 1981.

Democracy and Its Discontents: Reflections on Everyday America, by Daniel J. Boorstin. New York: Random, 1974.

Fair of Speech: The Use of Euphemisms, by D. J. Enright. New York: Oxford Univ. Press, 1985.

How to Argue and Win Every Time, by Gerry Spence. New York: St. Martin's, 1995.

I Must Say, by Edwin Newman. New York: Warner Bros., 1988.

JARGON: How to Talk to Anyone about Anything, by Joel Homer. Tree Communications, 1979.

Language in Thought and Action, by S. I. Hayakawa. San Diego, California: Harcourt Brace Jovanovich, 1972.

Language—The Loaded Weapon: The Use and Abuse of Language Today, by Dwight Bolinger. New York: Longman, 1980.

The Name Is the Game: How to Name a Company or Product, by Henri Charmasson. Homewood, Illinois 60430: Dow Jones-Irwin, 1988.

The New Doublespeak: Why No One Knows What Anyone's Saying Anymore, by William Lutz. New York: HarperCollins, 1996. Lutz's *Doublespeak: From Terminal Living to Revenue Enhancement* (HarperCollins, 1990) is equally useful.

"Politics and the English Language" from *A Collection of Essays by George Orwell.* New York: Harcourt Brace, 1946.

The Power of Words, by Stuart Chase. San Diego, California: Harcourt Brace Jovanovich, Inc. 1982.

They Laughed When I Sat Down: An Informal History of Advertising in Words and Pictures, by Frank Rowsome. McGraw Hill, 1959.

Trade Name Origins, by Adrian Room. Chicago: NTC Publishing, 1982.

Understanding and Using English, by Newman P. Birk. New York: Macmillan, 1972.

Paparazzi accused in

...ason to suspect any illegal activites. However, the issue remains unsettled a
...ow much involvement the press really had in the actual acci
...ics are not disclosing any further information about the
rumors do indicate that the limo had been under p

Nostalgia for yesterday's news

GROUP CALLS TV NEWS COVERAGE 'HARMFUL'

BY Arthur E. Diola
ARCOLA (AP) –

Things just ar
in a time gone
there was ofte
now it all com
Here and ther
it is not an iss
stolen from a
this is almost
until then, it
TV, radio, ma
broadcasting

Media makes minor mischief

the move does not involve any m
he right wing. In a similar in
draw the line somewhere.
to curb some of these

Gender

Teeth touch-up sho society's problem with imperfection

BY Albert J. Foster
SACRAMENTO (AP) — Although she has done a lot to foster her
never thought she would need dental reconstruction to continue
the general viewing public seems to agree. Although many of us
...respond that we do not believe 'you can judge

Springer's raunchy recipe for success

In today's TV market, ratings rule, and he who...

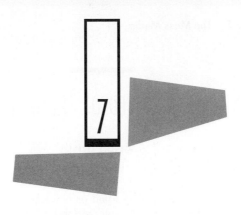

The Mass Media

Television, radio, movies, newspapers, magazines, books, and now the Internet have become something of a scapegoat. Politicians blame reporters when their ratings in the polls go down; parents blame violent heavy metal music for turning teenagers into delinquents; cancer patients blame advertisers for enticing them to smoke; the president of the United States blames talk radio for a "war of words" that's demoralizing the country, while criminals blame movies for giving them ideas or for making them lose control of their emotions. Actually, at least one murder has been traced to a victim's appearance on a television talk show, while another was apparently caused by a husband's jealousy over a radio talk show host (a "shock jock") sending roses to the husband's wife after the two had communicated by e-mail.

In spite of these negatives, the modern mass media also deserves plus marks. Never has there been such a chance for ordinary people to be tuned into the important affairs of their day, and never has there been such a chance to become educated without leaving the confines of one's home. The sheer volume of what is available has made some critics ask whether we are really better informed or just overwhelmed. Whole books, in fact, whole libraries, could be written on the ways that the mass media influences daily life. The articles in this chapter are little more than a sampling to illustrate some of the symbiotic relationships existing between language and the media.

TV Talk Shows Accused of Trivializing Troubles

Alison Bass

These five criticisms of talk shows were listed as a sidebar to Alison Bass's piece published in 1993 in the *Boston Globe*. As you read the article, see if Bass gives evidence to support these accusations. (1) They exploit people who are deeply troubled and in need of more than an hour's worth of sound-bite advice, say psychotherapists and some of the guests on these shows. (2) By focusing on childhood sexual abuse one day and transvestite weddings the next, the shows blur the line between major social problems and tangential or trivial issues, many mental-health professionals say. (3) Because these shows make a virtue of suffering and pain, they glorify victimization but often fail to show victims how to move beyond their pain, some psychotherapists say. (4) These shows feed into a growing preference of many Americans to view the world through the prism of personal feelings, rather than through intellectual ideas or scientific information, some say. This self-absorption spills over into politics, where many voters are more concerned with how they feel about a political candidate than with how that candidate stands on important issues. (5) Because these shows are increasingly the model by which Americans learn how to talk about intimate matters, they may be crippling the way people talk to each other. What viewers see on these shows is people talking at each other, not to each other, interrupting each other constantly, and rarely listening at length to what others have to say.

1   Alison Rubinstein used to watch Geraldo Rivera and Sally Jessy Raphael religiously. She liked *Geraldo* because it was scandalous, and she watched *Sally Jessy Raphael* because the host seemed "gentle and open, the opposite of Geraldo."

2   Then, two years ago, Rubinstein went on *Geraldo* herself. The topic was obscene phone calls, and Rubinstein had received some disturbing ones.

3   But her television experience spoiled talk shows for her forever.

4   "I don't watch them anymore," Rubinstein, a physical-care attendant who lives in Ashland, Massachusetts, said recently.

5   "Now, I know these shows are garbage."

6   It's hardly a secret that talk shows aren't serious. But like Rubinstein, more people are wondering whether such shows are worse than just mindless entertainment. Psychologists, sociologists, and even some viewers worry that the shows trivialize social issues while feeding on Americans' self-absorption.

ACCUSED OF EXPLOITATION

7   Critics say the shows also exploit troubled people, who often are presented as pathetic losers unable to tackle their problems.

8   Even some talk-show hosts are beginning to sound an alarm about what these shows may be doing to the nation's psyche.

9   "The talk shows deal with disillusion and destruction," Sonya Friedman, a psychologist and host of *Sonya Live,* a talk show on Cable News Network, said at a conference a few weeks ago. "They are the freak shows of American television."

10   Freak or not, talk shows are enormously popular. There now are 17 daytime talk shows on U.S. television, and they attract tens of millions of viewers daily.

11   *The Oprah Winfrey Show,* the highest-rated of the bunch, attracts an average of 19 million viewers each day, and *Sally Jessy Raphael,* the second-highest rated, draws about 11.7 million.

AFTER-SHOW CARE OFFERED

12   Freidman and others voice a wide range of criticims about most talk shows. And the producers of talk shows counter the criticism by saying most of their guests know what to expect when they appear. They also say they offer "after care" to guests who need it.

13   "We never leave these people," said Burt Dubrow, executive producer of *Sally Jessy Raphael.* "We will send them on our dime to therapists to help them out, to keep in touch with them."

14   Part of the problem, critics say, is the sheer number of shows and the enormous amount of air time they have to fill. Where once there were two talk shows, *Donahue* and *Oprah,* there now are 17, and each runs five days a week, 52 weeks a year. To fill time and stay competitive, critics say, the shows have had to reach further and further into the bizarre.

TOLD WHEN TO CLAP

15   They also have to work harder to create on-the-air drama. According to several people who have appeared on such shows, staff members often manipulate emotions at every point, even telling the audience when to laugh, when to scream at guests and when to clap.

16   Alison Rubinstein and others say the shows' staffs also instruct guests when and how much to cry. When she and her husband appeared on a *Geraldo* show two years ago, Rubinstein said, she was told at a commercial break that she was not crying enough, and both she and her husband were

encouraged to exaggerate the impact that obscene phone calls had had on their marriage, then only 4 months old.

"A CRASHING HALT"

17   "Geraldo kept saying to my husband, 'This destroyed your marriage, didn't it?' and Gary kept saying, 'No, but it was a rough time,' " Rubinstein said.

18   "Finally, Gary just gave in to him and said, 'Well, it brought everything to a crashing halt.' "

19   Jeff Erdell, a spokesman for the *Geraldo* show, denied in a telephone interview that Rivera manipulates his guests.

20   "That's the biggest load of baloney I've ever heard," Erdell said.

21   "Geraldo bends over backwards to make the show honest. For example, there are very few shows that do not pay people to appear, and Geraldo is one of them."

22   Other shows do not have similar scruples, Erdell said. He said, for example, that *Donahue* paid two of the policemen who were defendants in the Rodney King beating trial $25,000 to be on his show.

23   Phil Donahue said Monday that the police officers were paid, but he would not confirm the amount.

24   "Why should multinational corporations like Time Warner and General Electric get their software (talk-show guests) for free, when the money they make on the ratings generated by these interviews certainly benefits their stockholders?" Donahue asked in a telephone interview.

25   "I don't see the great moral agony here."

BAD BEHAVIOR FOR SHOW

26   That type of attitude, however, sends shivers through the spine of such talk-show critics as Wendy Kaminer, a social commentator and a fellow at the Radcliffe Public Policy Center in Cambridge, Massachusetts.

27   "In my darkest moments," Kaminer said, "I think people are going to start indulging in bad behavior simply to get on television."

28   What bothers her even more is that the shows feed into our culture's increasing preference for feelings over ideas, for individual experience over the common good. "The problem is that this mind-set carries over into the way we think about taxes and welfare reform and health-care reform," Kaminer said.

29   "There is no longer a sense that there is a public interest that may not be the same as our own personal interest, and I think talk shows contribute to this. They encourage us to view interests and movements in terms of what's good for me, not what's good for the USA."

COMPREHENSION

1. Words to talk about:

   - listed in a *sidebar*
   - an hour's worth of *sound-bite* advice
   - say *psychotherapists*
   - *transvestite* weddings
   - *tangential* or trivial issues
   - they glorify *victimization*
   - Americans' *self-absorption*
   - view the world through the *prism* of personal feelings

DISCUSSION

1. Look at each of the five criticisms of television talk shows that are outlined in the introduction and cite one or two bits of supporting evidence that Bass gives.
2. Does Bass take credit for thinking of the five criticisms? If not, who does she credit?
3. Which of the problem areas do you think is most influenced by television talk shows as opposed to other cultural factors? Why?
4. Do you agree with the statement that television talk shows are "the freak shows of American television"? What is your evidence, one way or the other?
5. Make a list of reasons both for and against paying those who appear on talk shows. After making your lists, try drafting a policy that would guide your behavior if you were the producer of such a show. You will need to decide such matters as whether you pay travel expenses, and if so, for how many people; whether you pay a flat fee or use a sliding scale depending on how much you want the guest; how you let people know whether or not money is involved; and how you go about screening guests and deciding on their pay.
6. Television talk shows vary considerably. If your teacher has time for such a discussion, you might watch two different shows and come to class ready to talk about such things as the mannerisms of the host, the choice of guests, the kind of audience participation that is encouraged, what impact you think a guest's appearance will have on his or her life, and what you got out of watching the show.

LIVING LANGUAGE 7.1

The Media Makes the News

As shown in these summaries, the media not only reports the news—sometimes it *is* the news.

- " 'I Always Believed the Press Would Kill Her,' Brother Says"; "Tabloid Media Blamed in Crash that Killed Diana," and "Did Paparazzi Chase Princess to Her Death?" were a few of the headlines after the death of England's Princess Diana on August 31, 1997. The media continue to play a part in the tragic story. As one commentator noted, she was truly the first world-wide celebrity; the televised coverage of her funeral was watched by more people than any other event in history. An ironic side note is that the advertising agency for Weight Watchers was left scrambling to cancel an advertising campaign featuring a comment by Fergie, the Duchess of York. Diana's former sister-in-law was quoted as saying that losing weight is "harder than out-running the paparazzi." (*Arizona Republic*, Sept. 4, 1997)
- While it has become standard wisdom to say that old technologies are not replaced by new technologies, in February of 1997, French maritime radio authorities sent out their last Morse code message, something the U.S. Coast Guard did in 1995. By February of 1999, Morse code with its famous SOS (dot-dot-dot, dash-dash-dash, dot-dot-dot) will be replaced throughout the world by radio and satellite communication. American Samuel Morse invented the telegraphic system in 1837, which by the early 1900s had become the principal medium of ship-to-shore communications. (Associated Press, Feb. 1, 1997)
- Undercover journalism received a blow in December of 1996 when a federal jury ruled that the American Broadcasting Corporation had committed fraud as it prepared a 1992 exposé for *PrimeTime Live* about unsanitary conditions at a Food Lion supermarket. At one of the company's supermarkets, two of the show's producers went to work wearing hidden tape recorders and cameras. They documented the selling of cheese gnawed by rats and of tainted chicken washed in bleach. The company, whose stores are mostly in southern states, claimed that the broadcast cost them between $1.7 billion and $2.5 billion in lost sales and lowered stock values. U.S. District Judge Carlton Tilley ruled that the store could not seek damages for lost business but could seek punitive damages plus compensatory damages from events prior to the broadcast. The case opens the door to various kinds of lawsuits in relation to news obtained through investigative reporting. (Associated Press, Dec. 21, 1996)
- While such politicians as Oliver North, Pat Buchanan, and Dick Morris may disagree, career radio people are saying that talk radio is moving away from politics. Ronald Elving, writing for the *Congressional Quarterly*, observed that "a big part of its appeal, especially on the nastier shows, has been the chance to do what most of us were taught not to do: raise our voices to interrupt other people

and talk back to those in authority." He said that such outrageous behavior was a catharsis for callers and a vicarious charge for listeners, "But when one has heard all this, and heard it repeatedly, the novelty and the naughtiness wear off." Talk show hosts are turning to sports; movie gossip; and such perennial concerns as sex, families, health, and careers. (*Arizona Republic,* May 28, 1997)

■ In what sounds like an answer to a won't-someone-say-something-good-about-us prayer, the headline on a *USA Today* story (April 23, 1996) read, "Pop Culture Gets Credit for IQ Gains." The story was based on findings reported at a conference cosponsored by Emory University and the American Psychological Association: "Americans score about 15 points higher on IQ tests than they did 50 years ago." However, "It's not that kids are getting smarter," explained a Yale University psychologist. Instead, "New cultural factors—TV, video games, even the changes in cereal boxes—are making them better test-takers."

■ "Oh, pulleeze, save us from choking on media-marinated catchphrases," wrote Leslie Savan for *Time* magazine (Dec, 16, 1996) under the title "Yadda, Yadda, Yadda." She started by quoting presidential candidate Bob Dole answering his own question about whether our economy was booming with, "I don't *think* so." The same answer was given the same week by a teenager in Madison, Wisconsin, when police ordered him to approach their squad car. "If pols and petty criminals use the same buzzphrases these days, they probably get them from TV, like everyone else," wrote Savan. Savan says that using such phrases as *No-brainer; Clueless; I hate when that happens; Same old, same old; Blah blah blah; Been there, done that; He's history; Not even close; Get over it;* and *Hel-lo-oh!* makes us feel clever and in control because, "It's as if they come with a built-in laugh track."

■ "Yesterday's News May Be Antidote to '90s Overload" was the headline on a Marc Fisher story for the *Washington Post* (Feb. 4, 1997) about Jane Pauley's MSNBC show, which for one hour each evening shows old news. The Fox News Channel is also showing old news, while for twenty-four hours a day the Classic Sports Network "recycles old Muhammad Ali fights, Michael Jordan's college games, Nolan Ryan no-hitters and the like." It's easy to understand why broadcasters use materials for which they've already paid the production costs, but why do viewers watch? Fisher proposes that "the phenomenon has tapped into a popular desire to slow down the march of events just enough to comprehend something. There's so much new news that no story, no character has time to jell in the public mind."

■ "Networks seem oddly indifferent to teen viewers," wrote Lawrie Mifflin in the *New York Times* (Dec. 17, 1996). Except for MTV, which is actually aimed at 18- to 24-year-olds, most networks sweep teenagers (those between 12 and 17) "into demographic bins with other groups, paying them no special heed." Advertisers,

continued

LIVING LANGUAGE 7.1

The Media Makes the News   continued

however, are encouraging the networks to look more toward this audience because they have money and "are often bellwethers for new fashions in all sorts of
products." "Who's surfing the Internet and knowing how to use computers in
most households?" asked an MTV executive. "Not parents. Teens and young
adults. They're the growth area for us and for our [advertising] clients."

■ In an attempt to pull herself and her show away from the increasingly sleazy reputation of television talk shows, Oprah Winfrey founded a book club where each
month she features a book and devotes practically a full hour to talking with the
author. She now kindly advises librarians and publishers ahead of time as to
what book will be featured, because in the beginning she caught everyone by
surprise. Librarians reported waiting lists of hundreds of patrons; some libraries
reported receiving ten or fifteen calls "within minutes—seconds—of her announcing each month's title." (*Arizona Republic,* March 26, 1997)

Do You Know a Kunz Out in Utah?

Phillip R. Kunz

"The number of Americans who report spending social evenings with neighbors has declined more than 30 percent from 1974 to 1996," said Tom Smith, director of the University of Chicago's General Social Survey project. His findings were corroborated by a study conducted by Ohio University and the Scripps Howard News Service (*Arizona Republic*, Aug. 14, 1997), which found that Americans now do most of their socializing and communicating on the job rather than with friends or neighbors. Rollin Hawley, director of the Washington, D.C., Archon Institute for Leadership Development, stated that the American "definition of friendship has evolved from the notion of someone with whom we live and experience life to mere acquaintances and business relationships." We spend so much time in our jobs and in commuting to work and then coming home to watch television, that we don't have the kinds of friends that our parents and grandparents had.

This article by Phillip R. Kunz, a sociologist living in Provo, Utah, illustrates some of the fall-out from the changing nature of friendship. His unusual experiment with Christmas cards and letters revealed that many Americans no longer know who their friends are, nor are they confident in the way they handle the social obligations of everyday life. The year after Kunz did his study, it was featured as a human-interest holiday story on several television and radio programs. As you read the article, think about whether a similar experiment could be conducted with other holiday greetings such as Hanukkah, Kwanzaa, Cinco de Maya, or the New Year's holidays celebrated by various groups.

T'was the week before Xmas
When thru-out the town
Came a bag full of mail
Delivered around.

Season's Greetings and Christmas joy
Who wished us all. But were so coy
Tho, you signed the cards
　We are no dunce—
　Just who in hell
Is Dr. and Joyce Kunz?

1　Thus read the cover of a Christmas card received by the author. Inside was added "And a Merry Christmas to you, too!" signed William and Dorothy

Tanner. I confess that I never knew them either. And the cards came from others—one hundred and seventeen—from Omaha, Nebraska and from Watertown, South Dakota. All came from people I never met—people I never knew.

2   What elicited this well wishing? This cheerful Season's Greeting? And who in Hell are Dr. and Joyce Kunz? I selected Omaha and Watertown for my study not because of some complex theoretical justification, but only because they were urban and rural, and the available *Polk Directory* from each area was of recent origin.

3   Six hundred families were randomly selected to receive my cards. Half were high status folks—doctors, lawyers, accountants, and railroad vice presidents. The other half were people who had blue collar jobs—truck drivers, janitors, and bicycle repairmen.

4   My cards were carefully selected—three types in all. The best was a snow covered bridge with pines and ice and frost and verse. The second [was] printed on card stock [with a] "Merry Christmas" and a hand traced candle and flame—not bad at all for home designed and press printed. Finally there was the same card stock with a "Merry Christmas" quickly written by my secretary with a big red "Marks-A-Lot." It was certainly not an artistic creation. I wasn't too proud to put my name on that, but I did. On one-half of each of the three types of cards was hand written "Dr. and Mrs. Phillip Kunz," a title to match those of the high status receivers in the sample. The remainder were signed "Phil, Joyce, Jay, Jenifer, Jody, Jonathan and Jana." With the absence of the title, "Dr.," and the addition of several children's names, the assumption was made that the sender would be perceived as lower class.

5   The response was surprising. First came the telephone calls— eleven of them in all, and none collect. "We have been thinking and thinking, but just can't remember who you are." They called during the day when I was at work so my wife had to answer. She wishes I would confine my sociological studies to the university!

6   On each of the envelopes I put an address sticker with my name and address, written to reflect the appropriate status. I decided to use my real name and address inasmuch as the return of a card, or some other like response, was the dependent variable for the study.

7   Then came the cards, one hundred and seventeen of them, in addition to the eleven phone calls. Some were just regular cards like "the Sister Madonna" and a name, printed "Mr. and Mrs. Andrew Follet"; or a Kaycrest Cotillion Card signed "The Paul Headmiller family." Others were signed too, but also wanted to know who we were. "For some reason we fail to recall that we know you, when you sent your Xmas card. Happy Holiday to you all anyway. May Peace reign." Or another, "We received your lovely X-mas card, but just can't seem to place you. Could you please let us know your maiden name and how you know us? Bill, Jan, Lari, Lynn and Brian."

8   There were colored photographs of new houses, new children, and pets. There were the cards with an apology for not having written sooner or regretting that "we see so little of you anymore." Some were confused at first but were able to work it out and knew who we were in the end.

> Dear Joyce and Phil:
>
> Received your Christmas card and was good to hear from you. I will have to do some explaining to you. Your last name did not register at first, so I had my niece stop on her way to Calif. to call you and ask if you were Dr. Ralph's daughter. She did, but a youngster answered the phone and she said she tried to explain that she was my niece. She said I had better write or you would be confused. Please forgive me for being so stupid for not knowing your last name. We are fine and hope you are well. We miss your father. They were such grand friends. Until I hear from you some more,
>
> Sincerely, Hubert and Ann.

9   Long letters came with some of the cards—letters telling of local news, family health, and children's progress in school. The record for length was a hand written letter of four pages. It closed with "It has been a long four years since we saw you."

10   One well wisher said he was going to drop off three children with us for a week while they went to California. Another replied as follows:

> Dear Phil, Joyce and family,
>
>   We received your holiday greetings with much joy and enthusiasm. We were so glad to hear from you again and we are very anxious to renew our old friendship.
>   Bev, I and the children (nine, now) have been wanting to travel the southwest next summer and need a place to stop over for a few days and refresh ourselves.
>   Provo will be just the right place for such a stop.
>   We leave here, June 1st, allow 2 days for travel and plan on us staying at least a week.
>   Good to hear from you again, as it fits right into our travel schedule. So on the way back the first part of July we could spend a few more days, resting and visiting with you.
>   Merry Christmas & Happy New Years.
>
>   Lou, Bev and the children
>
> P.S. We are bringing our 2 St. Bernards along, as we cannot bear to leave them at a kennel.

To these two respondents my reply was "Touché." No crank letters came from Nebraska, only from Watertown. A communicaster from the [Watertown] radio station called and later a newspaper editor. The radio commentator just mentioned in passing one day, "I got a Christmas card from a guy in Utah and I can't remember him." A later caller on the air said, "Me too!" Many others called the station to say that they, too, received cards from a Kunz out in Utah. Who was this mystery man? A former resident on the military base in Watertown? When was he here? Why can't we remember him?

11   Then the deputy sheriff called. "There is a family here with your same name—everyone is calling them and they are tired of it—who are you? What are you doing?" We talked a little and he said, "Interesting project! Merry Christmas," and then hung up. Three weeks after Christmas was over, the Kunz family from Watertown sent a card and letter and said it was tough at first, but now they were glad for the experience, and "good luck and a belated Merry Christmas to you." They weren't even part of my sample!

12   I sent a letter after Christmas to all of the people in the sample explaining the project so they could relax their thinkers.

13   Incidentally, I received a lot more replies with me as a doctor than from just plain me. Only nine percent of the doctor and lawyer types sent cards back, while thirty-two percent of the blue-collar people sent responses to my card. I probably won't send any cards this year, so a Merry Christmas to all of you!

COMPREHENSION

1. Words to talk about:

   - the *Polk Directory*
   - the *dependent variable* for the study
   - my reply was *"Touché"*

2. In what ways was Kunz's study made possible or affected by various kinds of media?

DISCUSSION

1. What does Kunz's study show about the changing nature of friendship in today's world? Does it support the idea expressed in the introduction that, today, many of us have "acquaintances" rather than "friends"? Give some examples of ways that modern media contribute to the blurring of lines that divide people we know and strangers.
2. Kunz quotes two letters in full—one he treats as serious and one as a spoof (note the *Touché*). What clues did he use to decipher the intentions of the writers?
3. Do you think these two letters came from people in different status groups? Why or why not?
4. If someone were to replicate Kunz's study, except to do it on e-mail, what do you think the results would be? Compare the clues that the receivers of the Christmas cards had with the clues that someone getting a holiday greeting on e-mail would have.
5. Kunz waits until the last paragraph to report on his formal findings. What were they? Are they surprising? Why didn't he report on the complete set of statistics he gathered?
6. Every year comedians and columnists make fun of the photocopied holiday letters that many families send out. Why? What are some of the challenges in writing such letters? Which ones were evident in the letters Kunz quoted?

Publishers Buy Word's Worth Not Wordsworth

Russell Baker

The changing nature of friendship and personal relationships may also be a contributing factor to the bad case of celebrity worship that afflicts many Americans. People seem to have transferred some of the emotions they used to save for close friends and family members to people they feel they know through the media. A by-product of celebrity worship, which is especially irritating to professional and aspiring writers, is that people buy the books by authors they recognize. However, the problem is that instead of looking for names of recognized authors, they look for the names of celebrities whether or not their celebritude relates to the subject of the book. In this July 1996 piece for the *New York Times*, syndicated columnist Russell Baker devoted his space to a court case between Random House publishers and television star Joan Collins.

1   After paying a soap-opera star a million or so to write some novels, Random House sued to make her give it back. Said the stuff she turned in wasn't quality, and otherwise heaped contumely on her authorial reputation.

2   We are talking of Joan Collins, who had once played the sex object in a TV show called *Dynasty* but had no known talent for writing fiction. She was what is known in the trade as a "celebrity author."

3   Celebrity authors make some of the biggest money in publishing. That's not because they are masters of prose, but because they are celebrities. Americans love celebrities. When they hear of a new book bearing a celebrity's name, they rush out to buy it right away.

4   It's fame that does the trick. If *Moby Dick* had been written by the famous whale, it might have been a smash at the bookstore. Alas, its cover bore the name of an unknown scribbler named Melville, and it didn't sell beans.

5   Why Random House dunned Collins to get its money back is hard to say, but a realist might suspect that she had lost her celebritude. Though the company said it was because her manuscript showed she couldn't write, this is not usually a deterrent. They don't expect celebrity authors to write.

6   Why should they? Being a celebrity is full-time work. Look at General Powell, the recent celebrity author whose book set sales records galore.

7   Who in his right mind would expect General Powell to interrupt his reflections about the wisdom of becoming president of the United States long enough to write a book?

8   Writing a book is not a lark, as running for president is this year. It means sitting alone in a darkened room for two or three years exploring the dimmest recesses of your brain. That's a lot of time in the dark when all the other celebrities are out running for president, starring on TV shows, leading wicked lives in Hollywood, etc.

9   And there is the toil of the thing. The work demands sleepless guard duty to prevent the infiltration of dangling participles. It means constant wrestling with the distinction between restrictive and nonrestrictive clauses. And much more.

10   We are talking heavy lifting done in a sitting position. If celebrity authors had to do it, the flow of blockbusters gushing off the presses would slow to a trickle. The last celebrity book written by a celebrity is thought to be the memoir of Ulysses S. Grant, and Grant was dying as he wrote it.

11   Publishers know it's folly to send a celebrity out alone and expect him to come back with a book, so they hire editors and skilled writers to put their books together.

12   Powell, in a rare display of generosity, gave credit on the jacket to Joseph E. Persico as his collaborator. Most celebrities don't, possibly because they don't know who did their books. The late Nelson Rockefeller is said to have written two books without reading either one.

13   For publishers, time is the enemy with celebrity books. Celebrity can wither faster than tomato blossoms in a blizzard.

14   The mystery is why Random House didn't give Collins's manuscripts the usual repair treatment. Her own lawyer said everybody realized she wasn't Ernest Hemingway and even suggested she was little more than a hack whose subject matter was limited to "money and sex, and power and sex, and intrigue and sex."

15   Well, once she'd been the sexy star of a big TV show. Having her name on books steamier than anything television could tolerate was probably an inspired money idea in that market. But the market changes quickly. One moment you are the toast of the masses; the next, the only people who ever heard of you are of an age that is hopelessly quaint and very, very downmarket.

16   There is a huge flood of new people coming on line just now when the boomers, looking down the barrel of 50, are more interested in Geritol than in sexy soap opera queens. As with J. R. Ewing and Jason the Vampire, celebritude passed Collins by.

17   In any event, the jury ruled against Random House, thus doing the culture a small, crude justice. Somebody should have to pay for turning literature into sausage.

COMPREHENSION

1. Words to talk about:
   - otherwise heaped *contumely* on her
   - a realist might suspect she had lost her *celebritude*
   - prevent the infiltration of *dangling participles*
   - wrestling with the distinction between *restrictive* and *nonrestrictive clauses*
   - hopelessly quaint and very, very *down-market*
   - when the *boomers*

2. Find a couple of metaphors that Baker used. "Translate" their meanings into ordinary language, then decide which of the metaphors was more effective.

DISCUSSION

1. Can you think of other evidence to support Baker's claim that Americans love celebrities? (See Living Language 7.2 for ideas.)
2. What did Baker achieve by alluding to Herman Melville and to Ulysses S. Grant? What joke is he making about "the famous whale"?
3. What does Baker say is involved in writing a book? Why don't celebrities write their own books?
4. With celebrity books, why is time the enemy? How do writers and publishers employ technology as aids in this fight against time?
5. Explain the meaning of Baker's concluding line.
6. Read the following summaries of news accounts relating to celebrity writing. The various incidents represent different approaches to the troublesome question of how to give credit. From the perspective of the ghost writers, rank the incidents from most fair to least fair. From the perspective of yourself as a member of the reading public, rank the books according to how much faith you would put in each one as expressing the thoughts of the person credited as author.
   (a) When rumors circulated that Hillary Clinton's *It Takes a Village* (Simon & Schuster, 1996) was ghost written, the White House invited journalists to come to Mrs. Clinton's private study to examine legal pads covered with Mrs. Clinton's handwriting. The reporters came away saying, "No doubt Mrs. Clinton wrote great parts of the book." Nevertheless, the White House later acknowledged that Barbara Feinman, who reporters described as "a veteran book doctor,"

had been hired by Simon & Schuster to help organize the book and to draft several chapters. It is known that Feinman stayed overnight at the White House and went with the Clintons on a summer vacation to Jackson Hole, Wyoming. All seemed to be going well, but a couple of months later Feinman was told that Mrs. Clinton was disenchanted with her reworking of some chapters. Rumors circulated about withholding one-fourth of Feinman's $120,000 fee—a charge the White House denies. Feinman cannot comment because of a confidentiality agreement; however, reporter Richard Lacayo finished his story on "The Ghost and Mrs. Clinton" by saying that nothing forbids Mrs. Clinton from citing her collaborator, "But her acknowledgement page thanks no one by name." (*Time* magazine, Jan. 22, 1996)

(b) In reference to a book that Sarah Ferguson, former wife of Prince Andrew and now the Duchess of York, "wrote" about the travels of Queen Victoria, reviewer Joe Queenan was quoted as explaining that a pivotal moment in Ms. Ferguson's career occurred in November of 1992 when she decided that "she would actually travel with her co-author, Benita Stoney, and learn something about the life of Queen Victoria, just in case anyone asked." She did not want "to fall into the trap set for themselves by such authors as Charles Barkley and O. J. Simpson, both of whom claimed to have been misquoted in their ghostwritten autobiographies—thus inviting jeers, catcalls and obloquy." Allan Starkie, Ferguson's financial advisor, was also quoted as saying, "The Duchess once bragged to me that she could field any question that was asked about her book on Victoria, even though she had never read it." (*The New York Times Book Review*, Jan. 5, 1997)

(c) Cartoonist John Callahan's name is the only one appearing on the dust jacket of his book *Don't Worry, He Won't Get Far on Foot* (Random House, 1989), but the copyright notice reads "copyright John Callahan and David Kelly." On the acknowledgments page, Callahan wrote: "Finally, David Kelly, working from hundreds of hours of my tapes, drafted each chapter and then rewrote it again and again and again and *again* until no trace of his own voice remained. 'We're not going to have one of those goddam *as-told-to* books,' he would snarl. And we don't."

7. Other news stories have complained about children's books being published by Carly Simon, Tom Paxton, Leontyne Price, John Travolta, and Michael Bolton. After reading these two authors' statements, explain why they feel especially irritated by celebrity writers.

(a) Author Elizabeth Koehler-Pentacoff complained about Bette Midler, Fergie, and Danielle Steel, who each wrote children's books. She was upset by the fact that some publishing houses won't buy a book until the "marketing department has viewed the author's *video clip*. No matter how good the book is, if the author isn't *media-genic*, the book will be rejected." Since Koehler-Pentacoff doesn't look like Christie Brinkley and can't get on *Jerry Springer* because she hasn't had, "an affair with a transsexual cross-dressing escaped convict," she was advertising for the reverse of a ghostwriter: someone "twenty-two, skinny and sexy. She can spend her time at the gym and the salon, while I slave away at the computer. She'll star in my video clip. After my book hits the shelves, she'll hit the road for the book tours. Meanwhile, I'll be in my old blue bathrobe, writing chapter seven of my next novel." (*San Francisco Examiner,* June 29, 1997)

(b) A prize-winning author of children's books, Kathryn Lasky stated her case against celebrity writers by saying, "It seems so unfair that somebody, for example, like Cher, might come into my field, but I don't get to go into hers. It's not a two-way street. I mean I know it sounds kind of silly, but then I've dreamed of my name in lights and all those neat costumes, not to mention the body. What would people do, for example, if Cher were appearing in Las Vegas, but she became ill and instead of Cher tonight it's going to be Kathryn Lasky reading excerpts to music from her recent novel? I come out on stage poured into this gold lamé dress (dream on, Kathryn!) with a kind of hood ornament on my head, and talk some about children's books and then sing 'I Got You, Babe.' I mean people would feel ripped off, wouldn't they? Well, that's kind of the way I feel about celebrities doing children's books." (Quoted from *Literature for Today's Young Adults,* fourth ed., by Alleen Pace Nilsen and Kenneth L. Donelson, HarperCollins, 1993.)

THE CELEBS' GOLDEN MOUTHPIECE

Martha Smilgis

If celebrities don't write their own books, who does? One person who does is William Novak, the subject of this article published in *Time* magazine in 1989. The subheading "William Novak spins best sellers out of other people's stories," acknowledges his success as the co-author of Lee Iacocca's *Iacocca: An Autobiography* (Bantam, 1984), Sydney Biddle Barrows' *Mayflower Madam* (Arbor House, 1986), Tip O'Neill's *Man of the House* (Random House, 1987), and Nancy Reagan's *My Turn* (Random House, 1989).

1   What do you say to an offer to ghostwrite Nancy Reagan's autobiography? "Just say yes," advised William Novak's wife Linda when Random House approached him a year and a half ago. Today *My Turn: The Memoirs of Nancy Reagan* has made headlines, sold some 400,000 copies and soared to the top of the best-seller lists. Yet if Novak went with a winner, so did Reagan. Novak, 41, came to the collaboration with credentials of his own. He is the golden mouthpiece of the nation's celebrities, a literary John Alden who can consistently woo—and win—the public in their behalf. In 1984, *Iacocca,* Novak's collaboration with auto executive Lee Iacocca, jolted the publishing world by selling 2.7 million copies. He followed that up with best sellers on Tip O'Neill and Sydney Biddle Barrows, the deb-styled Mayflower Madam. Paid a paltry $80,000 for the Iacocca book (which made $10 million to $15 million for its subject), Novak has since been rewarded with a much healthier cut of the profits he helps generate. For *My Turn,* he received a six-figure advance plus a percentage of the royalties.

2   Novak was prepared to dislike Reagan, assuming she was was cold, authoritarian, power hungry. Yet, he says, "I never encountered that 'off with your head' woman I heard about. She's not Imelda Marcos, Leona Helmsley or Marie Antoinette, and some poeple still don't understand that." Over eight months, Novak taped 250 hours of conversation at the White House, in the Carlyle Hotel in New York City, at the Reagan ranch near Santa Barbara, California, and, of course, over the phone. Reagan offered candid recollections of the day her husband was shot, her hospitalization for cancer and her mother's death.

3   At first she tried to dodge prickly questions about her reliance on astrology, her feuds with White House chief of staff Donald Regan and her troubled relations with her children. "When she'd say, 'Now, Bill, you're not going to

talk about this,' I'd use the editors: 'But the editors insist on these subjects,' "
says Novak. "The fact is, if you ask readers to pay $22 for a book, you have to
reveal new material. Ironically, the better known the person the more they
must reveal." Recalls Reagan: "There were tough, difficult times and good
times. But I wanted it honest and personal."

4   Novak is able to elicit such responses because he is a most unassuming,
amiable sort who leaves his ego at the door. He fits his approach to his subject. With the brusque, no-nonsense Iacocca, he conducted interviews in offices and conference rooms, never sharing a meal with him. With O'Neill, he
took drives around Cape Cod in the former Speaker's beat-up Chrysler and
listened to endless anecdotes over tuna sandwiches. "I worried that these
were only a wall of stories," he says. "I came to realize that Tip's opinions
were expressed through his stories." Novak arrived at the White House carrying a bag of Mrs. Fields chocolate chip cookies, Nancy Reagan's favorite.
When he met her at the Reagan's ranch, where she is known to favor jeans,
he showed up in jeans. "Bill's like a great character actor," says Peter Osnos,
his editor at Random House. "His self-effacing quality allows his subjects
their own expression. An extraordinary quality of intimacy with the person
is conveyed."

5   After doing exhaustive library research on a subject, Novak typically talks
to dozens of family members and friends to build up lists of questions for his
interviews. No muckraker, he uses challenging or contradictory material only
to try to jog his subjects's memory or trigger fresh stories. "I push as far as I
can go," he says. "I'm not trying to change a person's version of himself." Novak works from transcriptions of his interviews, occasionally going back to
the tapes to capture the subject's voice—one of his strengths, he believes. A
couple of months into a collaboration, he begins showing the subject drafts of
chapters. The subject usually offers changes and comments. ("Bill, this
stinks!" scrawled Iacocca). Novak tries to incorporate the lively ones and drop
the dull.

6   Toronto-born, Novak graduated from local York University intending to
be a writer ("No kid goes to bed at night dreaming he'll be a ghostwriter").
After earning an M. A. in comtemporary Jewish studies at Brandeis, he spent
ten years editing scholarly magazines and writing a string of financially unsuccessful books (among them: *High Culture,* about marijuana use, *The Great
American Man Shortage* and a compendium of Jewish humor). Just as he resigned himself to "finding a real job," an editor friend at Bantam suggested
Lee Iacocca. "Great! My kind of guy," said Novak, who had never heard of
Iacocca.

7   His success as a collaborator has brought him a comfortable life in an af-
fluent suburb of Boston that enables him, as he says, "to buy raspberries instead of apples." He is currently compiling an anthology of American humor
and mulling future celebrity sources. He muses about Mikhail Gorbachev
("But somehow I think he's busy right now"), and as a music lover who has

recently resumed piano lessons, he thinks about Paul McCartney or Barbra Streisand. "Or Elvis, if he can find him," wisecracks Ben, 10, one of Novak's two sons. As for a return to the solo byline of William Novak, he says it's not soon likely. "I get far more ego gratification and attention from these books than I ever did from my own." But aren't the celebrity books his own too? No. This John Alden, unlike the original, shrinks from speaking for himself. "I don't fool myself into thinking that *my* books are best sellers," he says. "The celebrities are the selling point."

Comprehension

1. Words to talk about:
   - a *six-figure advance*
   - far more *ego gratification*
2. When *Time* magazine editors wrote the subtitle to the article saying that William Novak *spins* best sellers out of other people's stories, what were they alluding to?
3. Other allusions to talk about:
   - Lee Iacocca
   - Sydney Biddle Barrows
   - Tip O'Neill
   - She's not Imelda Marcos, Leona Helmsley or Marie Antoinette
   - Mrs. Fields chocolate chip cookies
   - This John Alden

Discussion

1. When Novak was offered the chance to write Iacocca's biography, how was he prepared for this new career?
2. Once he gets an assignment for a book, what working method does Novak use?
3. What did Novak mean when he said that he was afraid Tip O'Neill's endless anecdotes "were only a wall of stories"?
4. When he gets some of the book on paper, what does Novak do? If you have worked with peer editing in a class, tell how his working method is similar, as well as how it's different.
5. While Novak good humoredly comments, "No kid goes to bed at night dreaming he'll be a ghostwriter," he seems relatively pleased with his career. Why?

It's Up Close and Misleading

Rita Braver

Rita Braver, chief White House correspondent for CBS News, wrote this op-ed (opinion editorial) piece for the *Washington Post* in March of 1996. While her piece is written in the format of a movie review of *Up Close and Personal*, which starred Michelle Pfeiffer and Robert Redford, the points that Braver is making extend beyond this particular movie. As you read it, think about the issues that underlie her thesis.

1   I went to see *Up Close and Personal* the other night. It wasn't billed as a horror movie, but it sure scared the heck out of me. Gorgeous, sexy Michelle Pfeiffer plays ingenue television reporter Tally Atwater. Tally is really named Sally, but for some reason she can't pronounce her own name, so the Robert Redford–type news director who hires her (who just happens to be played by Redford) orders her to substitute "T" for "S" so she won't get caught up on a little detail like saying who she is.

2   Redford, who believe it or not is named "Warren Justice" in the movie, is a former network White House correspondent who resigns over a matter involving his honor and journalistic integrity. This, however, does not stop him from hiring Sally/Tally, even though he knows that she has sent him a faked resume tape, which includes a clip of her wearing a really bad suit and telling prospective news directors that they should hire her because "I'm going to be a star." Redford/Justice agrees, offering Sally/Tally a job because she is so telegenic she "eats the lens."

3   Now here's the scary part: Because of the movie I am going to be besieged by even more desperately ambitious young women who aren't much interested in the news but who think they want jobs like mine. They will be like the beautiful, perfectly coiffed intern whom CBS executives asked me to talk to a few years ago.

4   "So," I opened the conversation, "you're interested in journalism?" Her contact lens green eyes grew wide. "Oh, no," she gasped. "I just want to do on-cameras, like you do."

5   I saw *Up Close and Personal* at a benefit screening where I was on a panel of journalists asked to talk about what it's like to be a real TV reporter who also happens to be a woman. Carole Simpson of ABC News and Margaret Warner of PBS' *NewsHour with Jim Lehrer* were on the panel, along with moderator Linda Werthheimer of National Public Radio.

6   I listened to their stories of taking crummy assignments, working nights and weekends and constantly having to prove themselves. I told a few tales of my own.

7   But mainly I was struck by the fact that what drew all of us to become reporters was that we wanted to understand the world and help explain it. We were curious. We wanted to talk to people about their lives. We wanted to expose the differences between what public officials said and what they did.

8   In fact, we wanted to do the same things that good male reporters wanted to do. But because we all came of age in a less-enlightened time, we women had to pry open a lot of news executives' doors that were slammed in our faces.

9   Which brings us to the other scary part of *Up Close and Personal*. It says that women are dopes who can succeed only if older, wiser men direct their every move.

10   Not only does Warren Justice tell Sally/Tally what to think and what to say, he also tells her what to wear. He takes her shopping and charges her clothes to the station. True, she does have a few spunky moments, and she has enough good sense to propose to Warren. But Tally is incapable of covering stories without him at her side. She leaves Warren in Miami to take a new job in Philadelphia, but she's so inexperienced that she bombs. Never fear, Warren flies in to the rescue.

11   Finally, Tally ends up covering a prison riot, all by herself. Sort of. We'll skip the part about how she gets into the prison without making the 60 or 70 set-up calls a real reporter would have to make. We won't dwell on the fact she and her trusty cameraman are magically able to broadcast from inside the prison without any of the necessary technical equipment. And we're not even going to try to explain how delectable Tally avoids being held hostage, raped or even threatened by the rampaging prisoners who kill eight of their fellow inmates.

12   The point is that just as the going gets tough, Warren arrives on the scene to speak slowly and steadily into Tally's earpiece and lead her through her live shots. Of course, rather than crouching down in the corner and letting the camera show the action transpiring in the prison the way any normal reporter would do, Tally thinks the way to cover the riot is to shove her mug in front of the camera and talk. But she only gets the guts to speak when Warren voices encouragement.

13   And, in a turn of events that is destined to send thousands of Tally wannabes stampeding out to their local prisons, Sally's Warren-managed performance results in her becoming a famous network anchorwoman. Her crowning achievement in her new role? She actually stands up in front of a huge audience of television executives and delivers a speech without using a teleprompter!

14   I know that films are make-believe. But too many women TV reporters have paid too many dues to let Tally Atwater stand as their symbol. She succeeds without ever working the phones, developing a source, covering a beat or even a single story for more than a few hours. It's true that Redford and

Pfeiffer were nice to watch, especially in those steamy love scenes. But their fun is over. I'm going to be sending all the starry-eyed job-seekers to them.

COMPREHENSION

1. Words to talk about:

   ■ a faked *resume tape*
   ■ a *clip* of her

LIVING LANGUAGE 7.2

Celebrities, Politics, and the Mass Media

As these stories show, while celebrities and the media are interdependent—one couldn't exist without the other—the relationship is sometimes rocky.

■ After an outpouring of criticism about the cross-over of thirteen journalists who played acting roles in the 1997 Robert Zemeckis movie *Contact,* which starred Jodie Foster as a scientist decoding messages from outer space, CNN made a new policy against their reporters appearing in movies. Marvin Kalb, who directs a center on the press and public policy at Harvard University, wrote, "If a reporter is to retain his credibility as a truth-teller, he has to stick to his craft and not confuse the viewer by playing an actor who plays a reporter telling fictional truths about space flight." Kalb also criticized Zemeckis for taking tapes of President Clinton speaking in totally different contexts and splicing them into the movie without White House permission. He warned that, in less playful hands, "the use of the presidential image and voice, deliberately misused for malicious purpose, could kick off a political or diplomatic crisis that no one needs." (*Arizona Republic,* July 27, 1997, comments originally contributed to *Newsday*)

■ When interviewed by the *Philadelphia Inquirer* in relation to the controversy over *Contact,* Jane Pauley said that she was a real journalist and would never portray a fictional one on TV or in the movies. "It blurs the line. Viewers are confused enough about the hair and the makeup and the glamour. We already confuse them so much without crossing the line and suddenly becoming make-believe." A few years back, Pauley also declined appearing in the *Murphy Brown* television sitcom where real women journalists were invited to the fictional baby shower for the famous title character played by Candice Bergen. (*Arizona Republic,* July 23, 1997)

- she is so *telegenic*
- to do *on-cameras*
- 60 or 70 *set-up calls*
- thousands of Tally *wannabes*
- without using a *teleprompter*

2. What's interesting about the name of the character played by Robert Redford? What do these kinds of playful names usually communicate?
3. What does Braver identify as "the other scary part" of *Up Close and Personal*?

- "Once viewed as the industry's dirty little secret, digital altering is so rampant that virtually every celebrity image circulated today has undergone some modification," wrote Mark Kennedy for an Associated Press story (Aug. 14, 1997) on how "celebrity-style makeovers are only a click of the mouse away." Anyone with a midprice desktop computer equipped with such software as PhotoShop can alter the content of photos. Controversial examples include the September 1989 cover of *TV Guide*, where Oprah Winfrey's face was put on Ann-Margret's body, and the May 1997 cover of *Allure* magazine, where model Mira Sorvino's image was changed to make her look like Joan Crawford. More common are such cosmetic changes as straightening Madonna's teeth for *Entertainment Weekly*, removing Harrison Ford's facial scar and realigning Jodie Foster's bellybutton (by three inches) for *Premiere* magazine. A highly publicized case occurred after the November 26, 1997, birth of septuplets to an Iowa couple, Bobbi and Kenny McCaughey. Bobbi's photo was shown on the cover of both *Time* and *Newsweek* magazines. On the *Time* cover, her front teeth were noticeably irregular, while on the *Newsweek* cover they had been digitally changed.
- On behalf of the media, *Washington Post* columnist Richard Cohen accepted part of the blame for the April 1996 death of seven-year-old Jessica Dubroff, the child who was killed while trying to be the youngest pilot to fly across the United States. He said bad decisions were influenced by a desire for "the themed record—the prize of publicity and, therefore, celebrity," but while we're blaming the mother, the father, and "the poor flight instructor," Cohen went on to ask, "what about the rest of us, all of us good guys who once thought the story was cute? . . . that poor little girl . . . was a prisoner of her own instant fame."

Discussion

1. It is always a problem to communicate with readers about a book or a movie that they haven't read or seen. What techniques did Braver use to tell the plot of the movie while getting on with the points she wanted to make?
2. How does Braver's piece differ from a regular movie review?
3. Do you think the movie inspired all these thoughts in Braver's mind, or did it remind her of things she had thought about before and wanted to communicate to the public? On what evidence are you basing your answer?
4. If Braver had relied only on her personal observations, would the essay have been as persuasive as when Braver tied her own experiences into those portrayed in the movie? Why or why not?
5. One of the problems with drama is the limited amount of time that producers have to tell their stories. They usually end up simplifying the background information so that they can focus on the plot and the characters. Have you seen a movie or a television program that included a presentation of a sport or some other endeavor you know more about than would the average viewer? If so, did you see the kind of simplification that bothered Rita Braver in *Up Close and Personal* in relation to broadcast journalism? If so, give some examples.
6. Read Living Language 7.2 about various issues relating to celebrities, politics, and the media. Which of the items relate to Braver's essay? In what ways?

The Power of Babble

Paul Gray

This article looks at the Bible, not as a religious document, but as an all-time best seller. As such, it cannot escape the effects of modern mass media because publishers, who are eager to get a piece of this lucrative market, are on the lookout for new and different ways to attract buyers. Paul Gray's article, reported by Richard Ostling, was published in *Time* magazine (Sept. 9, 1996) about a new edition under the subheading "The New Living Translation hit bookstores last month, another simplified Bible vying in a $400 million yearly market. What hath they wrought?"

1   Yea, verily, English-speaking Christians in search of Scripture suffered not long ago, few perturbations. Protestants reached for the Authorized, or King James, version of 1611. Roman Catholics consulted the Douay-Rheims translation, first issued in 1609 but revised during the 18th century to resemble or duplicate in most particulars the memorable cadences and phrasing of the King James. For some two centuries, readers of either of these Bibles could feel that the word they sought was the Word, that they had access to the linguistic unity enjoyed by humankind before the Tower of Babel, "And the whole earth was of one language, and of one speech."

2   No longer. The first modest assault on the long dominance of the King James version came in 1952, when the National Council of Churches of Christ in the U.S. released the Revised Standard Version. Thanks to 350 years of discoveries in archaeology and philology, the Revised Standard more accurately, if rather less poetically, reflected the original documents than did the King James. It quickly became the authorized text for most mainline Protestants. And after that trickle, the floodgates were opened.

3   There are now in print, according to *Publisher's Weekly*, some 450 English translations, paraphrases or retellings of all or parts of the Old and New Testaments. There is a New King James Version and a New Revised Standard Version, plus the New International Version, the New American Standard, the New American Bible, the New Jerusalem Bible, Today's English Version—also known as the Good News Bible—the Contemporary English Version and, well, the cup runneth over. These widely, wildly diverse texts chase the estimated $400 million that Americans spend each year on Bibles. And this proliferation of Bibles has in turn begotten a growing cottage industry in printed guides and videotapes intended to help both booksellers and customers sort

through the many different choices. The age of so-called niche Bibles has arrived.

4   A major new competitor for all that cash appeared in bookstores this summer: the New Living Translation (Tyndale House; 1,289 pages: $19.99). It comes with an initial print order of 950,000, a $2.5 million promotional budget and a fail-safe, backcover blurb from Billy Graham. The book is handsomely bound and printed and contains, at the end, a useful series of maps of biblical places. And anyone who remembers the King James will find some pretty startling things inside.

5   The New Living Translation is actually a revision and updating of The Living Bible (1972), Kenneth Taylor's loose, breezy paraphrase of the Old and New Testaments (*I Samuel 20:30:* "You son of a bitch"). It was frankly intended for readers who found Scriptural translations tough sledding, and those readers responded gratefully. The Living Bible has sold 40 million copies to date.

6   To put together this latest version, a team of 90 specialists checked Taylor's paraphrase against the original documents. The result thus carries more scholarly authority than The Living Bible, but it remains remarkably similar in language to its popular predecessor. And its radical difference from the King James is apparent from the outset. In *Genesis,* when God discovers that Adam and Eve have eaten the forbidden fruit, the King James conjures up a roar of rebuke: "And the Lord God said unto the woman, What is this that thou has done?" The Deity in the New Living Translation sounds like a parent scolding a child who has just tracked mud into the kitchen: "How could you do such a thing?"

7   If a certain loss of majesty has transpired here, as it does throughout, the editors remain unapologetic. "The translators have made a conscious effort to provide a text that can be easily understood by the average reader of modern English," they write. "The result is a translation of the Scriptures written generally at the reading level of a junior high school student." Since poetry is harder to grasp than prose, the poetry is rendered prosaically. Thus the King James version's "To every thing there is a season, and a time to every purpose under the heaven" (*Ecclesiastes 2:3*) must become, "There is a time for everything, a season for every activity under the heaven."

8   A defense of this practice might be that the editors of the New Living Translation are hardly alone. Most of the new Bibles flooding the market display a keen solicitude for their target readers, protecting them from tricky phrases that might call for a moment's reflection or, in some instances, from politically incorrect sentiments. Thus the 1995 New Testament and Psalms: An Inclusive Version renders God as "Father-Mother" and portrays Christ as ascending to sit at "the mighty hand" of the Father-Mother rather than "the right hand," thus keeping left-handed readers from feeling slighted.

9   The desire to make money is one reason to undertake a new biblical translation, but it is not, some observers believe, the only one. "Yes, there are commercial motivations because Bibles are big business," says John Wilson,

managing editor of the Evangelical journal *Books & Culture.* "But the overwhelming motivation behind all these versions is the conviction that this is the Word of God and people should be able to read it." Henry Carrigan, religion book-review editor of *Publisher's Weekly*, thinks the current spate of simplified Bibles "could be compared to what the King James Version did when it came out. It gave the people the Bible in their own language."

10   But what a language it was, the Renaissance English shared by a contemporary named Shakespeare, bursting with the energies and inventiveness of the just-ended Elizabethan Age. The 54 scholars who compiled the King James version strove for accuracy and directness and produced, in the process, some of the greatest poetry in the language. That Bible inspired, among so much else, John Wesley's hymns, *The Book of Common Prayer*, the speeches of Abraham Lincoln and the prose rhythms of Ernest Hemingway. It became the great resonator, the shared reference uniting English-speaking peoples around the world.

11   Will such religious and social influence be achieved by any of the new, simplified Bibles? The publishers' stated ideal of providing a text suited to the individual needs of each reader repudiates any such ambitions. The Bible must strive for democratic diversity, so the current thinking goes; the day is past when a dominant incarnation of it could, or should, exert a centripetal, unifying force on religious and social discourse.

12   How many of those now flocking to see the film adaptation of John Grisham's novel *A Time to Kill* know that the title comes from *Ecclesiastes 3:3* in the King James? Should they know, or care? If no one any longer reads the same words on the same page, on what basis will people talk to and understand each other? Will easy-read Bibles, rendering ancient mysteries and miracles in sitcom terms, inspire awe or channel surfing? Are many Good Books too much of a good thing?

THE TONGUES OF ANGELS

King James Version	New Living Translation
"And the LORD God said unto the woman, What is this that thou has done?"	"Then the LORD God asked the woman, 'How could you do such a thing?' "
	—Genesis 3:13
"The LORD is my shepherd; I shall not want."	"The LORD is my shepherd; I have everything I need."
	—Psalms 23
"After this manner therefore pray ye: Our Father which art in heaven, Hallowed be thy name. Thy Kingdom come . . ."	"Pray then in this way: Our Father-Mother in heaven, hallowed be your name. Your dominion come."
	—Matthew 6: 9–10

"Though I speak with the tongues of men and of angels, and have not charity, I am become as sounding brass, or a tinkling cymbal."

"If I could speak in any language in heaven or on earth but didn't love others, I would only be making meaningless noise like a loud gong or a clanging cymbal."

—I Corinthians 13:1

"For verily I say unto you, Till heaven and earth pass, one jot or one tittle shall in no wise pass from the law, till all will be fulfilled."

"With all the earnestness I have I say: Every law in the Book will continue until its purpose is achieved."

—Matthew 5:18

"Jesus wept."

"Tears came to Jesus' eyes."

—John 11:35

COMPREHENSION

1. Words and phrases to talk about:

   - suffered few *perturbations*
   - The age of so-called *niche* Bibles
   - a *fail-safe, backcover blurb* from Billy Graham
   - display a *keen solicitude* for their target readers
   - it became the great *resonator*
   - the day is past when a *dominant incarnation*
   - exert a *centripetal, unifying force*

2. What two Bibles were used almost exclusively for over 350 years? What is the difference between them?
3. What literary examples does Gray cite as being inspired by the Bible?

DISCUSSION

1. Find three or four examples of Biblical language in Gray's essay. What is their effect?
2. Read the excerpts from the two quoted versions of the Bible and see if you can figure out why the changes were made. What overall principles are at work?
3. What does it mean that the new translation is written, "At the reading level of a junior high school student," which is actually the level that standardized test makers say average adults read at. Why don't the editors say that it's written for the average adult reader rather than at "the reading level of a junior high school student"?

4. "Gender-neutral Bible Scuttled by Protests" was the headline on a *Raleigh News & Observer* story (May 29, 1997) saying that when conservative Christians heard about plans to replace *men* with *people* or *human beings* in a forthcoming edition of the NIV (New International Version) of the Bible, they "wrote letters, made phone calls and flooded the International Bible Society and Zondervan Publishing House with faxes." While there are already some gender-inclusive Bibles in print, "evangelical Christians were dismayed that the translation they most trust—the NIV—would soon be subject to the same cultural wars that have raged in society at large," wrote reporter Yonat Shimron. What does this reveal about "niche Bibles"?

5. Before the Bible was translated into English, all but a very few had to rely on their priests to tell them what it said. Do you agree that the newly produced, simplified Bibles are doing what the King James Version did by making it possible for common people to read the Bible? Why or why not?

6. Many eponyms are taken from the names of biblical characters (see Workshop 7.1). Will the various new editions of the Bible have as much of an effect on these eponyms as on other allusions or clichés? Why or why not?

7. Gray ended his essay with a series of questions. What is the effect of Gray using this technique instead of just telling readers what he thought?

WORKSHOP 7.1

Eponyms: How Words Come from Names

Eponyms are names, usually people's names that through various processes, acquire new meanings. For an eponym to work, it usually has to come from names of people or literary characters who are well known.

PART I: NAMES FROM ANCIENT STORIES

BRAIN TEASERS

1. Because more people have read the Bible than any other book in the world, it is a rich source of eponyms. Given below are ten fairly common English words that are eponyms based on Bible stories. With other class members, try to figure out the relationship between the meaning of the word and the biblical reference. Use the words in sentences that will illustrate their meanings.
   - an Adam's apple
   - raising Cain
   - a Delilah
   - a Jacob's ladder
   - the patience of Job
   - as old as Methuseleh
   - a good Samaritan
   - a scapegoat
   - a doubting Thomas
   - a Veronica move (in bullfighting)

2. The names of characters from Greek and Roman mythology have provided another rich source of eponyms. However, English is inconsistent in how long it keeps a capital letter on an eponym. In general, the longer a word has been in the language with its own meaning, the less likely it is to retain the capital letter showing that it was originally a name. Notice how the capitals have disappeared in some of these words associated with the myths. Try to identify the ten characters associated with these words. Again, use the words in sentences that will illustrate their meaning.
   - Achilles tendon
   - atlas
   - cereal
   - halcyon days
   - iris of the eye, the iris (flower)
   - janitor and January
   - narcissism
   - Sisyphean labors
   - to tantalyze
   - volcano, vulcanized rubber

PART II: HOW EPONYMS ENTER A LANGUAGE

It's easy to see how characters in biblical or mythological stories are so well known that speakers and readers can recognize the intended meaning when someone creates an eponym by alluding to an event or a character, but with real people, there has to be some kind of unusual circumstance to get the name known. Before the days of mass media, it might have been word-of-mouth. "Hobson's Choice" is used to describe a situation where there's no choice at all. It is an eponym from Thomas Hobson who, in the 1600s, ran a stable in Cambridge that rented horses to students wanting to ride into London. In the interest of keeping his best horses from being worn out, he operated on a strict rotation basis making each customer take the next horse in line. A contributing factor to the name getting well known was that Hobson dealt with hundreds of different students who learned his system. After they graduated from Cambridge, they scattered all over England spreading their use of "Hobson's choice."

During World War II, American soldiers wrote, painted, or scratched "Kilroy was Here!" on fences, crates, buildings, boards, trucks, trees, and whatever other surfaces they could find. American soldiers were attracted to the enigmatic message and the funny drawing; it was an inside joke that expressed their feelings of being "the little man" looking over a fence as the world disintegrated. After the war, the origin of the term was traced to a Massachusetts politician and shipyard inspector, James J. Kilroy, who started it all by putting the message on whatever crates he approved for overseas shipment. The soldiers took it from there.

continued

WORKSHOP 7.1

Eponyms: How Words Come from Names   continued

The Kilroy story is unusual in that the actual word written by its owner was spread throughout the world. What is more common is for the name of a famous person to be publicized through some kind of media. U.S. presidents appear in the news so often that their names even get made into adjectives. Under the headline "And How about *Doleful*," *Time* magazine (Dec. 11, 1995) cited a study that reporters did by running a word search through the Nexis database. They found 208 uses of *Kennedyesque*, 442 of *Nixonian*, 49 of *Carteresque*, 473 of *Reaganesque*, 273 of *Clintonesque*, and 536 of *Clintonian*. Because these eponyms can refer to so many different aspects of the presidents' policies or characteristics, they will probably not become a permanent part of the language as has the more specific *Eisenhower* jacket.

BRAIN TEASERS

Identify the various factors that helped to spread the use of each of the following words or phrases as eponyms. Notice that the kinds of media involved are more varied than just print and broadcast news accounts.

1. In the late 1800s, a young Presbyterian minister named Sylvester Graham preached a health food message. "Graham crackers" were named in his honor.
2. The "Gallup Poll" is named for the late Dr. George Horace Gallup, professor of journalism at Northwestern University.
3. Dr. Henry Heimlich, a Cincinnati doctor, was fifty-four years old when he developed and publicized the Heimlich maneuver to save people from choking.
4. *Pasteurized* and *pasteurization* come from the name of the French chemist Louis Pasteur.
5. The kind of spinal paralysis identified in medical dictionaries as Amyotrophic lateral sclerosis became known to the general public as Lou Gehrig disease after the well-loved baseball player died from it in 1941.
6. During World War II, Mickey Mouse's name was so famous it was used as the code name to identify the invasion of Normandy in 1944. But at the same time, "Mickey Mouse" also became a common way to speak disparagingly of things thought to be childish, silly, or second-rate, as in "Mickey Mouse rules" and a "Mickey Mouse college course." This connection was helped along by the Navy's use of M.I.C.'s (Military Indoctrination Centers) as a place to teach a multitude of petty rules to sailors.
7. *Sesame Street*, the most popular children's television program in the world, is named after the "Open Sesame" command with which Aladdin opens the door of the treasure cave in *Ali Baba and the Forty Thieves*.

8. *Rambo* has become an eponym for any exceptionally aggressive and capable an-tagonist. It comes from the hero in David Morrell's novel *First Blood* (Evans, 1972).
9. A *Scrooge* is any miserly person; the name comes from Ebenezer Scrooge in Charles Dickens's *A Christmas Carol*.
10. *Jumbo olives, jumbo hamburgers,* and *jumbo jets* are all named after the ele-phant Jumbo, who, for nearly 20 years, was exhibited at the London Zoo. Be-cause of his great size, he was given the Swahili name for "chief." In 1882, much to the consternation of the British, the zoo sold Jumbo to P. T. Barnum, who brought him to America as a star attraction in the circus. Walt Disney's cartoon elephant Dumbo is a play on Jumbo's fame.

continued

Workshop 7.1

Eponyms: How Words Come from Names   continued

PART III: CURRENT EXAMPLES

Understanding how eponyms are created and how their meanings evolve is important because the names of well-known people are often used to communicate basic ideas in current news stories. While most such references will not get into dictionaries as permanent words, readers or listeners who don't understand the process or who don't know the person will fail to understand what's being communicated.

BRAIN TEASERS

Given below are some eponyms that appeared as media references within the last decade. Either in small groups or as a class, try to figure out, first, whose name is being used, and second, what characteristic of the individual is serving as the base for the comparison.

1. Soldiers in the Gulf War complained about having to take *Johnny Weissmuller* showers.
2. Newscaster John Chancellor accused Ross Perot and his supporters of holding a *Daddy Warbucks* theory of presidential qualifications.
3. Trigger-happy police officers in Los Angeles were accused of having a *John Wayne* syndrome.
4. Women who give behind-the-scenes advice to their husbands or boyfriends are said to be "pulling a *Hillary.*" A few years ago it was a *Nancy,* a generation ago an *Eleanor.*
5. During the 1992 presidential campaign, *Murphy Brownism* was used as a term to accuse people of not supporting family values. The *Murphy Brown* factor may have contributed to the defeat of George Bush and Dan Quayle.
6. In the same campaign, President Bush referred to Clinton and Gore as "those two *Bozos.*" Commentators referred to the unfortunate name-calling, which damaged Bush's presidential image, as "The Bozo factor" and "Bozo politics."
7. When someone's guilt or innocence is judged through the media and public opinion, the situation is described as *trial-by-Oprah.*
8. In the summer of 1997 when the Russian space ship *Mir* was plagued with several mechanical problems, a high ranking U.S. official referred to it as a *Rube Goldberg* contraption. Apologies were soon in order.

Two Articles on Creating Names for Fun

These two articles from the *Washington Post* illustrate the kind of balance between creativity and regulation that is part of today's entertainment world. David Segal illustrates how the names of organized sports teams serve as a gathering point for community pride. But in spite of all the efforts that go into finding good team names, Segal questions the appropriateness of some of them. Vinnie Perrone shows how hard the owners of race horses work to find memorable and aesthetically pleasing names that will attract attention in the media as well as wagers at the betting windows. Before a thoroughbred can be entered in a sanctioned race in the United States, it must be registered through the Jockey Club in Lexington, Kentucky.

Who Put the "Jazz" in Utah?

David Segal

1   The National Hockey League recently announced that there would be two new expansion teams on the ice as early as next season. While the news drew huzzahs from hockey fans in the lucky new cities, Miami and Anaheim, Calif., in me it elicited only fear.

2   I'm afraid of what the teams will be named.

3   Why? Because naming a professional team is a perilous business, far trickier than most people think, and lots of teams in the past have blown it. A case in point is baseball's latest expansion teams in Colorado and Florida, which took their monikers from respectively, a geological formation and a fish. But the Rockies and the Marlins aren't the only ones to blow it. Before further damage is done, it's time to lay down some guidelines:

4   **Animal relevance:** You can use an animal if, and only if, it has some relevance to the region. No use coming up with any old beast just because it sounds zippy if it's not native to your town. Miami's marlin clearly passes this test (it fails another; see below), but the tiger, for instance, does not. I have never been to Detroit, but I get the sense the place is not exactly overrun with

LIVING LANGUAGE 7.3

Eponyms: An Unpredictable Game

As in the biblical scripture, "to he that has shall be given," eponyms have most often been based on the name of someone with prestige, regardless of who did the work. King James wasn't the one who did the work or even had the idea of translating the King James Bible, nor did Pope Gregory XIII figure out the astronomy and the mathematics for the Gregorian calendar, which corrected the inaccuracies of the Julian calendar. And as these other stories show, having one's name made into an eponym isn't always under the control of the person being "honored."

- In 1913, actor Harry Fox created a dance scene for a successful Broadway musical, then hired dance teacher Oscar Duryea to simplify the steps and introduce them to the public as the fox trot. His plan of creating an eponym for himself worked well, but few people know who the dance is named for. People who were asked offered such explanations as, "The steps are smaller than horses' steps," "Foxes move smoothly like good dancers," and "It's a borrowing from French *faux* meaning false—so a fake trot."
- Dr. Joseph Lister (1827–1912) developed the concept and the methodology of antiseptic surgery. He wanted to be remembered as the founder of the Lister Institute of Preventive Medicine. Instead, his name is most often spoken in relation to Listerine antiseptic mouthwash, a commercial product that he tried unsuccessfully to restrain from using his name.
- Dr. Joseph Ignace Guillotin (1738–1814) was a respected French physician who spoke out against the inhumane practice of tying people down and beheading them with a sword. In response to his pleas for a less painful and gruesome punishment, another doctor, Antoine Louis, designed a killing machine first called *La Louisette*. Dr. Louis died in 1792, the first year the machine was used. A popular song about the machine included the better-known Dr. Guillotin's name, and so the public picked it up and began calling the machine a guillotine. Dr Guillotin tried in vain to get his name removed from the gruesome apparatus, and so did his children. Instead, the French government gave the family permission to change their surname.
- John Duns Scotus, born in Scotland in 1265, was a forward-thinking scholar who attracted a following of intellectuals while teaching at Oxford and the University of Paris. For 200 years his ideas were well respected, but during the Renaissance, when new ideas were advanced and his followers refused to adjust their thinking, they were called dunces.
- Madame La Duchesse de la Valliere, the official mistress of King Louis XIV, was famous for her great beauty and for the jeweled pendants that she wore on chains around her neck. Her name recently came back into fashion for the lavalier microphones that hang around the necks of television performers.
- Joachim C. Neander was a beloved German poet and hymn writer who died in 1680. The Neander Valley *(Neander Thal)* near Dusseldorf was named to honor

his religious and scholarly contributions. In 1856, skeletal remains of the earliest form of Homo sapiens were found in the area and named Neanderthals.

- Although in the late thirteenth century Othman I founded the Ottoman Empire that lasted for over 600 years, the main use of his name is for the kind of large footstool that English speakers associated with the luxury of Turkish baths.

- On April 15, 1865, Samuel Mudd, a thirty-one-year-old doctor, lived in a Charles County, Maryland, farmhouse. John Wilkes Booth, who the night before had assassinated Abraham Lincoln, arrived at the farmhouse with a broken leg. Dr. Mudd set the leg in a splint and put the injured man to bed. Then he rode into nearby Bryantown and learned of Lincoln's death. When Mudd returned, the injured Booth was gone. Mudd was arrested, tried, and convicted for being part of the plot to kill Lincoln and for being an accessory after the fact. Mudd claimed innocence, and at the trial escaped hanging by only one vote. He died in prison, where he worked as a doctor. His name is generally thought to have given rise to—or at least to have popularized—the epithet, "Your name is mud!" In the 1990s his descendants went to court to prove his innocence.

- Names have a headstart in becoming memorable if, like Dr. Mudd's, they coincidentally have particularly appropriate connotations. For example, *sharpshooter* is based on the quality of the guns manufactured in the 1800s by the Sharps Company, while using the name *Maxim silencer* for guns invented by Hiram Percy Maxim (1869–1936) caught on because it sounds so much like a "maximum silencer."

- When American soldiers came home from World War I, they brought the word *crapper* with them for a toilet. It came from the name of Englishman Thomas Crapper, who did for flush toilets what Henry Ford did for automobiles. (See his story in Wallace Reyburn's *Flushed with Pride: The Story of Thomas Crapper,* Trafalgar, 1991.) As a manufacturer, Crapper proudly identified his product with his name. The word *crap* was already in the English language having come from Dutch *krappe,* meaning "scraps," to refer to excrement or discards from butchering.

- *Draconian,* to describe anything harsh and unreasonable, comes from Athenian legislator Draco, who in 621 B.C. was assigned to collect and catalog Athens's unwritten laws. The laws were extremely harsh, and Draco was blamed for this harshness, though he really only gathered and wrote them down.

- *Rastafarian* comes from the pre-coronation name (Ras Tafari) of Ethiopian Emperor Haile Selassie (1892–1975). Rastafarianism is a religious belief system practiced by Jamaicans, who revere Selassie, but many American speakers know the word only to name a kind of music or hair style.

- In 1812, Massachusetts Governor Elbridge Gerry, running for re-election, redistricted the state so as to better advantage himself. The new word *gerrymander* was born through blending after a newspaper editor showed a map to painter

continued

LIVING LANGUAGE 7.3

Eponyms: An Unpredictable Game   continued

Gilbert Stuart. Stuart added a head, wings, and claws to one of the districts making it look like a salamander.

- Pantalone, an early Christian doctor who worked with the poor and was condemned to death by the Romans, became the patron saint of medicine. Because the literal meaning of his name is "all lion," the producers of the famous *commedia dell'arte* (a playful, improvised drama tradition in renaissance Italy) applied his name in jest to their main buffoon who wore bloused trousers. From this usage came the word *pantaloons*, eventually shortened to pants.
- The first teddy bear was made in 1902 by a Brooklyn candy store owner, who fashioned the toy after a cartoon drawing by *Washington Post* cartoonist Clifford K. Berryman. It showed Teddy Roosevelt turning away from shooting a helpless cub.
- Samuel Maverick was the colorful pioneer mayor of San Antonio, Texas, who refused to brand his cattle. Critics assumed he wanted an excuse to claim any unbranded cattle, but because he owned 385,000 acres of ranch land, perhaps the job of finding his cattle—much less branding them—was simply too daunting. Today a maverick is anyone who refuses to comply with rules and expectations.

---

safari animals straight off the Serengheti Plains. Cincinnati, for that matter, couldn't have all that many bengals, and I'll eat my shorts if you can show me a bruin in Boston.

5   **Indians:** Enough Indians. America has a multitude of cultures and people with as yet no team named after them, and maybe it's time to cut some of them in. I propose something like the Anaheim Hispanics or the Miami Jews.

6   **Events:** Only the good Lord knows what the Montreal Expos were thinking when they named their team after the 1967 World's Fair but surely they must regret it now. Fewer and fewer people even remember the occasion and a lot of those who do got sick on the rides. The 49ers have confused more than a few folks with their California Gold Rush reference (I was never confused myself, but I keep thinking they'll break out of the huddle with sifting pans). Montreal and San Francisco do, however, get points for opening up a whole range of possibilities. If you can name a team after an event, you can name it after just about anything—a disease, an inert gas, my mom, whatever. Don't name your team after an event.

7   **A name that can't be singularized:** I hate to harp on these guys, but the Expos—and while we're at it, the Twins and the Rockies—are wretched names because they make the identity of individual players incomprehensible. What does it mean for one of them to say, "I am an Expo"? Logically, this would seem to mean, "I am a world's fair," but that's what the team as a whole

is supposed to be. Is each player a different pavilion? Food from a different country? It's hard to figure how any Montreal player knows who he is, and frankly I wouldn't be surprised to hear that a lot of them are in therapy.

8   **Death:** Sports are fun. Death is not. So for the most part, intimations of death in team names are to be frowned on. You'd think, this would be obvious, but tell it to the Chicago Bulls, who, wittingly or not, named their team after an animal the city used to be famous for slaughtering. It was also—how to put it?—inappropriate, for Washington, a city with one of the nation's highest homicide rates, to keep the name the Bullets once the team moved here from Baltimore—which come to think of it is not exactly a model of safety either. In this vein, the new hockey team in Florida would do well to avoid, for instance, the Miami Riots.

9   **Birds:** Using a type of bird to name your team is absurd because all birds are monumentally indifferent to games. Except pigeons. Blue jays, cardinals, orioles—none of these birds, given a choice, would be caught dead in a sports stadium, so using them to christen teams is folly. No more bird names.

10   **Fish:** No more fish, either.

11   **An imponderable:** A name need not be a Stonehengian mystery, understood by ancient elders, a riddle to modern man. Undoubtedly someone knows the derivation of the Royals and the Dodgers, but are they around to tell us? If not, did they write it down somewhere? And what did Buffalo have in mind when it named its football team the Bills? What's a Bill? If the team is named after Buffalo Bill Cody, why? The guy is most closely associated with Rochester. Buffalo Bob, Howdy Doody's sidekick, was from Buffalo, so the Buffalo Bobs might be more appropriate. If they just wanted a nice familiar-sounding guy's name, what would have been so wrong with the Buffalo Daves?

12   **Local occupations:** Sometimes these work, sometimes they don't. For instance, the Pittsburgh Steelers is a winner because you could sort of imagine guys in that line of business knocking heads together and playing a mean game of football. The Mariners, on the other hand, is a stinker because, while ship navigators generally perform ably at sea, it's hard to imagine a guy in a macintosh and yellow hat hitting for the cycle or turning a double play. The Senators was an ill-conceived idea too, not so much because legislators make lousy athletes but because the name added a somewhat sordid dimension to all the talk about stealing and scoring. Handle with care.

13   **Sox:** A tip for future baseball fans. Sox are so much a part of the game's tradition that no one bothers to correct the weird spelling anymore. For a new expansion team, however, a sox name would appear ridiculous because it would invoke another era; it'd be like calling a Bauhaus office building "Ye Old Shoppe." And there's always the danger that a pastel-addled city like Miami would go with the Framboise Sox. Sox names are off limits.

14   And finally, here's a bit of advice for all teams: If things don't work out in your present location and you end up changing hometowns, please, in the name of all that is just, change the name too. When the Jazz were in New Orleans they had a good name; now that they're in Utah they have a ridiculous

name. The Lakers worked in Minnesota; it doesn't in L.A. And whatever Dodgers turn out to be, they couldn't exist in plenitude in towns as different as Los Angeles and Brooklyn. No doubt it costs big bucks to change the uniforms and the programs and all that, but for the right name it's really worth it.

No Easy Task to Name Names

Vinnie Perrone

And Scepter is moving like a tremendous machine!
—The famous 1973 Belmont Stakes call Chick Anderson almost made.

1   Had Penny Chenery had her way, Secretariat wouldn't have been named Secretariat. The Triple Crown winner of 1973 and one of the greatest thoroughbreds in history would have been known then and forever as Scepter, in deference to his regally named parents, Bold Ruler and Somethingroyal.

2   The Jockey Club, which approves the naming of all registered thoroughbreds, rejected Scepter because the name already was in use. On the same grounds it then refused Royal Line, Something Special, Games of Chance and Deo Volente before accepting Secretariat, a name suggested by Chenery's personal secretary, Elizabeth Ham.

3   "She liked the sound of it," Chenery said recently from Lexington, Ky. "I wasn't crazy about the name Secretariat. But after the name came back, I figured it was an okay name. By the time the horse had finished racing, of course, it was a marvelous name."

4   The naming of a thoroughbred can be as restrictive as it is imaginative, an often-overlooked art form subjected to Jockey Club censorship. Among the numerous constraints: No horse can have a name exceeding 18 characters, including spaces and punctuation. They can't take the name of a "famous" horse—the world will know only one Man o' War—nor the name of a former racehorse who's been dead fewer than 10 years (five if the horse was a gelding). The name of a living person requires that person's authorization, which is how Willard Scott, Art Buchwald, Chris Evert and Don Rickles became horses. Trade names are not allowed nor are copyrighted names nor those "which are suggestive of or which have a vulgar or obscene meaning."

5   In that regard, The Jockey Club has let a few slip through.

6   The Jockey Club will process more than 40,000 name applications this year, facing its busiest period next month when it will handle some 800 name

requests per day, according to Jim Peden, director of communications. The Jockey Club recently extended the naming deadline to Feb. 1 of a horse's two-year-old season, after which a $50.00 late charge is assessed.

7   Each application allows six names to be listed in order of preference. According to Peden, a computer verifies that no identical or similar name is in use, then examines whether the name is phonetically acceptable.

8   From that check a name is tentatively approved and forwarded to the registry floor, where it is considered by six of the 35 application processors. If they accept the name, it goes to registrar Buddy Bishop for final approval.

9   Peden said the six-person "floating committee" is purposefully diverse in age and background. "The Grateful Dead might not mean that much to a more elderly person," he said, "just as the name Toots Shor might be unfamiliar to a younger one."

10   When the breeding business peaked in the mid-1980s and more than 50,000 name applications were submitted annually, the Jockey Club's likelihood of overlooking a questionable name rose as well. "Once in a while something does slip through that is undesirable or incorrect, or whatever," Peden said.

11   Although Peden declined to be specific, The Jockey Club was said to be embarrassed at having accepted the name Bodacious Tatas, particularly after she gained recognition as a stakes winner. (Years earlier, it authorized that a filly be named Cold as a Witch's; bred to Banquet Table, her ensuing foal was named Titular Feast.) While phonetically sensitive, The Jockey Club somehow confirmed Up Your Assets.

12   Peden called the process of scrutinizing so many applications "a fairly monumental task" and said the ever-increasing number of registered names makes it more difficult for owners to have their first choice accepted.

13   Legendary horseman Alfred Vanderbilt, owner of the 1950s superhorse Native Dancer and one of the masters of the name game, said that sheer numbers have encumbered a once-artful pursuit. "Occasionally you can have some fun with what are oftentimes considered clever names," he said. "I enjoy doing it. I spent a lot of time at it. But it's become so much more difficult."

14   Still active at 86, Vanderbilt has jousted with The Jockey Club for more than half a century, testing the boundaries of the double entendre. "They could be pretty arbitrary about what was good taste and what was not," he said. Vanderbilt, however, found no resistance to the name Social Outcast after breeding Pansy to Shut Out, while two unions between The Axe II and Top o' The Morning produced Splitting Headache and Chipper.

15   According to Peden, about three names are submitted on average before one is approved. Harry Meyerhoff, a bridge fanatic, wanted to name his Bold Bidder colt Seven No Trump; rebuffed, he chose Spectacular Bid. John Hay Whitney secured No Robbery after having Fair Exchange rejected.

16   Vanderbilt said the true challenge of naming rests in the ability to select clever titles that distinguish pedigree. Some recent examples by other

horsemen were Axe Me Nicely (by Hatchet Man out of Joanne Behave); Dixieland Bandit (Dixieland Band–Masked Moment); Freezer Burn (It's Freezing–Smillie's Revenge); Muffler (Stop the Music–Fur Scarf); Whiz Taylor (Taylor's Special–Whiz Along); Slashing (Blade–Young Empress) and Wire Tap (Phone Trick–Probably Magic).

17   There seems a curious correlation between classic names and outstanding thoroughbreds. A number of this country's finest horses from the 20th century had names that helped carry their legend: Citation, Man o' War, Whirlaway, Secretariat, War Admiral, Seattle Slew, Forego, Affirmed. "You have to have decent names," Chenery said, "or you don't get any respect."

18   Scott Regan, a Maryland trainer whose family runs a small breeding operation, knew there was little hope of getting a fast horse from the planned romance between Thirty Eight Paces and Maureen B. So Regan ventured to name the colt Nyuk Nyuk Nyuk, a Curlyism from The Three Stooges.

19   "I was pretty sure I'd get it," Regan said. "I didn't think anybody else could possibly pick a name that stupid."

20   Nyuk Nyuk Nyuk was accepted, and the three-year-old has proceeded into a perfectly forgettable career.

21   "You don't ever see a real good horse with a stupid name," Regan said. "There's a subtlety behind it. I suppose I went the opposite way with Nyuk Nyuk Nyuk knowing he was a cheap homebred. He would have had another name if I were hoping for a Secretariat."

TO NAME A FEW

Sire	+	Dam	=	Foal
Topsider	+	Anesthesiologist	=	Going Under
Damascus	+	Perfect Roux	=	Dam Perfect
Cortan	+	Kissing Lizzie	=	Kiss My Tan
Roaring Spring	+	Aunt Lyd	=	Babbling Brook
Hatchet Man	+	Red Light Girl	=	Loose Lizzie
Spend a Buck	+	Suite of Dreams	=	Creative Act
Petite Roche	+	I Can't Wait	=	A Little Impatient
Bold Agent	+	Dashing Denise	=	Blown Cover
Maudlin	+	Twice Before	=	Twice Too Many
Oh Say	+	Low Cut	=	Ogle
Shelter Half	+	Fuel to Burn	=	Half Lit
Hatchet Man	+	La Grande Finale	=	Finita La Musica
Island Whirl	+	Merry Chase	=	Burning Sensation
Blue Ensign	+	Bridal Party	=	Naval Engagement
Affirmed	+	Adored	=	Marriage
Known Fact	+	Home on the Range	=	Known Ranger

Jaklin Klugman	+	Rubies Mildred	= Oscar Oscar Oscar
Sham	+	Mach Three	= Mockery
What a Threat	+	Breath of Scandal	= Kneecap Tony
Cannon Shell	+	Two Skips	= Badaboom
Linkage	+	Dance Troupe	= Line Score
Center Cut	+	My Big Twin Sister	= Rump Cut
Rollick 'n Roll	+	In My Water Bed	= Bedrock
Iron Constitution	+	Root Toot Toot	= Constitoot
Nodouble	+	Distinctiveness	= Broke The Mold
Tunerup	+	John's Other Girl	= Points N Plugs
It's Freezing	+	Proudly Hailed	= Hailing
Kid Colin	+	Tinsley's Island	= Isle Kid You Not
Double Zeus	+	Safely Home	= Safe On Second
Dimaggio	+	Dusty Row	= Fifty Six Ina Row
Muscovite	+	You Won't Be Sorry	= Gorby

COMPREHENSION

1. Words to talk about:

   - the news drew *huzzahs*
   - off the *Serengheti Plains*
   - a *Stonehengian* mystery
   - a guy in a *macintosh*
   - a *Bauhaus* office building
   - go with the *framboise sox*
   - *triple-crown* winner
   - boundaries of the *double entendre*

2. Why does the Jockey Club have a diverse committee reviewing requests?
3. What are the restrictions placed on the naming of horses?
4. What restrictions does Segal place on the naming of teams?

DISCUSSION

1. When naming horses, why does it make sense to outlaw trademarks and to require that permission be obtained before using the names of living people?
2. Of the many examples of double entendre given in the articles, pick out a couple and explain their cleverness.

3. Besides being amused at Segal's observations, careful readers can use the information he provides to come up with several good observations about names that appeal to the public. Combine your knowledge of the world with what Segal says to decide why team owners chose the names on the left instead of those on the right:

Miami Marlins	Miami Fish
Cincinnati Bengals	Cincinnati Tigers
St. Louis Cardinals	St. Louis Birds
Boston Bruins	Boston Bears
Buffalo Bills	Buffalo Bobs or Buffalo Daves

4. In hopes of drumming up support for a National League baseball expansion team in Arizona, Phoenix Suns president Jerry Colangelo invited the public to suggest possible names. Explain the appropriateness behind these names considered clever enough to be featured in news stories:

Phoenix Dry Sox	Sun Strokes
Hot Wind	Zonies
Sandbaggers	Diamondbacks

5. Part of the fun of athletics is the mental gymnastics involved in choosing clever names. On Chinese New Years in Albuquerque, the New Mexico Race Walkers sponsor an annual New Year Wok, while in Big Sur, California, sponsors of a marathon solicited names relating to classical music in honor of the orchestras and pianists that provide music along the route. Suggestions included such names as The Unfinished Hill, Crescendo at De Endo, Go-for-Baroque Hill, and Trouble Cliff. Given below are team names used over the last few years in the Nike Capital Challenge, an amateur foot race held in Washington, D.C. Match the names with where the team members worked at the time of the race.

Team Names	Participating Groups
Appellate Briefs	Bureau of Alcohol, Tobacco, and Firearms
The Boxer Shorts	Rep. Barbara Boxer's office
Elliott Fit Ness's Runtouchables	Circuit Court of Appeals
The Kinder, Gentler Soles	C-Span Broadcasting
Peacock Strutters	George Bush White House
Running Concurrently	National Broadcasting Company
See Span Run	Supreme Court
Writ Runners	U. S. Sentencing Commission

6. ESPN sports broadcaster Chris Fowler nominated the following high school team names for a "Scholastic Sports America" Nickname Hall of Fame. Listed alphabetically on the left are the team names while the towns they represent are listed on the right. Match them up by figuring out the connections.

Team Name	Town
Awesome Blossoms	Speedway, Indiana
Bats	Miami Beach, Florida
Bubblers	Highland Home, Alabama
Cavegirls and Cavemen	Chillicothe, Illinois
Flying Squadron	Carlsbad, New Mexico
Ghosts and Spooks	Boiling Springs, Pennsylvania
Hi-Tides	Blooming Prairie, Minnesota
Sparkplugs	Belfry, Montana

7. Games and sports have contributed a goodly number of metaphors to English. A recent one is the Nintendo effect, based on the video game and used to describe an insensitivity or hardening of personal feelings about war and terrorism because of the excessive viewing of explosions on television as part of a game. Make a list of at least ten other sports or game metaphors and explain how they do a good job of communicating.

SEX SELLS, BUT HOW FAR WILL WE LET IT GO?

Scot Lehigh

In relation to entertainment and the mass media (movies, television, pornographic magazines and books, popular music, and the Internet), there's probably no more contentious
issue than that of protecting children, and perhaps adults, from sexually explicit or sexually titillating material. In this article published in the *Boston Globe* in 1995, Scot Lehigh
discusses mass media sexuality, not so much from the point of view of a censor wanting
to protect young people (see Chapter 3 for comments on censorship), but from a more
overarching view of what society wants for itself.

1 Doesn't that nearly nude couple having Better Sex know how hard it is to
   read with them carrying on like that on the next page—and inviting you to
   join them?
2   And those lovers sprawled across two pages of entangled ecstasy in the
   perfume ads—shouldn't they pull the sheet up just a bit?
3   How about the Good Vibrations woman who has plunked herself down
   to play with erotic toys in the back of magazines everywhere? And what in
   the world is going on with those Naughty Victorians up there in the corner?
   Is the woman silhouetted in the window really spanking her consort? Don't
   they know the curtains are open?

SECOND PARADISE

4 These days you can't open a magazine to pursue a little of the wisdom that
   renaissance scientist Pracelsus called the second paradise of the world without being beckoned thither to sample the products of the first. Even the *New
   Yorker,* that bastion of civility, includes in a recent issue a nitty-gritty look at
   the inner workings and evolutions of the burgeoning pornographic film industry.
5   The growing acceptance of a rapidly relaxing sexual climate is equally evident on the airwaves. The young hipsters who populate prime-time chat and
   joke about sex with a candor that would have made their media forebears
   pop a vacuum tube.

6   To the delight of some and the horror of others, there has been an efflorescence of nudity, sexual talk and carnal advertisement in American culture.
Call it the new eroticism or a plague of permissiveness, a refreshing sexual
frankness or a perverse coarsening of culture, the standards we steer by are
once again in motion, as a confluence of technology, commerce and libertarian impulse help redefine what's hot, what's acceptable. And with each passing week, the category of what's "acceptable" seems to grow.

7   ABC's *NYPD Blue* has garnered much of the attention for occasionally revealing flesh that theretofore came uncloaked only on cable. But the new sexual frankness is perhaps better seen—or rather, heard—in sitcom conversations.

8   Janice Irvine, an associate professor of sociology at the University of
Massachusetts at Amherst who teaches about sexuality in society, says the rapidity with which the change has come is astonishing. "It has really changed
amazingly over just the last couple of years," Irvine said. "The number of references to sexuality and to homosexuality is just phenomenal."

TERRACE TRYST

9   Take the hit NBC show *Friends,* a sitcom tracking the lives of a group of twen-
tysomething Manhattan pals. In recent weeks, it's been revealed that Monica had a tryst on the outdoor terrace (and left her underwear there), Joey
once took a bit part in a porn film (which the friends then watch) and, after
weeks of worry, Ross has finally had sex with his new girlfriend (twice in one
night).

10   On *Seinfeld,* Jerry and George and Elaine and Kramer regularly discuss
their lives and loves—and the allusions range from the now famous bet about
who can abstain from autoeroticism longest to "the move," Jerry's highly effective but closely guarded sexual technique.

11   And to think, just a generation or so ago, poor Laura and Rob Petrie (*aka*
Dick Van Dyke and Mary Tyler Moore) couldn't even have a double bed in
the master suite. Lucy was forbidden to mention she was pregnant; "expecting" was the proper form. And Jack Paar stormed off the *Tonight Show* because NBC decided to cut a joke with an allusion to a "WC," or water
closet—a bathroom by another name.

12   Why have the standards changed? Against the backdrop of '60s and '70s
legal redefinition of obscenity, Irvine argues that causes like the feminist and
gay and lesbian movements have made discussion of sex more commonplace,
while issues such as sex education, abortion and AIDS have all made it more
acceptable, and even imperative, to discuss sex more openly.

13   A '60s generation that shed parental and religious inhibitions about sex
has likely also played a role, others say. "Through the '60s and '70s with
the sexual revolution, sex became more OK to talk about," said Michael

Gonzales, a University of California at Irvine psychologist. "We then raised a generation who think more openly about sexuality."

14   Support for that theory comes from Lily Pond, publisher of *Yellow Silk*, a quarterly of high-brow erotic fiction based in Albany, Calif. "Baby boomers, that's where the difference is," declares Pond. "We redefined for our generation what sexuality was about."

15   Pond said she started her publication to fill a void she saw in contemporary literature. "To me when I was in high school, writing class and literature were important, but so was making out in the back seat. I didn't see why that shouldn't be part of what I considered to be my literature."

16   *Libido*, the franker and more sexually explicit Chicago erotic quarterly, "is geared toward arousing on both an intellectual and a physical level," said editor Marianna Beck. Thus *Libido*'s favorite advertising forum: *Harper's* magazine.

17   Beck says most of her subscribers are well-educated, broad-minded people striving to keep long-term relationships zestful. Shirley Zussman, former president of the American Association of Sex Educators, Counselors and Therapists, and a practicing sex therapist, agrees that long-term couples are increasing consumers of erotica.

18   As Zussman sees it, the sexual revolution reduced shame about sex, while AIDS has increased fear of promiscuity. As a result, "People have become more aware of how they can enhance sexuality with their partner."

19   But whatever the growing receptivity to a new eroticism, it is far from universal. *Libido* counts a circulation of only 10,000 while *Yellow Silk* boasts about 16,000. For most people, the principle exposure to those journals has been through their advertisements, which run in thoughtful publications, such as *Harper's*, the *Atlantic Monthly* and the *New Republic*.

CLASH OF VALUES

20   A broader receptivity for erotic advertisements shouldn't, of course, be mistaken for wholesale cultural acceptance. Rather, a resounding clash of values continues between libertarian leanings and censorious impulse, between conservative religious morality and a more latitudinarian mindset.

21   Among many conservatives, the change from a buttoned-up culture to one that is increasingly unzipped has created real distress. "You have got several people in high positions who are amoral, if not immoral, and who live a certain lifestyle and hope that everybody else will live that lifestyle," said the Rev. Donald Wildmon, president of the American Family Association, based in Tupelo, Miss., which tries to pressure sponsors to drop offending shows. Wildmon says some of his group's strongest support comes from conservative New Englanders repulsed by what they see on TV.

22   But others say Hollywood is reflecting, rather than leading, the cultural change. "I think there is a more open sexual frankness around," said Alan Holliday, an assistant professor of mass communication at Boston University. "I think for the *Melrose Place/Seinfeld*-age audience, this is not shocking or new. It is just something they live with all the time."

23   Part of it, certainly, is technology, which has helped emancipate the libido. The videocassette recorder, in particular, has made erotic material far more accessible to regular people.

24   "Twenty years ago if you wanted to see anything like that, you had to go to a porno theater," said cultural critic Steve Stark, who is writing a book about TV. "Now you can get it on your VCR, you can get it on-line, you can get it on your cable system. That has had the effect of greatly liberating standards."

25   Adds Gonzales, the University of California psychologist: "If you go to the adult section of your neighborhood video store, it is not just dirty old men. There are women and men of all ages."

ADULT VIDEOS SCORE

26   "Sex in America," a University of Chicago study released last year, offers some evidence of just how prevalent adult movies have become. Of the 3,400 people surveyed, the study found that 41 percent of men and 16 percent of women had spent money on some sort of erotica in the past year. X-rated movies or videos led the list, with 23 percent of men and 11 percent of women spending on them.

27   Advertisement of explicit videos is becoming more and more commonplace in mainstream publications. The best examples are the sexually explicit videos offered in publications like *US*, the *New York Times Book Review*, and the *Boston Globe Magazine*. Those series are billed as sexual self-help works.

28   Well, sometimes. As one couple fondles each other on the "Loving Better" series, Dr. Sheldon Kule narrates: "There approaches a point, if stimulation continues unimpeded, where a great deal of muscular tension takes place within the body and the level of excitement increases tremendously." Just so.

29   The "Better Sex" video series doesn't pretend to that level of didacticism. All most people really need, intones Dr. Judith Seifer, "is permission to talk about sex with their partners—and enough information to communicate what it is they want sexually from one another. Well, we provide this service."

30   In abundance. Various couples (some porno stars in other incarnations) parade across the screen, all providing service. The videos also feature people acting out their sexual fantasies: from sex outdoors to sex in the hot tub. The message is clear: I'm OK, you're OK, our fantasies are fine.

31   Which brings up the question: Just what isn't OK?

32   There, the absolute standard may be difficult to define. But, to paraphrase former Supreme Court Justice Potter Stewart, we tend to know it when we see it.

33   Designer Calvin Klein found that out last summer. Klein has long used an emaciated group of underdressed androgyny to pitch products. But when he launched a new campaign that flirted with kiddie-porn atmospherics, the outrage was immediate and sustained. Sex wasn't selling, it was rebelling.

34   A chastened Klein pulled the ads.

COMPREHENSION

1. Words to talk about:

   - spanking her *consort*
   - The young *hipsters*
   - an *efflorescence* of nudity
   - *confluence* of technology, commerce, and libertarian
   - who can abstain from *autoeroticism*
   - a more *latitudinarian mindset*
   - an *emaciated group*
   - underdressed *androgyny*

2. What different kinds of media does Lehigh cite to support his thesis that sexuality is more visible in today's society than it was a generation ago?

DISCUSSION

1. Lehigh lists these four descriptions of today's sexual attitudes. How do they differ in connotations?

   - a new eroticism
   - a plague of permissiveness
   - a refreshing sexual frankness
   - a perverse coarsening of culture

2. Lehigh gives three sociological reasons that have contributed to more openness about sex. What are they?

3. Lehigh also gives technological reasons that have contributed to more openess about sex. What are they?

4. Lehigh described "a resounding clash of values" between "libertarian leanings and censorious impulse." In the next paragraph, he says

almost the same thing metaphorically. What metaphor does he use? Is it effective? Why does he repeat the idea?

5. Lehigh says that different groups of people are now buying erotic material. Who are they? What has brought about the change?

6. Lehigh used the controversial Calvin Klein ads as an example of what is *not* acceptable. Can you generalize from this one example to tell something about the values that society still holds?

7. Look at the following news summaries and explain how they relate to Lehigh's essay.

   (a) "The industry finally caved in this week to viewers' concerns— but only under a federal threat," is the way *USA Today* (July 11, 1997) characterized changes being made in the television viewing code to become effective October 1, 1997. In addition to the current age-based ratings of G, PG, TV-14 and MA, networks will label shows with V (violence), S (sexual content), L (strong language), and D (suggestive dialogue). Warning icons in the top left of the screen will be larger and last longer. For children's shows, Y will continue to denote shows for all youths, with Y-7 indicating appropriateness for ages 7 and up. An FV label will flag cartoons and other shows for fantasy violence. As part of the agreement, parents will join a review committee to look at networks not complying with ratings.

   (b) According to the *Sydney Morning Herald* (July 9, 1996), all TV sets being sold in Australia are to be equipped with a chip that will allow viewers to filter out violent programs. "While parents and church groups welcomed the move to tighten controls on celluloid violence—including the introduction of a V-chip, delayed screening times and the reclassification of some films— they shared the view of censors and film organisers that the legislation was unlikely to have any effect at all in helping to limit actual violence in society."

   (c) *ImageCensor* is the name of a new antiporn software designed to be used with Windows. *School Library Journal* (August 1997) said that according to *Wired* magazine, the software "employs an image-detecting algorithm developed by scanning thousands of nude photos." Supposedly the software will block images of genitalia whether on disk, CD-ROM, or on-line. Librarians are interested in finding out about such software because they are under pressure to keep young people who use library computers from accessing pornography. At its 1997 summer conference, the American Library Association approved a resolution opposing filters on library computers; however, Judith Krug, Executive Director of ALA's Office for Intellectual Freedom, still talked about installing filters in children's room computers, while still allowing children to use other computers within the library. She compared the situation to having special children's rooms but letting children also check out books from the regular collection.

(d) Ironically, as the level of sexual content has increased in movies, rock music, television, and now on the Internet, parents, who are increasingly anxious to control what remains in their jurisdiction, have become more active in censoring books and asking that certain titles be removed from reading lists and school libraries. According to various issues of the American Library Association's *Newsletter on Intellectual Freedom*, between January of 1986 and December of 1995, thirteen formal requests were made for removal from schools and libraries of Judy Blume's *Forever* (Bradbury Press, 1975), a story of first love, which was criticized for being "sexually explicit" and "erotic" and for "condoning premarital sex." Robert Cormier's *The Chocolate War* (Pantheon, 1974) was the subject of eleven such requests, some centering on its "negative view of life," while others objected to references to masturbation. The third most censored novel for young adults was Nancy Garden's *Annie on My Mind* (Farrar, Straus, & Giroux, 1982), the story of two young women who have a lesbian love affair.

TWA CONSPIRACY SPREADS ON INTERNET

Jonathan Vankin and John Whalen

Vankin and Whalen's article illustrates the growing interrelationships between the Internet and standard news sources. The two authors have also written a book, *The 60 Greatest Conspiracies of All Time* (Citadel Press, 1997). Their interest in conspiracies drew them to news stories and rumors about the 1996 TWA crash, but while investigators from the Federal Aviation Authority were combing the ocean floor for evidence of what happened, Vanking and Whalen were combing the Internet for evidence of a different kind. They were searching for relationships between computers and print and broadcast journalism. They wanted to see how this kind of intermingling makes it possible for rumors to gain worldwide acceptance in the same amount of time that stories used to take to filter through a neighborhood. Their article was first published in the *New York Times Magazine,* December 1996.

1   On the night of July 17, TWA Flight 800 exploded and crashed off the coast of Long Island, N.Y., killing everyone.

2   For months investigators have focused on three possible causes—a bomb, mechanical failure or a terrorist missile. On Nov. 20, with 95 percent of the wreckage recovered, the lead FBI investigator said it is now "less likely that a bomb or missile" downed the plane.

3   Yet barely 36 hours after the disaster, a message posted on an Internet discussion site called "rec.aviation.piloting" suggested a darker possibility.

4   "Did the Navy do it?" wrote someone from New York who identified himself as Evan B. Gillespie. "It is interesting how much evidence there is that it was hit by a missile."

5   Actually there wasn't any weightier evidence for this than for the other two theories. But reports from eyewitnesses—who said they saw a streak of light approaching the jet—prompted investigators to entertain the idea that someone shot it down. Within days of the crash, numerous Net writers mulled over the witness reports and made a startling leap.

6   They speculated that the jet was downed by accidental "friendly fire" from a U.S. Navy ship on a training cruise.

7   Such a horrifying blunder, according to the evolving theory, was quickly covered up by a conspiracy involving federal investigators, the military and President Clinton.

8   Even by conspiracy standards, this one was pretty weak. But as a study in how conspiracy theories mutate in the age of easy global communication, the friendly fire story is a gem.

9   On the Internet, conspiracy theories gestate almost instantly, and spread with dizzying speed. The theorists seize on and often distort mainstream media reports, make gross assumptions about the government's allegedly boundless capacity for malevolence and, occasionally, fabricate reports outright.

10   In the case of Flight 800, the process happened so fast and with such intensity that the conspiracy theory, which once might have bounced around harmlessly on the fringe, briefly elbowed its way into mainstream coverage.

11   In September and again in October, prompted by the Internet's conspiratorial buzz, journalists felt compelled to ask officials about friendly fire. The authorities labeled it "an outrageous allegation."

12   News organizations, which subsequently took a closer look, agreed. But the fact that friendly fire came up at all says a lot about the power of the Internet.

13   Here is a chronological review of how a theory catapulted to 15 minutes of fame.

JULY 17–23: A PENNY FOR YOUR PLOTS

14   In the immediate aftermath of the crash, unhinged speculation was cheap. Some theorists suggested that the true target of the TWA "attack" was Henry Kissinger, who was supposedly on board. He wasn't.

15   Over time, the theories included such notions as the jet being zapped by a death ray possibly operated by a consortium of Russians, North Koreans and the Japanese Aum Shinrikyo cult. Predictably, some asserted that a UFO was responsible.

16   But only the friendly fire theory developed real legs, thanks largely to a July 21 *Jerusalem Post* story in which unnamed "French Defense Ministry experts" asserted that "the infrastructure needed to fire a missile powerful enough to hit a plane at that altitude is only possessed by Army units."

17   The story was clearly presented as "what if" speculation, but many conspiracy theorists took it as confirmation that the U.S. government had shot down Flight 800. The *Post* is available on the World Wide Web, and the story spread rapidly all over the planet.

18   "I think it's pretty obvious," stated one contributor to the "talk.politics.guns" news group, "that TWA 800 was taken down by a SAM (surface-to-air missile). . . . Friendly fire, as it were."

JULY 24–29: TROOPERGATE

19   A posting in the news group "alt.conspiracy" made a more startling claim: President Clinton was probably involved.

20   "Two of the passengers were former Arkansas state troopers on Bill Clinton's security detail," it read, explaining that the men were on their way to Paris to tell all to *Le Monde*. The "source" for this shocker? The *Miami Herald*.

21   The "Troopergate" message generated excitement among Net conspiracy theorists, many of whom believe Clinton to be capable of anything. "Suddenly the TWA 800 explosion got a whole lot less mysterious," wrote one correspondent in "misc.survivalism."

22   Over in "alt.politics.org.batf," an America Online subscriber wondered, "How many (total) does that make now of people who have previously known our Komrad Klinton who are now pushing up daisies?"

AUG. 2: CYBERHOAX

23   The *Miami Herald* quickly exposed the trooper message as a hoax. The *Herald* traced it to the Net address of Gene Hilsheimer, a Florida resident.

24   The *Herald* said, "Hilsheimer denied creating it," though he did opine later that the posting was probably designed to bait "conspiracy nuts." Despite this particular debunking, friendly fire kept on going. Other writers surged ahead with the unsupported claim that "there is a report of sailors at sea routinely locking on to airliners during mock missile practice."

AUGUST 22: RUSSELL TAKES CHARGE

25   Friendly fire might have stalled if not for an anonymous message that began circulating in late August. "TWA Flight 800 was shot down," one version stated, "by a U.S. Navy guided-missile ship which was in area W-105 . . . a Warning Area off the southeast coast of Long Island." The message was attributed to "a man who was safety chairman for the Airline Pilots Association for many years and he is considered an expert on safety."

26   In fact, it was written on America Online by Richard Russell, a 66-year-old Floridian and former United Airlines pilot. Russell later told reporters that he never intended his message—a private e-mail communication sent to about a dozen friends who were aviation accident investigators—to be widely distributed. Nonetheless, replicated countless times by unknown Netizens, it spread like a viral contagion.

AUGUST 28-SEPT. 1: FRIENDLY FIRE SKYROCKETS

27   As the crash investigation of TWA 800 entered its second month, friendly fire talk began to move beyond the Internet. It was helped along, inadvertently, by news reports of more eyewitness anomalies, including the murky snapshot taken by Linda Kabot, a Long Island secretary. Blown up and distributed on

the Net, it showed a blip, supposedly a long cylinder streaking through the night sky, allegedly in the vicinity of the doomed jet.

28   About this time, multiple copies of the hijacked Russell opinion began arriving in newsrooms via fax and e-mail. With populist speculation about friendly fire becoming a roar, major media outlets decided to take a closer look.

29   On Sept. 1 *Newsday* launched a preemptive strike on the friendly fire theory, quoting a "senior federal source" who advised, perhaps wishfully, "You can put that to bed."

SEPT. 5–7: GOING UP, UP, UP

30   Another mainstream report—this one by a local TV reporter helped amplify the Net buzz about friendly fire. On Sept. 5 Marcia Kramer of WCBS-TV in New York broadcast that investigators were examining whether a missile from "a U.S. military plane" might have torn through the jet without exploding. Her sources? Unnamed officials close to the investigation. Kramer's report was ignored by most of her colleagues, a fact that inflamed Net suspicion. "This news item did not show up anywhere else on radio or TV during the following day," one Net surfer wrote. "Shades of censorship?"

SEPT. 8–17: RUSSELL FIZZLES

31   In the next several days *Newsday, Newsweek,* the Associated Press, Reuters and CNN decided they had to take a hard look at friendly fire.

32   "Because so many people were talking about it we felt it was the responsible thing to do, to revisit this question," says Ron Dunsky, a CNN producer whose network investigated friendly fire in July, found no evidence to support it and didn't run a story.

33   Why did it come to the fore again, with no new evidence? "The Internet was part of the reason," he says, "one of the factors that tipped the scales."

34   At a Sept. 16 news briefing on Long Island, FBI and National Transportation Safety Board officials found themselves under unfriendly fire from a fixated press corps. The investigators responded to at least four straight questions about the theory— including one from CNN, which later that day ran a serious report on friendly fire. It mentioned the Russell-authored message and conveyed emphatic denials from the government.

35   Russell can't be accused of courting publicity. He says he has been contacted by several major TV shows, but they've all lost interest because he won't give up his source. Unless Russell decides to say more, or his claimed source comes forward, his now-notorious e-mail message has to remain filed under "Rumors: Unsubstantiated."

AFTERMATH: IT LIVES!

36   Though the Russell-gram seemed at a dead end, the Net has made it immortal.

37   On Sept. 27 Tom Snyder, on his *Late Late Show*, announced that he'd found the message on the Net and wondered aloud—albeit skeptically—about a cover-up.

38   Then on Nov. 8, friendly fire made headlines again. This time it was Pierre Salinger—the noted journalist and John F. Kennedy administration press secretary—who went public with the theory.

39   Salinger, according to news accounts, said his source was a document given to him by "someone in French intelligence in Paris," written by an American who "was tied to the U.S. Secret Service, and has important contacts in the U.S. Navy."

40   But apparently, the document was the Russell message, or at least a clone of it.

41   CNN showed Salinger a copy of the message and he said: "Yes. That's it. That's the document. Where did you get it?"

42   He also told other reporters that he learned only after he went public on Nov. 7—U.S. media ran the story the next day—that the same document had been on the Net for weeks. He said the message was dated Aug. 22—the same day Russell sent his famous e-mail.

43   As Net writers might say: "Interesting!!!"

Comprehension

1. Words to talk about:

   - conspiracy theories *mutate*
   - conspiracy theories *gestate*
   - boundless capacity for *malevolence*
   - *fabricate* reports outright
   - a theory *catapulted* to *15 minutes of fame*
   - though he did *opine* later
   - replicated countless times by unknown *Netizens*
   - news reports of more eyewitness *anomalies*
   - *Newsday* launched a *preemptive strike*

2. Allusions to talk about:

   - *Troopergate*
   - to Paris to tell all to *Le Monde*
   - people who have previously known our *Komrad Klinton*
   - guided missile ship which was in *area W-105*

3. How soon after the TWA crash was a conspiracy message posted on the Internet?

DISCUSSION

1. What storytelling techniques did Vankin and Whalen use to make their account interesting?
2. Proving a negative (the idea that the plane was not shot down by a missile) is very hard to do. Is that what Vankin and Whalen are trying to prove, or is it something else? If so, what?
3. What does the story from the *Jerusalem Post* illustrate?

LIVING LANGUAGE 7.4

The Internet Becomes Mass Media

As these stories show, the mass media is no more immune from the effects of the Internet than is the rest of society. More information about how computers are influencing language practices appears in Chapter 8, "Technology and Language Change."

- In July of 1997 when the Pathfinder landed on Mars, 45 million visits were made to the 21 identical Web sites run by the Jet Propulsion Laboratory where NASA's Mission Operations Room was housed. The night of the landing, the number of visitors increased ten-fold and stayed strong all week, making it the most popular event ever covered on the Web. Amy Harmon, writing for the *New York Times* (July 14, 1997), compared this pivotal moment to the 1861 attack on Fort Sumter, which heightened the importance of newspapers, the 1941 Japanese attack on Pearl Harbor, which did the same for radio, and the 1963 assasination of President Kennedy, which showed how a whole country could be united through television.

- The editors of *Publishers Weekly* received a happy surprise when they conducted an extensive three-month long survey to measure the reading habits of middle-class Americans. They contacted people by telephone, in interviews as they left bookstores, and over the Internet. "The mean number of books purchased by indivduals each year was twelve, but the people contacted over the Internet purchased three times as many." Chief editor Nora Rawlinson said, "There's always been a concern that people who used computers a lot would read less, but now it's obvious they make up for computer time by eliminating some other leisure activity, maybe like watching less television." (*Fort Worth Star-Telegram*, June 15, 1997)

4. Why wasn't it censorship when other news agencies did not report what Marcia Kramer reported about investigators "examining whether a missile from 'a U.S. military plane' might have torn through the plane"?
5. When Pierre Salinger announced his "document," he said it came from someone who "was tied to the U.S. Secret Service and has important contacts in the U.S. Navy." How does this description of Russell compare with the earlier one?
6. Can you give examples of other rumors that you have seen on the Internet? From reading this article, do you have any ideas of what to look for as you try to decide whether something is factual versus a rumor? Explain some of the clues that Vankin and Whalen looked for.
7. Rumors about celebrity clothing designers making racist remarks have circulated for years like urban legends, but today they move much

---

- Author John Updike stuck "his head into the mouth of the electronic lion" when he went on-line in partnership with a bookseller who was sponsoring a $143,000 contest for wannabe authors. Updike started a story for contestants to complete. Each day a winner of $1,000 would have his or her paragraph(s) posted. At the end of 43 days, Updike was to write a conclusion and a $100,000 prize was to be awarded in a drawing from contestants and Web site visitors. (*Arizona Republic*, July 30, 1997)
- "Reporters now regularly troll the Internet for stories in the same way they used to prowl the corridors of City Hall," wrote David S. Jackson in an article about readers talking back to newspapers and magazines. The information highway has become a two-way street, and reporters find that, no matter what they write on controversial issues, they will be flooded with angry e-mail. (*Time* magazine, Spring 1995)
- From Belgrade, Yugoslavia, the news of the political revolt continued to pour out after, "President Slobodan Milosevic, faced with large anti-government demonstrations, tried to shut down the last vestiges of an independent news media." When he put the independent radio station, B-92, off the air, it began digital broadcasts in Serbo-Croatian and English over audio Internet links. "It was the home page put out by B-92 that saved the revolution now under way in Serbia," said Sasa Vucinic, managing director of the Media Development Loan Fund, a nonprofit group that supports independent news and information outlets in Eastern Europe. (*New York Times*, Dec. 8, 1996)

faster because someone puts them on the Internet. Tommy Hilfiger is a recent victim, but Liz Claiborne has also been targeted. Hilfiger is supposed to have said on *Oprah* that his clothes look better on white people. In spite of his and Winfrey's denials, the rumor keeps spreading. Patricia Turner, a professor of African-American Studies and author of *I Heard It Through the Grapevine: Rumor in African American Culture* (University of California Press, 1993), offers the explanation that such rumors are a kind of backlash against "elaborate, sophisticated campaigns to get us to spend money on clothing." Some people feel comfortable in looking at a price tag and saying, "No way am I spending this amount of money," but for others who are sorely tempted, a statement like, "You know what he said on *Oprah*," makes it easier to leave the clothes on the rack (*Los Angeles Times*, April 2, 1997). Does this explanation make sense to you? Can you think of equally credible reasons underlying people's willingness to believe and pass on rumors? If so, what are they?

SUGGESTED TOPICS FOR WRITING

1. The subject of ghost writing or "as told to" books brings up two of the trickiest issues that writers face whether they are in a college writing class or on a serious writing assignment where the work is too difficult and time consuming for one person to handle. The two problem areas are plagiarism and the sharing of credit. You might choose either one of these topics to write about. As you explore the issues involved, you will be preparing yourself for decisions you will probably have to make.

   Plagiarism: It has always been a challenge to do research and to incorporate other people's ideas into your work without using their words or plagiarizing their ideas. Today there are factors that make it even harder. Investigate some of these factors and write a paper showing the complications. For example, when you hear something on the radio or on television, you probably don't jot down the time, the program, and the speaker because it doesn't occur to you until later that here is an idea that fits with a topic you are developing. Also, when you find information in a book or a magazine, it is easier to cite sources and give appropriate credit than when you take something off the Internet. And when some of the most admired people in the world are clearly taking credit for writing done by "ghosts," "book doctors," "editors," or "speechwriters," why should you be so different? And when numerous sites on the Internet offer term papers all ready for downloading, are you just being old-fashioned and foolish not to take advantage? Find out if your department or your teacher has a statement defining plagiarism. If so, examine it and see whether you agree with it and whether you think its guidelines are reasonable. Are they ones that you can follow? If your department does not have such a statement, perhaps you can outline the points that might go in such a policy statement.

Sharing credit: A troublesome problem for people who are working together is how the decision making and the credit should be shared. Even people with long experience in co-authoring articles or books have trouble in deciding such matters as whose name goes first and whether particular individuals should be listed as co-authors or acknowledged in some other way. Some people advise deciding such matters "up front," so that, as people work, they will know how much credit they will get. Others advise that it is better to wait until the work is done and then decide on the basis of who has done the most work. In most cases, the person whose name goes first is considered to be the primary author (sort of like having first chair in an orchestra), but in some fields the person whose name is last is considered the primary author. Some people say alphabetical order is appropriate, but those are nearly always people whose names come early in the alphabet. Some co-authors take turns, while others say the person who had the idea should have his or her name first. The only rule that is universally appropriate is that of giving honest credit for honest work. Write a paper explaining what this means. You might think that it doesn't matter for a small class project, but if you haven't thought about the matter ahead of time, you may find yourself left out and resentful on a later project where it does matter.

2. Choose an important news event that is in the process of unfolding. Read about it in print format; for example, in a daily newspaper or in a news magazine that advertises a web page. Find that source's web page and read about the same event. Write a comparison showing what you got from the printed version and what you got from the "soft" version. So as not to be overwhelmed with information, you should probably limit yourself to one particular day. Think of your audience as someone who hasn't used the Internet and is deciding whether it is worth the expense and the trouble of going online. Explain the advantages and the disadvantages of each format.

3. A similar assignment could be to find two accounts of the same event in different print sources and then compare them; for example:

   ■ Different newspapers such as a local weekly paper and a big city national paper or a tabloid
   ■ An editorial compared to a news account

- A historical account compared to one written at the time of the incident
- A national news magazine and a hometown local paper

Answer such questions as: Which is the more dramatic and the most personal? Which has the most emotional appeal? Which does the best job of answering *who, when, where, what,* and *why?*

4. Write a review of a movie you have enjoyed or one that has diappointed you. See if you can be as efficient as Rita Braver was in telling just enough of the plot so that readers can relate to what you say about the movie. The best reviews, the ones that people enjoy and remember, usually put across a focused point. Weaker, less interesting reviews resemble what children are prone to do. When asked about a movie, they give little more than a long rambling account of the plot.

5. Do some research on a successful journalist whose career you admire. Tell the story of his or her career preparation. Restrict yourself to talking about professional matters or you might end up feeling that you need to write a whole book to get everything in.

6. Find three different versions of a common biblical story such as Adam and Eve, Noah's Ark, David and Goliath, or Daniel in the Lion's Den. You might look at a children's bible, at a big illustrated book for family reading, and at the newest "translation" or edition that is in your local library. Read the three versions and compare them. You might start by considering such basic issues as what audience each one is written for, how successful the author is in aiming toward this audience, and what techniques are used.

7. Think back to your own childhood. How did you learn the "facts of life"? What memories do you have? If you are well acquainted with some children today, compare their experience with yours. Is it different? If so, can you tell whether the differences are in any way related to the factors that Lehigh outlined?

INFORMATION SOURCES FOR WRITING

American Media and Mass Culture: Left Perspectives, edited by Donald Lazere. Berkeley: Univ. of California Press, 1987.

Amusing Ourselves to Death: Public Discourse in the Age of Show Business, by Neil Postman. New York: Viking, 1985. Postman has also published a book *The Disappearance of Childhood* (New York: Delacorte, 1982) about the effects of mass media on children. A related video recording is available from Instructional Media Center of the National College of Education.

Blackface: Reflections on African Americans and the Movies, by Nelson George. New York: HarperCollins, 1994.

Breaking the News: How the Media Undermine American Democracy, by James Fallows. New York: Random, 1996.

Chronicle of the Cinema, by Robyn Karney. New York: Dorling Kindersley, 1995.

Communication as Culture: Essays on Media and Society, by James W. Carey. New York: Routledge, 1992.

Dictionary of Catchphrases, by Nigel Rees. Cassell/Sterling, 1995.

The Global Village: Transformations in World Life and Media in the 21st Century, by Marshall McLuhan and Bruce R. Powers. New York: Oxford Univ. Press, 1989.

Media Circus: The Trouble with America's Newspapers, by Howard Kurtz. New York: Times Books, 1993.

The Plug-In Drug, by Marie Winn Miller. New York: Viking Penguin, 1985.

Prime Time: How TV Portrays American Culture, by S. Robert Lichter and Linda Lichter. Washington, D.C.: Stanley Rothman, 1994.

A Reporter's Life, by Walter Cronkite. New York: Knopf, 1996.

Same Time . . . Same Station: An A to Z Guide to Radio from Jack Benny to Howard Stern, by Ron Lackman. New York: Facts on File, 1996.

Thou Improper, Thou Uncommon Noun: An Etymology of Words that Once Were Names, by Willard R. Espy. New York: Clarkson S. Potter, 1978.

Tube of Plenty: The Evolution of American Television, by Erik Barnouw. New York: Oxford Univ. Press, 1975.

AMERICANS 'SCIENTIFICALLY ILLITERATE,' LAWMAKER SAYS

it may well

ASU struggles with 'private' e-mails

BY Tony Toberier
STATE PRESS

cyberspace

Metric system inches way in

BY Arnold Lane
STATE

Altho
it was
an insi
still far
the year
in ques
for all
there m

Web site created to fight cyberhate

BY Reginald A. Groster

Man charged with his daughter's murder after Internet confession

BY Troy McLure
(AP)-LONDON —After an exhaustive effort by London's finest, it was an

Student satellite in final stages

BY Jay Uttal, Washington Tribune

TECHNOLOGY AND LANGUAGE CHANGE

While speaking to a group of college English teachers meeting in St. Louis, Jon Franklin, formerly a science writer for the *Evening Sun* in Baltimore and now a teacher of journalism at the University of Maryland, noted that in recent years more than half the books that won the Pulitzer Prize in nonfiction have been science books. He went on to explain how the increasingly important role of scientific writing in newspapers and magazines is changing basic concepts of journalism. The upside-down pyramid, in which the key points are stated first and the details filled in later (so an editor can cut the story whenever the available space is filled) does not work for science writing. This is because, with today's advanced technology, most scientific developments and concepts are too complex for readers to understand unless they get the supporting details first.

Franklin worries about a new kind of elitism based on scientific literacy. He believes that when readers do not understand something they are likely to dismiss it as unimportant or to resent or reject all scientific concepts. Judith Stone, who wrote the first article in this chapter, points to the temptation we all feel to ridicule things that frighten us or make us feel stupid. John Allen Paulos, author of the second article, worries more about gullible readers and listeners who don't have the skill and confidence to ask common sense questions in relation to the many numbers they are confronted with daily. Other articles in this chapter explore computers and the tremendous changes they are bringing to communication strategies.

If U Cn Rd Ths, U Undrstnd Scnce

Judith Stone

Judith Stone is the author of *Light Elements: Essays in Science from Gravity to Levity* (Ballantine, 1991) from which this essay is taken. In the introduction, she confesses, "I used to be the kind of person who didn't recall—or care—whether it's on*tology* or on*togeny* that recapitulates Phil Donahue. I thought that gluons were false eyelashes and that Brownian motion was discovered by Betty Crocker (if I bothered to think at all about the random travels of microscopic particles suspended in a liquid or a gas). . . . In other words, along with 95 percent of the American public, I was a scientific illiterate." Partly because she was offered money and partly because she "felt uncomfortable living among natural and technological phenomena" that she didn't understand, she embarked on the explorations that became *Light Elements*. After writing the book, she confided that "there are two ways to approach a subject that frightens you and makes you feel stupid: you can embrace it with humility and an open mind, or you can ridicule it mercilessly. I'm still deciding which I prefer."

1   You say you don't know a proton from a crouton and you can't tell gravity from levity? You're not alone. A recent nationwide survey funded by the National Science Foundation shows that fewer than 6 percent of American adults can be called scientifically literate. The rest think DNA is a food additive, Chernobyl is a ski resort, and radioactive milk can be made safe by boiling.

2   "Only one in twenty adults knows enough about science to function effectively as a citizen and consumer when asked to help formulate public policy about issues like nuclear power or toxic waste," says Jon Miller, director of the Public Opinion Laboratory of Northern Illinois University, who conducted the study.

3   Certainly I have no right to be smug; I have, after all, been known to whine that if God wanted us to use the metric system, He would have given us ten fingers and ten toes. But, honestly, do you want these people voting on where to stash the leftover plutonium? More to the point, would you like to ride a chair lift or hoist a frosty, glow-in-the-dark malted with them? Well, they're us.

4   Miller's subjects, just plain folks, answered three sets of questions. The first measured their knowledge of the process of science. "What does it mean to study something scientifically?" people were asked; their responses had to include some mention of testing hypotheses, formulating theories, and using

experiments or systematic comparative study. Those who answered correctly were then asked whether astrology was scientific. Only about 12 percent got both parts of the section right. (The rest must have been Geminis; they always have trouble with two-part questions.)

5   Twenty-eight percent passed the second part, which tested knowledge of scientific terms and concepts, mostly through true-false questions such as "The earliest human beings lived at the same time as the dinosaurs" (37 percent correctly answered false) and "Electrons are smaller than atoms" (43 percent correctly answered true). Also included were multiple-choice questions, like whether the earth travels around the sun or vice versa. Those who knew that the former is true were asked whether this event takes one day, one month or one year. Forty-five percent got it right; the rest had really enjoyed Mel Gibson in *The Day of Living Dangerously.*

6   Half the respondents aced the part that gauged their understanding of how science and technology affect their lives. That's where the radioactive milk came in; 36 percent weren't worried about its half-and-half life.

7   Age wasn't a factor in determining who was scientifically illiterate, although sex was; men scored somewhat higher than women did. Miller attributes the difference to the way science has traditionally been presented in schools—as a stereotypically male realm that girls are subtly discouraged from entering. The best predictor of a high score was having taken a college science course.

8   At least we're not getting dumber; Miller conducted similar studies in 1979 and 1985 and finds little difference in scores then and now. And a nearly identical survey of 2,000 Britons, conducted in 1988 by Oxford University, revealed that they know as little as we do. A slightly higher percentage of Brits grasp the impact of science on society, but twice the number of Americans—about half—know what software is. More important, we know that Benny Hill just isn't funny.

9   (We may soon have a chance to see how we measure up to the Japanese; Miller is trying to arrange a study there. You'll be relieved to know he thinks the Japanese scientific literacy rate will turn out to be "not much more than twice ours.")

10   Miller's figures are fascinating, but I wanted to learn more about what people thought they knew. So for a few months, wherever I traveled, I asked people questions about science—some from Miller's study and others inspired by recent news stories. I talked to people on airplanes, at restaurants, on the beach, and on the street—basically anyone who didn't pull a knife when I said, "Hi, what's the ozone layer?" My study of nearly 150 unarmed Americans, ranging in age from three-and-a-half to sixty-seven, was rather informal but highly revealing. I was heartened to see how many respondents (just under oodles) could define the scientific method but demoralized to discover how few seem to apply it to their lives. All answers are totally serious, except those followed by the words "Just kidding."

11   First came my tricky reworking of one of Miller's questions: "How," I asked, "did the earliest human beings fight off dinosaurs?" You and I know that the last of these creatures vacated the planet more than fifty million years before *Fredus flinstoniensis* moved in. But only about half the folks I polled had gotten the news. A twenty-eight-year-old actress/waitress at a Manhattan restaurant insisted that coexistence wasn't a problem since dinosaurs were vegetarians. According to an eighteen-year-old advertising major at San Francisco State University, "Early human beings would hide in caves, set up traps, or play dead when dinosaurs came upon them." (If a dinosaur came upon me, I'd probably play dead, too. Talk about your sticky situations.)

12   Thank heavens for Andrew, a three-and-a-half-year-old San Francisco nursery school student majoring in fire engines, who declared, rather condescendingly, "There *weren't* any people. I saw a show." His father explained that they'd recently seen a play about dinosaurs at the University of California's Lawrence Hall of Science in Berkeley. Parents take note; otherwise your kid could end up like Buddy, an Alabama man visiting Pensacola, Florida, the southern tip of what the locals refer to as the Redneck Riviera. "First," Buddy said, "early man called the dinosaurs names—'you ugly bastards!' Then he ate their eggs." He took a pull at his Bud Light and inhaled a handful of Zapp's Crawtater Chips. "Just kidding."

13   More people correctly defined the ozone layer than any other scientific term; a librarian at the University of Virginia and a retired auto mechanic in Portland, Oregon, even knew that it's oxygen with an extra O. But a twelve-year-old member of a Kilgore, Texas, church group identified it cryptically as "the middle layer." I believe she confused *ozone* and *Oreo*, a slip even Nobel laureates sometimes make.

14   When asked to identify Isaac Newton, nearly all adults surveyed mentioned gravity (without going into further detail), and they correctly linked Charles Darwin with the theory of evolution. But a St. Louis man told me, sans elaboration, that Darwin was "known for his use of force," and a twelve-year-old Kilgore boy stated confidently that the two men were actors—scientific method actors, no doubt. I know I especially enjoyed Chuck "the Enforcer" Darwin in *The Originator.*

15   Recognizing Chernobyl would be a lead-pipe cinch, I thought, but I included the item anyway since in a recent Gallup poll a fair number of high school students thought it was Cher's real name. More kids drew a blank on this one than I expected. And a thirty-nine-year-old accountant returning to San Francisco State as a freshman really did think it was a ski resort. My favorite answer, from his megamellow nineteen-year-old classmate: "A Russian nuclear power plant that totally blew up, dude."

16   DNA, you'll be interested to learn, is a sickness (a nine-year-old girl from Little Rock said that), the smallest known molecule (according to a twenty-six-year-old woman from Philadelphia), a food additive (another

Philadelphian recently overheard in a Chinese restaurant saying, "I'll have the Hunan beef, but go easy on the DNA"), and an airport. (This puzzling answer from a Kilgore third grader, was explained by an older friend. "I think she's thinking of DFW—Dallas–Fort Worth.") Among the cognoscenti, the term *genetic blueprint* won the prize for Most-Bandied-About. An architect from Baton Rouge made a fashion statement: "It's the double helix that holds all our genes together."

17   Oddly, this question yielded the only vaguely hostile answer, from the head of a New York public relations firm who hollered in a French restaurant, waving his *boudin* for emphasis, "I don't know what DNA is and I don't want to know!" Most people were either apologetic or oddly proud of their ignorance, but always good-natured.

18   The hardest question on the survey, one I myself couldn't answer extempore even if you threatened to make me watch an endless loop of "Hello, Larry" reruns, was "Explain how television works." You can guess how many wags from coast to coast felt compelled to say, "You push the button"; I got quiplash. The typical response was in the ballpark, but not quite complete, like this one from a thirty-year-old woman who is art director of a Baton Rouge business publication: "Radio waves are sent through the air and electronically reorganized in your television." A Texas eight-year-old said simply, "Microchips," which was more than one child's answer to more than one question. "It's done with mirrors and broadcasting," said a San Francisco man. And on the Redneck Riviera, one answer sparked a lively debate. "Radio waves are sent and received," said good old Buddy. "But if they're *radio*," asked a companion, "how do they know when to turn into a picture?" "How," said Buddy sagely, "does a thermos know when to keep something hot and when to keep it cold?"

19   I especially enjoyed the responses of Gail Sipes's third-grade class at the A. B. McDonald Elementary School in Moscow, Idaho, a generally canny crew that included one young *civis indignatus* who, when asked which is heavier, a pound of bricks or a pound of feathers, wrote, "Bricks!! Of Course!!!!" The kids also revealed that software is either "plastic knives and forks" or "clothes that keep us warm," and that the ozone layer "separates bad air from good air."

20   How alarmed should we be at these answers? Does an inability to explain DNA make you an awful person? Is it more important to recognize the name Chernobyl or to have the psychological savvy to judge the guy with his finger on the nuclear button? Just what, in this large loaf of data-nut bread that is the modern world, do we need to know?

21   Miller worries that citizens who think the answer to the question "How long does it take the earth to revolve around the sun?" is "A long time" will have trouble making public policy decisions involving science. (Political leaders could do better, too, he believes. "I think members of congressional committees who deal with science would do quite well on my test. But our last

president would have failed the first question on my survey; he didn't know that astrology isn't a science. That alone qualifies him as scientifically illiterate and should have disqualified him from being president.")

22   Look, we can't all be Einstein (because we don't all play the violin). At the very least, we need a sort of street-smart science: the ability to recognize evidence, gather it, assess it, and act on it. As voters, we're de facto scientific advisors. In the next few years we're going to be making, directly or indirectly, vital decisions about the greenhouse effect, acid rain, the pesticides that taint our foods, genetically engineered organisms, how much to spend on mending our torn ozone layer. (Or Oreo layer.) If we don't get it right, things could go very wrong. The oceans will rise, the trees shrivel, the snow turn to steam; nothing will taste good. If we don't get it right, they'll be shedding their thermal software in Antarctica.

LIVING LANGUAGE 8.1

Communication and Technology

There is hardly an area of our lives, including communication, that is not affected by modern science and technology, as indicated in this sample of news summaries.

- "Junk science often wins, and genuine science often loses when juries decide," wrote C. W. Griffin in a guest editorial advocating that America follow Britain's lead in banning jury trials in technically complex civil cases. Griffin, who sometimes serves as an expert witness in construction litigation, advocates arbitration panels for trials where technology is an issue. He cited, as an example of "spectacular stupidity," a recent case where a jury awarded a Philadelphia psychic $1 million because she claimed that a hospital CAT scan destroyed her ability to predict the future. He also said that Judge Lance Ito's disqualifying of "regular newspaper readers" from the O. J. Simpson criminal jury displayed a "judicial obsession with bias at the expense of intelligence." (*Arizona Republic*, Dec. 15, 1996)

- The scientific phrase *Occam's razor* got a new lease on life when it played a prominent part in the 1997 movie *Contact*, directed by Robert Zemeckis. William of Occam (c. 1280–1349) was an English philosopher and Franciscan, who was such a careful thinker and debater that he was said to dissect every question with a razor. Newspaper columnist Steve Wilson headlined a piece, "Logically, Occam's razor cuts through the garbage." He explained that the concept "also called the law of parsimony, says that the simplest theory fitting the facts is usually the right one." (*Arizona Republic*, July 25, 1997)

- "Cursive writing is limping along in computer age" headlined the *Chicago Tribune*. "Is the end at hand? Hurry-up world cramps art of penmanship," headlined

COMPREHENSION

1. Words to talk about:

   - you don't know a *proton* from a *crouton*
   - where to stash the leftover *plutonium*
   - among the *cognoscenti*
   - the double *helix* that holds
   - we're *de facto* scientific advisors

2. Why did kids draw a blank on identifying Chernobyl?
3. What does Stone define as the minimum for "street-smart" science?

---

the *Northwest Florida Daily News,* and "Penmanship slipping through fingers" headlined the *Arizona Republic.* All three articles were about the way schools are simplifying or skipping instruction in penmanship. Some schools take children directly from manuscript print into computer keyboarding. (*New York Times,* Dec. 12, 1996)

- One of the newest pop music stars in Japan is DK-96, a computer-generated fabrication. Her initials stand for both Digital Kid and Date Kyoko. As might be expected she makes most of her appearances on-line, with a few MTV-like videos being shown on TV talk shows. No one seems to mind that her voice is that of a real singer with the group Summer of Love. DK-96 has a combined Western/Eastern look, and is shown dancing and walking through New York almost as often as through Tokyo. (*Arizona Republic,* Dec. 7, 1996)
- As a sidebar to a science piece about black holes, the *Arizona Republic* (Dec. 16, 1996) pointed out that English is deficient in not having words to describe numbers the size that astronomers use. Our numbering system is very precise, and there's no end to what can be represented with mathematical symbols. But once we get past a trillion (a 1 followed by twelve zeros: 1,000,000,000,000), we're short on words. Our vocabulary makes a big jump going to a *googol* (a one followed by a hundred zeros), which is the estimated number of years before the universe goes dark. It's probably because he didn't want to talk about a "googol" that Carl Sagan kept repeating "billions and billions."

DISCUSSION

1. Jon Franklin, the science writer mentioned in the chapter introduction, has made a two-pronged proposal for alleviating the high level of scientific illiteracy in the United States. First, he said that science writers must work harder to make their material interesting and understandable to keep readers engaged past the headline and the first couple of paragraphs. Second, readers must develop more skill and patience as they read science materials. Describe and illustrate with specific examples at least three techniques that Stone used to keep readers' interest.

2. As to Franklin's second point about readers developing skill and confidence so that they can comprehend and evaluate science writing, what did you learn from Stone's essay that will help you the next time you read a piece about science or technology?

3. Why did Stone write her title leaving out most of the vowels? What other amusing techniques did she use to make her piece sound "high-tech"?

4. List four or five amusing allusions that Stone made. Did you enjoy her humor or did you find it distracting?

5. Although Stone doesn't follow an obvious comparison and contrast organization, her essay is nevertheless based on comparison and contrast. She is showing the difference between what people know and what she thinks they ought to know if they are going to participate as voters in a society increasingly dependent on technology. Find at least three examples of facts she thought people should know but don't. What techniques, what guide words, did she use to clarify for her readers the differences between what people should know and what they do know?

More Dismal Math Scores for U.S. Students: X, Y, and U

John Allen Paulos

John Allen Paulos, a professor of mathematics at Temple University, has written several popular books about mathematical literacy, or more accurately, illiteracy. In the book from which this essay is taken, *A Mathematician Reads the Newspaper* (Doubleday, 1995), Paulos gives ten well-developed reasons that Americans love lists of ten. He refers to those endless surveys we read as "Societal Gas Laws," and also illustrates how fond we are of the "meaningless precision" that made a museum guide tell visitors that a dinosaur was 90,006 years old. When questioned as to how the age was figured, the guide explained that when he started working six years earlier, he was told that the dinosaur was 90,000 years old. In this essay, Paulos talks more generally about the importance of being able to "read" mathematically. He is also the author of *Innumeracy* (Random House, 1990).

1   Such headlines [More Dismal Math Scores for U.S. Students] remind me of the children's riddle about Pete and Repeat.

> *First Child:* Pete and Repeat are walking down the street. Pete falls down. Who is left?
>
> *Second Child:* Repeat.
>
> *First Child:* Pete and Repeat are walking down the street. Pete falls down. Who is left?
>
> *Second Child:* Repeat.
>
> *First Child:* Pete and Repeat are walking . . .

2   Looked at in the right way, it might almost be humorous. Some eminent commission issues a warning that the mathematics (or science) performance of American students is dismal. Then the stylized expressions of alarm are voiced, after which the subject is quickly forgotten until the next, even more dismaying, report is announced. Pete and Repeat.

3   Why should we really care? As a mathematician, I'm often challenged to come up with compelling reasons to study mathematics. If the questioner is serious, I reply that there are three reasons or, more accurately, three broad

classes of reasons to study mathematics. Only the first and most basic class is practical. It pertains to job skills and the needs of science and technology. The second concerns the understandings that are essential to an informed and effective citizenry. The last class of reasons involves considerations of curiosity, beauty, playfulness, perhaps even transcendence and wisdom.

4   And what are the costs incurred if we as a society continue in our perversely innumerate ways?

5   The economic cost of mathematical ignorance is gauged, in part, by people who, though they can perform the basic arithmetical operations, don't know when to do one and when to do another: clerks who are perplexed by discounts and sales taxes, medical personnel who have difficulty reckoning correct dosages, quality control managers who don't understand simple statistical concepts. The supply of mathematically capable individuals is also a factor in the U.S.'s position in many new scientific technologies, among them fuel-efficient engines, precision bearings, optical glasses, industrial instrumentation, laser devices, and electronic consumer products.

6   As Labor Secretary Robert Reich and others have written, those jobs and job classifications requiring higher mathematics, language, and reasoning abilities are growing much more rapidly than those that do not. (It should be admitted, however, that although their rate of growth is higher, the number of such jobs still doesn't compare with the huge number that require lesser skills.) Nevertheless, enrollment in college-level mathematics is down, and fewer and fewer American students are majoring in math or in the growing number of fields that require it.

7   The social cost of our mathematical naïveté is harder to measure (although I try to in this book), but gullible citizens are a demagogue's dream. Charlatans yearn for people who can't recognize trade-offs between contrary desiderata; who lack a visceral grasp of the difference between millions of dollars for the National Endowment for the Arts and hundreds of billions of dollars for the savings-and-loan bailout; or who insist on paralyzing regulation of rare and minuscule health risks, whose cumulative expense helps to ensure the incomparably greater health hazard of poverty. As this book shows, almost every political issue—health care, welfare reform, NAFTA, crime—has a quantitative aspect. And, as I mentioned earlier and as the FDA is just now recognizing, the worst drug problem in this country is not crack or cocaine but cigarette smoking, which kills 400,000 Americans annually, the equivalent of three fully loaded jumbo jets crashing each and every day of the year. Or consider Lani Guinier's mathematical suggestions regarding the Voting Rights Act, or the possible economic and ecological implications of chaos theory, or the statistical snares inherent in the interpreting of test results, whether they be for academic achievement or the presence of drugs.

8   Regarding the third class of reasons, I think it's only fair to say that the "cost" of the philosophical impoverishment resulting from mathematical il-

literacy is one that millions of Americans gleefully assume. Still, there is evidence that people respond enthusiastically to mathematical topics as long as they are not labeled as such. People enjoy complicated numerical and mechanical puzzles (Rubik's Cube, for example, the number of whose possible states—4×10^{19}—is greater than the distance in inches that light travels in a century); crossword puzzles and word play (including certain kinds of humor); board games; all sorts of gambling; paradoxes and brain teasers. Part of the enjoyment is traceable to their quasi-mathematical charm. We have an innate attraction to pattern, structure, and symmetry that mathematics and science develop and refine. Certainly Bertrand Russell is not alone in prizing the subject's "cold and austere beauty," and many are excited by Andrew Wiles's likely proof of Fermat's last theorem, even if it is of little earthly use.

9   With these reasons to study mathematics, why don't American students do better? Enough's been written about our many social problems, so rather than plunging into that dreary story let me end this segment with five misconceptions about mathematics. Cumulatively, they contribute significantly to poor pedagogy in school and needless handicaps on the job.

10   Probably the most harmful misconception is that mathematics is essentially a matter of computation. Believing this is roughly equivalent to believing that writing essays is the same as typing them. Or, to vary the analogy, imagine the interest in literature that would be engendered if every English class focused exclusively on punctuation. Of course, this is not to say that calculating mentally or with paper and pencil is not important. Nor is it meant to discourage the excellent habit of estimating quantities. It is merely to assert that in mathematics, as in other endeavors, the big picture is seldom presented.*

11   Another misconception about the subject is that it is strictly hierarchical; first comes arithmetic, followed in lockstep by algebra, geometry, calculus, and differential equations, after which arrive abstract algebra, complex analysis, and so on. There is undeniably a cumulative aspect to mathematics, but it is less significant than many think. A third misconception concerns what, for lack of a better term, I'll call storytelling. An effective educational strategy since ancient times, storytelling places a question into context, demonstrates

---

*Although details are very often critically important, an inability to stand back and "chunk" facts leads to a myopic favoring of minutiae over ideas in many contexts. As I've mentioned, computation is valued above conceptual understanding in mathematics; in politics, smart tactics bring greater rewards than wise policies; technical hocus-pocus in the stock market attracts more attention than does analysis of fundamentals; for those with a religious temperament, rules, rites, and rituals obscure wonder, awe, and mystery; in sex, lust and fetishism are mistaken for love. I grant that the first element in each of these oppositions does sometimes rightfully take precedence over the second, but generally too little stress is placed on the second. It's much easier to put the jigsaw puzzle together after you've seen the whole picture (assuming there's one to see).

its relation to other questions, and concisely lays out some seminal idea. The rigid view that draws a sharp distinction between formal math and narrative may explain why this plain means is too seldom employed in mathematics education and why the topic of this book will seem strange to many people.

12   Parental expectations can be effective in thwarting the effects of the next misconception, which is frequently signaled by comments such as "I'm a people person, not a numbers person" or "Math was always my worst subject." Although it is undoubtedly true that some people have considerably more mathematical talent than others, mathematics is not only for the few. There are also disparities in writing ability, but people rarely counsel students to give up on their English courses because they're not going to make it as novelists.

13   The last misconception is the romantic belief that a concern with mathematics is somehow numbing, making one unresponsive to, say, stone farmhouses in the late afternoon sun. Asking How Much, How Many, or How Likely is thought to make one a member of Napoleon's despised "nation of shopkeepers." Sentiments such as these are as potent as they are baseless.

14   I'll forgo discussing the curricular and pedagogical suggestion that follow from this discussion, except to note that the newspaper is an undervalued source of examples and ideas for mathematics classes at various levels. Once an idea or notion is grounded in some real-life situation, it can later be generalized, idealized, and aestheticized.

15   Pete and Repeat . . . Let's not.

COMPREHENSION

1. Words to talk about:

   - trade-offs between contrary *desiderata*
   - lack a *visceral* grasp
   - traceable to their *quasi-mathematical* charm
   - *Andrew Wiles's* likely proof of *Fermat's* last theorem
   - *myopic* favoring of *minutiae* over ideas
   - a member of Napoleon's despised *"nation of shopkeepers"*

2. Explain the reference to Lani Guinier.
3. Paulos was careful in this essay to keep informing his readers where he was going. Make an outline showing the points he talked about. Why did he put the part about "chunking" facts in a footnote?
4. What did Paulos say he wasn't going to talk about? By mentioning the topics, did he remind you of arguments you have already heard? If so, what are they?

Discussion

1. What are the three "broad classes of reasons" that Paulos gives for studying mathematics?
2. Paulos says only the first reason is practical? Would Judith Stone say the first and second reasons are practical? If you agree, explain why.
3. Talk about Paulos's statement that "almost every political issue—health care, welfare reform, NAFTA, crime—has a quantitative aspect." Give some examples that illustrate his point.
4. When something is measured and numbered do you feel more confidence in its authenticity? How many of us really understand all those numbers we study on the labels of food packages? A point that Paulos makes in another of the essays is that recipes calling for "a handful of this," "a pinch of that," and "seasoning to taste," conclude with a kind of "meaningless precision" by saying something like "recipe yields four servings, each with 373 calories, 224 mgs. sodium, and 11.6 grams of fat." Why does Paulos say this is "meaningless precision"? Can you think of similar examples? Do you feel better about getting a grade when there is a point scale even if the teacher arbitrarily decides on how many points to award?
5. When they were conducting sensitive hearing tests, workers and clients in the Speech and Hearing laboratory at Arizona State University were often interrupted by noise coming from students in the hallways. Signs were put up restricting the hallway to clinic workers and patrons, but still students kept taking shortcuts and making noise in the hallway. They stopped only when the glass was frosted and the sign in the photo on page 392 was put up. What is there about the new sign that makes it look more forbidding or authoritative?
6. A generation ago, it was believed that humans couldn't remember numbers longer than five digits. This is why telephones have both alphabetical letters and numbers on them. Telephone numbers were given with a word and a five-digit number; for example, Alpine 3–6011. Has the human brain gotten more skilled at remembering numbers or have expectations changed? What numbers do you need to remember on a daily basis? Do you think one of the reasons that most of us don't envision the quantities of whatever is being discussed is that we use numbers as identification codes almost more often than as measures of quantity?
7. Give some examples of the kinds of measurements that most of us can't process but that Paulos says are important to the future of our country.
8. As you read the incidents in Living Language 8.2 and look at the photos, talk about whether the numbers are used primarily for measuring

or for identification purposes. Which of the usages are meant to suggest a high-tech connection? Do they succeed? What do the numbers mean in the names of the Philadelphia 76ers and the San Francisco 49ers? Why are Heinz 57 Varieties and V8 Juice effective trademarks? Can you think of show business names that include numbers? What numbers have a kind of magic in addresses or in the names of streets or roads? Why do we like to rank things from 1 to 10 or create top-ten lists? If you work with computers, try making a list of company names that use numbers; for example, Gateway 2000, which named its Web site GW2K, and the Intel Company with its Pentium (Greek for "five") computer chip.

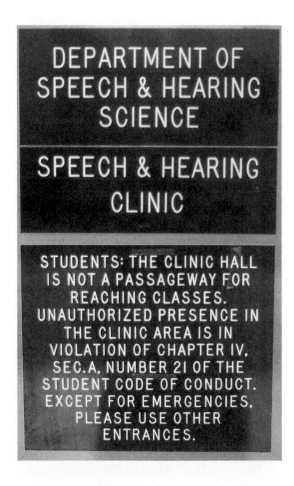

DEPARTMENT OF
SPEECH & HEARING
SCIENCE

SPEECH & HEARING
CLINIC

STUDENTS: THE CLINIC HALL
IS NOT A PASSAGEWAY FOR
REACHING CLASSES.
UNAUTHORIZED PRESENCE IN
THE CLINIC AREA IS IN
VIOLATION OF CHAPTER IV,
SEC.A, NUMBER 21 OF THE
STUDENT CODE OF CONDUCT.
EXCEPT FOR EMERGENCIES,
PLEASE USE OTHER
ENTRANCES.

THE RECYCLING OF WORDS IN CYBERSPACE

Alleen Pace Nilsen

Estimates for new computer-related words or usages run as high as 25,000 in English alone. Both on-line and in-print dictionaries document these thousands of new terms and meanings, but few have been coined as new sound combinations. Instead, most are adaptations in which new meanings are given to words and ideas already known to speakers. This article explores one of the semantic areas from which such terms have come. It is based on an earlier article "Literary Metaphors and Other Linguistic Innovations in Computer Language" written with Kelvin Nilsen and published in *English Journal* (October 1995).

1   "Forget antiwar protests, Woodstock, even long hair. The real legacy of the sixties generation is the computer revolution," wrote Stewart Brand under the title "We Owe it All to the Hippies," which was published in a *Time* magazine special issue: Welcome to Cyberspace (spring 1995). Brand, speaking as part of the Woodstock generation (he edited the popular *Whole Earth Catalog*), laughs about how his generation perverted JFK's inaugural exhortation into "Ask not what your country can do for you. Do it yourself." He added,

> Our ethic of self-reliance came partly from science fiction. We all read Robert Heinlein's epic *Stranger in a Strange Land* as well as his libertarian screed-novel, *The Moon Is a Harsh Mistress*. Hippies and nerds alike reveled in Heinlein's contempt for centralized authority. To this day, computer scientists and technicians are almost universally science-fiction fans. And ever since the 1950s, for reasons that are unclear to me, science fiction has been almost universally libertarian in outlook.

Brand went on to make a persuasive case for how today's nonhierarchical and democratically run Internet is a direct result of the counter-cultural beliefs of early computer hackers who changed the computing landscape by wresting power from centralized mainframe computers under the control of IBM and giving it to millions of individuals with PC's. Marshall McLuhan, adored as a "hot-gospeller of technology," not only predicted but helped shape the future with his writings about the power of media to create a global village.

LIVING LANGUAGE 8.2

Our Love/Hate Relationship with Numbers

While math phobia may be endemic to our culture, as shown in the photos here and on page 395, we are nevertheless fond of numbers, especially when they are used in combination with initials that lend an air of authority or technological sophistication (for example, the World War II B-29 bomber or the WD-40 household solvent, named because it was the fortieth formulation of a water displacement compound developed to protect Atlas missiles).

- Joseph Heller chose the inspired name of *Catch-22* for the paradox explored in his 1961 antiwar novel. Dictionaries now define Catch-22 as "a problematic situation for which the only solution is denied by a circumstance inherent in the problem." In Heller's book, the way to get out of flying bombing missions was to be insane. However, Catch-22, "specified that a concern for one's own safety in the face of dangers that were real and immediate was the process of a rational mind," proving one's sanity and hence the necessity of flying more bombing missions. Heller gave his *Catch-22* a number to make it sound official and army-like. He chose the alliterative *22*, because it seemed far enough down a list to fit with other army regulations, but not so far down as to be unimportant.
- Karl Malone, basketball player for the Utah Jazz, is called The Mailman "because he always delivers." An extra little joke when the nickname was coined is that his number 32 matched the price of a first-class stamp.
- The perfume Chanel No. 5 has a name that is both romantic and high-tech. The romantic feeling comes from the last name of Coco Chanel (1883–1971), a

continued

Living Language 8.2

Our Love/Hate Relationship with Numbers
continued

French designer and perfumer, while No. 5 subtly communicates that this is a quality product, because by the fifth formula, it must have been perfected.

- With cars, today's code numbers or letters are considerably more sophisticated than in 1909, when Henry Ford marketed his Model-T. With the Infiniti Q45, the 45 identifies the displacement of the engine while the Q identifies the size and body style. The BMW 740i is from the company's seventh series (their largest sedan) and has a 4.0 liter, fuel-injected engine. Because these vehicles are upscale and respected, they helped establish a pattern seen in such other names as the Chevy S-10 and the Mazda RX-7.

- X is a mathematical sign for the unknown. Ever since 1896 when German scientist Wilhelm Konrad von Roentgen discovered a shortwave ray whose nature he could not understand and so named it an X-ray, X has been used to suggest a high-tech connection. Because its name is usually spoken, it is often treated as a code as in the Nissan Maxima GXE and Pulsar NX and the Honda Accord LX. The name of the Ford Ranger XLT has the extra advantage of looking like an abbreviation for "excellent."

- "Get your Kicks on Route 66," is the slogan for the most famous highway name in America, which during the 1950s and 1960s took millions of Americans from Chicago to Los Angeles. Even though Interstate 40 has stolen most of the traffic from what was labeled "The Mother Road," "The Glory Road," and "America's Main Street," there is still enough nostalgia for Historic Route 66 to support a sizable tourist industry winding through Illinois, Missouri, Oklahoma, Texas, New Mexico, Arizona, and California.

2   From a language standpoint, what's interesting is how a love for science fiction along with 1960s values is reflected in computer language. In the sixties, popular music played a crucial role in the counter-culture, and rock musicians had little respect for standard language customs. When Buddy Holly chose the name Crickets for his group because they were "a happy kind of insect," John Lennon enviously wished he had thought of it because the popularity of cricket as an English game would have made a clever tie-in for a group from London. Then Lennon thought of beetles, as being similar to crickets, and of spelling the word Beatles "to make it look like beat music, just as a joke."

3   The success of that uniquely spelled name inspired the altered spelling in The Monkees and later The Byrds and The Black Crowes. Then came Led Zeppelin followed by Def Leppard. Such creative spelling seemed so natural to computer hackers that when they felt it was important to distinguish in writing between a bit and a bite, they changed the spelling of the latter to byte. The

y gave the new word distinction; it looked like computer talk and so they followed suit by spelling nibble as nybble. Next they created luser to name computer neophytes from a blending of user and loser, followed by *turist* as a term for someone who scans the network looking for interesting groups to join.

4   For rock musicians, even more unusual than their creative spelling was the way they drew together incompatible images and concepts, shown in such names as:

Blind Melon	Blue Oyster Cult
The Circle Jerks	Grateful Dead
Parliament/Funkadelic	Pearl Jam
Sly and the Family Stone	Stone Temple Pilots
The Velvet Underground	The Who

5   Judging from a list released during the 1992 scare about the Michelangelo virus, the names that today's hackers use for computer viruses look a lot like revolutionary band names. These examples come just from the first three letters of an alphabetical list.

Adolph	AIDS II	Ambulance Car
Animus	Anthrax	Armageddon
Attack	Bad Boy	Beware
Black Monday	Black Wizard	Bloody
Brazilian Bug	Casper	Catman
Code Zero	Crazy Imp	Creeper

6   One of the most natural ways to communicate about new or unnamed concepts is to create metaphors or make allusions based on common understandings. A study of the second edition of *The New Hacker's Dictionary* (edited by E. Raymond and published in 1993 by MIT Press) lends support to Brand's statement that hippies read bucketfuls of science fiction. It takes an acquaintance with science fiction and fantasy to understand a surprisingly large number of computer-related allusions.

7   Words coming from various science fiction sources include *Martian* to describe a network packet received from an unidentifiable source, *hyperspace* for errant memory access, *cyberpunk* for an imagined world in which anthropomorphized computers participate in human interactions, and *cyberspace* for a world in which humans communicate with the computer as if by mental telepathy. Writer William Gibson invented this latter term and made it famous in his 1984 novel *Neuromancer* after watching kids hunched over video games so involved that they looked as though they had entered into another realm.

8   Archaic operating systems that print only uppercase letters are called Great Runes, a usage probably influenced by the writings of J. R. R. Tolkien, who has contributed more words to hacker language than has any other author. Ever since the days of the Great Runes, computer programmers have had a unique attitude toward upper- and lower-case letters. They invented the

practice of bicapitalization in which capitalized words are joined together without spacing in between, or caps are inserted inside words as with these trademarks: CompuServe (playfully spelled Compu$erve as a criticism of its cost), dBase, FrameMaker, GEnie, NeXt, TeX, VisiCalc, and WordPerfect. The capitals save spaces as in FrameMaker and WordPerfect; plus they attract attention and guarantee uniqueness so the words can be registered as original trademarks. While the practice was initially motivated by the grammar of programming languages that dictated items that had to stay conjoined were not to have spaces between them, it is now so common that noncomputer companies are following suit: HarperCollins publishers; DreamWorks media, and Project NExT (New Experiences in Teaching). How fast the practice came into general public use is illustrated by the bicapitalized name of JonBenet Ramsey, which appeared in headlines all around the country as police officers tried to solve the 1996 Christmas murder of the six-year-old beauty queen from Boulder, Colorado.

9   Going back to J. R. R. Tolkien's contributions, because of sound similarity, Hobbit is used to refer to the "high-order bit of a byte." Elvish, the name of the fictional language that Tolkien created in *The Lord of the Rings,* was first used to refer to a particularly elegant style of printing but is now used more generally for any odd or unreadable typeface produced through graphics. An infamous 1988 bugging of the Internet was called The Great Worm, named after Scatha and Glaurung, Tolkien's powerful and highly feared Middle Earth dragons. Printers, and especially the people who use printers to provide unnecessary paper copies, are called Tree-killers, based on what Treebeard the Ent called the Orcs.

10   *Heavy wizardry* is a term used to talk about the integration and maintenance of components within large and complicated, but poorly documented, software systems, while *deep magic,* a term borrowed from C. S. Lewis's Narnia books, refers to the implementation of software that is based on difficult-to-understand mathematical principles.

11   *Code police,* a comparison to the *thought police* in George Orwell's *1984,* take upon themselves the responsibility of enforcing idealized styles and standards for programming language codes. The term is generally used pejoratively, and the feeling among the hacker community is that those who are most likely to assume this role are outsiders (management and ivy-tower academics) who rarely participate in the practice of software development. A closely related term is *net police,* which describes members of the network community who assume the role of enforcing protocol and etiquette standards in public e-mail and electronic bulletin board forums by shaming, or "flaming," anyone who violates the established expectations.

12   When there is a need for a random number that people will recognize as such, 42 is often used because that's what Douglas Adams had his computer give as "The Answer to the Ultimate Question of Life, the Universe, and Everything" in *The Hitchhiker's Guide to the Galaxy.* Grok from Robert Heinlein's *Stranger in a Strange Land* is used to mean that a computer program un-

derstands or is "one with" a particular idea or capability. Often, older versions of commercial software products can't grok data files produced by newer releases of the same product. In a more playful usage from Heinlein's *The Moon Is a Harsh Mistress,* the acronym tanstaafl has become a quick and socially acceptable way to tell someone "There Ain't No Such Thing As a Free Lunch." Another Heinlein usage is Waldo, taken from the title of his 1942 story in which he invented mechanical devices working under the control of a human hand or foot. When these were first invented for the nuclear industry in the mid-1940s, they were called Waldos, but today NASA uses such terms as *telefactoring, telepresence,* and *telecommunication.* A human user on earth manipulates a mechanical arm belonging to a robot on the moon and the robot sends back visual and sensual feedback providing the illusion that the operator is actually present on the moon.

13   Science fiction and fantasy stories that have been adapted into movies and television are naturally known by more people and so serve as a rich source for allusion. A Godzillagram, named after the hero of 1950s Japanese monster movies, is a network packet of maximum size or one broadcast to every conceivable receiver. Aspiring teenage hackers are called Munchkins, based on the little people in *The Wizard of Oz.* Those who make problems for others by programming something to keep repeating itself might be called Wabbits, from cartoon character Elmer Fudd's "You Wascawwy wabbit!" while a program that accidentally repeats itself is said to be in Sorcerer's Apprentice mode, a reference to Walt Disney's *Fantasia.*

14   The movie *Star Wars* is another rich source of allusions. Someone who uses computer skills for devious purpose is called a dark side hacker (as opposed to a Samurai), meaning the person is like Darth Vader in having been seduced by the "dark side of the force." UTSL is a shorthand way to send someone the message that they should do some research before they send out a network call for help. It is an acronym for "Use the Source, Luke!" a play on "Use the Force, Luke!" An Obi-Wan error, taken from the name of Obi-Wan Kenobi, refers to any computation that is off-by-one, as when a programmer starts counting a particular quantity at 1 instead of 0. By analogy, in an Obi-Wan alphabetical code letters are used that are one off from the original so that HAL might stand for IBM as many viewers thought it did in the movie *2001.*

15   *Vulcan Nerve Pinch* comes from the original *Star Trek* television series in which this special pinch was used to paralyze people. In computer talk, the term describes the keyboard action of simultaneously pressing on three keys as when rebooting with the control, alternate, and delete keys. Droid from android, a science fiction term since the 1920s, was also popularized in the *Star Trek* television series. Computer hackers frequently use droid or the suffix -oid in a derogatory way to imply that a person is acting mindlessly, as though programmed. Marketdroids and sales droids promise customers things which can't be delivered, while a trendoid offers Twonkies. A Twonkie is a software addition that is essentially useless but nevertheless appealing in some way, perhaps for marketing purposes. Its meaning is made clear by its

resemblance to *Twinkie*, which has become almost a generic term for junk food. However, its source is thought to be the title of Lewis Padgett's 1942 short story "The Twonky," which has been frequently anthologized since its original publication in *Astounding Science Fiction.*

16   The new generation of computer hackers grew up watching *Sesame Street*, as shown by their calling someone who won't share a system with others a Cookie Monster. Double Bucky is a play on the Sesame Street Rubber Duckie song. It originated as a joke when designers were trying to figure out how to get more characters from the same size keyboard and someone suggested adding foot pedals to serve as extra shift keys.

17   Somewhere between *Sesame Street* and science fiction, hackers must have read *Alice in Wonderland*, because from Lewis Carroll's "Hunting of the Snark" they took snark as an appropriate name for any unexplained foul-up that they have to go searching for.

18   Cinderella is the name of a real-time management program, while Piglet is the name for an artificial intelligence program based on Personalized Intelligence Generation of Little Explanatory Texts. Subunits of the program are named after other characters from *Winnie the Pooh.* In the 1960s, people spoke of IBM and the Seven Dwarves with the dwarves being Burroughs, Control Data, General Electric, Honeywell, NCR, RCA, and Univac. In a classic computer hacker story about a conflict between Motorola and Xerox, two hackers at Motorola wrote a pair of "bandit" background processes they affectionately named Robin Hood and Friar Tuck. These two processes took over the Xerox developers' main computer system. The point was to get the attention of the Xerox team in order to deliver an important message that had been repeatedly ignored during the several months prior to the attack.

19   The Trojan Horse legend provides the name for a program that is designed to get around security measures by sneaking into a system while disguised, perhaps as a game or a useful utility. When the program is invoked, in addition to providing the advertised functionality, it does unexpected and unwanted harm to a computer system.

20   One of the relatively few references to a piece of traditional literature is moby, to mean something immense or huge. This comes from Herman Melville's *Moby-Dick.* It was popularized in precomputer days by model train fans who used it to describe large layouts and by pickle lovers who described large dill pickles as Moby. Hackers use it in such sentences as "The disk crash resulted in moby data loss" and "Writing a new back-end for the compiler will be a moby undertaking!" Several years ago when the University of California Library System named its library access program Melvyl after Melvyl Dewey, developer of the Dewey Decimal System, some users assumed a connection to Herman Melville because it was such a moby data base.

21   There's always a lag between the popularization of a term and its being adapted to a new use. However, today's instant communication shortens the lag, as shown by two fairly recent references. Feature Shock is a play on the title of Alvin Toffler's book *Future Shock.* It describes a user's reaction to a

program heavy on features, but light on explanations. The other recent usage is Sagan from the name of the late Carl Sagan, star of the TV series *Cosmos*, who often repeated the phrase *billions and billions*. His name is used as shorthand for any large number, as in "There's a sagan different ways that computers are going to affect the languages of the world."

22   Of course not all the new words needed to talk about computers have come from literary references. As will be shown in Workshop 8.1, many of them developed from more typical sources as when we create acronyms to replace long descriptions, when we borrow words from old technologies to name new technologies, and when we compare human and machine relationships and behaviors.

COMPREHENSION

1. Words to talk about:

   - Forget antiwar protests, *Woodstock*
   - Welcome to *Cyberspace*
   - JFK's inaugural *exhortation*
   - Heinlein's *libertarian screed-novel*
   - today's *nonhierarchical* and democratically run
   - adored as a *"hot-gospeller* of technology"
   - computer *neophytes*
   - *anthropomorphized* computers

2. What point is the author making by giving so many examples of words taken from science fiction and fantasy that are given new meanings in relation to computers?

DISCUSSION

1. Do you agree with Stewart Brand's observation that the Internet is non-hierarchical and decentralized? Why or why not?
2. A larger group of people can relate to the allusions taken from movies and television than to the ones taken from books. Why?
3. Boys have always read more science fiction than girls have. Do you think there is any relationship between this and the fact that the first generation of computer experts were predominantly men? What other reasons might there be?
4. Are more women reading science fiction and entering the computer field today? What kinds of evidence do you have?

WORKSHOP 8.1

Filling Lexical Gaps

Because of the newness of computers and the speed with which they spread throughout the world, the language that has been developed to talk about computers provides an interesting illustration of language development. The processes used to fill lexical gaps in the computer world are the same that have been used whenever people have new experiences. Some of these basic processes are described below in relation to general language followed by exercises related specifically to computers.

PART 1: ANALOGY

With analogy, speakers create words to fit into what appears to be a common English pattern. *Oldster,* for example, was created as a matching term to *youngster.* The *afterword* and *headnotes* in books are terms based on the more common *foreword* and *footnotes. Input* has come into use as an analogous term to *output,* and *early on* has been created to match *later on.*

BRAIN TEASERS

1. Computers fit well into the general definition of *hardware.* What analogous term was created to name the programming for this *hardware?* What are some further analogous terms based on *ware?*
2. What are some analogous terms based on *hard?* What two other terms are suggested by the name of the television news program *Hard Copy?*
3. What analogous words do people jokingly use based on *e-mail?*
4. *Bug* came into use as the name of a glitch or a problem in a computer from the early days when computers were so big that they filled whole rooms and actual bugs were attracted to the warmth inside the machines. What English prefix was used to create an analogous way to say that corrections were being made?

PART II: COMPOUNDING

Some of the most common words in English were created through putting two or three smaller words together. For example, the first meal of the day is the one in which people break the night's fast. But instead of talking about breaking the fast, people began to use the more efficient compound to break fast. Gradually the compound began to be used as a noun, and today few people recognize the verb and noun combination in the word *breakfast. Halloween* is a shortened version of the compound All Hallows Eve, the holy evening before All Saint's Day on November 1. Christmas is a compound from Christ's mass, and Thursday is a compound of Thor's Day, after the Norse god of thunder and weather.

When compounding, speakers aren't restricted to using full words. They might use the parts of words called morphemes (the smallest units of language that carry meaning), including affixes and suffixes.

While most compounds are the result of two words being used together so frequently that speakers begin to think of them as a single unit, some compounds come directly into the language as one word; for example, *superhighway*, which fits with such modern exaggerations as *supermarket, superstar, superpower,* and *supertanker. Superman,* a term coined by George Bernard Shaw for his 1903 play *Man and Superman* and then later made famous in the comics and on television, probably contributed to making this a productive pattern.

Cyber has proven to be an unusually productive morpheme in computer language. It is based on a Greek word for "pilot" or "one who steers" and came into modern English in the 1940s in the form of cybernetics, which referred to the automatic control of bodies through the nervous system and the brain. In a kind of metaphor, it also means mechanical-electrical communications systems. In the 1980s, science fiction writer William Gibson thought of cyberspace, and since then, we've seen such compounds as cyberslang, cybertalk, cyber-smear, cyber-surfing, cyberseconds, cybersex, cyberjunkies, and even Cyberia.

BRAIN TEASERS

1. Name three or more compounds used to describe the process through which groups of people communicate with each other by e-mail or through the Internet.
2. When two ordinary words (*down* and *load*) are put together, what computer term do they form? How does its meaning relate to such ordinary terms as *unload* or *lift down*? Is there enough of a connection that you could figure out the computer meaning even if you hadn't been told? Look at the articles and the Living Language boxes in this chapter and try to think of five or six other examples of ordinary words that now have unique computer-related meanings as compounds.
3. What compound that includes *friendly* has been adapted beyond computer language? How did it fill a general need?
4. Name a couple of compounds made with *hyper*. What are their meanings?

PART III: CLIPPING (AND BLENDING)

A process that often goes along with, or precedes, compounding is the clipping of long words and phrases; for example, it's easier to say *typo* than *typographical error, perks* than *perquisite,* and *exam* than *examination.* The most common process is to

continued

WORKSHOP 8.1

Filling Lexical Gaps   continued

clip the end of a word, as when people refer to an automobile as an *auto* and to a delicatessen as a *deli*, but with *bus*, the beginning happened to be clipped. The same is true with *cycle* for *motorcycle* and *plane* for *airplane*. Occasionally, the pronunciation will be changed to make the clipped form easier to say as in *bike* and *trike* from *bicycle* and *tricycle*.

A severe kind of clipping results in nothing being left but the initials. With hard-to-pronounce foreign words, clippings are especially helpful as with the AK-47 or Ak-Ak gun for the Russian *Avtomat Kalashnikova*. During the 1996 Whitewater investigation hearings, a witness made repeated references to Potus and Flotus. When Counsel asked, "By Potus, do you mean the president?" the witness answered affirmatively. Apparently the terms were acronyms from President of the United States and First Lady of the United States.

Before Windows 95, computer users had to type in WIN to open their programs. This clipping was not only easy to remember, it was also a persuasive bit of salesmanship. The most common kind of clipping in computer language is acronyming. Computer specialists even have acronyms for acronyms. TLA stands for Three Letter Acronym while YABA stands for Yet Another Bloody Acronym. When companies choose new names they check to make sure they are "YABA compatible," meaning the initials can be pronounced easily and won't make a suggestive or unpleasant word.

An acronym important to the history of computers is GUI for Graphics User Interface, the process that allows people to control their computers by clicking on an icon (a picture) rather than doing everything through words. The acronym WYSIWYG for "What You See Is What You Get" was popular for the previous generation of computers, but it is already falling out of use because better technology has led users to expect all computers to print what the screen shows.

BRAIN TEASERS

1. Do you know, or can you figure out, the meanings of the following acronyms that are part of cyberslang?

   "Careful, that may be a CLM!"

   "He's suffering from a GFR problem."

   "Yes, I got your ROTFL suggestion."

   "It's GIGO!"

   "RTM!" (Note: This means almost the same as UTSL and is often written in its less polite form, RTFM!)

2. See if you can figure out the meaning of these acronyms that are part of the Neti-quette used by chat groups. They are shortcut ways of saying often repeated phrases.

AFAIK	OIC
BCNU	RUOK
BTW	THK
CUL or CUL8R	

PART IV: SEMANTIC SHIFT—NARROWING OR BROADENING

Sometimes meaning changes take place without the words changing. Instead the thoughts in people's heads change so they use the old words with different meanings. Some of these changes occur so slowly that only when old meanings are compared to current meanings are they noticeable. In Shakespeare's time, *meat* was a general term for food. When people would ask for meat and drink, they were asking for food and drink. *Disease* used to be a simple compound whose meaning could be figured out from its parts: *dis,* meaning "out of" or "away from," and *ease,* meaning "comfort." When someone's shoes didn't fit or when the weather was hot and muggy, people could be described as diseased, but today a diseased person has a specific illness, probably caused by an organism growing in the body. The main meaning of *plastic* used to be "moldable." It was when this was its primary meaning that doctors adopted *plastic surgery* to describe reshaping or molding a part of someone's body. But in the 1940s and 1950s, technology was improved to create an oil-based substance that could be molded into various shapes. Since the most outstanding property of the sub-stance was its adaptability to being shaped, it was called *plastic.* The substance proved to be so versatile and useful that most people come in contact with some form of it every day and so think of it when they hear the word. They are surprised to learn that plastic surgery is in no way connected to the substance called plastic.

In all of these cases, the main meaning of the word was made narrower. With the opposite process of broadening (also called generalization) the word probably keeps its original meaning, but also takes on additional meanings. *Dilapidated* comes from Latin *lapis,* meaning "stone." Originally it was used only in reference to the wearing away of stone, but today we talk about dilapidated schools, dilapidated cars, and dilapidated couches, only one of which could be made from stone.

Generalization seems to work faster than specialization especially in relation to changing conditions and technological developments. The *linens* of today (tablecloths, napkins, sheets, and towels) are not made from linen but from cotton usually blended

continued

WORKSHOP 8.1

Filling Lexical Gaps   continued

with synthetic fibers. Most of us *butter* our bread with margarine, while we wear *glasses* made of plastic and eat with *silverware* made from stainless steel.

Because narrowing is a slower process, in computer language we won't see as many examples of narrowing as of broadening. But perhaps the computer-related meaning of *hacker* is pushing out the older meanings. A *hack* was a common or worn-out horse (c.f. hackney cab), or an unskilled person (c.f. a Grub Street hack or a hacker in tennis or basketball), but today when most people hear the word *hacker*, they think of a computer whiz. While some computer scientists interpret the word positively (they want to use a different word, cracker—as in safecracker—for those with criminal intent), the general public seems to associate the word with bad behavior. This may be because of the negative connotations associated with the old meanings.

Icon used to be used mainly in religious contexts, where it referred to pictures or statues of deities or some other religious symbol. Today more people use it in reference to the pictures or symbols that appear on computer screens.

BRAIN TEASERS

1. Try to think of five or six terms connected with paperwork and office management that have been broadened to include new computer-related meanings. Explain the differences between the general meanings and the new meanings.
2. Try to think of five or six terms connected with transportation that have been broadened to include new computer-related meanings. Explain the differences between the general meanings and the new meanings.

PART V: ASSOCIATION OR METAPHOR

When people use someone's name to create an eponym or to make a metaphorical allusion, other speakers must have some kind of an association or they won't understand or remember the reference. Metaphors are efficient in focusing attention on a similarity between basically dissimilar items. Some metaphors resemble the hyperbole of cartoonists, such as when you describe someone as being bent out of shape or a successful person as pulling himself up by his own bootstraps. When metaphors have been in the language so long that they no longer trigger people to think of the original base, they are called dead or buried metaphors such as, "He was brought in to be the hatchet man," or "Public dissatisfaction has mushroomed." A specific kind of association is shown through synecdoche (when a part of something is used to stand for the whole thing), as when we refer to a television set as the screen, the tube, or the box; to a softbound book as a paperback; to an athlete as a jock, or to a woman as a skirt. Metonymy is similar, except a quality rather than an physical part is referred to; however, the two processes blend together because it's not always easy to decide whether a feature is a quality or an integral part of something.

BRAIN TEASERS

1. In the early 1980s, when Mitch Kapor developed a method of making spreadsheets, what flower did he choose as a metaphorical name? How is it appropriate?

2. Explain the metaphorical allusions underlying these computer terms:

booting	dedicated terminal
handshaking	memory
motherboard	second (or third) generation
smart (or dumb) terminal	a computer virus

3. What is going on when computer programmers refer to their employers as *the suits?* Why do the suits sometimes get even by calling programmers *propeller heads?* What is the implication?

PART VI: FUNCTIONAL SHIFT

Conversion or functional shift is the process through which words are used beyond their established or expected parts of speech. The process has been going on for hundreds of years, yet it isn't automatically accepted. Language purists object to such sentences as "He offices down the hall from me," (a noun used as a verb) and "Updike makes for a good summer read" (a verb used as a noun). If a friend tells you that his car "has been totalled," he is using an adjective as a verb, while if someone else describes a friend as "an intimate," she is using an adjective as a noun. Affixing brings about a particular kind of functional shift as when such prefixes as *un-, de-, sub-,* and *post-* are used to make new words; for example, *unzip, dehumanize, subzero,* and *postdate.* Suffixes such as *age, ism, ize,* and *less* are also used to make new words such as *mileage, localism, modernize,* and *humorless.*

BRAIN TEASERS

1. Explain what functional shift has resulted in the italicized words and phrases in these sentences:
   - I'm finally getting good at *keyboarding*.
   - He thinks he can *debug* the program in a couple of hours.

continued

WORKSHOP 8.1

Filling Lexical Gaps   continued

- *Scroll down* until you find it.
- My computer came with some pre-installed *plug-ins.*
- I'm going to *log on* now.
2. Look at the essays and the Living Language sections in this chapter and find three or four other examples of words or phrases that have undergone functional shift. Identify the shift.

PART VII: COINING

While coining new sound combinations would seem to be an obvious way to create new words, it actually doesn't happen very often because newly coined words are too hard for people to learn and remember. Most neologisms (new words) are in some way related to words already in the language. For example, *snob* is said to be a coined word, but is so similar to *snub, snoot, snotty,* and *nob* that one might argue that it was really created through blending rather than coining. A. A. Milne is credited with coining a new word for elephant when in *Winnie the Pooh* he had Christopher Robin call his elephant a *heffalump.* The word caught on and is listed in the supplement to the *Oxford English Dictionary,* but notice how it uses basically the same sounds as *elephant,* has the same number of syllables, and ends with *lump,* which is fairly descriptive of an elephant. The same kind of connections can be found in the playful words that Dr. Seuss created including *Jivvanese* for a new language, *smogulous* for a kind of smoke and *skeegle-mobile* for a vehicle.

For a coining to succeed, it has to have a sponsor of some kind such as an author, a songwriter, or a television personality. Companies can act as a "sponsor" when they create names for themselves or their products and spend money in advertising. But even with names, there is usually some connections to words already in the language.

BRAIN TEASERS

1. Look on page 409 at the product names photographed from T-shirts given to the participants of a 1997 computer conference. What processes were used to create these names? Which ones are compounds? Is there evidence of clipping and blending? Are any of them coined? Do they remind you of words already in the language? If so, in what ways?
2. Look back at the essays in this chapter and find three or four examples of words coined for some other purpose and then adopted into computer language.
3. The most original coining that has taken place is with *emoticons,* created by the writers of e-mail messages. Standard keyboard symbols are used to make side-

ORACLE®

ways faces. Their popularity is growing because they are an efficient way to hint at the tone intended by the sender. Try figuring out the meaning of the following:

```
:-)  or  :-))          :-/
;-)                    :-0
I-0                    :-(  or  :-((
```

REIN IN BOSSES WHO SPY ON E-MAIL

Philip L. Bereano

Philip L. Bereano is a professor in the Department of Technical Communication at the University of Washington in Seattle. He has a law degree from Columbia University and, as this article shows, is interested in protecting individuals' privacy. He is a member of the National Board of Directors of the American Civil Liberties Union (ACLU). This article was first published in *Newsday* and then in various newspapers as an op-ed (opinion editorial) piece.

1   In Kitsap County, Wash., a county commissioner uses a government computer during business hours to surf 130 dirty-sex Internet sites.

2   At prim Princeton University, officials try to prevent staff, students, and faculty from using the computer system for "personal political discourse."

3   And in the private sector of "cyberia," Michael Smyth is sacked for an after hours e-mail to a co-worker about bosses who were "back-stabbing bastards."

NEW TECHNOWORLD

4   All this provokes a question: Don't workers have privacy rights in the new technoworld, similar to those they have with old familiar systems like the telephone? And if they don't, shouldn't they? Would Smyth be an unemployment statistic if he had penned rather than e-mailed his note to his office mate? And would it have mattered if the pen had been supplied by his employer rather than brought from home?

5   The answers are critical because privacy is under assault in America today. Big Brother and Big Sister know a lot about each of us. Records of our illnesses, our charitable donations, the concerts we attend and the videos we rent, for example, can be obtained by others, often without our knowledge or consent. Indeed, such information is a hot commodity, bought and sold by people who want to control our social, political and consumer behaviors.

6   And many of us are worried about this situation. A 1994 report by the American Civil Liberties Union concludes that concerns about personal privacy "run deep among the American people." This year, the ACLU says, "the protection of spheres of individual privacy and autonomy is a core civil liberties concern." And 80 percent of us do not think that an employer has the

right to consider off-duty activities in hiring or firing decisions. So lots of folks would think that Smyth got a raw deal.

7   But, corporations contend the computer systems are their equipment. We need, they say, to control its use to promote efficiency and honesty in the workplace, to prevent trade secrets from being divulged and to ensure that employee time and attention aren't diverted so that we get the full measure of the labor power we have purchased.

PRIVACY IS A CONCEPT

8   And, anyway, the corporations add, privacy is a concept that may be applied to prevent government snooping; the private sector isn't limited by the Fourth Amendment's protection of private "papers and effects" and the First Amendment rights to free speech.

9   But there is much to be concerned about as regards the privacy of employees in the private sector. As the ACLU notes, "The need for . . . employee protection is acute because many private employers have power and influence comparable to that of governmental entities, and because even the smallest private employer can exercise enormous control over employees. . . . Employers' violations of employees' privacy can have particularly grievous effects, due to the large part of an employee's life spent in the workplace and the lack of anonymity there."

10   Certainly, a reasonable position is that what workers do on their own time should be of no interest to the boss. In this regard, the monitoring of employee activity should only be for legitimate business reasons—safety, efficiency, job evaluation, prevention of theft or fraud—and then should only be done after notice to the employee (unless notice would inherently undercut the purposes of the monitoring).

11   In other words, while recognizing that employers have some legitimate interest in knowing what use workers are making of electronic communications networks, employers should only focus on what is clearly work-related.

ELECTRONIC FILE CABINET

12   Often in law and policy making, when examining the rules most suitable for a new technology, we look to existing technologies for models or analogies. Is computer e-mail like the telephone? Are the computer's information storage and handling capacities a kind of "electronic file cabinet"?

13   New technologies do not appear as acts of God or nature. They are purposeful human creations, specifically designed to alter existing social or natural environments. The technologies that are developed reflect the interests and agendas of groups that were powerful enough in society to marshal the resources to lead to their creation. Computer networks, for example, are the result of enormous governmental research and development subsidies,

especially by the military. The Internet, in particular, was a Defense Department artifact, discarded as inadequate and later picked up by civilian interests.

14   Technologies bear the stamp of their origins. Despite the claims of cyber-junkies that computers are somehow inherently equalizing and democratic, a moment's reflection shows that they are highly centralized technical systems designed for manipulation of information, memory, surveillance and control over people and social systems.

15   Computer technologies will never be readily available to most Americans because of high cost. For instance, many American households do not have a telephone. Also, despite the growing use of computers, the population at large still fails to have a significant need for them. That's not surprising since most Americans don't regularly work on spreadsheets. So, computer systems will be most intensively used by the corporate sector, and they will be increasingly employed to keep track of our activities. To acknowledge this danger is not hysterical but historical.

RATIONAL EXPECTATIONS

16   There is a great threat in existing court cases about computer use that suggests that somehow the boundaries of privacy depend on a person's "rational expectations." If employers (as well as hospitals, insurance companies, telemarketers and government) can habituate us to low expectations of privacy protections, violations by such parties will become the accepted legal and social norms. What is needed is a rallying point for workers and unions to demand privacy rights on the job and thus to help nourish their expanded legal recognition.

17   Employers can meet their legitimate business interests by measures oriented to results (is the worker productive or not?) without fostering a workplace atmosphere of suspicion, distrust and stress-related illness.

18   America's devotion to human dignity and integrity, and the private protections needed to assure these ends, requires our continued efforts to make the workplace a zone of freedom. Otherwise, the "back-stabbing bastards" win.

COMPREHENSION

1. Words to talk about:
   - in the private sector of *"cyberia"*
   - in the new *technoworld*
   - *Big Brother and Big Sister* know a lot
   - such information is a *hot commodity*
   - a Defense Department *artifact*

2. What three reasons does Bereano give for companies saying they need to monitor the work done by their employees?
3. How do companies view themselves as different from governmental agencies in relation to privacy?

DISCUSSION

1. Is Bereano making a one-sided argument? What clues are there to his belief?
2. Why did Bereano open with an incident that appears to be supporting the need for surveillance?
3. The article "Recycling in Cyberspace" cited the creators (or really the adapters) of the Internet as "computer geniuses," but Bereano calls them "cyberjunkies." What is implied by the different tone? How does he argue against the idea that the Internet is democratic and nonhierarchical?
4. What point is Bereano making about court decisions being based on people's "rational expectations"? Is he saying that if someone thinks something is private, then the courts will lend them protection?
5. Talk a little about the rationale behind courts basing decisions on a person's expectations, then read the following news summaries dealing with some aspect of computers and privacy and discuss them in relation to how they contribute to general expectations about privacy.
   (a) "Companies' Productivity Caught in Net" was the headline on a story about how increasing numbers of companies are providing Internet access for employees but have failed to spell out what is and is not acceptable. Don Wetmore, president of Connecticut-based Productivity Institute, said, "Productivity typically drops from 5 to 15 percent when employees are given Internet access," because people who don't want to be at work look for distractions, and surfing the net is a less obvious way to goof off than standing around the water cooler. (*Arizona Republic,* June 16, 1997)
   (b) "Another Attack on E-Mail Privacy" read the headline on a story about brokerage houses testing software that will read all e-mail messages sent and received by employees. Dean Witter and Oppenheimer & Co. said that they want to make sure that employees are not violating Securities and Exchange Commission rules, but critics think the companies also want to filter out politically incorrect messages because stockbrokers have been notorious for telling questionable jokes as a way of developing rapport with potential buyers. (*Arizona Republic,* July 21, 1997)

Living Language 8.3

News Clippings About the Internet

Hardly a day goes by that newspaper readers don't see one or two stories related to the Internet. Here is just a sampling.

- In late June of 1997, defenders of academic freedom and free speech were relieved when the Supreme Court rejected the 1996 Communications Decency Act, which had not been enforced since being approved in February of 1995. The law was designed to protect children from pornography on the Internet, "But in doing so, it appeared to put at risk a wide variety of materials available in one way or another through college computers, such as students' personal home pages on the World Wide Web, images stored on college servers for art-history classes, and discussion lists for faculty members in the humanities." Colleges were also worried that it would inhibit lectures and discussions integrated into distance education classes. But on the other side of the issue, many parents are still worried about their children's free access to sexual material and are committed to finding either legal or technical measures that will help them screen materials. Congress and many state legislatures have vowed to try again with a differently worded law. (*Chronicle of Higher Education,* July 3, 1997)

- Two 30-second audio clips (*Discotheque* and *Wake Up Dead Man*) from an album that U2 was still recording were smuggled onto the Internet by a fan in Hungary who got hold of some private videotapes. "In cyberseconds, the clips were on sites worldwide and, despite their iffy quality, were playing on radio and MTV and selling on the streets of London for $10." In the midst of protesting and asking the media not to air the songs, Island Records refuted charges that the tapes were leaked for the sake of prerelease publicity. (*Time* magazine, Dec. 2, 1996)

- "Teenagers need only retreat to their rooms, boot up the computer and click on a cartoon bumblebee named Buzzy to be whisked online, to a mail-order house in Los Angeles that promises the scoop on 'legal highs,' 'growing hallucinogens,' 'cannabis alchemy,' 'cooking with cannabis' and other 'trippy, phat, groovy things,' " wrote Christopher S. Wren in a story lamenting the fact that all this is available at the same time that "parents, teachers and government officials urge adolescents to say no to drugs." (*New York Times,* June 22, 1997)

- "The agency that enforces Quebec's language laws has warned a computer store that its English-language Web site violates a law requiring businesses to use French." The owners were given one month to provide a French version or be fined up to $1,000. The store manager said the store's position is that the agency does not have the right to control what goes on the Internet. Since reports of the warning surfaced in Montreal media, "The watchdog agency has received a wave of electronic hate mail." (*Arizona Republic,* June 19, 1997)

- One of the reasons that the U.S. government considers Iran to be headquarters for international terrorism is that "Thanks to highly sophisticated surveillance capabilities, American intelligence agencies intercepted numerous telephone messages from Iran ordering acts of terrorism." However, in late summer of 1996, the terrorists stopped using telephones and switched to using codes on the Internet. A frustrated expert on international terrorism explained, "There's so much crazy screwball stuff on the Internet that it's practically impossible to track down and isolate the dangerous terrorists. No government can analyze those millions and millions of messages." (*Parade Magazine,* Sept. 29, 1996)

- "If you instruct AltaVista, a powerful Internet search engine, to scour the Web for references to Microsoft's Bill Gates, the program turns up an impressive 25,000 references. But ask it to look for Web pages that mention God, and you'll get 410,000 hits. Look for Christ on the Web, and you'll find him—some 146,000 times." All this wrote *Time* magazine editors is just part of the "delicate dance of technology and faith—the marriage of God and the computer networks," which is allowing believers to re-examine, debate, argue, and create new ways to convey their deepest thoughts. (*Time* magazine, Dec. 16, 1996)

- Heartrending pleas on the Internet that are written in chain letter form are often counterfeit as when "Jessica Mydek, only seven years old and dying of cancer" supposedly sent out a message urging readers to live their lives more fully and to pass her message on to as many other e-mail recipients as possible. The letter said that several corporate sponsors, along with the American Cancer Society, would each contribute three cents toward cancer research for every message forwarded. The American Cancer Society had nothing to do with the message, nor did the chair of a department at the University of South Carolina, whose name and address were given. Such messages seldom ask for money, since that would be breaking United States Postal Inspection rules. What the perpetrators are most interested in is collecting e-mail addresses to use for marketing purposes, and it doesn't hurt that the respondents have "been prescreened for gullibility." (*New York Times,* July 14, 1997)

- "Home Pages for Hate: A campaign to limit the voices of white supremacists on the Internet has defenders of the First Amendment worried," began a *Time* magazine article (Jan. 22, 1996) describing contrasting opinions about the ways that hate groups participate on the net. Rabbi Abraham Cooper, associate dean of the Simon Wiesenthal Center, the world's largest Jewish human rights organization, has campaigned for the development of a code of ethics that would squelch Web sites that promote bigotry and violence. He claims such an approach would be similar to current practices where most mainstream newspapers and magazines will not run ads from racist or hate groups. Speaking to the other side of the issue, Sameer Parekh, president of Community ConneXion in Berkeley, California, says, "The answer to hateful speech is more speech." If you ban hate groups, "You are promoting the idea that they might actually have something valuable to say." A separate issue to the one about groups having their own pages, is the fact that members infiltrate other discussion groups "to troll for new members" and to play with "shock value."

- An embarrassing string of events began on Friday afternoon, June 5, 1998, when House Majority Leader Dick Arney introduced Representative Bob Stump, who

continued

LIVING LANGUAGE 8.3

News Clippings About the Internet   continued

had been asked to make the sad announcement that Bob Hope had died. While various congressmen stood up to eulogize Hope's contributions, the 95-year-old performer was home in California eating a late breakfast and getting ready to go out and hit a couple of golf balls. The mistake occurred because the Associated Press had written an obituary of Hope to have ready when he died. The writer accidentally pushed the wrong "save" key, so the obituary went to the Associated Press Web site instead of to a "file for future use" site.

Bob Hope was amused, but people worry that tragic or dangerous consequences could result from such errors.

(c) In Decatur, Illinois, a computerized lunch payment system allows parents to know what their children buy for lunch. In the middle and high schools, students pay with cards bearing individual bar codes. When they check out, a warning is signaled if the students choose foods their parents prefer they not eat. A more thorough record is kept in elementary schools where students' names and barcodes are kept in a book. At check out, a worker punches computer keys identifying what food the student has selected and then runs a wand across the student's bar code. (*Arizona Republic,* Jan. 16, 1997)

(d) Across the country, some 12,000 school systems have purchased the PhoneMaster system since it became available in 1983. It is a computerized truant officer that reads attendance records in schools' computers, then dials the homes of students with unexcused absences and "rattles off a standard message" about a student missing one or more classes on a given day. (Associated Press, Feb. 17, 1997)

(e) A woman in Pahrump, Nevada, C. J. Prime, purchased a used IBM personal computer through an Internet auction for $159 and was surprised when she turned it on to find the medical records (names, addresses, social security numbers, and prescriptions) of 2,000 patients from a pharmacy in Arizona. Prescriptions included AZT for AIDS patients, Antabuse for alcoholics, and numerous antidepressants, psychotropic drugs, and narcotic prescriptions. Because she once lost a job when an employer learned she had multiple sclerosis, Prime embarked on a crusade to trace the history of her computer and to alert authorities to the privacy issues that were apparently unrecognized when two groups of pharmacies merged, and as many as thirty-four computers were returned to a leasing company. (*New York Times,* April 5, 1997)

A Neo-Luddite Reflects on the Internet

Gertrude Himmelfarb

To understand the title of this essay you need to know the story of Ned Ludd, who in 1811 in Leicestershire, England, led a movement in which workers destroyed labor-saving machinery as a protest. It isn't clear just why they were called "*Luddites,*" but their name has come down through history to stand for anyone who is opposed to change, particularly change related to technology. In creating her title, Himmelfarb added *neo*, meaning "new"—as in *neologism, neo-Nazi, neo-impressionism,* and *neo-classic.* Himmelfarb, a retired professor of history at the City University of New York, published her article in the *Chronicle of Higher Education* read by college teachers and administrators. Her article elicited several letters to the editor. As you read the article, think of what people might have said in such letters.

1   On the subject of our latest technological revolution, cyberspace, I am a neo-Luddite. Not a true Luddite; my Luddism is qualified, compromised. I revel in the word processor; I am grateful for computerized library catalogues; I appreciate the convenience of CD-ROMS; and I concede the usefulness of the Internet for retrieving information and conducting research. But I am disturbed by some aspects of the new technology—not merely by the moral problems raised by cybersex, which have occupied so much attention recently, but also by the new technology's impact on learning and scholarship.

2   Revolutions come fast and furious these days. No sooner do we adapt to one than we are confronted with another. For almost half a millennium, we lived with the product of the print revolution—the culture of the book. Then, a mere century ago, we were introduced to the motion picture; a couple of decades later, to radio and then to television. To a true Luddite, those inventions were the beginning of the rot, the decline of Western civilization as we have known it. To a true revolutionary, such as Marshall McLuhan, they were giant steps toward a brave new world liberated from the stultifying rigidities of an obsolete literacy. To the rest of us, they were frivolities, diversions, often meretricious (as some popular culture has always been), but not threatening to the life of the mind, the culture associated with books.

3   Not that the book culture has been immune from corruption. When the printing press democratized literature, liberating it from the control of clerics and scribes, the effects were ambiguous. As the historian Elizabeth Eisenstein pointed out in her seminal 1979 work *The Printing Press as an Agent of Change,*

the advent of printing facilitated not only the production of scientific works, but also of occult and devotional tracts. It helped create a cosmopolitan secular culture and, at the same time, distinctive national and sectarian cultures. It stimulated scholarship and high culture, as well as ephemera and popular culture. It subverted one intellectual elite, the clergy, only to elevate another, the "enlightened" class.

4   Yet for all of its ambiguities, printing celebrated the culture of the book—of bad books, to be sure, but also of good books and great books. Movies, radio, and television made the first inroads on the book, not only because they distracted us from reading, but also because they began to train our minds to respond to oral and visual sensations of brief duration rather than to the cadences, nuances, and lingering echoes of the written word. The movie critic Michael Medved has said that even more detrimental than the content of television is the way that it habituates children to an attention span measured in seconds rather than minutes. The combination of sound bites and striking visual effects shapes the young mind, incapacitating it for the longer, slower, less febrile tempo of the book.

5   And now we have the Internet to stimulate and quicken our senses still more. We channel-surf on television, but that is as naught compared with cyber-surfing. The obvious advantage of the new medium is that it provides access to an infinite quantity of information on an untold number and variety of subjects. How does one quarrel with such a plenitude of goods?

6   An information-retrieval device, the Internet is unquestionably an asset, assuming that those using it understand that the information retrieved is only as sound as the original sources—an assumption that applies to all retrieval methods, but especially to one whose sources are so profuse and indiscriminate. Yet children and even older students, encouraged to rely upon the Internet for information and research, may not be sophisticated enough to question the validity of the information or the reliability of the source. A child whom I saw interviewed on television said that it was wonderful to be able to ask a question on one's home page and have "lots of people answer it for you." Before the age of the Internet, the child would have had to look up the question in a textbook or encyclopedia, a source that he would have recognized as more authoritative than, say, his older brother or sister (or even his mother or father).

7   As a learning device, the new electronic technology is even more dubious—indeed, it may be more bad than good. And it is dubious at all levels of learning. Children who are told that they need not learn how to multiply and divide, spell, and write grammatical prose, because the computer can do that for them, are being grossly miseducated. More important, young people constantly exposed to "multimedia" and "hypermedia" replete with sound and images often become unable to concentrate on mere "texts" (known as books), which have only words and ideas to commend them. Worse yet, the constant exposure to a myriad of texts, sounds, and images that often are only tangentially related to each other is hardly conducive to the cultivation of logical, rational, systematic habits of thought.

8   At the more advanced level of learning and scholarship, the situation is equally ambiguous. Let me illustrate this from my own experience. I used to give (in the pre-electronic age) two sequences of courses: one on social history, the other on intellectual history. In a course on social history, a student might find electronic technology useful, for example, in inquiring about the standard of living of the working classes in the early period of industrialization, assuming that the relevant sources—statistical surveys, diaries, archival collections, newspapers, tracts, journals, books, and other relevant materials—were on line (or at least that information about their location and content was available).

9   This kind of social history, which is built by marshaling social and economic data, is not only facilitated, but actually is stimulated, by the new technology. One might find oneself making connections among sources of information that would have had no apparent link had they not been so readily called up on the computer screen (on the other hand, now one might not make the effort to discover other kinds of sources that do not appear).

10   But what about intellectual history? It may be that the whole of Rousseau's *Social Contract* and Hegel's *Philosophy of History* are now on line. Can one read such books on the screen as they should be read—slowly, carefully, patiently, dwelling upon a difficult passage, resisting the temptation to scroll down, thwarting the natural speed of the computer? What is important in the history of ideas is not retrieving and recombining material, but understanding it. And that requires a different relation to the text, a different tempo of reading and study.

11   One can still buy the book (or perhaps print out a hard copy from the computer), read it, mark it up, and take notes the old-fashioned way. The difficulty is that students habituated to surfing on the Internet, to getting their information in quick easy doses, to satisfying their curiosity with a minimum of effort (and with a maximum of sensory stimulation) often do not have the patience to think and study this old-fashioned way. They may even come to belittle the intellectual enterprise itself, the study of the kinds of books— "great books," as some say derisively—that require careful thought and study.

12   Perhaps I am exaggerating the effect of the electronic revolution, just as critics have said that Elizabeth Eisenstein has exaggerated the effect of the print one. She sometimes seems to suggest that printing was not only an agent of change, but the primary agent. Without the printing press, she has implied, the Renaissance might have petered out or the Reformation been suppressed as yet another medieval heresy. "The advent of printing," she notes, preceded "the Protestant revolt."

13   The electronic media cannot make that claim to priority. The intellectual revolution of our time, postmodernism, long antedated the Internet. Nonetheless, the Internet powerfully reinforces postmodernism: it is the postmodernist technology par excellence. It is as subversive of "linear," "logocentric," "essentialist" thinking, as committed to the "aporia," "indeterminacy," "fluidity," "intertextuality," and "contextuality" of discourse, as deconstruction

itself. Like postmodernism, the Internet does not distinguish between the true and the false, the important and the trivial, the enduring and the ephemeral. The search for a name or phrase or subject will produce a comic strip or advertising slogan as readily as a quotation from the Bible or Shakespeare. Every source appearing on the screen has the same weight and credibility as every other; no authority is "privileged" over any other.

14   The Internet gives new meaning to the British expression describing intellectuals, "chattering classes." On their own home pages, subscribers can communicate to the world every passing reflection, impression, sensation, obsession, or perversion.

15   Michael Kinsley, editor of the new cyberspace journal *Slate*, defensively insists that his magazine will retain the "linear, rational thinking" of print journalism. To have to make that claim is itself testimony to the non-linear, non-rational tendency of the new medium. Each article in *Slate* gives the date when it was "posted" and "composted" (archived). Composted! One recalls the computer-programming acronym a few years ago—GIGO, for "garbage in, garbage out." (As it happens, the articles in *Slate* are not garbage, but much on the Internet is.)

16   One need not be a Luddite, or even a neo-Luddite, to be alarmed by this most useful, most potent, most seductive, and most equivocal invention.

Comprehension

1. Words to talk about:

   - world liberated from the *stultifying rigidities*
   - they were frivolities, diversions, often *meretricious*
   - the longer, slower, less *febrile tempo* of the book
   - constantly exposed to *"multimedia"* and *"hypermedia"*
   - gives the date when it was *"posted"* and *"composted"*

2. What does Himmelfarb mean when she says that no source is "privileged" over another? Do you agree?

Discussion

1. Expound a bit on the author's statement that "Revolutions come fast and furious these days." Make a more specific timeline for the innovations she lists: books, motion pictures, radio, then television.

2. What major cultural difference does Himmelfarb ascribe to the production of books?

3. Do you agree that the quickness and the visual effects of television inca-
   pacitate young minds for the kind of concentrated thought that is required for serious reading?
4. Why does Himmelfarb say that the new kinds of electronic media
   would be helpful to students taking her class in social history but
   would be harmful to students taking her class in intellectual history?
5. Why does Himmelfarb say the Internet reinforces postmodernism?
6. What is the contrast between these two sets of terms that Himmelfarb
   uses to depict the Internet:

Subversive of:	Committed to:
linear thinking	aporia
logocentric thinking	indeterminacy
essentialist thinking	fluidity
	intertextuality
	contextuality

Give some specific examples that either support or contradict her observation. You can take the examples either from her essay or from your
own experience.
7. Talk about the differences in doing research through books and magazines in a library and through doing computer-assisted research, which
   would include using material from Web pages as well as from bulletin
   board or news groups on the Internet, finding print citations through
   something like Nexus, and requesting information or help through e-
   mail. What are the advantages and the disadvantages of each source?
8. In relation to Himmelfarb's point about authenticity, consider these interesting language tidbits forwarded by friends who picked them up on the
   Net. Since none of them came with documentation or with cited sources,
   what various ways could be used to check their authenticity? Under
   what circumstances would someone be likely to go to the trouble of
   checking? Which ones do you believe without checking somewhere else?
   Which ones seem questionable? How is getting these items from the Internet different from hearing them in class or in a casual conversation?
   (a) Clans of long ago that wanted to get rid of unwanted people with-
       out killing them used to burn their houses down—hence the ex-
       pression "to get fired."
   (b) The word *checkmate* in chess comes from the Persian phrase *Shah
       Mat*, which means "The king is dead."
   (c) No word in the English language rhymes with either month, or-
       ange, silver, or purple.
   (d) The term *the whole nine yards* came from WWII fighter pilots in the
       South Pacific. When arming their airplanes on the ground, the .50
       caliber machine gun ammo belts measured exactly 27 feet before
       being loaded into the fuselage. If the pilots fired all their ammo at a
       target, it got "the whole nine yards."

(e) *Stewardesses* and *reverberated* are the two longest words (twelve letters each) that can be typed using only the left hand.
(f) The longest word that can be typed using only the right hand is *lollipop. Skepticisms* is the longest word that alternates hands.
(g) The combination *ough* can be pronounced in nine different ways. The following sentence contains them all: "A rough-coated, dough-faced, thoughtful ploughman strode through the streets of Scarborough; after falling into a slough, he coughed and hiccoughed."
(h) Dr. Seuss pronounced *Seuss* such that it rhymed with *rejoice.*
(i) Sherlock Holmes never said, "Elementary, my dear Watson."

Suggested Topics for Writing

1. As Judith Stone mentioned, Americans have been loathe to adopt the metric system. But actually, bits and pieces of it are sneaking in. We buy soda pop and water in "liter bottles," police report confiscated drugs in kilos, measuring utensils for cooking come marked in both systems, many medicines and medical procedures are measured metrically, people who have imported bicycles and cars buy tools made for metric measurements, automobile speedometers come with both markings, and track, swimming, and equestrian sports are measured in meters. As much as anything, it's probably fear of the unknown that makes most people reject the idea of moving along with the rest of the world (except Liberia and Burma) into the metric system. Do some research and write a piece that will clarify for readers what would be different if the United States moved fully to a metric system. You might do a persuasive paper by choosing to support either side of the issue: "Yes, Americans Should Continue Moving to the Metric System" or "No, Americans Should Resist a Move to the Metric System."

2. Write an essay exploring your personal feelings about numbers. You might get inspired by looking at Living Language 8.2 (pages 394–396). Do you have a fondness for things that come in threes? If so, why? Could it relate to all those stories you heard as a child—"The Three Little Pigs," "Goldilocks and the Three Bears," "Three Billy Goats Gruff"—or do you think the stories reflect some inner feeling that people have about "a pair and a spare"? Population planners came up with such a hypothesis when they found it hard to convince parents that a family with two children was the ideal size. How about the number seven? Do you think of it

as a lucky number? What about ten? Does it have a stamp of authority for you?

3. One of the essays in John Allen Paulos's *A Mathematician Reads the Newspaper* is a list of ten reasons that Americans like lists of ten. Think of the "lists of ten" you have seen or heard. They probably range from The Ten Commandments to the funny lists that David Letterman gives in his late-night monologues. See if you can write an essay modeled on Paulos's idea. This should be tempting because one of the reasons in Paulos's list was that the creators of such lists don't have to worry about transitions. The numbers serve as sign posts telling readers to be prepared for a new and perhaps totally unrelated idea. After you've written your essay, just for fun you could find Paulos's book and see how the reasons you've thought of compare with those that Paulos lists.

4. Choose a semantic area from a field of endeavor that you are better acquainted with than most people, perhaps through employment or a hobby, and write about how the lexical gaps have been filled in that field. You might start by making a list of unusual words or adaptations of ordinary words. Your writing will probably go more smoothly if you group similar items together. The examples from computer language in Workshop 8.1 were organized according to the process of their development, but you may want to have a different pattern if you wish to focus your readers' attention on the relationship of the new field of endeavor to an older field or if you want to make a statement about the kinds of people who created the new words.

5. The human mind is clever at extending comparisons to make analogies based on more than a single point. In the early nineties, many people, including Vice President Al Gore, talked about the coming of an "information superhighway." Professor Raymond Gozzi and his students in the Television-Radio Department of Ithaca College collected news clippings about this information superhighway and found the following related metaphors:

- different technologies were to serve as *on ramps*
- broadcast studios who feared a negative impact on their services warned about *drive-by shootings*
- companies who feared some of their enterprises would be taken over worried about becoming *road kill*
- small companies *merged* to guarantee themselves a *lane* on the *superhighway*
- when the merger between Bell-Atlantic phone company and TCI cable was canceled in February of 1994 the *New York Times* headlined *An Information Detour*

Other terms that Professor Gozzi and his students found applicable included *toll booths, hackers hitching a ride, public roads vs. private ways,* the cable box serving as the *steering wheel,* measuring *cargo-carrying capacity,* and getting in *gridlock* or *graphic jams.* In the fall 1994 issue of *Et cetera,* he went on to point out several discrepancies between the concept of a superhighway and the realities of the "collection of wires, computers, and telephone switching stations" that will "carry video, audio, computer data, and 2-way message capacity into the home." His concern was that people were going to be disappointed because the metaphor leads them to expect the same kind of economic improvements from the information superhighway that were brought about by the actual Interstate Highway System in the 1950s, 1960s, and 1970s. As people began to understand the differences and to perhaps experience some of the problems, the term fell out of popularity so that today most people refer to *the Web* or *the Internet.* Write an essay in which you illustrate how the three names (Web, Internet, or information superhighway) trigger people to think differently about their involvement. If you prefer, you could work with such other terms as *cyberspace* and/or the *electronic frontier.* Can you find extended metaphors or analogies growing out of the alternate names? Why did information superhighway serve as such a productive source for analogies?

6. As Philip L. Bereano pointed out in his essay, a key issue for legislators and others struggling to develop policies about e-mail privacy is whether e-mail should be treated like the telephone or like letters. Should a computer's information storage be considered the same as any other company file cabinet except that it is electronic? Try your hand at clarifying the issue by writing a piece that illustrates the similarities and the differences. To simplify matters, you might want to focus on only one of the alternatives (choose either the telephone or letters) and then explore how e-mail is both alike and different from the medium you are looking at.

7. Although in the summer of 1997 the Supreme Court struck down as unconstitutional the Communications Decency Act (CDA), which had been passed by Congress and signed by President Clinton, there promise to be many more controversies over freedom of speech on the Internet. Write a persuasive paper either defending or speaking against freedom of speech on the Internet. As part of your evidence, you might explore and compare the Internet to other media.

8. Look on the Internet and find two home pages that you like. Make copies of them and then do an analysis of their likenesses and differences. You will be able to make more interesting points if you choose pages produced by individuals or organizations with similar goals. Of course there will be big differences between a Web page from a hate group and a Web page from a publisher promoting children's literature. Based on your analysis of the two sites you examine, decide which one is the most effective in reaching its goals. Explain why.

INFORMATION SOURCES FOR WRITING

The Book of Scientific Anecdotes, by Adrian Berry. New York: Prometheus, 1993.

The Children's Machine: Rethinking School in the Age of the Computer, by Seymour Papert. New York: Basic, 1993.

Conscientious Objections: Stirring Up Trouble about Language, Technology, and Education, by Neil Postman. New York: Knopf, 1988.

I Sing the Body Electronic: A Year with Microsoft on the Multimedia Frontier, by Fred Moody. New York: Viking, 1996.

The Internet: How to Get Connected & Explore the World Wide Web, Exchange News & Email, Download Software & Communicate On-Line, by Brian Cooper. New York: Dorling Kindersley, 1996.

Light Elements: Essays in Science, by Judith Stone. New York: Ballantine, 1991.

A Mathematician Reads the Newspaper, by John Allen Paulos. New York: HarperCollins, 1995; Anchor paperback, 1996.

The Order of Things: How Everything in the World Is Organized . . . into Hierarchies, Structures & Pecking Orders, by Barbara Ann Kipfer. New York: Random, 1997.

Silicon Snake Oil: Second Thoughts on the Information Highway, by Clifford Stoll. New York: Doubleday, 1995.

Using the Internet Online Services & CD-ROMs for Writing Research & Term Papers, by Charles Harmon. New York: Neal-Schuman, 1996.

The Wired Neighborhood, by Stephen Doheny-Farina. New Haven: Yale Univ. Press, 1996.

Your Guide to Getting Better Grades Using the Internet and Online Services: Your Personal Net Study, a Michael Wolff Book. New York: Wolff New Media, 1996.

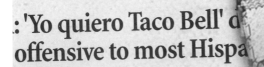

: 'Yo quiero Taco Bell' d
offensive to most Hispa

(AP) - The Rocky Mountain Poll gauges Arizona's mood on the majo
e day: President Clinton's performance, who would make the best g
rating the economy, and now that little dog that just loves Taco Bell.
Hispanic leaders are complaining that the little chihuah
rious commercials is d

2 pesos

Honda, Mazda,
lead local car sa

BY Reginald Fulberginer
State Press

A local impartial survey body has determined that residents are looking ou
in efforts to increase domestic purchases, the Joint Council of Independant Aut
this may help bring consumers back home into the American auto market, ho
It is uncertain how long this will last, but experts estimate
if not, the auto industry in

Karaoke
Replaces
Disco

'Euromyths' running ram

BY Timothy Tucker
(AP) — Houston
Transportation
may not stay the
different kind of
in the distance is
the needed materi
short on items wh
the new system is
the people of Nel
In a few short y
how well can onl
a measurement sy
capable of increas

STUDENT'S AUTO SHANGHAIED
AT GUNPOINT ON CAMPUS

ning home from class was accosted at the corner

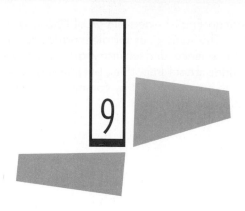

CHANGING WORDS IN A CHANGING WORLD

The fact that it took centuries for smallpox to travel from Europe to the vast areas of North and South America, while it took only a decade for AIDS to become a worldwide health problem, illustrates how modern transportation has truly made the world one large neighborhood. And what's true for the spreading and movement of actual goods and people, including their diseases, is even more true for words and processes of communication.

Workshop 9.1—beginning with the earliest caravans and shipping routes and ending with the marketing of today's cars—illustrates how commerce, along with its accompanying migration of people, encourages the blending of languages. But such blending does not come without pain. French speakers, whether from Montreal or Paris, are regularly embroiled in campaigns against the use of English. And within the last few years, the Canton city government in China, and the mayor of Moscow, have outlawed English names on buildings. And, in spite of the confidence that Americans feel when they read a headline such as Bill Bryson's "English as a World Language," the fact that over sixty U.S. cities or states have passed "Official Language" or "English-Only" laws reveals that we have similar insecurities to those of other peoples.

Language is a two-way process, and so, of course, the increasing numbers of immigrants to the United States are going to influence communication practices. Also, when a language is spread through so many countries as is English, it is bound to pick up many different influences. In 1996, the Oxford University Press published *A Dictionary of South African English on Historical Principles* and also a *Dictionary of Caribbean English Usage*. Without the definitions, American English speakers would have a hard time recognizing many of the terms. The same goes for dictionaries specialized to such professions as computer science and culinary arts. As this chapter shows, geographical boundaries are still important, but in many cases, modern technology has allowed them to be superceded by commercial, professional, religious, political, and educational interests.

ENGLISH AS A WORLD LANGUAGE

Bill Bryson

Bill Bryson is an American who lives and writes in England, which gives him an advantage when writing about variations in his native language. His best-selling *The Mother Tongue: English & How It Got That Way,* from which this essay is taken, was published in 1990.

1   In Hong Kong you can find a place called the Plastic Bacon Factory. In Naples, according to the *London Observer,* there is a sports shop called Snoopy's Dribbling. (The name becomes fractionally less alarming when you know that *dribbling* is the European term for moving a soccer ball down the field), while in Brussels there is a men's clothing store called Big Nuts, where on my last visit to the city it had a sign saying: SWEAT—690 FRANCS. (Closer inspection revealed this to be a sweatshirt.) In Japan you can drink Homo Milk or Poccari Sweat (a popular soft drink), eat some chocolates called Hand-Maid Queer-Aid, or go out and buy some Arm Free Grand Slam Munsingwear.

2   In Sarajevo, Yugoslavia, a largely Muslim city seemingly as remote from English-speaking culture as any place in Europe, you can find graffiti saying HEAVY METAL IS LAW! and HOOLIGAN KINGS OF THE NORTH! In the Europa Hotel in the same city, you will find this message on every door: "Guest should announce the abandonment of theirs rooms before 12 o'clock, emptying the room at the latest until 14 o'clock, for the use of the room before 5 at the arrival or after the 16 o'clock at the departure, will be billed as one night more." Is that clear? In Yugoslavia they speak five languages. In not one of them does the word *stop* exist, yet every stop sign in the country says just that.

3   I bring this up here to make the somewhat obvious observation that English is the most global of languages. Products are deemed to be more exciting if they carry English messages even when, as often happens, the messages don't make a lot of sense. I have before me a Japanese eraser which says: "Mr. Friendly Quality Eraser. Mr. Friendly Arrived!! He always stay near you, and steals in your mind to lead you a good situation." On the bottom of the eraser is a further message: "We are ecologically minded. This package will self-destruct in Mother Earth." It is a product that was made in Japan solely for Japanese consumers, yet there is not a word of Japanese on it. Coke cans in Japan come with the slogan I FEEL COKE & SOUND SPECIAL. A correspondent of *The Economist* spotted a T-shirt in Tokyo that said: O.D. ON BOURGEOISIE MILK BOY

MILK. A shopping bag carried a picture of dancing elephants above the legend: ELEPHANT FAMILY ARE HAPPY WITH US. THEIR HUMMING MAKES US FEEL HAPPY. Some of these items betray a distinct, and yet somehow comforting, lack of geographical precision. A shopping bag showing yachts on a blue sea had the message SWITZERLAND: SEASIDE CITY. A range of products manufactured by a company called Cream Soda all used to bear the splendidly vacuous message "Too fast to live, too young to happy." Then some spoilsport informed the company of its error and the second half of the message was changed to "too young to die." What is perhaps most worrying is that these meaningless phrases on clothing are invading the English-speaking world. I recently saw in a London store a jacket with bold lettering that said: RODEO—100% BOYS FOR ATOMIC ATLAS. The jacket was made in Britain. Who by? Who for?

4   So how many people in the world speak English? That's hard to say. We're not even sure how many native speakers there are. Different authorities put the number of people who speak English as a first language at anywhere between 300 million and 400 million. That may seem sloppily imprecise, but there are some sound reasons for the vagueness. In the first place, it is not simply a matter of taking all the English-speaking countries in the world and adding up their populations. America alone has forty million people who don't speak English—about the same as the number of people in England who *do* speak English.

5   Then there is the even thornier problem of deciding whether a person is speaking English or something that is *like* English but is really a quite separate language. This is especially true of the many English-based creoles in the world, such as Krio, spoken in Sierra Leone, and Neo-Melanesian (sometimes called Tok Pisin), spoken in Papua New Guinea. According to Dr. Loreto Todd of Leeds University in England, the world has sixty-one such creoles spoken by up to 200 million people—enough to make the number of English speakers soar, *if* you consider them English speakers.

6   A second and rather harsher problem is deciding whether a person speaks English or simply *thinks* he speaks it. I have before me a brochure from the Italian city of Urbino, which contains a dozen pages of the most gloriously baroque and impenetrable English prose, lavishly garnished with misspellings, unexpected hyphenations, and twisted grammar. A brief extract: "The integrity and thus the vitality of Urbino is no chance, but a conservation due to the factors constituted in all probability by the approximate framework of the unity of the country, the difficulty of communications, the very concentric pattern of hill sistems or the remoteness from hi-ghly developed areas, the force of the original design proposed in its construction, with the means at the disposal of the new sciences of the Renaissance, as an ideal city even." It goes on like that for a dozen pages. There is scarcely a sentence that makes even momentary sense. I daresay that if all the people in Italy who speak English were asked to put up their hands, this author's arms would be one of the first to fly up, but whether he can fairly be said to speak English is, to put it charitably, moot.

7   So there are obvious problems in trying to put a figure to the number of English speakers in the world. Most estimates put the number of native speakers at about 330 million, as compared with 260 million for Spanish, 150 million for Portuguese, and a little over 100 million for French. Of course, sheer numbers mean little. Mandarin Chinese, or Guoyo, spoken by some 750 million people, has twice as many speakers as any other language in the world, but see how far that will get you in Rome or Rochester. No other language than English is spoken as an official language in more countries—forty-four, as against twenty-seven for French and twenty for Spanish—and none is spoken over a wider area of the globe. English is used as an official language in countries with a population of about 1.6 billion, roughly a third of the world total. Of course, nothing like that number of people speak it—in India, for instance, it is spoken by no more than 40 or 50 million people out of a total population of 700 million—but it is still used competently as a second language by perhaps as many as 400 million people globally.

8   Without any doubt, English is the most important language in the world, and it is not hard to find impressive statistics to prove it. "Two thirds of all scientific papers are published in English," says *The Economist*. "Nearly half of all business deals in Europe are conducted in English," says *The Story of English.* "More than seventy percent of the world's mail is written and addressed in English," says Lincoln Barnett in *The Treasure of Our Tongue.* "It is easy to let such impressive figures run away with us. *The Story of English* notes that the main television networks of the United States, Britain, and Canada enjoy audiences that "regularly exceed one hundred million." Since the population of the United Kingdom is 56 million and that of Canada only a little over 25 million, that claim would seem to be exaggerated. So too almost certainly is the same book's claim that "in total there are probably more than a billion speakers of English, at least a quarter of the world's population."

9   The simple fact is that English is not always spoken as widely or as enthusiastically as we might like to think. According to *U.S. News & World Report* [February 18, 1985], even in Switzerland, one of the most polyglot of nations, no more than 10 percent of the people are capable of writing a simple letter in English.

10   What is certain is that English is the most studied and emulated language in the world, its influence so enormous that it has even affected the syntax of other languages. According to a study by Magnus Ljung of Stockholm University, more than half of all Swedes now make plurals by adding *-s*, after the English model, rather than by adding *-ar*, *-or*, or *-er*, in the normal Swedish way. The hunger for English is gargantuan. When the BBC English-teaching series *Follow Me* was first broadcast in China, it drew audiences of up to one hundred million people. (This may also tell us a little something about the quality of alternative viewing in China.) The presenters of the program, Kathy Flower, an unknown in England, is said to be the most familiar British face in China after the queen. At all events, there are more people learning English in China than there are people in the United States. The teaching of English,

according to *The Economist,* is worth 6 billion pounds a year globally. It is estimated to be Britain's sixth largest source of invisible earnings, worth some £500 million a year.

11   English words are everywhere. Germans speak of *die Teenagers* and *das Walkout* and German politicians snarl "No comment" at German journalists. Italian women coat their faces with *col-cream,* Romanians ride the *trolleybus,* and Spaniards, when they feel chilly, don a *sueter.* Almost everyone in the world speaks on the telephone or the telefoon or even, in China, the te le fung. And almost everywhere you can find hamburgers, nightclubs, and television. In 1986, *The Economist* assembled a list of English terms that had become more or less universal. They were: *airport, passport, hotel, telephone, bar, soda, cigarette, sport, golf, tennis, stop, O.K., weekend, jeans, know-how, sex appeal,* and *no problem.* As *The Economist* put it: "The presence of so many words to do with travel, consumables and sport attests to the real source of these exports—America."

12   Usually English words are taken just as they are, but sometimes they are adapted to local needs, often in quite striking ways. The Serbo-Croatians, for instance, picked up the English word *nylon* but took it to mean a kind of shabby and disreputable variation, so that a nylon hotel is a brothel while a nylon beach is the place where nudes frolic. Other nations have left the words largely intact but given the spelling a novel twist. Thus the Ukrainian *herkot* might seem wholly foreign to you until you realized that a *herkot* is what a Ukrainian goes to his barber for. Similarly, unless you heard them spoken, you might not instantly recognize *ajskrym, muving pikceris,* and *peda* as the Polish for ice cream, the Lithuanian for moving pictures, and the Serbo-Croatian for payday. The champion of this naturalization process must be the Italian *schiacchenze,* which is simply a literal rendering of the English *shake hands.*

13   The Japanese are particular masters at the art of seizing a foreign word and alternately beating it and aerating it until it sounds something like a native product. Thus the *sumato* (smart) and *nyuu ritchi* (newly rich) Japanese person seasons his or her conversation with *upatodatu* expressions like *gurama foto* (glamour photo), *haikurasu* (high class), *kyapitaru gein* (capital gain), and *rushawa* (rush hour). . . . But for the most part the Japanese use the same sort of ingenuity in miniaturizing English words as they do in miniaturizing televisions and video cameras. *So modern girl* comes out as *moga, word processor* becomes *wa-pro, mass communications* becomes *masu-komi,* and *commercial* is brusquely truncated into a short, sharp *cm. No-pan,* short for *no-panties,* is a description for bottomless waitresses, while the English words *touch* and *game* have been fused to make *tatchi geimu,* a euphemism for sexual petting.

14   This inclination to hack away at English words until they become something like native products is not restricted to the Japanese. In Singapore, transvestites are known as *shims,* a contraction of *she-hims.* Italians don't go to a nightclub, but just to a *night* (often spelled *nihgt*), while in France a self-service restaurant is simply *le self.* European languages also show a curious tendency to take English participles and give them entirely new meanings, so that the

French don't . . . engage in a spot of sunbathing, but rather go in for *le bronzing*. A tuxedo or dinner jacket in French becomes *un smoking,* while in Italy cosmetic surgery becomes *il lifting.* The Germans are particularly inventive at taking things a step further than it ever occurred to anyone in English. A young person in Germany goes from being in his teens to being in his *twens,* a book that doesn't quite become a best-seller is instead *ein steadyseller,* and a person who is more relaxed than another is *relaxter.*

15   Sometimes new words are made up, as with the Japanese *salryman* for an employee of a corporation. In Germany a snappy dresser is a *dressman.* In France a *recordman* is not a disc jockey, but an athlete who sets a record, while an *alloman* is a switchboard operator (because he says, "allo? allo?"). And just to confuse things, sometimes English words are given largely contrary meanings, so that in France an *egghead* is an idiot while a *jerk* is an accomplished dancer.

16   The most relentless borrowers of English words have been the Japanese. The number of English words current in Japanese has been estimated to be as high as 20,000. It has been said, not altogether wryly, that if the Japanese were required to pay a license fee for every word they used, the American trade deficit would vanish. A count of Western words, mostly English, used in Japanese newspapers in 1964 put the proportion at just under 10 percent. It would almost certainly be much higher now. Among the Japanese borrowings:

erebata—elevator

nekutai—necktie

bata—butter

beikon—bacon

sarada—salad

remon—lemon

chiizu—cheese

bifuteki—beefsteak

hamu—ham

shyanpu setto—shampoo and set

17   Not all languages have welcomed the invasion of English words. The French have been more resistant than most. President François Mitterand declared in 1986, perhaps a trifle excessively: "France is engaged in a war with Anglo-Saxon." The French have had a law against the encroachment of foreign words since as early as 1911, but this was considerably bolstered by the setting up in 1970 of a Commission on Terminology, which was followed in 1975 by another law, called the Maintenance of the Purity of the French Language, which introduced fines for using illegal anglicisms, which in turn was followed in 1984 by the establishment of *another* panel, the grandly named Commissariat Général de la Langue Française. You may safely conclude from all

this that the French take their language very seriously* indeed. . . . More than one observer has suggested that what really rankles the French is not they are borrowing so many words from the rest of the world but that the rest of the world is no longer borrowing so many from them. As the magazine *Le Point* put it: "Our technical contribution stopped with the word *chauffeur.*"

18   The French, it must be said, have not been so rabidly anglophobic as has sometimes been made out. From the outset the government conceded defeat on a number or words that were too well established to drive out: *gadget, holdup, weekend, blu jeans, self-service, manager, marketing,* and many others. Between 1977 and 1987, there were just forty prosecutions for violations of the language laws, almost always involving fairly flagrant abuses. TWA, for instance, was fined for issuing its boarding passes in English only. You can hardly blame the French for taking exception to that. The French also recognize the global importance of English. In 1988, the elite Ecole Centrale de Paris, one of the country's top engineering academies, made it a requirement of graduation that students be able to speak and write fluent English, even if they have no intention of ever leaving France.

19   It would be a mistake to presume that English is widely spoken in the world because it has some overwhelming intrinsic appeal to foreigners. Most people speak it not because it gives them pleasure to help out American and British monoglots who cannot be troubled to learn a few words of their language, believe it or not, but because they need it to function in the world at large. They may like a few English words splashed across their T-shirts and shopping bags, but that isn't to say that is what they want to relax with in the evening.

20   Go to Amsterdam or Antwerp or Oslo and you will find that almost everyone speaks superb English, and yet if you venture into almost any bookstore in those cities you will usually find only a small selection of books in English. For the most part, people want to read works in their own language. Equally they want to watch television in their own language. In the coastal areas of Holland and Belgium, where most people can both speak English and receive British television broadcasts, most still prefer to watch local programs even when they are palpably inferior to the British product (i.e., almost invariably). Similarly, two English-language satellite networks in Europe, Sky TV and Super Channel, had some initial success in West Germany, but as soon as two competing satellite networks were set up transmitting more or less the same programs but dubbed into German, the English-language networks' joint share slumped to less than 1 percent—about as much as could be accounted for by English-speaking natives living in West Germany. The simple fact is that German viewers, even when they speak English well, would rather watch Dallas dubbed badly into German than in the original English. And who can blame them?

21   In many places English is widely resented as a symbol of colonialism. In India, where it is spoken by no more than 5 percent of the population at the

*See the next article, by Simmons. —Ed.

very most, the constitution was written in English and English was adopted as a foreign language not out of admiration for its linguistic virtues but as a necessary expedient. In a country in which there are 1,652 languages and dialects, including 15 official ones, and in which no one language is spoken by more than 16 percent of the population, a neutral outside language has certain obvious practicalities. Much the same situation prevails in Malaysia, where the native languages include Tamil, Portuguese, Thai, Punjabi, twelve versions of Chinese, and about as many of Malay. Traditionally, Malay is spoken in the civil service, Chinese in business, and English in the professions and in education. Yet these countries are almost always determined to phase English out. India had hoped to eliminate it as an official language by 1980 and both Malaysia and Nigeria have been trying to do likewise since the 1970s.

Comprehension

1. Words to talk about:

   - many English-based *creoles*
   - to put it charitably, *moot*
   - affected the *syntax* of other languages
   - alternately beating it and *aerating* it
   - take English *participles*

2. What do speakers in Serbia and Croatia mean by a nylon hotel? Have you heard things in America described as chintzy or sleazy? These two adjectives are also taken from particular kinds of cloth. How are they similar to the nylon hotel example?
3. Explain the meanings of these German words that are based on English: *twens, steadyseller, relaxter.*
4. What is an *alloman* in French?

Discussion

1. Why is it so hard to determine how many people speak English?
2. What's the difference in world impact between the way English is spoken by some 330 million people and the way Mandarin Chinese is spoken by some 750 million people?
3. What do the various "foreign" spellings of English words reveal about the complexities of changing to a system of phonological spelling?
4. From looking at the Japanese equivalents to the English words listed on page 433, what observations can you make about the Japanese sound system?

5. Look at the pictures on this page and on page 437. At the time they were taken in Kabul, Afghanistan, the Soviet Union had not yet invaded, and ambitious merchants were trying to court business from English speakers. Other signs posted in Afghanistan at the same time as the ones pictured include: Fipst Aid Station, Plumbery, Workshp, Kandaharp Aint House, and Watches Maker. Try to figure out the underlying reasons for the mistakes in English.

6. Use the same possibilities to try to explain these other confusions. John Murphy, a names consultant in London, has a collection of products whose English names are "unusual." From Morocco he has a hair straightener named Stiff and from Japan a moisturized tissue named Pocket Wetties. *Japanese Jive: Wacky and Wonderful Products from Japan,* a book by Caroline McKeldin (Tengu Books, 1993), cites Crunky Kids as the name for a crunchy chocolate bar, Dew Dew dried apples, NFL Grease hair dressing for men, and Brown Gross Foam hair mousse. Richard Lederer collects "Anguished English" (see his books *Anguished English* [Dell, 1989] and *More Anguished English* [Delacorte, 1993]), including such signs as these from hotels around the world:

Ladies are kindly requested not to have their babies in the cocktail bar. (Beirut)

Swimming is forbidden in the absence of a savior. (French Riviera)

We highly recommend the hotel tart. (Torremolinos)

Hot and cold water running up and down the stairs. (Italy)

7. As you read Living Language 9.1 explain where each incident fits in relation to Bill Bryson's claim that English is "without any doubt . . . the most important language in the world," or in relation to his cautionary statement that, at the same time, it "is not always spoken as widely or as enthusiastically as we might like to think."

LIVING LANGUAGE 9.1

It's a Small, Small World

As these examples show, when speakers from different languages interact, they will leave their "footprints in the sand."

- Few of the American children who play with Lego building blocks know that the name comes from Danish *leg godt,* which means "play well." Nor do the players of the Pac Man video game know that its name comes from the Japanese slang word *paku-paku,* which describes the opening and closing of a mouth while eating. The almost-as-popular Donkey Kong, which features an aggressive gorilla, was supposedly misnamed through a translation problem. If someone hadn't confused a *d* with an *m,* the game would have been named Monkey Kong in honor of King Kong.

- How small the world has grown is shown by the problems that the Anheuser-Busch company ran into when selling Budweiser beer throughout Europe. Back in the 1870s, founders of the American company chose Budweiser as their product name "in honor" of the area around Budweis, Czechoslovakia (now named Ceske Budejovice), which since medieval times has been known for its beer. When the Soviet Union broke up, the Czechoslovak brewery that for 150 years has had the name of Budweiser began expanding throughout Europe causing a trademark war. The small brewery refused to sell their company to Anheuser Busch so that today the American company can sell Budweiser in ten European countries that recognize its trademark, while selling Bud in eight that do not. Germany and Austria allow neither trademark preferring to drink the Czech Budweiser.

- "Welcome to the National Hockey League, a United Nations sport if ever there was one," read a newspaper story about foreign players joining American teams. When Coyotes goalie Nikolai Khabibulin, who was born in the former Soviet Union, joined the team he knew not one word of English. The same was true for Oleg Tverdovsky and Igor Korolev. The three players, who have now been in the States for several years, said they learned the language of hockey first because of all the repetition during practice. Nevertheless, they felt left out when team members would joke, and sentences spoken on television sounded "like all one word." The players still find it hard to go to a doctor, rent a house, or buy a car. In 1995, 372 NHL players came from Canada as compared to 107 from the United States, 46 from Russia, 27 from Sweden, 23 from the Czech Republic, 12 from Finland, and 1, 2, or 3 from Germany, Slovakia, England, Latvia, Ukraine, Northern Ireland, Norway, Poland, Scotland, South Africa, and South Korea. (*Arizona Republic,* Sept. 28, 1996)

- "Language Woes Threaten Air Safety," was the headline on a story about how "an unfamiliar turn of phrase, a heavy accent, an overly abbreviated command in the exchange between pilots and air-traffic controllers," can have deadly consequences. While English is the de facto language of world-wide aviation, some countries (France, for example) still allow traffic controllers to speak in the native language to pilots of their own airline. Other pilots object because when there's another plane in the air they need to know "where that aircraft is and what it's going to do." And even when all parties are using English, there can still be problems. A 1990 crash of an Avianca jet in Cove Neck, New York, was probably caused by a pilot saying, "We're running out of fuel." If he had said, "Fuel emergency!" he would have been cleared for immediate landing. The deadliest crash in the world (in 1977 at the Tenerife Airport in Spain 582 people died) is also thought to have resulted from a communication misunderstanding. Pilots and air-traffic controllers from around the world are working to devise a standardized phrase book. (Associated Press, Nov. 16, 1996)

- *Umami,* a Japanese word meaning "delicious" and pronounced "ooh-mommy," has been chosen as the name for that "savory sensation that swaddles your mouth after devouring the first bite of a piping hot pizza with all the extras." Scientists at the University of Miami medical school are exploring the thousands of taste buds imbedded in the human mouth. They say that *umami* is fifth in line for recognition, after sweet, sour, salty, and bitter. It is the taste associated with monosodium glutamate (MSG), the flavor enhancer often found in Asian foods. (Knight-Ridder Newspapers, June 29, 1997)

- *Occhi di lupo,* Italian for "wolf's eyes," is metaphorically used to describe large tubes of pasta; *shiro goma* is Japanese for "white sesame seeds" (*kuro goma* for black); and *foofoo, foufou, fufu,*and *foutou* are all West African for a thick porridge made from ground cassava, corn, rice and/or yams. They are only a few of the 16,000 definitions in *Webster's New World Dictionary of Culinary Arts* (Prentice-Hall, 1997). It took the co-authors (Sarah Labensky, Gaye Ingram, and Steve Labensky) three years to do the research. Previous food dictionaries had been Eurocentric. While this one includes all the standard French terms, it also includes words from Thai, Vietnamese, Japanese, Hindi, and Swahili. (*Arizona Republic,* June 15, 1997)

- When the British officially left Hong Kong in July of 1997, they left behind many English names. For the past two decades Hong Kong teenagers have been choosing their own Western style names as a way of "asserting their individuality, and their independence" from parents. Even those who speak little English have chosen names from dictionaries and magazines. *New York Times* reporter Barbara Basler found young people named Sherlock, Lenin, Apple, Psyche, Creamy, and Cinderella. A man named Civic Wong, explained that he had originally chosen Civil but "Civic just sounded better." A medical student rejected his professor's advice that Westerners would not take him seriously and insisted on keeping his chosen name of Onion. (*New York Times,* Oct. 28, 1993)

continued

LIVING LANGUAGE 9.1

It's a Small, Small World   continued

■ "Along with *Coke, CNN* and *Visa, stress* is rapidly spreading throughout the world. Or at least the word for it is," wrote Richard A. Schweder. "From tongue to tongue there are, of course, variations in the voicing and stressing of *stress*," but that doesn't keep it from being "on loan to most of the major languages of the world," where it is replacing such words as *angst* and *Weltschmerz*. Schweder wrote, "Imprecise and evasive language may be a disaster for science, but it is a boon in everyday life. 'I am stressed out.' is non-accusatory, apolitical and detached." It's a "low-cost way" to release tension. (*New York Times,* Jan. 26, 1997)

■ In the late 1980s, two dozen different spellings appeared in news stories about Libya's leader known variously as Qaddafi, Qadhafi, Gaddafi, Kaddafi, Quaddafi, Al-Gathafi, and El-Gadhafi. The *New York Times, The Wall Street Journal,* the Library of Congress, and the two English newspapers in Libya each used different versions. The problem resulted from the fact that the English language has no sound exactly matching the gutteral sound with which the name begins.

BAR ENGLISH? FRENCH BICKER ON BARRICADES

Marlise Simons

Bill Bryson's book *The Mother Tongue* was published in 1990. Since he did his research, the French government instituted yet another new campaign designed to protect "the purity" of the French language as described in this 1994 article from the *New York Times*. The law, which was being debated at the time this article was written, received formal approval. Other countries have expressed similar sentiments but have focused mainly on signs. For example, in the mid-1990s, the city of Canton in China banned foreign names from restaurants, bars, and buildings. The Wall Street Financial Plaza, Monte Carlo Villas, and Manhattan Plaza were held up as especially unsuitable names, which had to be changed. According to the *Baltimore Sun* (April 4, 1997), the mayor of Moscow also instituted a campaign against English signs that used such words as *supermarket, minimarket, drugstore, pub,* and *shop.*

1   The French official, elegant as always, walked into the Foreign Ministry salon, bowed slightly and began, "Le briefing est off the record "

2   Soon, official use of such a phrase will be against the law if the Culture Ministry has its way. So will Fun Radio's un-French name and its babble about "le listing" on "le hit parade." Not to mention Ford Motor Company's advertisement for a new car equipped with "le air bag."

3   France's old and losing battle against the English language has moved into a new and touchy phase now that the Government has presented a draft law to put up a barrier against further foreign incursions.

4   The proposed law, which faces a vote in the National Assembly this spring, would ban foreign words from virtually all business and government communications, radio and television broadcasts, public announcements and advertising messages whenever a "suitable local equivalent" exists in French.

5   Labels and instructions for products would have to include French. So would conferences and publications arranged by French citizens. Violators could be punished with fines, so far unspecified, or lose state financing.

6   In a nation where debates over language keep many people entertained, writers, singers, politicians and teachers have already warmed to the issue, and participants have split into several camps. One sees itself—and English— as modern, hip, flexible; another identifies with the glory of French culture.

7   A third camp holds that while the other two exaggerate their claims, the world's cultural diversity is threatened by increasingly standardized products and advertising-speak.

8   The proposed law is "pas tres cool," grumped le "disque-jockey" of the popular radio station Sky-rock.

9   The novelist Jean d'Ormesson, who has always defended his national tongue, says the bill is ridiculous. "Borrowed words have always enriched the language," he said. "We have accepted good foreign words like sofa and opera."

10   *Informatin,* a new Paris tabloid, sniffed, "All proposals designed to legislate on the use of language give off a stale smell."

11   But the Government, heartened by its victory last December in retaining the right to levy taxes and set quotas on imports of American-made movies, television programs and music recordings, seems determined to win passage of the law in the name of defending French culture.

"AN ACT OF FAITH"

12   Recently the National Assembly adopted a law stipulating that a minimum of 40 percent of the songs broadcast by radio stations be in French.

13   A majority of lawmakers in the conservative-dominated National Assembly are in the Government camp on the language bill, as are a number of intellectuals. Among them is Claude Hagège, a prominent linguist, who said that while he was not against the introduction of loan words, "we should act against excesses."

14   Last week, Prime Minister Edouard Balladur inaugurated a Higher Council of the French language and solemnly told its 29 members that defending their tongue was "an act of faith in the future of our country." Maurice Druon, a secretary to the French Academy, the traditional arbiter of language, has suggested that "observers" start monitoring usage on radio and on television.

15   The enemy, unnamed in the draft law, is English, of course, which has burrowed its way into music, sports, commerce and science, undercutting elaborate French words and phrases with snappy expressions like "le marketing," "le cash flow," "le stress," "le kit" and "le brainstorming."

16   Advertising agents and scientists seem flummoxed by the proposed ban. Officials at the Pasteur Institute, the renowned medical research center, said they were unsure, that under the new restrictions, they could continue three specialized publications that have English titles and largely English texts.

17   "We don't know where we stand," said Nadine Peyrolo, one official. "It will be very expensive if we must provide simultaneous translation for every colloquium."

18   France has had linguistic purges before, repressing its regional tongues until early in this century and turning against English in the 1960s, when American culture and technology started galloping across Western Europe.

19   *Le Canard Enchaîné,* the satirical weekly, said the proposed law would have no more effect than a 1975 measure banishing foreign words from advertising and radio and television news.

20   "Language, like French genius, comes and goes," the weekly said. "At the moment, neither is in good shape. Like the English, we can't get used to the idea of being a second-rank nation."

THE MARAUDING ANGLO-SAXONS

21   Culture Minister Jacques Toubon, the bill's promoter, makes the opposite case, saying the law would permit France to "better assume its responsibility" at the forefront of countries in which French is still widely used. Forty-seven countries attended the summit meeting of francophone nations in Mauritius last October.

22   "The use of a foreign language is not innocent," Mr. Toubon said. He said the "Anglo-Saxon" countries, far from being satisfied with the hegemony of English, were making "considerable efforts" to conquer new linguistic territory. English is so popular in France that almost 80 percent of high school students choose it as their foreign language of study.

23   Despite its air of general disapproval, the French Academy regularly published neologisms and borrowed words that it has approved.

24   Wordsmiths have in many cases come up with French alternatives for innovations like the microchip ("puce," which means flea) and software ("logiciel"). The name of the train that is to ferry passengers through a tunnel under the English Channel is to change its name from Le Shuttle to La Navette.

25   This week the Delegation for the French Language, appointed by the Culture Ministry, is to publish a dictionary of French terms it recommends as substitutes for English words adopted in France.

26   Government officials insist that the campaign is not anti-American but part of an effort to help French people who are often unfairly confronted with job contracts or product information in a foreign language.

27   But the movement seems to be aimed chiefly at suppressing "Franglais," a hybrid born of the French penchant for borrowing English words and adding something to them or subtly changing their meaning. In France, "le pressing" is the dry cleaner, "le footing" means jogging, and "loger" is computer-speak for "to log on."

28   Because the French love words, the issue has led to endless debate on portentous questions like: Does language determine the way people think and act? Are the French more elegant in expression or just long-winded?

29   To a foreigner, the French substitutes proposed for some English expressions may seem cumbersome as well as longer. If the Government triumphs, cars will no longer be equipped with an air bag, but the "coussin gonflable de protection."

Some English words commonly used in France, and the French equivalents recommended by a government panel.

AIRBAG = coussin gonflable de protection

BEST SELLER = succès de librairie

BRUNCH = grand déjeuner

COOKIE = sablé américain

CAMERAMAN = cadreur

COCKPIT = habitacle

DATABANK = banque de données

FAST FOOD = restauration rapide

JUMBO JET = gros-porteur

MARKETING = mercatique

PARKING (to mean "parking lot") = parc de stationnement

POPCORN = maïs soufflé

PRIME TIME = heures de grande écoute

TALK SHOW = causerie

COMPREHENSION

1. Words to talk about:

   - further foreign *incursions*
   - standardized products and *advertising-speak*
   - provide *simultaneous translation*
   - satisfied with the *hegemony* of English
   - regularly published *neologisms*

2. In France, what are the three major opinions or "camps"?

DISCUSSION

1. What recent successes related to protecting French language and culture gave the government confidence that it could get the proposed language rules approved?

2. Which of the actions do you think will be the most effective? Which will be the easiest to enforce? Why?
3. What factors encouraged the French adoption (and adaptation) of these particular terms?

le marketing	le cash flow
le stress	le kit
le brainstorming	le footing
loger	le pressing

4. What are some of the complications of the new law?
5. English began as a Germanic language, but after the French conquered England in 1034, many French words came into English. Look in the chart at the preferred "French" terms. How many of the words seem at least vaguely recognizable to English speakers? What are some English cognates related to these words? What does this show about the "purity" of language?
6. In the article, did anyone use humor to argue a point? If so, where?
7. How effective do you think the dictionary that is to be published of French terms to replace English words will be? Could it have the opposite effect of publicizing the English words and increasing their use by people who are not in sympathy with the law?

THE OFFICIAL LANGUAGE CONTROVERSY

While Americans are not concerned in the same way as the French, the Chinese, and the Russians are about words from other languages coming into English, we too are protective of our language and culture. The most visible manifestation has been the passing of laws declaring English as our official language. By the end of 1996, 23 states and more than 40 cities had enacted "Official English" or "English-Only" laws, described by many observers as symbolic and unenforced. In December of 1996, the U.S. House of Representatives passed such a law (voided by the Senate) called "English Empowerment Act of 1996."

Eight years earlier, 50.5 percent of Arizona voters had said "yes" to an Official Language constitutional amendment, Proposition 106, which stated, "The English language is the language of the ballot, the public schools and all government functions and actions." The Amendment was more restrictive than most, and was challenged in Federal Court and declared unconstitutional. Arizona Governor Rose Mofford declined to appeal the decision, but one of the groups that had originally promoted the law appealed the Federal Court decision to the U.S. Supreme Court. Arguments were presented in 1996, and in July of 1997, the Court voided the 9th Circuit Court's ruling on grounds related to legal procedures. This sent the case back to the Arizona Supreme Court, which in June 1998 declared the law invalid. In the meantime, it is likely that the U.S. Supreme Court will accept other cases asking for an answer as to whether Official Language laws violate the U.S. Constitution's guarantee of free speech.

Because Arizona's law was the first to go before the U.S. Supreme Court, and because the arguments occurred at about the same time that the U.S. House of Representatives passed its "English Empowerment Act," public interest was high. Reprinted here are items from various public forums all treating the topic of English as an official language. As you read them, notice how they differ in tone and style. Also, notice how many underlying issues come into the picture. It's similar to what hikers say about descending into the Grand Canyon; the deeper down they go the bigger it seems to get.

The first article, written by a sociolinguist who teaches at Arizona State University, has been excerpted from a bulletin meant to inform English teachers about the issue. This is followed by a sample of "letters to the editor," then soundbites from activists on both sides of the issue.

English-Only: As American as Apple Pie?

Karen L. Adams

1   The Arizona campaign for Proposition 106 made clear to those watching and listening that language choice is a "political issue," not because people were asked to cast a vote, but because when people anywhere elect one language to a status different from another language they also elect the speakers of that language to a different status.

2   How can that be? Proponents of 106 (mostly U.S. English, a national organization, and the affiliated Arizonans for Official English) told us that making English the Official Language was really no different from choosing a state bird or flower. They argued that since English is the common language of the nation, why not recognize that fact legally? The law would only be a recognition of existing conditions. They claimed also that language is a neutral code for communication like Morse code, and the selection of English merely expedient.

3   But a "symbolic" law is not a neutral one especially when the symbol is language. Language itself is a symbol, not the neutral code that people claim. Language is a symbol of social identity, including one's friends, family, ethnicity, race, class, gender identification, religion, and occupation. It is a symbol of all social identities and relationships mediated by language. By making English the Official Language of a state or a country, voters give it privileges as a symbol of social identity above all others.

4   The images we saw before the election in 1988—Nazis goosestepping across our TV screens, American flags on both pro and con bumperstickers, and second-generation Americans proudly explaining on television and radio how their parents learned English when they came to the United States—reflected the intensity of feelings both for and against the amendment. The flag image was especially interesting because both sides used it. On a personal level, opponents to the amendment associate the U.S. flag with their viewpoint because of their own patriotism. Hispanic organizations such as LULAC (League of United Latin American Citizens) and MALDEF (Mexican American Legal Defense and Education Fund) and some Asian American organizations see no conflict in a desire to value their culture and heritage and their languages while being devoted American citizens.

5   For many Arizona communities, the claim of a special status for English was insulting because their non-English speaking communities existed long before the English speaking ones. These include Native American, as well as some Hispanic, communities. Since the increase in Official English language

laws at state levels and the continued lobbying for a federal English Language Amendment, the U.S. Congress recognized the irony of placing English above indigenous languages. In October of 1990, it passed the Native American Language Rights Act. Many Native American communities have also developed language policies to counter pressure from omnipresent English use.

6   Opponents of Official English in Arizona were also concerned for the kinds of bilingual services that would be eliminated with the passage of an Official English amendment. Many vital services—hospital, police and fire emergency numbers, driver's license tests, employment and unemployment applications—are now available in bilingual or trilingual formats. Losing these services would be devastating to many citizens. Critics noted that elderly people and women in minority communities would suffer the most because their lives are often more restricted, which means they are more likely not to have learned English.

7   Not surprisingly, the proponents of Official English consider their position equally "apple pie" and American flag. They perceive that among the growing non-white population, a large number do not speak English, and, worse yet, they do not want to speak English. They see newcomers demanding and receiving special language treatment that was not given to earlier immigrants. They think bilingual policies, especially those related to education and voting rights, discourage and postpone the acquisition of English.

8   These concerns, deserve serious consideration. Let's turn first to the perception that recent immigrants are not learning English. While there is a steady influx of immigrants from non-English speaking countries, the consensus of studies done on these populations is that as they continue to live in the United States they become fluent in English and lose their skill in their native languages at approximately the same rate as earlier immigrant groups.

9   Even without considering the benefits of better occupational opportunities, non-English speakers are highly motivated to learn English, and many find themselves on long waiting lists for classes because there are not enough community programs and teachers. Contrary to the perceptions of Official English supporters, special efforts are needed to help people maintain their native languages such as Navajo, Hopi and Zuni. This is also true for such languages as Tagalog, Thai, and even Spanish. Since skill in another language is both an economic and an intellectual resource for individuals and the country, the maintenance of skills in languages other than English is important.

10   Like the flag, bilingual education is used as an arguing point on both sides of the issue. This is possible because the evaluation of such programs has not been uniform. Supporters of Official English think that bilingual education programs cost excessive amounts of money while discouraging students from learning English. They argue that full immersion into English worked for earlier immigrants and will now. However, one of the most comprehensive studies published in 1991 by David Ramirez ("Study Finds Native Language Instruction Is a Plus," *NABE News* 14:5, 1, 20–23), shows that

children's acquisition of English was less successful in immersion programs (where almost all teaching is in English) and in early-exit programs. The development of language skills was about the same for students who transferred in two or three years to English-only classrooms as it was for those who stayed in bilingual classrooms until sixth grade. However, those who had bilingual instruction until sixth grade had a higher level of achievement in mathematics.

11   Some supporters of Official English are genuinely concerned about the rights of non-English speaking populations. For example, a liberal area in California voted for an advisory policy against multilingual ballots because they were convinced by Official English information that ballots printed in different languages gave politicians who spoke minority languages control over the information that voters received. This perception resulted from a lack of understanding of the workings of multilingual communities, where information from English-speaking groups is spread by bilingual speakers.

12   Of course, minority voters are concerned about issues of quality education and equal access to the American economy. When lobbying groups convince them that Official English will somehow improve their opportunities, they may vote for it, but typically not when they learn that the underlying intent of many of those who promote Official English is to eliminate bilingual education and services.

13   Another area of concern among proponents is the belief that the existence of many languages within one country is correlated with civil strife. Surveys of the nations of the world indicate that there are few monolingual nations, and in multilingual countries there are only a few where conflicts have linguistic overtones. A study by Joshua Fishman and F. Solano (published in *Language and Ethnicity in Minority Sociolinguistic Perspective*, Philadelphia: Multilingual Matters, LTC, 1989) found contributing factors to strife to be a combination of deprivation, authoritarianism, and modernization. When these factors exist, then language and other cultural factors such as religion and race are often exploited to mobilize people to support competing sides. In other words, balkanization is much more complicated than a matter of people speaking different languages. Not all proponents of Official English believe such studies, but we need to recognize that multilingualism does not of necessity lead to conflict and that conflict can exist in countries which are monolingual as shown by our own civil war.

14   Proponents are also concerned about protecting the rights of English speakers. *The U.S. English Newsletter* reports cases of discrimination against English speakers in the workplace and elsewhere. Ironically, these are the same concerns that opponents of Official English have. The opponents also point to what seem to be increases in discrimination since the passage of Official English legislation in some states. Both proponents and opponents seek to secure language and individual rights, but each group sees the opposite effect coming from Official English language legislation.

15   The Official English movement is not likely to go away. U.S. English is still actively pushing for a federal language amendment as well as for state legislation, and it is unclear what either state or federal legislation would entail. Even before the Arizona law was declared unconstitutional, the Attorney General said he would argue for its interpretation in the most limited sense; i.e., that only official government acts (legislation, lawsuits, and rules) be in English. Work leading to such acts would not have to be carried out in English.

16   The hope of those who are promoting Official Language laws is that enough states will pass such laws that the way will be eased for an amendment to the U.S. Constitution, the ELA (English Language Amendment). Opponents fear that if such an amendment were passed, support for bilingual education, balloting, and other policies would shortly disappear.

17   In America, this is not a new issue. The founders of the U.S. government held heated debates about whether to designate English an Official Language and whether to create a language academy like those in France and Spain. The new nation was linguistically diverse with German speakers making up at least 6 percent of the population. The intensity of the original debate is shown by this statement against the Pennsylvania Dutch (from *Deutch* meaning "German") made in 1751 by Benjamin Franklin, and quoted by K. Karst in Volume 64:304 (1986) of the *North Carolina Law Review:*

> Why should the Palatine bores be suffered to swarm into our settlements, and, by herding together, establish their language and manners to the exclusion of ours? Why should Pennsylvania, founded by the English, become a colony of aliens who will shortly be so numerous as to Germanize us instead of our Anglifying them?

The founders of the United States worked their way through even such impassioned outbursts as this. They were wise about many issues. Perhaps we should follow their lead and let English continue to win people over because of its role, not only as the language of the majority, but also as the language of wider communication and world-wide status.

A Sampling of Letters to the Editor About Arizona's Proposition 106

1   This is an English-speaking country, and a person who doesn't learn English will have pretty much a dead-end life. We all knew that long before someone dreamed up Official English. Why, then, was Official English ruled unconstitutional if all it did was confirm what already exists?

2   Because that wasn't all it did. Because in the guise of promoting language unity, it tried to gut the First Amendment and the dignity of other languages. If two State of Arizona employees talked about state business in private in a language other than English, it would have been illegal. If the state hosted a trade delegation from a foreign country, offering greetings in the language of that country, it would have been illegal. If an information officer at the state capitol building spoke some language other than English in giving directions to a non-English-speaking tourist, it would have been illegal. The examples go on and on.

3   Of course, Official English proponents say that none of these examples are what they intended. However, saying that no government action can be in any language other than English means exactly what it says. That's why the courts threw Official English out. It was a glossed-up attempt to restrict free speech and to meddle in people's lives under the guise of promoting language unity. It promoted divisiveness and exclusionism, not unity.

4   People cite Quebec as an example of what can happen without language unity. However, there is no valid comparison to be drawn. Separatist sentiment is as old as Quebec itself. It involves much more than just language, and it exists in spite of, not because of, the bilingualism legislation that Canada's Parliament enacted in the late 1960s. Forcing everyone in Quebec to speak English would solve the separatism problem about as effectively as burning down your house would fix a leaky faucet.

5   Whether new immigrants or just tourists passing through, we will always have people whose English skills leave something to be desired. There are surely much better ways to communicate with these people than to tell them, as Official English tried to, to speak English or get lost.

Sid Lachter
Phoenix Gazette, March 26, 1996

6   In 1915 my father was an immigrant from Germany. He married a German woman, so I'm 100 percent German. He didn't cost our government one penny because he was a skilled machinist that our country needed. He applied for a job in his skill and was told that he had to learn to speak English first. Then he worked in a coal mine and studied English. He studied a year and then qualified for the machinist job and was hired.

7   Today, many states are printing ballots and other official items in a foreign language, or more than one language, costing us tax dollars. Some schools have foreign-language teachers teaching a foreign language to our children. This is not the melting pot that made this country great. Although my father and mother could speak German perfectly, they only spoke English to me, and I never even learned the German language.

8   At the same time, foreign immigrants moved into my neighborhood. My father said he wanted to be 100 percent American, so he changed our name

to Brown. I attended grade school with German, Polish, French, English, American, Scottish and Italian students.

9   We had American English-speaking teachers and we learned to communicate in the English language. This was called the melting pot because we all learned to speak and communicate in English.

10   When World War II began, most of us entered the military. To communicate on the ground and in the air on radio was a life or death matter. We had no problems because we all understood each other speaking English.

11   If we had a war today many immigrants would be useless because of their inability to speak English. They couldn't even be trained to fight.

12   Although the ability to speak other languages helps us in competing in the world's economy, we must have a common language.

Richard F. Brown
Phoenix Gazette, June 25, 1996

13   I have a friend who asserts that "America would be stronger if it were more united, especially linguistically." The notion of "English Only" is an issue simmering just below the surface of American society, especially in border states.

14   True supporters of the English Only movement often cite costs associated with printing bilingual ballots, which perhaps is a reasonable concern from an economic point. But if one errs in tinkering with democracy, I would hope the error would be toward more inclusiveness, not less.

15   I respectfully disagreed with my friend and made my own assertion: "America is strong because of its linguistic diversity." Then I told my friend a story that really got him to thinking.

16   In the early 1900s, the official government policy toward American Indians could be summed up in one word—*assimilation*. Complete assimilation into the fabric of the dominant English-speaking society. Speaking their native tongue was discouraged and in many settings it was not tolerated. The Indians resisted and held on to their language and culture, as they do today.

17   Now skip ahead a few years to 1939 and World War II, and the attack on Pearl Harbor of Dec. 7, 1941, which made clear that America was now at war, ready or not. As the war got uglier and more dangerous, America had a continuing and urgent need to transmit information that could not be understood or "decoded" by the enemy. Enter the Navajo code talkers, who played a key role in America's victory.

18   What if the Navajos and their offspring had let their language die and fade into history, as official government policy dictated just a generation or so earlier?

19   America is strong because of its linguistic diversity, not despite its linguistic diversity. My friend insisted on a real-life example and so I told him this story.

Stephen C. Ponton
Arizona Republic, Jan. 3, 1996

Soundbites About National Legislation

1 "Language other than English is used in official government business only to promote vital interests, such as national security, law enforcement, border enforcement, civil rights, or to assure access to government services, such as police protection, public safety, health care, and voting. Government business conducted only in English would decrease administrative efficiency and exclude taxpaying Americans who are not proficient in English from education, employment, voting, and equal participation in our society."

> Bill Clinton, Presidential Candidate
> Associated Press, Oct. 11, 1996

2 "A common language is one of the strongest ties that binds us together as Americans. As president, I intend to have English declared the official language of the United States and to reform federally financed bilingual education programs to help students completely master English in a timely fashion."

> Bob Dole, Presidential Candidate
> Associated Press, Oct. 11, 1996

3 "This is not a First Amendment case. This is an employers' speech case. We're talking about the language of government. The measure requires only that official government acts, such as documents, be in English."

> Robert Park, Chairman
> Arizonans for Official English,
> *Arizona Republic*, Jan. 6, 1996

4 "The political crowd wanted something tough-minded to take back to the hustings. So the House passed the English Empowerment Act of 1996, which names English as the official language in the land of E Pluribus Unum. Is it needed? No. Will it play in Podunk? Probably. These are decidedly anti-immigrant times."

> Editorial, *Arizona Republic*, Aug. 7, 1997

5 "The bill is extremely divisive, and it doesn't accomplish what its supporters say their aim is, which is to bring immigrants into the American mainstream. It is so hypocritical to us that the people who are promoting this are the same ones who slashed the budgets for English as a second language and bilingual education."

> Karen Narasaki, Executive Director
> National Asian Pacific American Legal
> Consortium, *Washington Post*, Aug. 2, 1996

6   [After citing a General Accounting Office study showing that 97 percent of the U.S. population speaks English well] "The measure is unnecessary and dangerous. The English language in the United States is not in jeopardy. . . . It [the bill] is being done for the sake of symbolism and for the sake of trying to earn cheap political points."

Cecilia Munoz, speaking for the National
Council of La Raza, *Washington Post*, Aug. 2, 1996

7   "As Official English advocates, we are merely trying to legislate common sense. If someone uses a few words of Urdu to explain something to an elderly person, we don't mind. The question is one of government entitlement."

James Boulet Jr., Executive Director of English First
Washington Post, Aug. 2, 1996

8   "What sort of message is the House sending to other governments—the very ones the United States tries to win over in the war for international trade?"

Editorial, *Arizona Business Gazette*, Aug. 1, 1996

Comprehension

1. Words to talk about:

   ■   relationships *mediated* by language
   ■   Nazis *goosestepping* across our TV screens
   ■   placing English above *indigenous* languages
   ■   pressure from *omnipresent* English use
   ■   *monolingual* and *multilingual* countries
   ■   *Balkanization* is much more complicated
   ■   *Palatine* bores
   ■   our *Anglifying* them
   ■   back to the *hustings*
   ■   land of *E Pluribus Unum*

2. What is the difference in connotation between: English-Only law, Official Language act, and English Empowerment act?

Discussion

1. Why isn't designating English the official language similar to designating a state flower or a state bird?

2. Make a list of the various issues that Adams brought up in her essay. Find at least three examples in the letters to the editor or in the soundbites where what people said illustrated one of the issues that she discussed.
3. Choose some examples from the letters to the editor or from the soundbites to illustrate how people's personal experiences influence their political decisions. The soundbites are so short that most of your clues will have to come from the person's affiliation or identification.
4. Do you find yourself attracted to the statements that reinforce ideas you already held before you read this section? What came closest to giving you new insight or to making you change your mind? Why?
5. Will the issue be settled if, and when, the Supreme Court renders a decision on the matter of Official English in relation to the United States Constitution's guarantee of free speech? Why or why not?
6. Adams cites Fishman and Solano's finding that deprivation, authoritarianism, and modernization contribute to civil strife. Why or how can these factors make for problems?
7. Explain the different perceptions of the following issues that are held by supporters and opponents of English-Only laws: a definition of patriotism; the effects of bilingual education; the role language plays in political strife; how fast immigrants learn English.

BUT A LANGUAGE SHOULDN'T CHANGE THAT FAST

William W. West

As this English teacher found when he returned to Japan after having been away for forty years, a lot can change over four decades. Just as many, or even more, changes took place in his native language of English, but because he learned about them gradually they didn't seem as startling. His article was published in the *English Journal* in 1986. Because of increased international communication between Japan and its trading partners, if he returned today he would probably find a whole new set of changes.

1   It was an ego trip last summer when I was—at 60—the oldest person involved in an exchange program at Showa University in Fujiyoshida, Japan. In Japan, most people retire at 55, so in many situations I was the senior person present. When I went to Japan 40 years ago at the age of 19, I was usually the youngest. You can imagine my surprise when in a mixed group of Japanese and Americans I was called upon to describe life in Japan in 1945.

2   One of the first communication problems between Gaijin (Westerners) and the Japanese came in 1549 when the Portuguese missionary, Saint Francis Xavier, came from India to Kagoshima. Realizing that Japanese had no word quite equivalent to the Portuguese *theos* for the concept of the Christian God, St. Francis determined to introduce both the concept and a new word at a huge outdoor gathering.

3   Even at that time, the Japanese had a surprisingly high literacy rate, so the sainted missionary hired a sign painter to produce a banner bearing kanji symbols for the new word. He intended, at the appropriate moment, to signal acolytes to raise the banner and thus reinforce the sound of the new concept with Japanese symbols.

4   Unfortunately, Japanese sounds do not include the full range of Western sounds, nor do Japanese writing systems (they now have four) permit their expression. Consequently, the painter had to search for symbols—always complete syllables ending in either a vowel or an *n*, and without the *th* and *l*, and several other consonants which do not exist in Japanese. (Japanese often have trouble with Western names. The transliteration *ma-ka-sa* was as close as they could come to General Douglas MacArthur's name, and *ma-ka-sa* was the closest they could come to Joseph McCarthy's name. You can imagine the confusion in Japan during the Army-McCarthy hearings in the early 1950s.)

5   In any case, either the painter had a limited kanji vocabulary—or an active sense of humor. The sounds he chose for the word *theos* was the Japanese phrase *dai uso*. At the instant St. Francis exhorted the congregation to accept, worship, and adore the "new" God, the acolytes elevated the banner, and the congregation began to titter, then to chuckle, next to laugh aloud, and finally to guffaw. The kanji which expressed the sounds of *dai uso* triggered the Japanese meaning of "the great lie."

6   Another classic misunderstanding near the end of World War II was originally revealed in the *Atlantic Monthly* ("The Great Mokusatsu Mistake"). Despite the fact that it was debunked by Admiral Zacharias, America's World War II expert on things Japanese, it has been cited in countless language arts texts as an example of both the problems and the importance of accurate communication. According to the story, the Potsdam Declaration by Churchill, Truman, and Stalin gave the Japanese an ultimatum: surrender unconditionally or accept the consequences. In closed chambers the Japanese discussed the communication, but when a reporter surprised Premier Suzuki by asking, "What are you doing about the Potsdam Declaration?" Tanaka, off-the-cuff, responded with an ambiguous Japanese term: "We are giving it *mokusatsu*." The term might mean either "We are considering it" or "We are ignoring it." The reporter, so the story goes, chose the latter meaning, and as a result, Hiroshima and Nagasaki were targeted.

7   And, of course, there is the classic story of the murder trial in Washington or Oregon in which a Japanese emigrant on trial for his life was asked directly, "You did murder this man, didn't you?" His answer followed the Japanese pattern: *yes*—which means, "Yes, I *didn't* murder him." (A narrator always gives this story a happy ending: The Supreme Court overturned the guilty verdict.)

8   My own problems with the Japanese language are less significant than these and undoubtedly less amusing. Nonetheless, since 1945 when I was a 19-year-old paratrooper with the 11th Airborne Division and entered Japan from Luzon via Okinawa about a week before the signing of the peace treaty on the *U.S.S. Missouri,* it has been one of the splendid fictions of my life that "I speak 'a little Japanese.' "

9   I remember sitting with Senator Hayakawa at the Conference on English Education luncheon in San Francisco and trying a little of that language on the great semanticist. Though he understood me, he disclaimed for himself any skill in conversational Japanese, even as he mentioned that his aged mother spoke it fluently. I continued with presumptuous bravado speaking in Japanese to him until somehow out of nowhere Edwin Markham's line, "What to him is the swing of the Pleiades," came suddenly to me. And since I couldn't even express the idea in Japanese, let alone discuss its philosophical or aesthetic implications, I realized—as if I didn't already know—the limitations of my ridiculously low-level syntax and limited vocabulary. But the Senator was kind. Nonetheless, we all live by little fictions, and that has been one of the more pleasant ones in my life.

10   I did, however, study Japanese for nine months in 1945–46 under a Canadian missionary, and last summer I tried, for the first time outside of a Japanese steak house, to use the little language I learned at that time. My problems undoubtedly had multiple sources: (a) I didn't learn very much originally, and I learned it inadequately; (b) I learned a *hogen,* or dialectal form; (c) I had not been sensitive to levels of usage or degrees of politeness, (d) but, especially over 40 years, the language has changed. A language shouldn't change that much.

11   Here are a few of my embarrassing misuses. If anyone out there speaks Japanese and can give me insight into the reasons for my problems, I'll be appreciative. In the meantime, I shall offer the following experiences as examples of the surprising rapidity of linguistic change and, as such, interesting examples of language.

12   The first time I elicited guffaws as I tried to use Japanese was at Narita Airport when I inquired at an information desk how to get to the station (*teishaba*) to catch a train into Tokyo. Came the sudden laugh and the apologetic explanation: "*Teishaba* old-fashioned word. New word *eki.*" And so it was: in five weeks in Japan, the only time I heard the "old-fashioned word" for railroad station was when I used it.

13   I encountered a similar problem in Aomori when I inquired the way to the *watashi-bune,* or ferry, from Honshu to Hokkaido. In Japanese, a "crossing" is *watashi*—which is perhaps confusing, since it sounds very much like the informal word for "I," *watakushi,* reduced to *watashi*—and *bune,* "ship." Forty years ago, I had learned that a "crossing ship," or "ferry," is a *watashi-bune.* But in 1985 everyone laughed when I said *watashi-bune.* "Watashi-bune old-fashioned word. New word *ferry.*" And so it was.

14   Again, at a railroad station I ran into problems with the word for restroom (or toilet or powder room). Now, I knew well enough not to use the word *benjo,* a term we boys might use among ourselves—perhaps equivalent to John—so I dredged from my memory, *gomen kudasai. Gofujo wa doko desu ka?* ("Pardon me. Where is the ladies' room?"). The information officer in Sendai doubled up with laughter. "*Gomen kudasai* stressful apology word. Simple apology word for 'pardon me,' *sumimasen.*" A light came into his eyes, and he stopped halfway through the word. "Oh, I see. You want *gofu kurubu* (club)," and he pantomimed a golfer following through on a powerful slow-motion swing. "No, no," I protested. "*Kanai wa . . .* " And as soon as I mentioned the rather low, impolite word for my own wife instead of the elevated word for someone else's he realized what I wanted. He laughed loudly. "*Gofujo* old-fashioned word. New word *te-arai,* meaning 'hand-washing place.' "

15   I noticed many examples of simplification from the older forms of the language which I had learned 40 years ago:

1. *Ikaga desu ka?* (How are you?) as a greeting seems less common now than the simpler *O genki desu ka.* (Honorable good health exists?)

2. *So de wa arimasen ka* (the tag question asking for agreement, much like the French *n'est-ce pas*, the German *nicht wahr*, the Spanish *no es verdad*, or the English *isn't it* had become first *ja arimasen ka* and then elided to *ja nai*.

16   The use of pronouns is somewhat different in Japanese from the patterns in English. The Japanese are inclined to dispense with most pronouns in which context makes the meaning clear. I had learned forty years ago, however, that to refer to a specific woman where we would use *she*, it was perfectly all right to use *ano onna*, or *that woman*. When I used the form this time, however, it elicited gasps of surprise. "Old form very impolite. New form *ano josette*." It sounds French to me, but I have no idea of its origin or even its correct transliteration in Roman symbols.

17   Perhaps my worst moments were when I attempted to fall back on my 40-year-old-vocabulary without checking the meaning of the words in current Japanese. At breakfast one morning, I asked one of the sweet young students about a pitcher standing between the corn flakes and the coffee: *Kore wa chichi desu ka?* ("This is milk?" I was trying to determine whether it was milk for the cereal as opposed to cream for the coffee.) She gasped, looked horrified, and told me emphatically "*Iiye.*" I learned later that I had asked if it was *mother's breast milk*. I don't know whether the word has changed in 40 years or if some prankster long ago booby-trapped me by deliberately teaching me the wrong word.

18   My final example is one which I, fortunately, was sensitive enough not to use in a potentially embarrassing situation. I long ago learned that the word for hand is *te* (remember the *te-arai*, "the hand-washing place?"). The word for *paper* is *kami* and the two combined *tegami* is *hand paper*, or *stationery*. Similarly, the word *te* means *hand* and when coupled with the word *fukero*, meaning *sack* or *bag*, becomes *tebukero*, that is to say, a *sack for the hands*, or *mittens*. The same word *fukero*, meaning *bag*, can be surrounded with the Japanese honorific to become *o-fukero-san*, the slang term 40 years ago for *okasan*, or *mother*. This etymology tells us that obviously, 40 years ago *honorable bag* was a slang term, so I waited to use it in a properly informal situation with the appropriate audience in a festively informal mood. At last I found a group of close friends American and Japanese—when we had been toasting our friendships and engaging in community singing in a *karaoki* (*empty orchestra*) bar. . . .

19   But such is the transient nature of slang. When I attempted to employ this example of my knowledge of the nuances of informal Japanese, I was foiled. In 40 years, the word had vanished.

20   Truly, language changes—and at an amazing rate. We don't perceive the changes when we are immersed in a culture, but to return to a country after a hiatus of 40 years is to be made acutely aware of language change. Rip van Winkle slept, I think, for 20 years, and his language became archaic. I was away from Japan for twice that period, and I was at least double his figure of fun.

COMPREHENSION

1. Words to talk about:

   - *theos* for the concept of the Christian God
   - a banner bearing *kanji* symbols
   - to signal *acolytes*
   - after a *hiatus* of 40 years

2. West said he had learned a *hogen* or dialectal form of Japanese. What would a *hogen* be for someone learning English?
3. Explain the construction of the Japanese words *tegami* and *tebukero.*

DISCUSSION

1. What purpose in the essay is filled by the story about Saint Francis Xavier coming to Japan in 1549?
2. What is it about the Japanese sound system and Japanese writing systems that contributes to confusions between Japanese and English speakers? How does this relate to what the Japanese thought about the McCarthy hearings in the early 1950s?
3. Explain "The Great Mokusatsu Mistake." Does this relate to a difference in sound systems or to some other kind of difference? Explain.
4. What is West communicating when he says, "We all live by little fictions"? What was the "little fiction" that gave him pleasure but was put to the test when he went back to Japan?
5. In reference to the "mistakes" that West made, can you see any patterns to the kinds of changes that had occurred? If so, illustrate the patterns with one or two specific examples.
6. Although their surface structures won't be the same, try to think of changes that have occurred in English that are similar in pattern or type to some of the Japanese changes that West wrote about.
7. Most of the incidents described in Living Language 9.2 are simply mistakes that could happen when people try to communicate with someone they don't know very well. However, some of these "mistakes" were also influenced by differences in cultural expectations. Which ones?

Mistakes the World Could Have Lived Without

Communication among strangers has never been foolproof, as shown by these misunderstandings.

- It has long been assumed that Columbus named the people he found in the New World "Indians" because he thought he had reached the Indies of Asia. A recent theory that is flattering in its political correctness, but hardly believable, is that he devised the name from the Italian *una gente in Dios,* meaning "a people of God."

- In the 1800s, English-speaking missionaries in Africa taught new converts the game of Bingo, alongside lessons in Christianity. Many of the converts, who were also learning English as a foreign language, got the two endeavors confused and thought that shouting "Bingo!" was like shouting "Hallelujah!" or "Amen!" and so began using Bingo as a name for the Christian Heaven.

- In American Samoa, Pango Pango was the name of the harbor until the 1800s when English-speaking missionaries came and began transliterating the native language and printing maps and guidebooks. Because the Samoan language has many *n*'s, typesetters ran out and deleted *n*'s wherever they judged them to be nonessential, hence the name Pago Pago.

- *Nome,* Alaska, got its name when the British navy sent a ship to map Alaska and one of the cartographers wrote "Name?" above a cape that apparently didn't have a name. The London printer misunderstood and identified the marked place as Cape Nome. The name stuck and was later given to the port that previously had been called Anvil City.

- Reykyavik, which is the name of the capital city of Iceland, means "smokey bay." The name was given to the area in the year 874 by Ingolfur Arnarson, the first permanent settler. From a distance, he saw steam rising from hot springs and assumed it was smoke.

- Guinea pigs came from Guyanna, a country whose pronunciation doesn't fit well with English. Speakers simplified the name to the more familiar Guinea, also seen in guinea fowl and the name for a British coin. The name of Guinea was itself a mistake. When Portuguese explorers arrived at the area along the west coast of Africa, local tribesmen came out to meet them. The explorers pointed to the shore asking the name of the area. The tribesmen thought they were pointing to the women standing on shore and responded with *Guine,* their word for "women" (probably related to *queen* and *gynecologist*). The explorers duly recorded and publicized Guinea as the country's name.

- In the Philippines, Magellan's men asked an old fisherman the name of the place nearest them. He replied, "Luzon?" which in Tagalog means, "What did you say?" They thought he was giving them the name of the island, hence the name Luzon. There are similar stories about the naming of the llama, the kangaroo, and the country of Yucatan.

- The state of Alaska has had a long-running debate with the federal government over the name of North America's highest peak (20,320 feet). While the federal government says the name is Mt. McKinley, the state of Alaska officially uses the name of Denali, a Native American word meaning "high place." This was the mountain's name until a trapper arbitrarily gave it the name of McKinley in 1896 in hopes of furthering William McKinley's presidential campaign. McKinley never saw the mountain, but congressional delegates from his home state of Ohio have been adamant about keeping the name. Congress voted to name the surrounding park Denali. Critics view the compromise as absurd because Denali means "high place."

WORKSHOP 9.1

Selling in a Global Market

While modern media and advances in methods of travel have increased the speed with which words from different languages are being intertwined, there has always been a mixing of languages, especially in relation to trade and shipping, where items were given names that are in effect geographical eponyms.

PART I: MARKETING FOODS

For centuries people have used place names as a way of identifying various kinds of food, just as we do today when talking about Boston baked beans, Long Island iced tea, Tex-Mex Spanish food, Manhattan or New England clam chowder, Buffalo wings, (Kentucky) Derby pie, and Chicago hot dogs and pizza. Most such names are taken from the place where the food originates, but because of people's creativity there can also be other relationships, as when an American chef figured out how to pickle beets and named them Harvard beets because their color matched the university's football uniforms. Sandwiches are indirectly named after a place. In the 1700s, the British diplomat John Montagu, the Fourth Earl of Sandwich, liked to gamble so much that he didn't want to stop to eat. He instructed servants to bring his food between two slices of bread surely one of the best inventions ever.

BRAIN TEASERS

From the brief descriptions given below, see if you can think of the geography-based food names that are commonly used in American English.

(a) In the summer of 1885 at the Erie County Fair held near the town of Hamburg, New York, two sandwich vendors ran out of pork and substituted beef.

(b) Chinese gardeners developed a new citrus tree that produced small and very sweet oranges.

(c) Cheese makers in Parma, Italy, figured out how to make a hard and dry kind of cheese that they were able to ship all over the world. Today it is often grated and served on various kinds of Italian food.

(d) In the 1800s, immigrants from the province of Limburg in Belgium brought their fondness for well-aged cheese to America.

(e) Since 1591, a heavy dessert wine has been shipped from the city of Oporto in northern Portugal. Although it comes in different colors, the most common is a deep red.

(f) Before this breakfast food got its present name, it was variously called Spanish toast, German toast, and Nun's toast.

(g) When European explorers went to Lima, Peru, they found the natives raising a large white bean.

(h) Cooks in the county of York in northern England began placing a heavy kind of bread under their roasts so that it would absorb the meat juices. The term first appeared in a 1747 cookbook and is often seen in British stories about grand feasts.

PART II: MARKETING CLOTH

In the early days of international commerce, it was even easier to trade cloth than food because cloth doesn't spoil and so can go on long ocean voyages or ride overland atop camels and wagons. One of the reasons the English vocabulary is so rich is that we have words for similar kinds of cloth coming from different parts of the globe as when pants are referred to as jeans, denims, dungarees, and Levis. Jeans is derived from Genoa, Italy, where this heavyweight cloth was first woven. At Nimes, France, a similar kind of cloth was called *serge de Nimes,* from which we get *denim.* In the Hindi language of India, *dungri* was the name for tent cloth, and from this we get *dungarees.* During the 1850s California gold rush, an enterprising young man named Levi Strauss noticed how easily the miner's pants snagged and tore as they worked in the rough terrain. He bought some tent cloth and began making and selling *Levi's* pants.

BRAIN TEASERS

From the brief descriptions given below, see if you can think of the geography-related names of cloth that came into either American or British English.

(a) Workers in the city of Madras, India, have for centuries woven designs into a fine cotton cloth used for shirts, dresses, bedspreads, and tablecloths.

(b) Sheep of different colors with fairly tough wool were raised near the Tweed River in Scotland.

(c) Near the Worsted parish and village in Norfolk, England, the sheep produce long fibers that skilled workers combed and carded to make a smooth napless fabric.

(d) This 45-square-mile island in the English Channel, gave us not only a kind of sweater, but also a kind of milk cow and a name for an important city and state in the northeastern United States.

(e) A kind of dotted cloth is thought to be named after a Polish dance in which the dancers quickly move from one spot to another.

continued

Workshop 9.1

Selling in a Global Market   continued

PART III: NAMES FOR GENERAL CONCEPTS

Intercultural words reveal some of the ways our linguistic ancestors related to each other.

BRAIN TEASERS

See if you can figure out what fairly common words or phrases came into English in relation to the following historical facts. There were usually small changes in pronunciation, and many of them have taken on metaphorical meanings.

(a) During medieval times many Slavic people in Central Europe were held in bondage.
(b) The Vandals were Germanic tribes who in the first four centuries A.D. moved southward from Scandinavia wreaking havoc throughout Gaul, Spain, North Africa, and Rome.
(c) During the late 1800s sailors under the influence of drugs or alcohol were often kidnapped and placed on board departing ships. The furthest and most exotic port was chosen as the term for such kidnappings.
(d) Napoleon's plan to conquer the world ended when he suffered a complete defeat in the 1815 Battle of Waterloo in Belgium.
(e) The Maelstrom is a place off the Lofoten Islands on the west coast of Norway where ocean currents join to form a permanent whirlpool.
(f) Lesbos is a Greek island that in 600 B.C. was a center of civilization and culture. Although several philosophers and poets all lived there at various times, it is the woman scholar and poet Sappho who is responsible for the island's fame and the word based on its name. Sappho taught and wrote poetry, much of it romantic, with a group of intellectual young women.

PART IV: SELLING CARS

Prior to the mid-1950s, Americans bought and drove almost exclusively American cars, but then the German Volkswagen company began importing cars and vans. In the 1960s, the VW van was almost as important to the hippie movement as was long hair and jeans. However, effects on the American automobile industry went far beyond this most visible manifestation. These small cars challenged fundamental practices by making smallness a virtue and by keeping the same designs year after year. Americans gave them the humorous nicknames of bug and beetle, and although the company never officially used the names on the vehicles they used them in advertis-

ing. Later, when the Volkswagen company began to manufacture different models, they continued to use playful names. For example a 1974 jeep-like vehicle named the Thing was advertised under the slogan, "The cost of every Thing is going down." When after two decades the sedan replaced the bug, it was named the Volkswagen Rabbit, while later models were named the Fox and the Colt—a step up from bugs and beetles, but still a long ways from the big and powerful connotations that American manufacturers prefer. When in 1998 the Volkswagen company released a newly designed bug, the advertisements were clever enough to win an international award for the way they played on the idea of an old friend that has been out of touch for the last nineteen years.

continued

WORKSHOP 9.1

Selling in a Global Market   continued

BRAIN TEASERS

Use what you have observed about cars and their marketing to figure out the answers to the following questions:

(a) Actually, there are so many cars—many more today than fifteen years ago when Blumberg wrote his article—that it's possible to find sets of names to prove almost any thesis. What do the names in this set have in common? What characteristics would the people have who are being targeted as buyers?

Buick *Park Avenue Ultra* and *Riviera*

Cadillac *Coupe* (and *Sedan*) *de Ville*

Chevrolet *Corsica, El Camino Malibu,* and *Monte Carlo*

Honda *Del Sol*

Lincoln *Continental*

Pontiac *LeMans*

(b) Can you think of other sets of names that might attract buyers with particular dreams or characteristics? What about an admiration for royalty? How about names that indicate business success or prestige?

(c) Successful names attached to well-made vehicles inspire imitation. The British-made Landrover and Range Rover were among the first four-wheel drive, heavy-duty wagons. What vehicle names can you think of that have similar connotations?

(d) When the Honda Company of Japan named its Acura car to sell to an American market, it worked with the French *acutesse,* the Italian *acutezza,* and the English *accurate* and *acumen,* all with meanings related to intelligence, sharpness, and acuteness. What in the history of East/West relations, made it important to choose a name that would be associated with the idea of high quality engineering? What other advantages does the name have?

(e) Several years later, General Motors came up with Geo, from the Greek *gaia,* meaning "earth," as seen in words with engineering connotations including *geodesic* and *geometric* as well as in the more commonplace *geography.* An extra boost in creating the desired message, is that the *o* in *geo* is drawn with latitude and longitude markings to resemble a globe. What do you think General Motors wanted to communicate with the new name?

(f) It has been serendipitous that many new words created for car names have the advantage of being easy to protect against copying, plus they can suggest positive qualities without any need for proof. For example, the Nissan Altima was taken from Latin *altus,* suggesting a higher order, as in English *altitude.* The creators also hoped it would make buyers think of ultimate, while Sentra would make them think of a sentry standing guard, and Maxima of something like maximum value. Think of some other car names and speculate on what thoughts the manufacturer was hoping to trigger in customers' minds.

(g) As you read about these less-than-perfect names for cars, describe the problem. Is it related to an actual confusion between languages or to differing connotations?

Chevrolet Nova: Only after the company was well into production and advertising did it learn that in Spanish *no va* means "won't go."

Hyundi: Its pronunciation is unclear, and in one version sounds like *high and dry,* a nautical term meaning "stranded." Also, some Japanese speakers resent this Korean name because they think it was purposely designed to borrow the positive connotations of Honda.

Mercury Merkur: Ford dropped this luxury German-made car in 1989 because of poor sales, which were in part attributed to problems with the name. *Merkur* is German for "mercury" (pronounced "Mare-cure"), and English speakers never felt comfortable with it.

Saab: As in the old joke, "What you do when it's time to make the payments."

Toyota MR2: When said in French, the last part of this name sounds like a French word for excrement and so this model is no longer marketed in France.

Yugo: Looks and sounds too much like yucko, which plays into comedian's jokes.

Zchiguli: This best-selling car in Russia is named after the place on the Volga River where the factory is located, but when the manufacturers began exporting the car they discovered that Europeans translated the name as *gigolo.* Models built for export are now named Lada, a feminine first name.

In the Canon, for All the Wrong Reasons

Amy Tan

Amy Tan is a second-generation American, who grew up in California. Her best-selling books include *The Joy Luck Club* (1989); *The Kitchen God's Wife* (1991); *The Hundred Secret Senses* (1996); and *The Moon Lady* (for children). Her essay is placed last in the book because she asks the fundamental questions that we ask throughout this text about language and reading and what it means to be American.

1   Several years ago I learned that I had passed a new literary milestone. I had made it to the Halls of Education under the rubric of "Multicultural Literature," also known in many schools as "Required Reading."

2   Thanks to this development, I now meet students who proudly tell me they're doing their essays, term papers, or master's theses on me. By that they mean that they are analyzing not just my books but me—my grade-school achievements, youthful indiscretions, marital status, as well as the movies I watched as a child, the slings and arrows I suffered as a minority, and so forth—all of which, with the hindsight of classroom literary investigation, prove to contain many Chinese omens that made it inevitable that I would become a writer. Once I read a master's thesis on feminist writings, which included examples from *The Joy Luck Club*. The student noted that I had often used the number four, something on the order of thirty-two or thirty-six times—in any case, a number divisible by four. She pointed out that there were four mothers, four daughters, four sections of the book, four stories per section. Furthermore, there were four sides to a mah jong table, four directions of the wind, four players. More important, she postulated, my use of the number four was a symbol for the four stages of psychological development, which corresponded in uncanny ways to the four stages of some type of Buddhist philosophy I had never heard of before. The student recalled that the story contained a character called Fourth Wife, symbolizing death, and a four-year-old girl with a feisty spirit, symbolizing regeneration.

3   In short, her literary sleuthing went on to reveal a mystical and rather Byzantine puzzle, which, once explained, proved to be completely brilliant and precisely logical. She wrote me a letter and asked if her analysis had been correct. How I longed to say "absolutely."

4   The truth is, if there are symbols in my work they exist largely by accident or through someone else's interpretive design. If I wrote of "an orange moon rising on a dark night," I would more likely ask myself later if the image was a cliché, not whether it was a symbol for the feminine force rising in anger, as one master's thesis postulated. To plant symbols like that, you need a plan, good organizational skills, and a prescient understanding of the story you are able to write. Sadly, I lack those traits.

5   All this is by way of saying that I don't claim my use of the number four to be a brilliant symbolic device. In fact, now that it's been pointed out to me in rather astonishing ways, I consider my overuse of the number to be a flaw.

6   Reviewers and students have enlightened me about not only how I write but why I write. Apparently, I am driven to capture the immigrant experience, to demystify Chinese culture, to point out the differences between Chinese and American culture, even to pave the way for other Asian American writers.

7   If only I were that noble. Contrary to what is assumed by some students, reporters, and community organizations wishing to bestow honors on me, I am not an expert on China, Chinese culture, mah jong, the psychology of mothers and daughters, generation gaps, immigration, illegal aliens, assimilation, acculturation, racial tension, Tiananmen Square, the Most Favored National trade agreements, human rights, Pacific Rim economics, the purported one million missing baby girls of China, the future of Hong Kong after 1997, or, I am sorry to say, Chinese cooking. Certainly I have personal opinions on many of these topics, but by no means do my sentiments and my world of make-believe make me an expert.

8   So I am alarmed when reviewers and educators assume that my very personal, specific, and fictional stories are meant to be representative down to the nth detail not just of Chinese Americans but, sometimes, of all Asian culture. Is Jane Smiley's *A Thousand Acres* supposed to be taken as representative of all of American culture? If so, in what ways? Are all American fathers tyrannical? Do all American sisters betray one another? Are all American conscientious objectors flaky in love relationships?

9   Over the years my editor has received hundreds of permissions requests from publishers of college textbooks and multicultural anthologies, all of them wishing to reprint my work for "educational purposes." One publisher wanted to include an excerpt from *The Joy Luck Club,* a scene in which a Chinese woman invites her non-Chinese boyfriend to her parents' house for dinner. The boyfriend brings a bottle of wine as a gift and commits a number of social gaffes at the dinner table. Students were supposed to read this excerpt, then answer the following question: "If you are invited to a Chinese family's house for dinner, should you bring a bottle of wine?"

10   In many respects, I am proud to be on the reading lists for courses such as Ethnic Studies, Asian American Studies, Asian American Literature, Asian

American History, Women's Literature, Feminist Studies, Feminist Writers of Color, and so forth. What writer wouldn't want her work to be read? I also take a certain perverse glee in imagining countless students, sleepless at three in the morning, trying to read *The Joy Luck Club* for the next day's midterm. Yet I'm also not altogether comfortable about my book's status as required reading.

11   Let me relate a conversation I had with a professor at a school in southern California. He told me he uses my books in his literature class but he makes it a point to lambast those passages that depict China as backward or unattractive. He objects to any descriptions that have to do with spitting, filth, poverty, or superstitions. I asked him if China in the 1930s and 1940s was free of these elements. He said, No, such descriptions are true; but he still believes it is "the obligation of the writer of ethnic literature to create positive, progressive images."

12   I secretly shuddered and thought, Oh well, that's southern California for you. But then, a short time later, I met a student from UC Berkeley, a school that I myself attended. The student was standing in line at a book signing. When his turn came, he swaggered up to me, then took two steps back and said in a loud voice, "Don't you think you have a responsibility to write about Chinese men as positive role models?"

13   In the past, I've tried to ignore the potshots. A *Washington Post* reporter once asked me what I thought of another Asian American writer calling me something on the order of "a running dog whore sucking on the tit of the imperialist white pigs."

14   "Well," I said, "you can't please everyone, can you?" I pointed out that readers are free to interpret a book as they please, and that they are free to appreciate or not appreciate the result. Besides, reacting to your critics makes a writer look defensive, petulant, and like an all around bad sport.

15   But lately, I've started thinking it's wrong to take such a laissez-faire attitude. Lately I've come to think that I must say something, not so much to defend myself and my work but to express my hopes for American literature, for what it has the potential to become in the twenty-first century—that is, a truly American literature, democratic in the way it includes many colorful voices.

16   Until recently, I didn't think it was important for writers to express their private intentions in order for their work to be appreciated; I believed that any analysis of my intentions belonged behind the closed doors of literature classes. But I've come to realize that the study of literature does have its effect on how books are being read, and thus on what might be read, published, and written in the future. For that reason, I do believe writers today must talk about their intentions—if for no other reason than to serve as an antidote to what others say our intentions should be.

17   For the record, I don't write to dig a hole and fill it with symbols. I don't write stories as ethnic themes. I don't write to represent life in general. And I certainly don't write because I have answers. If I knew everything there is to know about mothers and daughters, Chinese and Americans, I wouldn't have

any stories left to imagine. If I had to write about only positive role models, I wouldn't have enough imagination left to finish the first story. If I knew what to do about immigration, I would be a sociologist or a politician and not a long-winded storyteller.

18   So why do I write?

19   Because my childhood disturbed me, pained me, made me ask foolish questions. And the questions still echo. Why does my mother always talk about killing herself? Why did my father and brother have to die? If I die, can I be reborn into a happy family? Those early obsessions led to a belief that writing could be my salvation, providing me with the sort of freedom and danger, satisfaction and discomfort, truth and contradiction I can't find in anything else in life.

20   I write to discover the past for myself. I don't write to change the future for others. And if others are moved by my work—if they love their mothers more, scold their daughters less, or divorce their husbands who were not positive role models—I'm often surprised, usually grateful to hear from kind readers. But I don't take either credit or blame for changing their lives for better or for worse.

21   Writing, for me, is an act of faith, a hope that I will discover what I mean by "truth." I also think of reading as an act of faith, a hope that I will discover something remarkable about ordinary life, about myself. And if the writer and the reader discover the same thing, if they have that connection, the act of faith has resulted in an act of magic. To me, that's the mystery and the wonder of both life and fiction—the connection between two individuals who discover in the end that they are more the same than they are different.

22   And if that doesn't happen, it's nobody's fault. There are still plenty of other books on the shelf. Choose what you like.

COMPREHENSION

1. Words to talk about:

    - In the *canon*
    - More important, she *postulated*
    - rather *Byzantine* puzzle
    - a *prescient* understanding
    - Chinese culture, *mah jong*
    - assimilation, *acculturation*
    - *Tiananmen Square*
    - *Pacific Rim* economics
    - a point to *lambast* those passages
    - such a *laissez-faire attitude*

A Tossed Salad

As shown by the Official Language controversy, as well as by these news summaries, many Americans are replacing the old metaphor of the melting pot with a newer metaphor, such as a tossed salad, in which people can blend together but still keep their individuality.

- When Japanese immigrants arrived in America in the late 1800s and early 1900s, they were desirous of fitting into their new culture. Instead of building Buddhist Temples as they would have done at home, they established the Buddhist Churches of America, held Sunday services, installed pews and organs, and called their clergy "Reverend." But today several congregations are quietly returning to the word temple, because as the Reverend Lee Rosenthal, a priest at the Arizona Buddhist Church explained, "The Buddhist temple is not literally, by the nature of the word, a house of God." Buddhists do not worship God or Jesus. Their belief system presents a spiritual path through which to seek wisdom and enlightenment. (*Arizona Republic*, July 19, 1997)

- In his book *My Own Country: A Doctor's Story of a Town and Its People in the Age of AIDS* (Simon & Schuster, 1994), Dr. Abraham Verghese, an immigrant from India, shares a tip that he got from a fellow immigrant about how to find an Indian restaurant in a strange American city. You count the number of *Patels* in the phone book and multiply by sixty, which tells you how many Indian-Americans live in the area. "Take my word: less than ten Patels means no Indian restaurant. If more than ten, you call, say you are from India, ask them where to go to eat."

- "A guy walks in with a bowler hat on, a beard, a coat coming down to his knees," said New York Sheriff James Kralik. "He looks like something out of *Fiddler on the Roof*." The person being talked about is Deputy Shlomo Koenig, probably the only Hasidic police officer in the United States. He is 35-years-old, and before taking the 600-hour training program at the Rockland County Police Academy, worked as an unofficial liaison between the sheriff's department and Rockland's growing community of over 35,000 members of Hasidic and other ultraconservative Jewish sects. He translates not only language, but customs. He explained that there is mistrust between police and the Hasidim because, "We've been brought up in countries where the government was not our friend." From the other side, he tries to help police officers understand what is happening when, for example, a man abandons his car on the side of a highway and begins walking. He may be an Orthodox Jew who is late getting home on Friday night and is forbidden to drive after sunset. And when a woman refuses to accept a speeding ticket from an officer, she may just be upholding the rule against contact between the sexes. If the officer sets the ticket down, she will pick it up. (Associated Press, Feb. 9, 1997)

- "Let's see if we've got it all straight: Don't hug a Vietnamese when greeting him, but peck a Portuguese on both cheeks. Don't ever wear black to a Chinese wedding (the color suggests death), and use discretion in handing out yellow flowers (to an Armenian they mean you miss her; to an Iranian, they mean you hate her). Don't clean your plate in a Cambodian's dining room unless you really want more food, and fill the plate of your Salvadoran guest, who expects that of a good host." So began Clyde Haberman's review of *Multicultural Manners: New Rules of Etiquette for a Changing Society,* by Norine Dresser (John Wiley & Sons, 1996). Haberman concluded, "For all its value, this book can push cultural tolerance to the breaking point." For example, knowing that in Iraq wives and children "are often considered possessions of the men" is of little use to either the district attorney or to the former wife of an Iraqi man who has just run off with their son. (*New York Times Book Review,* Feb. 18, 1997)

■ American advertisers pride themselves on the skill with which they direct advertisements to distinctive groups. But with Asian-Americans, they feel particularly challenged because there are so many subtle nuances that communicate different things to different groups. For example, a company that passed out complimentary packages of four golf balls found that to Chinese and Japanese the number four is considered unlucky because the words "four" and "death" sound the same. Surnames are often used to draw up lists for direct-mail, but such a name as *Lee* can be Korean, black, white, or Chinese, and people resent being misidentified. If potential Korean customers are encouraged to call for more information on free 800 numbers, a company should provide a Korean speaking operator. For Chinese calls, the operator needs to be able to communicate in Mandarin or Cantonese, but because most Japanese take pride in being westernized and up-to-date it would probably be counter-productive to hire a Japanese-speaking operator. (*Philadelphia Inquirer,* April 6, 1997)

■ Religion News Service writer James Rudin thinks, "It's time to retire one of our most popular verbal icons: *Judeo-Christian tradition.*" He used to view the term as "a convenient, albeit superficial, way to affirm religious pluralism." But as he points out, "Although there are certainly many Christians in the world, how many Judeos are there?" What worries him even more is that "the expression Judeo-Christian is now the last refuge of some public officials who seem deeply troubled by recent demographic changes in the religious makeup of the American population." They are using the term not to include, but to exclude. (*Arizona Republic,* April 5, 1997)

■ "Islamic council takes Nike to task on logo that looks like Arabic," was the headline on a story about a logo on athletic shoes that resembles the word *Allah* in Arabic script. "Nike said the logo was meant to look like flames for a line of shoes to be sold . . . with the names Air Bakin', Air Melt, Air Grill and Air B-Que." Nike said it had caught the problem six months earlier, before the shoes went into production, and altered the logo; however, Nihad Awad, president of the Council on American-Islamic Relations, displayed a pair of the controversial shoes and said they were still seen in retail stores. Adding to the protest through a public letter was Hakeem Olajuwon, a Muslim who endorses another brand of athletic shoe. He wrote to Nike President Tom Clarke, "It is offensive to us when a major corporation such as Nike publicly shows disrespect for Allah's name." Two years earlier, Nike had removed a controversial billboard near the University of Southern California that showed a basketball player with the heading, "They called him Allah." (Knight-Ridder Newspapers, April 10, 1997)

2. Does Tan think she is in the literary canon only for the wrong reasons? Or is she there for some of the right reasons, too?

Discussion

1. Gordon Allport has said that labels of primary potency "act like shrieking sirens, deafening us to all finer discriminations that we might otherwise perceive." Racial designations are one of those labels. Find two or three places in Tan's essay where she demonstrates the expectations that some people have for her and her writing based on the fact that she is of Chinese ancestry.
2. What's wrong with the question: "If you are invited to a Chinese family's house for dinner, should you bring a bottle of wine?"
3. What do you think about the man's opinion that it is "the obligation of the writer of ethnic literature to create positive, progressive images"? What does Tan think about it?
4. What does Tan mean when she says, "If I knew everything there is to know about mothers and daughters, Chinese and Americans, I wouldn't have any stories left to imagine"?
5. What does Tan say is "the mystery and the wonder of both life and fiction"? How does this relate to changing conditions in today's world?
6. As you read the news accounts summarized in Living Language 9.3, think about how these incidents relate to the fact that an increasing number of Americans are bilingual and bicultural. Explain how the incidents show a rejection of the old metaphor about America becoming "a melting pot."

Suggested Topics for Writing

1. Write an essay explaining why English is so widely spoken around the world. Use both historical and contemporary information.
2. Write an essay in which you use linguistic evidence to develop the point that the world is one big neighborhood. You can glean much of your supporting data from this chapter, but try to find at least two or three other examples from current news stories or from interviewing people who have lived in other countries.

3. After you have pondered the various issues relating to the "Official Language" controversy, write your own letter to the editor. You will have a better chance of getting it published if you tie it in with a current news story in your local area. Also, realize you will need to limit the scope of what you say. Notice how in her essay Karen L. Adams was able to treat several facets of the problem, while the letter writers had to be more focused on either one or two points.

4. Go back to the essay, "Propaganda: How Not To Be Bamboozled" in Chapter 6 (p. 262). Study the various kinds of persuasive techniques that Donna Woolfolk Cross discusses, then write an essay in which you analyze some of the persuasive techniques that are being used by either or both sides in the "Official Language" controversy. Look especially at where people make claims of cause and effect where, in fact, there may be only correlations.

5. Look around at current marketing practices and see if you can find an area to write about that reflects how advertisers take advantage of the thought behind the proverb, "The grass is always greener on the other side of the fence." What do advertisers do to cash in on our sense of wanderlust and our longings for new and exotic experiences? Perhaps you can do research through the Internet or can interview international students to find out (1) how an American product is being marketed in a particular country or (2) how the marketing of an imported item differs in this country from the way it is sold at home.

INFORMATION SOURCES FOR WRITING

The City in Slang: New York Life and Popular Speech, by Irving Lewis Allen. New York: Oxford Univ. Press, 1993.

Forgotten English: A Merry Guide to Antiquated Words Packed with History, Fun Facts, Literary Excerpts, and Charming Drawings, by Jeffrey Kacirk. New York: William Morrow, 1997.

Japanese Jive, by Carolyn McKeldin, foreword by George Fields. New York: Tengu, 1993.

The Kitchen God's Wife, by Amy Tan. New York: Putnam, 1991. Along with Tan's earlier *The Joy Luck Club, The Kitchen God's Wife* provides readers with glimpses of the immigrant experience of a Chinese-American family.

Made in America: An Informal History of the English Language in the United States, by Bill Bryson. New York: Avon paperback, 1994.

The Mother Tongue: English & How It Got That Way, by Bill Bryson. New York: William
    Morrow, 1990; Avon paperback, 1991.
The New Age of Communications, by John Green. New York: Holt, 1997.
The Next Century, by David Halberstam. New York: Morrow, 1991.
Scholastic Dictionary of Idioms, by Marvin Terban. New York: Scholastic, 1996.
The Story of English: A Companion to the PBS Television Series, by Robert McCrum,
    William Cran, and Robert MacNeil. New York: Viking/Penguin, 1986.
Take My Words: A Workaholic's Guide to the English Language, by Howard Richler. Van-
    couver, B.C., Canada: Ronsdale, 1996.
The Thesaurus of Slang: Over 165,000 Uncensored Contemporary Slang Terms, by Esther
    Lewin. New York: Facts on File, 1994.
Whistlin' Dixie: A Dictionary of Southern Expression, by Robert Hendrickson. New
    York: Facts on File, 1993. This is Volume 1 in a Dictionary of American Regional
    Expression Series, which also includes *Dictionary of the American West,* by Win-
    fred Blevins.
*Wise Words and Wives' Tales: The Origins, Meanings and Time-Honored Wisdom of
    Proverbs and Folk Sayings, Olde and New,* by Stuart Flexner and Doris Flexner.
    New York: Avon paperback, 1993.
The Woman Warrior, by Maxine Hong Kingston. New York: Knopf, 1975.
Word Watch: The Stories Behind the Words of Our Lives, by Anne H. Soukhanov. New
    York: Henry Holt, 1995.

CREDITS

Karen L. Adams, "English-Only: As American as Apple Pie?" Adapted from *Arizona English Bulletin* (Winter 1992), vol. 34, no. 2. Reprinted by permission.

William F. Allman, "The Mother Tongue," from *U.S. News and World Report* (November 5, 1990). Copyright, Nov. 5, 1990, U.S. News and World Report.

Maya Angelou, excerpt from *I Know Why the Caged Bird Sings*. Copyright © 1969 by Maya Angelou. Reprinted by permission of Random House, Inc.

"Anti-Gay Policy Hinders Classroom Talk" (March 4, 1996). Reprinted by permission of Associated Press.

Chris Arthur, excerpt from "Ferrule," from *The American Scholar* (Summer 1996) 65, no. 3. Copyright © 1996 by the author. Reprinted by permission.

Russell Baker, "Publishers Buy Word's Worth, Not Wordsworth," from *The New York Times* (February 17, 1996). Copyright © 1996 by The New York Times Co. Reprinted by permission.

James Baldwin, "If Black English Isn't a Language, Then Tell Me, What Is?" from *The New York Times* (July 27, 1979). Copyright © 1979 by The New York Times Co. Reprinted by permission.

Dennis Baron, "Word Law," from *Verbatim* (Summer 1989). © Copyright 1989 by *Verbatim*, The Language Quarterly.

Regina Barreca, "In Celebration of the Bad Girl," from *They Used to Call Me Snow White . . . but I Drifted: Women's Strategic Use of Humor*, Viking, 1991. Reprinted by permission of the author.

Alison Bass, "TV Talk Shows Accused of Trivializing Troubles," from *The Boston Globe* (October 16, 1993). Reprinted courtesy of the Boston Globe.

Philip L. Bereano, "Rein in Bosses Who Spy on E-Mail," from *Arizona Republic* (November 12, 1996). Reprinted by permission of the author.

Erma Bombeck, "Four Dialogues," from *At Wit's End* by Erma Bombeck. Copyright © 1967 by Newsday, Inc. Used by permission of Doubleday, a division of Bantam Doubleday Dell Publishing Group, Inc.

Joseph Boskin, "Our Private Laughter: American Cynicism and Optimism," from *The World and I* (August 1992). Reprinted by permission of the author.

Rita Braver, "It's Up Close and Misleading," from *The Washington Post* (March 14, 1996). © 1996 The Washington Post. Reprinted with permission.

Bill Bryson, "English as a World Language," from *The Mother Tongue: English and How It Got That Way* by Bill Bryson. Copyright © 1990 by Bill Bryson. Reprinted by permission of William Morrow & Company, Inc.

Sandra Cisneros, "My Name," from *The House on Mango Street*. Copyright © 1984 by Sandra Cisneros. Published by Vintage Books, a division of Random House, Inc., New York, and in hardcover by Alfred A. Knopf in 1994. Reprinted by permission.

Donna Woolfolk Cross, "Propaganda: How Not to Be Bamboozled," from *Word Abuse: How the Words We Use Use Us*, Coward, McCann & Geoghegan, 1979. Reprinted by permission of the author.

David Crystal, "Acquiring Language," from *The Cambridge Encyclopedia of Language*. Cambridge University Press, 1997. Reprinted with the permission of Cambridge University Press.

Index